lonely pk P9-BYB-369

South Australia & Northern Territory

DISCARDED

WORTHINGTON LIBRARIES

Darwin &
the Top End
(p142)

Uluru &
Outback
Northern
Territory
(p179)

Outback
South Australia
(p129)

Western
South Australia
(p120)

Barossa Valley
& Southeastern
South Australia
(p99)

Adelaide
& Around
(p52)

Anthony Ham & Charles Rawlings-Way

Contents

PLAN YOUR TRIP

MATT MUNRO/LONELY PLANET ©

ALICE SPRINGS P196

NEALE COUSLAND/SHUTTERSTOCK ©

ADELAIDE P53

ON THE ROAD

Contents

Aboriginal and Torres Strait
Islander people should be
aware that this book may
contain images of or refer-
ences to deceased people.

Welcome to South Australia & Northern Territory

Welcome to Australia's epic centre, the country's heartland, a wild and beautiful place tamed only by wineries and remote desert trails.

The Wild Interior

Call that Australia? *This* is Australia. Ever since *Crocodile Dundee* brought Kakadu to the world's attention, the outback and Top End have been on the radar for their impressive portfolio of quintessentially Aussie land forms: Uluru and Kata Tjuta rising improbably from the desert; the great sandstone escarpments and pristine coastline of Arnhem Land; the soulful Flinders Ranges; the vast stretches of outback with sand dunes and flood plains and monsoonal mangroves. All providing a stirring backdrop to some of Australia's best wildlife watching, from crocs to kangaroos. It's hard to escape the feeling that in this land lies eternity...

Indigenous Culture

It is the Indigenous population of the Northern Territory (NT) that gives the outback soul. These are a people whose lives remain inextricably tied to a land that their people have inhabited for millennia. And, unlike elsewhere in Australia, in the NT it's relatively easy to cross the cultural frontier and meet Indigenous Australians on their terms: it could happen on an intimate exploration of country led by an Indigenous guide, in quiet conversation with artists at work in one of the NT's many art centres, or in the timeless rituals and ceremonies of a festival.

The Sophisticated South

When you imagine Australia, South Australia (SA) is hardly the first thing that springs to mind. But here on the outback's fringe in SA are some big-ticket attractions. Take, for example, some of the country's premier wine-producing regions (perfect for slaking that outback thirst), among them the Barossa Valley, McLaren Vale, Clare Valley and the Coonawarra. There's also wonderful Kangaroo Island and, at the heart of the south, is Adelaide, where you can experience a torrent of creative energy through its amazing festivals, arts scene, pubs and foodie culture.

Outback Dreaming

While it's easy to identify the more obvious elements of the outback's appeal, there's one thing that's less easy to quantify: its strange, almost mystical allure. There's something about this place, an intangible call that defies easy explanation, something spiritual that echoes through so many moments out here. Perhaps it will touch you when you first lay eyes on Uluru. Or as the sun dips below the horizon beyond the escarpments of Kakadu. Or when you pull off the road in the middle of nowhere and find yourself enveloped by silence. In such moments lies the mysterious call of the outback.

Why I Love South Australia & Northern Territory

By Anthony Ham, Writer

God I love this place. There is something in the outback wilds that calls to me in ways I barely understand. It happens out on the lonely Carpentaria Hwy or down by the Victoria River near Timber Creek. It grips me every time I pass a turn-off out into the desert and find myself longing to take it. It's the possibility that a fabulous sighting of wildlife could happen at any moment. Boiled down to its essence, it is this: this is a wild land whose natural and human history are writ large on an impossibly beautiful canvas.

For more about our writers, see p288

Above: Driving the Old Andado Track (p46)

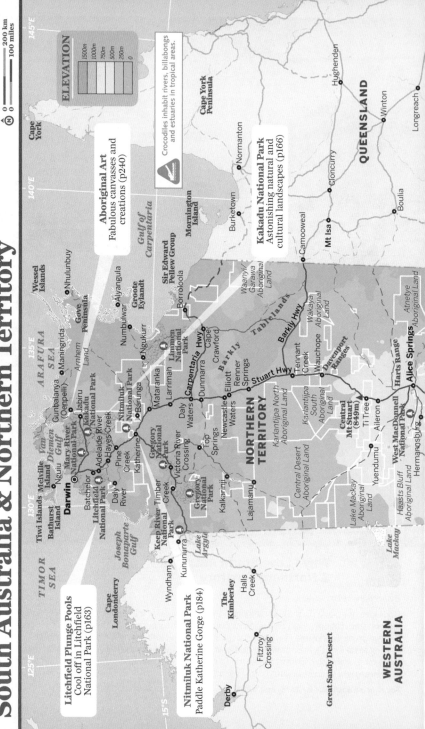

South Australia & Northern Territory

Litchfield Plunge Pools
Cool off in Litchfield National Park (p163)

Aboriginal Art
Fabulous canvasses and creations (p240)

Crocodiles inhabit rivers, billabongs and estuaries in tropical areas.

Kakadu National Park
Astonishing natural and cultural landscapes (p166)

Nitmiluk National Park
Paddle Katherine Gorge (p184)

ELEVATION

1500m
1000m
750m
500m
250m
0

200 km
100 miles

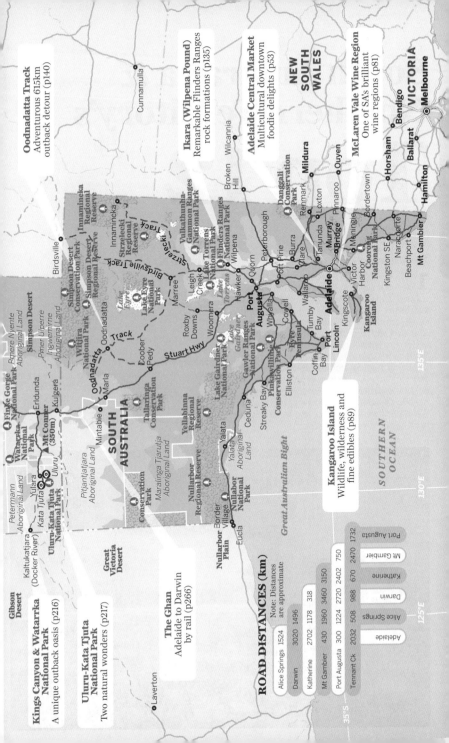

Kings Canyon & Watarrka National Park
A unique outback oasis (p216)

Uluru-Kata Tjuta National Park
Two natural wonders (p217)

The Ghan
Adelaide to Darwin by rail (p266)

Oodnadatta Track
Adventurous 615km outback detour (p140)

Ikara (Wilpena Pound)
Remarkable Flinders Ranges rock formations (p135)

Adelaide Central Market
Multicultural downtown foodie delights (p53)

McLaren Vale Wine Region
One of SA's brilliant wine regions (p81)

Kangaroo Island
Wildlife, wilderness and fine edibles (p89)

Gibson Desert

Laverton

Petermann Aboriginal Land

Kaltukatjara (Docker River)

Kata Tjuta ◉ Yulara ◉ Uluru

Uluru-Kata Tjuta National Park

Finke Gorge National Park

Watarrka National Park

Mt Conner ▲ (350m)

Erldunda

Kulgera

Pirnere Nyente Aboriginal Land

Pirner Uiperre Ingwemre Aboriginal Land

Pitjantjatjara Aboriginal Land

Maralinga Tjarutja Aboriginal Land

Mintabie

Marla

Oodnadatta

Oodnadatta Track

Coober Pedy

SOUTH AUSTRALIA

Great Victoria Desert

Nullarbor Regional Reserve

Yalata Aboriginal Land

Border Village

Eucla

Nullarbor Plain

Tallaringa Conservation Park

Yellabinna Regional Reserve

Yalata

Ceduna

Streaky Bay

Elliston

Coffin Bay

Port Lincoln

Cummulla

Birdsville

Simpson Desert Conservation Park

Witjira National Park

Simpson Desert Regional Reserve

Innamincka Regional Reserve

Strzelecki Track

Strzelecki Regional Reserve

Innamincka

Birdsville Track

Marree

Oodnadatta Track

Roxby Downs

Woomera

Stuart Hwy

Lake Eyre National Park

Lake Eyre (Kati Thanda)

Leigh Creek

Hawker

Wilpena

Flinders Ranges National Park

Vulkathunha-Gammon Ranges National Park

Broken Hill

Wilcannia

NEW SOUTH WALES

Lake Torrens National Park

Lake Torrens

Quorn

Port Augusta

Port Pirie

Peterborough

Burra

Clare

Tanunda

Gawler Ranges National Park

Lake Gairdner National Park

Lake Gairdner

Pinkawillinie Conservation Park

Whyalla

Cowell

Tumby Bay

Eyre Peninsula

Port Augusta

Danggali Conservation Park

Renmark

Loxton

Pinnaroo

Murray Bridge

Meningie

Victor Harbor

Tanunda

Wallaroo

Adelaide ◉

Kangaroo Island

Kingscote

Mildura

Ouyen

Bordertown

Coorong National Park

Kingston SE

Naracoorte

Beachport

Mt Gambier

Horsham

Hamilton

Ballarat

Bendigo

VICTORIA

Melbourne ◉

SOUTHERN OCEAN

Great Australian Bight

35°S

125°E   130°E   135°E

ROAD DISTANCES (km)
Note: Distances are approximate

	Adelaide	Alice Springs	Darwin	Katherine	Mt Gambier	Port Augusta
Alice Springs	1524					
Darwin	3020	1496				
Katherine	2702	1178	318			
Mt Gambier	430	1960	3460	3150		
Port Augusta	300	1224	2720	2402	750	
Tennant Ck	2032	508	988	670	2470	1732

South Australia & Northern Territory's
Top 12

Kakadu National Park, NT

1 Kakadu (p166) is more than a nature reserve: it's an adventure into a natural and cultural landscape like no other. Weathered by successive seasons of Wet and Dry, the sandstone ramparts of Kakadu and neighbouring Arnhem Land have sheltered humans for aeons, and an extraordinary legacy of rock art remains. Represented are mysterious figures of the Dreaming, hunting stories, zoological diagrams, and 'contact art' – records of visitors from Indonesia and more recent European colonists. Kakadu's Ubirr and Nourlangie galleries are of World Heritage significance and are accessible to all. Below: Ubirr at sunset (p168)

Uluru-Kata Tjuta National Park, NT

2 Australia's most recognised natural wonder, Uluru (Ayers Rock; p222) draws pilgrims from around the world like moths to a big red flame. No matter how many postcard images you have seen, nothing prepares you for Uluru's immense presence, character-pitted epidermis and spiritual gravitas. Not far away is a mystical clutch of stone siblings known as Kata Tjuta (The Olgas; p224). Deeply cleaved with narrow gorges and decorated with tufts of vegetation, these 36 pink-red domes majestically flaunt their curves and blush intensely at sunset.

ETER EVE/TOURISM NT ©

TERRA IMAGES/SHUTTERSTOCK ©

WENDY MEDER/SHUTTERSTOCK ©

Wine Regions, SA

3 If you're into wine, get into South Australia (p33). Persecuted Lutherans on the run from Prussia and Silesia first had the bright idea of planting vines here. Lo and behold – one of the world's great wine societies was born! Coonawarra cabernet sauvignon, Barossa Valley and McLaren Vale shiraz, Adelaide Hills sauvignon blanc, Clare Valley riesling ... The quality is sky-high, and the experience of wobbling between cellar doors and their adjunct restaurants and B&Bs is an indulgent delight. Put simply, these are among Australia's premier wine regions and are a pleasure to visit. Above: Vineyard, McLaren Vale

Nitmiluk (Katherine Gorge) National Park, NT

4 Paddling a canoe upstream, through one gorge and then another, leaving the crowds behind, you will be drawn into the silence of the towering cliffs that squeeze the waters of the Katherine River (p184). Take a break on a sandy river beach, walk up to a viewpoint or take a helicopter flight for an eagle's-eye view. The wider Nitmiluk (Katherine Gorge) National Park has even more to offer, such as the Jatbula Trail, a five-day walk from the gorge to the wonderful Leliyn (Edith Falls).

Adelaide Central Market, SA

5 Lift the lid on multicultural Adelaide with a visit to the city's world-class food market (p53). Beneath one vast roof you'll find cheese wrights, pasta stalls, delis, locally farmed fruit and veg, yoghurt shops, family-run seafood vendors and sausage stands that have been here for decades. Italian, Greek, German, French, Hungarian ... it's crowded, in-your-face trading, but never intimidating or claustrophobic. Right next door is Adelaide's Chinatown: hit the food courts for a steaming laksa, forage for a new mobile-phone cover or settle in for a Friday-night beer.

ANDREW WATSON/GETTY IMAGES ©

ANDREA IZZOTTI/SHUTTERSTOCK ©

Kings Canyon, NT

6 Central Australia's lesser-known geological wonder (p216) lies isolated and hidden within the low George Gill Range, in Watarrka National Park between Alice Springs and Uluru. Yet it is a jaw-dropping spectacle for those who undertake the journey. Centuries of changing climates have sliced the canyon out of the reddish sandstone like a knife through butter, leaving the 100m-high walls extraordinarily smooth. Above the canyon rim are fascinating 'beehive' formations, while beneath the imposing cliffs permanent waterholes nourish rare and beautiful plants and shy animals.

Kangaroo Island, SA

7 'KI', as it's known, makes a delightful detour from mainland SA's established tourist trail. Just a 45-minute ferry chug across the Backstairs Passage from Cape Jervis, the island (the 131st-biggest island in the world – about half the size of Crete) is a haven for wildlife, wineries, weird rock formations and wild ocean beaches. The ferry tickets are pricey and the locals are begging for progress, but we like KI (p89) the way it is: unspoiled, untouristy and unsophisticated in the best possible way.

STANISLAV FOSENBAUER/SHUTTERSTOCK ©

The Ghan, SA & NT

8 The legendary *Ghan* – named after central Australia's pioneering Afghan cameleers – is one of the world's great train journeys (p267). Begun in 1877, the old line from Marree, north of Adelaide, to Alice Springs suffered from wash outs and shoddy construction before a shiny new line replaced it in 1980. The Alice-to-Darwin section followed in 2004: now there's 2979km and 42 hours of track between Adelaide and Darwin. The *Ghan* isn't cheap or fast, but the experience of rolling through the vast, flat expanse of central Australia's deserts is magical.

Oodnadatta Track, SA

9 Feeling adventurous? Craving some off-road action but don't want to get ridiculously remote? Take a two-day trip along SA's Oodnadatta Track (p140) – an unsealed 615km desert drive between Marree in the northern Flinders Ranges and Marla on the main Adelaide–Darwin Stuart Hwy. There's plenty of history and natural heritage here: threadbare railway towns, remarkable old pubs, natural springs, the astonishing Lake Eyre... But the drive itself is the true reward – an essential Australian desert-heart experience. You'll need a 4WD to do it justice.

Litchfield Plunge Pools, NT

10 Step into a glossy tourist brochure and take the plunge into an Eden-like rock pool complete with sparkling waterfall and surrounding foliage. Even if you don't have the toned, young body featured in the brochure the setting is picture-perfect. Litchfield National Park (p163) is renowned for its shimmering cascades and gin-clear pools teeming with fish and it's so close to Darwin you can be back in town by nightfall. Other stirring rock formations make this one of the Top End's most beautiful corners. Below: Florence Falls (p163)

Ikara (Wilpena Pound), SA

11 The geologic highlight of the Flinders Ranges is Wilpena Pound (p135), known to the area's Adnyamathanha people as Ikara. The local camping ground is shaded by native pines, the Wilpena resort is interesting and affordable and there are bushwalks to suit everyone from overachievers to the terminally lazy. But the real lure is Ikara itself: an astonishing formation of purple-brown rock escarpments encircling a vast, dusty bowl full of arid scrub, homestead ruins and wandering emus. On a camera-wielding flight or a picturesque hike, the Pound is seriously scenic.

FRITZ16/SHUTTERSTOCK ©

SOUTHERN LIGHTSCAPES AUSTRALIA/GETTY IMAGES ©

Indigenous Art, NT

ANDREW WATSON/GETTY IMAGES ©

12 The Northern Territory's numerous art centres are vital focal points for Aboriginal culture and one of the easiest entry points into the Indigenous world for outsiders. The paintings alone make these centres art galleries of singular power and beauty, offering so many windows into local culture. But spend enough time here and you may be able to sit, watch and talk with the region's finest artists as they create their masterpieces. Injalak Arts & Crafts Centre (p176), in Gunbalanya in western Arnhem Land, is one outstanding example among many. Left: An Aboriginal artist at work at the Mindil Beach Sunset Market (p154)

Need to Know

For more information, see Survival Guide (p253)

Currency
Australian dollar ($)

Language
English

Visas
All visitors to Australia need a visa (except New Zealanders). Apply online for a three-month ETA or eVisitor Visa, or standard 12-month Tourist Visa.

Money
ATMs widely available, especially in larger cities and towns. Credit card and Eftpos purchases accepted in most hotels and restaurants.

Mobile Phones
European phones will work on Australia's network, but most American or Japanese phones won't. Use global roaming or a local SIM card and prepaid account.

Time
Central Standard Time (GMT/UTC plus 9½ hours)

When to Go

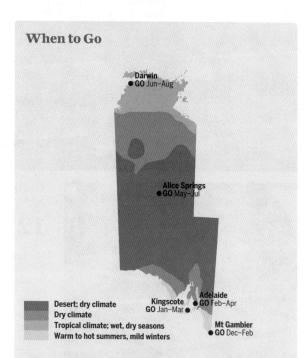

Darwin
● GO Jun–Aug

Alice Springs
● GO May–Jul

Kingscote
GO Jan–Mar ●

Adelaide
● GO Feb–Apr

Mt Gambier
● GO Dec–Feb

Desert; dry climate
Dry climate
Tropical climate; wet, dry seasons
Warm to hot summers, mild winters

High Season
➡ In the south, summer (Dec–Feb) is high season. SA accommodation prices jump as much as 25%.

➡ In the deserts and tropical north, winter (Jun–Aug) is high season: warm days, low humidity. Uluru and Kakadu accommodation prices leap 25%.

Shoulder
➡ March, April and May bring clear skies and shorter queues.

➡ Spring (Sep–Nov) is particularly atmospheric around Adelaide, but can still be wet in the Top End.

➡ Local business people are relaxed, gearing up for (SA) or recovering from (NT) peak tourist trade.

Low Season
➡ In the south, winter (Jun–Aug) brings cool rainy days, meaning few tourists. Restaurants and attractions keep slightly shorter hours.

➡ Up in the tropical north, summer (Dec–Feb) brings the Wet and its heavy rains. Most unpaved roads are impassable.

Useful Websites

Lonely Planet (www.lonely planet.com/australia) Destination information, hotel bookings, traveller forum and more.

Bureau of Meteorology (www. bom.gov.au) Weather forecasts and warnings.

South Australian Tourism Commission (www.south australia.com) Accommodation, activities, events and tours.

Travel NT (www.northern territory.com) NT travel guide.

Department of Environment, Water & Natural Resources (www.environment.sa.gov.au/ parks/Home) SA national parks .

Parks & Wildlife (www.nt.gov. au/leisure/parks-reserves) NT national parks.

Important Numbers

Australian phone numbers have two-digit area codes followed by eight-digit numbers. Drop the initial 0 when calling Australia from overseas.

Country code	✆61
International access code	✆0011
Emergency	✆000
NT road conditions	✆1800 246 199
Directory assistance	✆1223

Exchange Rates

Canada	C$1	$0.99
China	CNY1	$0.19
Euro zone	€1	$1.42
Japan	¥100	$1.17
New Zealand	NZ$1	$0.96
UK	UK£1	$1.66
USA	US$1	$1.32

For current exchange rates see www.xe.com.

Daily Costs

Budget: Less than $150

➡ Dorm bed: $25–35 per night

➡ Double room in pub/budget hotel: $80

➡ Budget pizza or pasta main course: $15

➡ Adelaide or Darwin bus ride: $3–$5

Midrange: $150–275

➡ Double room in midrange hotel/motel: $130–250

➡ Midrange restaurant main course with glass of wine: $35

➡ Small-car hire per day: $35

➡ Short taxi ride: $25

Top End: More than $275

➡ Double room in top-end hotel: more than $250

➡ Top-end restaurant main course with glass of wine: $50

➡ Tickets to a show: $20–150

➡ 4WD hire per day: from $100

Opening Hours

Banks 9.30am to 4pm Monday to Thursday; until 5pm on Friday

Cafes 7am to 5pm

Petrol stations & roadhouses 8am to 10pm; some 24 hours

Post offices 9am to 5pm Monday to Friday; some from 9am to noon on Saturdays

Pubs & bars Open for drinking from lunchtime until late; food from noon to 2pm and 6pm to 8pm

Restaurants Noon to 2pm and 6pm to 9pm, often later

Shops & businesses 9am to 5pm Monday to Friday; until noon or 5pm on Saturday

Supermarkets 7am until at least 8pm

Arriving in South Australia & Northern Territory

Adelaide Airport (ADL) Prebooked private **Adelaide Airport Flyer** (p75) minibuses connect the airport with the city ($35; 6am to 11.30pm). Public **Adelaide Metro** (p274) JetBuses ply the same route ($3.20 to $5.10; 6:30am to 11pm). Taxis charge around $30 into the city (15 minutes).

Darwin Airport (DRW) Private **Darwin City Airport Shuttle** (p156) minibuses connect the airport with the city ($15; 24 hours); prebooking recommended. Taxis charge around $40 into the city (15 minutes).

Getting Around

Outback Australia is vast: buses and trains can shuttle you between the major centres, but you'll be getting behind the wheel for most other destinations.

Car & 4WD To explore SA and the NT properly you'll need your own wheels (4WDs for outback tracks). There are car-hire outlets in cities and most large towns. Drive on the left.

Bus Useful, affordable, regular connections between major centres: good for covering long distances on a budget.

Train Expensive, infrequent long-distance routes: more for romance and scenery than expedience.

For much more on **getting around**, see p267

First Time

For more information, see Survival Guide (p253)

Checklist

➡ Sign up for a local roadside-assistance network.

➡ Buy one of the excellent Hema Maps that cover outback roads and tracks.

➡ Inform your debit-/credit-card company.

➡ Arrange for appropriate travel insurance.

➡ Check if you can use your mobile/cell phone.

➡ Check weather and road conditions before setting out.

What to Pack

➡ Sturdy walking shoes – there are many excellent walks, long and short.

➡ Warm clothes – the desert nights are surprisingly cold in winter.

➡ Hat, sunglasses and sunscreen.

➡ Water bottle.

➡ Australian electrical adaptor.

➡ Binoculars and wildlife field guides.

Top Tips for Your Trip

➡ Don't be too ambitious – outback Australia is a *big* place, and trying to see everything can lead to frustration (and exhaustion).

➡ Weather matters out here – pay close attention to the forecasts.

➡ On long drives don't forget to stop regularly to reboot the brain.

➡ Avoid driving at night. The empty landscape teems with car-wrecking kangaroos, while cattle find the sun-warmed roads a fine place to rest on a cold desert night.

➡ Book well in advance if you need accommodation (and/or rental vehicles) for any of the festivals in Adelaide or remote communities.

➡ If booking a rental vehicle, especially in Darwin, and you want unlimited kilometres, you may need to book through a travel agency or the local tourist office.

What to Wear

It will be no surprise to learn that the theme is casual; however, it is not 'anything goes' and many dining and entertainment venues will require covered shoes or sandals (no flip-flops or singlets). The central deserts are very cold in winter, with subzero temperatures at night. As soon as the sun sets winter woollies are needed. Sensible and stylish under the outback sun is the broad-brimmed hat and, if you are travelling in summer, bring a bathing costume to cool off in the waterholes and swimming pools.

Sleeping

There are excellent accommodation possibilities, but choice is limited outside major towns and tourist sites.

➡ **Hotels, motels and pubs** Hotels are often restricted to major cities. Pub accommodation is usually very basic and motels are typically clean, convenient, conventional and everywhere.

➡ **Roadhouses** One-stop shops along the highways; from camp sites to basic dongas (small, transportable buildings) with shared facilities to modern motel rooms.

➡ **Caravan parks** Most caravan parks have cabins as well as caravan and camping sites. Many have swimming pools and restaurants.

➡ **Hostels** Found in the more major towns, hostels tend to be highly social affairs ideal for young travellers.

Bargaining

Gentle haggling is fairly common in weekend markets, secondhand shops and often when purchasing arts and crafts from the artist, but it's not the done thing in most Indigenous art centres, where prices are fixed. It's common practice to ask for a discount on expensive items when paying cash (not that you are guaranteed to get one). In most other instances you are expected to pay the stated price.

Tipping

Tipping is far from ingrained in Australian society, and most people in the outback don't bother. The only place where tipping is considered normal is restaurants; taxi drivers also appreciate you rounding up the fare.

➡ **Hotels** Not usually expected.

➡ **Restaurants** For excellent table service tip 5% to 10%.

➡ **Taxis** Not expected, but the drivers will appreciate you rounding up the fare

Alcohol

Check whether alcohol rules apply when visiting an outback community. You may be breaking the law even with unopened bottles in your vehicle.

Smoking

Smoking is banned in many public places, including on public transport and in pubs, bars and eateries.

KRZYSZTOF DYDYNSKI /GETTY IMAGES ©

Adelaide Arcade

Etiquette

➡ **Greetings** Usually a simple 'G'day' or 'Howzitgoin?' suffices. Shake hands with men or women when meeting for the first time. Australians expect a firm handshake with eye contact. However, when visiting an Aboriginal community this can be seen as overbearing. Here, a soft clasp with little arm movement, and virtually no eye contact can be expected. The best advice is to take it as it comes and respond in like manner.

➡ **Shout** Australians like to take it in turn to buy ('shout') a round of drinks for the group and everyone is expected to take part.

Eating

Eating in outback Australia can be as pricey or prudent as you like: a roadhouse hamburger can taste just as good as a fine-dining morsel in a haughty winery bistro. Bookings are really only necessary in Adelaide's or Darwin's top restaurants.

➡ **Restaurants** Adelaide, SA's wine regions and Darwin have excellent restaurants. Elsewhere, pickings are slim. The Centre has a small selection of fine-dining restaurants found within the better hotels in Alice Springs and Yulara.

➡ **Roadhouses** More of a necessity than a recommendation, roadhouse fare (think burgers and steaks) suffers from the tyranny of distance, whereby fresh ingredients and reliable cooks are hard to source. Nevertheless, there are some pearls.

➡ **Pubs** Pubs serve a similar purpose to roadhouses (hearty, no-nonsense meals); the food is generally secondary to the beverages.

If You Like...

Beaches

Bookending outback Australia to the north and south are long, convoluted coastlines studded with beautiful beaches. In South Australia you can surf and swim; Northern Territory beaches are better suited to sitting and reading.

Snelling Beach On Kangaroo Island's sheltered north coast is this hidden gem: take a dip or snooze under an umbrella. (p95)

Pondalowie Bay Some of SA's best surf peels into Pondalowie, on the southern tip of Yorke Peninsula. (p122)

Glenelg Adelaide's big-city beach is a rambling tram ride from the CBD. White sand, pubs, boutiques, bikinis ... (p59)

Ninety Mile Beach Fronting the Southern Ocean in Coorong National Park is this roaring surf beach. Bring your 4WD. (p116)

Cobourg Peninsula Watch for sea turtles and whales (and crocs!) at this isolated stretch of paradise. (p177)

Mindil Beach Darwin's Mindil Beach is a beaut spot to chew a few satay sticks. (p147)

Carrickalinga Beach Southeast of Adelaide is this underpopulated 2km beach: good fishing, beachcombing and swimming. (p85)

Wine Regions

Wine is hard-wired in South Australia's DNA. Even if you're more of a beer boffin, your visit here will undoubtedly involve dipping into a wine region or three.

Barossa Valley More than 80 wineries in this German-settled enclave, home to some of Australia's greatest reds. (p102)

Clare Valley Clare Valley riesling rocks! Skillogalee is our fave, with a fab cellar-door restaurant. (p106)

Coonawarra Cabernet sauvignon is the name of Coonawarra's game, with 100-year-old vines as thick as your leg. (p119)

Adelaide Hills Cool-climate grapes (sauvignon blanc, pinot noir) dapple the slopes in Adelaide's backyard. (p76)

McLaren Vale Famously weighty shiraz grows an hour south of Adelaide, with a string of beaut beaches nearby. (p81)

Aboriginal Art & Culture

The Northern Territory is home to the country's richest traditions of Aboriginal art and the numerous art centres both showcase the artworks and provide a meeting point of cultures. South Australia has some intriguing options too.

Uluru Aboriginal Tours Learn all about Uluru from knowledgable Indigenous guides. (p218)

Kakadu Animal Tracks Tours through Kakadu's famous Aboriginal rock-art galleries and wetlands, departing Darwin or Jabiru. (p167)

Barunga Festival Aboriginal cultural and sports festival near Katherine. Music, dance, arts, storytelling, crafts, football and spear throwing. (p20)

Injalak Arts & Crafts Centre Terrific gallery, shop and a chance to sit with the artists while they paint. (p176)

Ghunmarn Culture Centre One of the NT's best, with an exceptional exhibition of art and culture from West Arnhem Land. (p191)

Museum & Art Gallery of the Northern Territory Darwin art gallery with a collection of astonishing richness. (p147)

Papunya Tula Artists Beautifully presented Alice Springs gallery of paintings from the Western Desert. (p206)

Bookabee Tours Aboriginal-run day tours of Adelaide, plus longer jaunts into the Flinders Ranges. (p61)

Wildlife

You'll see a whole lotta native wildlife on your central Australian road trip: emus, goannas, snakes, koalas, seals, parrots, frill-necked lizards, cockatoos, dolphins... And that's before you hit the wildlife parks!

Cahill's Crossing Croc central at East Alligator River, where Kakadu National Park meets Arnhem Land. (p169)

Seal Bay Conservation Park On Kangaroo Island, home to a malodorous colony of Australian sea lions. (p96)

Whale watching Seeing a southern right whale breaching is unforgettable. Scan the seas off Victor Harbor or Head of Bight, west of Ceduna in SA. (p128) (p86)

West MacDonnell Ranges Black-footed rock wallabies, dingoes, red kangaroos and great birding. (p209)

Cobourg Peninsula Marine mammals, including six different turtle species, in an unspoiled setting. (p177)

Pungalina – Seven Emu Wildlife Sanctuary Fabulous birding and unusual mammals in a deliciously remote setting. (p197)

Fogg Dam Conservation Reserve Bird-rich wetlands close to Kakadu. (p160)

Alice Springs Desert Park The surprising abundance of desert life is on show here. (p199)

Territory Wildlife Park Meet the residents of wetlands, woodlands and monsoon vine forests just south of Darwin. (p162)

PLAN YOUR TRIP IF YOU LIKE...

Top: Thorny Devil lizard

Bottom: Snelling Beach, Kangaroo Island (p95)

Arts Festivals

The best arts festivals aren't always the ones with the loftiest ambitions. Sure, go highbrow if you like, but central Australia also celebrates the offbeat and the downright ridiculous.

Adelaide Festival The big one with the big names and world-class performances. (p61)

Darwin Festival The Top End's best theatre, literature, music, cabaret, comedy and visual arts. (p148)

Garma Festival One of Australia's best Aboriginal festivals out in Eastern Arnhem Land. (p178)

Barunga Festival Katherine celebration run by the local Jaywoyn people. (p22)

Stone Country Festival Accessible West Arnhem Land festival with a focus on the arts. (p177)

Tjungu Festival Yulara celebration of Indigenous culture within sight of Uluru. (p219)

Alice Desert Festival The desert delivers offbeat cinema, street art, bush foods and arts and crafts. (p203)

Adelaide Fringe Hip, off-kilter and unfailingly entertaining, Adelaide's Fringe is second only to Edinburgh's. (p61)

WOMADelaide Arguably Australia's best live-music festival with acts from across the globe. (p61)

Alice Springs Beanie Festival Lots of local arts and crafts. (p203)

Beautiful Landscapes

Big rocks, gaping chasms, wildlife-rich billabongs, lurid lakes and astonishing caves: central Australia wrote the book on wonders of the natural realm.

Uluru Sure, you've seen it on TV, but you'll still do a double-take when you spy it on the horizon. (p222)

Kata Tjuta The tallest of these 36 jaw-droppingly big boulders is higher than Uluru. (p224)

Kings Canyon One of the true wonders of Australia's natural world and utterly unforgettable. (p216)

Remarkable Rocks Kangaroo Island's spectacular weather-gouged rocks. Remarkable! (p98)

Kakadu National Park The view from the Ubirr escarpment at sunset is one of Australia's truly iconic images. (p167)

Yellow Water wetlands Kakadu National Park's famed wetlands are fertile and festooned with wildlife. (p172)

Blue Lake Mt Gambier's undisputed highlight, a 75m-deep lake that turns ludicrously blue in summer. (p117)

Naracoorte Caves World Heritage–listed limestone caves in southeastern South Australia. (p118)

Limmen National Park Remote park with two 'lost cities' of bizarre and very beautiful rock pinnacles. (p192)

Rainbow Valley Conservation Reserve Dazzling colour changes in a remote corner of the outback. (p215)

Quirky Small Towns

'Woah … how do people live out here?!' Not an uncommon thought in remote central Australia. But isolation breeds small towns with community spirit, quirkiness, charm and (usually) a good pub.

William Creek On SA's Oodnadatta Track, there's not much here: an airstrip, a petrol pump and an amazing old pub. (p140)

Wycliffe Well On the Stuart Hwy 380km north of Alice Springs, Wycliffe Well is a UFO-spotting hot spot. (p197)

Coober Pedy With its subterranean, opal-obsessed locals, Coober Pedy in SA is truly one of a kind. (p138)

Melrose Two pubs, a national park, a derelict brewery and inexplicable gravitas: is Melrose SA's perfect small town? (p133)

Humpty Doo The name is glorious, there's a Big Boxing Crocodile and the pub is self-proclaimed 'world famous'. A cute fuel stop on the road to Kakadu. (p160)

Daly Waters The pub here claims to be the NT's oldest (1893). 120 years later it's still a worthy pit stop. (p195)

Borroloola On the Gulf of Carpentaria, Borroloola has an art centre, barramundi fishing and very little else. (p193)

William Creek Hotel (p140)

Bushwalking

If the sun's not scorching and the heavens aren't delivering a deluge, there are some brilliant bushwalks in central Australia. Just get your timing right!

Base Walk Take your time on this lap of Uluru: for such a monstrous monolith the atmosphere is surprisingly intimate. (p223)

Valley of the Winds A 7.4km loop weaving through Kata Tjuta's wondrous rockscapes. (p224)

Jatbula Trail An intense, five-day jaunt through 66km of Nitmiluk National Park. (p185)

Barrk Walk Challenging 12km walk through the Nourlangie

area in Kakadu National Park. (p171)

Waterfall Gully Track Traipse past waterfalls on the way up/down the surprisingly perky Mt Lofty (727m) behind Adelaide. (p79)

Markets

To market, to market, to buy a fat...[insert gourmet/boutique item of choice]. Right across central Australia you'll find fabulous markets to blow your dollars at: food, produce, and arts and crafts.

Adelaide Central Market A true Adelaide highlight, the Central Market is a food-lover's paradise. (p53)

Parap Village Market In suburban Darwin is this unexpected, claustrophobic Asian street mart complete with smoky aisles, art galleries and tropical flowers (p154)

Mindil Beach Sunset Market Darwin during the Dry? Tail the crowds to this famed evening market: food, live music and loads of fun. (p154)

Gilles Street Market Hip fashion and design in downtown Adelaide at this monthly market (twice monthly in summer). (p74)

Willunga Farmers Market On the doorstep of McLaren Vale wine region is Willunga, a cute-as-a-button sandstone town with a pumping Saturday-morning market. (p83)

Month by Month

January

South Australia and the central deserts are hot and dry; the Top End is hot and wet with many tourism-related business and even some hotels closed. In SA, locals head to the cricket.

☆ Tour Down Under

SA's six-stage version of the Tour de France. People line the streets to watch the lycra-clad lads whizz past, with picnic rugs, champagne and Euro vibes. (p61)

February

February is central Australia's warmest month: hot and sticky in the Wet up north, while central regions swelter in dry desert heat. Many roads are impassable in the north, especially Arnhem Land. Locals go back to work.

☆ Adelaide Fringe

All the acts that don't make the cut (or don't want to) for the highbrow Adelaide Festival come to the Fringe. Comedy, music, theatre, buskers and the hyperactive Garden of Unearthly Delights. Second only to the Edinburgh Fringe. It's that good. (p61)

March

March is harvest time in SA's vineyards and festival time in Adelaide: international visitors drag the city onto the world stage. It's still wet up north and the countryside is sodden; many unsealed roads remain impassable.

☆ Adelaide Festival

Culture vultures absorb international and Australian dance, drama, opera and theatre performances at this ultra classy annual event. Australia's biggest multiarts event. (p61)

☆ WOMADelaide

Annual festival of world music, arts, food and dance, held over four days in Adelaide's luscious Botanic Park. Eight stages and more than 400 world-music acts: very family friendly, and you can get a cold beer too. (p61)

☆ Crush

Fine wine and music at this Adelaide Hills festival, billing itself as the 'stylish alternative'. Our advice: pick your winery and stay put – racing the crowds from winery to winery ain't stylish. (p76)

☆ Tiwi Grand Final

Proof that life very much continues in the Wet comes at one of rural Australia's most celebrated footy finals. It's a real local event with plenty of visitors from the mainland and art exhibitions as well. (p158)

☆ Clipsal 500

Mulleted bogans rejoice as Adelaide's city streets become a four-day Holden-versus-Ford racing track. High-pitched engine whine resonates through the suburbs. (p61)

April

The Adelaide Hills are atmospheric as European trees turn golden then maroon. Up north the rain is abating and the desert temperatures are becoming manageable, but it's still low season. Easter = pricey accommodation everywhere.

🎊 Barossa Vintage Festival

Biennial festival held in odd-numbered years that has processions, maypole dancing, traditional dinners and much Barossa Valley wine (...shoot for a sip of Penfolds' famous 'Grange'). (p102)

🎊 Tjungu Festival

April sees the dynamic Tjungu Festival take over Yulara with a focus on local Aboriginal culture. (p219)

May

The Dry begins in the Northern Territory bringing relief from humidity and returning tourists. This is a great time to visit Uluru, before the tour buses arrive in droves.

☆ Alice Springs Cup Carnival

Five days of racing and an abundance of social activities is a good excuse to dust off the old suit/frock and sink a few cold ones under a shady marquee while the horses do their stuff. (p203)

🍷 Clare Valley Gourmet Weekend

Long-running food-and-wine festival run by local wineries and some of SA's top restaurants. Book your B&B early! (p106)

🏃 Whale Watching

Along the South Australian coast, migrating southern right and humpback whales come close to shore to feed, breed and calf. The whales are here between May and October; see them at Victor Harbor and west of Ceduna. (p86)

☆ Country Music in Katherine

Country music finds a temporary spiritual home in Katherine with live performances and plenty of big hats. It's usually in May but sometimes moseys on into June. (p181)

☆ Uluru Camel Cup

Camel races within sight of Uluru are a fabulous if rather ungainly sight at this festival that never takes itself too seriously. (p203)

June

Winter brings peak season in the tropical Top End and central deserts. Many hotels and tour operators reopen after a long hiatus. Waterfalls and outback tracks are accessible (accommodation prices less so). Chilly across South Australia.

🎊 Adelaide Cabaret Festival

Unique cabaret festival supporting local and interstate music and theatre. Everything from stockings-and-suspenders burlesque shows to intimate concerts by top crooners. (p62)

🎊 Barunga Festival

Fabulous Aboriginal cultural and sports festival. Music (battle of the bands!), dance, arts, storytelling, crafts, football, athletics and spear throwing. Camp or day-trip from Katherine. (barungafestival.com.au)

☆ Finke Desert Race

Two-day, off-road bike, car and dune-buggy race through the desert from Alice Springs to the Apatula Community. It draws all sorts and brings remote communities to life. (p203)

🍷 Sea & Vines Festival

Wine, seafood and live music in McLaren Vale wineries over the June long weekend. Can get insanely crowded: book your transport and accommodation many moons in advance. (p82)

July

Pubs with open fires, cosy coffee shops and empty beaches down south; packed markets, tours and accommodation up north. Pack warm clothes for anywhere south of Alice Springs.

☆ Alice Springs Camel Cup

Unpredictable camel racing and beer drinking kicks up the dust in Alice Springs. This is Alice at its most rambunctious best. (p203)

☆ Darwin Cup Carnival

Darwin's Fannie Bay racecourse erupts with six days of thundering hoofs and fine-lookin' folk. Wear your shiny shoes and your best hat. (p149)

🎊 Darwin Fringe Festival

Offbeat culture in the Top End: theatre, visual arts, dance, music and poetry fill the city's streets. (p149)

🎊 NAIDOC Week

The National Aboriginal & Islander Day Observance Committee conducts performances, exhibitions and talks in communities around SA and the NT (www.naidoc.org.au).

☆ Royal Darwin Show

Darwin's show is when rural Northern Territory comes to the city with farm animals at every turn and much entertainment tacked on to broaden the appeal. (www.darwinshow.com.au)

🎊 Walking with Spirits

One of the outback's best festivals with an Indigenous focus. The waterfalls near Beswick are a fab setting for this explosion of traditional dance and music and other entertainment. (p191)

☆ Beer Can Regatta

Sandy high jinks and beer-can boats at Darwin's Mindil Beach. Help the locals empty a few cans to build the boats for next year. (p149)

August

Southerners, sick of winter's grey-sky drear, head north for some sun. Last chance to visit the outback and tropical Top End before things get too hot or wet (or both). Kakadu, anyone?

🎊 Darwin Festival

Two weeks of theatre, comedy, cabaret, dance, music, food and workshops – an artistic cavalcade! A focus on Aboriginal, Asian and outdoor events. (p148)

Top: Performer at the WOMADelaide festival (p61)
Bottom: Performance at the Garma Festival (p178)

⚒ Garma Festival

Out in remote East Arnhem Land, Yirrkala launches the Garma Festival, one of the largest and most vibrant celebrations of Indigenous culture in the Top End. (p178)

⚒ SALA Festival

The South Australian Living Artists Festival zooms in on contemporary art (no dusty old canvasses here). Look for SALA posters in cafes/bars/theatres/pubs around the state. (p62)

⚒ Stone Country Festival

This fine festival in Gunbalanya is one of the more accessible Arnhem Land festivals, with artistic traditions and performances very much the centrepiece. (p177)

September

Spring heralds a rampant bloom of wildflowers and mild temperatures across the outback, especially in the Flinders Ranges. It's cool and windy down south; starting to get hot and sticky up north.

⚒ Alice Desert Festival

Central Australian visual arts, music, dancing, exhibitions and street performers. Runs right through September, spilling into August and October. (p203)

🏃 City to Bay

A sweaty, heart-pumping 12km dash from downtown Adelaide to the beach at Glenelg. Bettser start training! (p62)

☆ Henley-on-Todd Regatta

Alice Springs' iconic 'boat' races on the (usually) bone-dry Todd River. Watch from the riverbanks, or build your own boat and join in. (p203)

☆ Royal Adelaide Show

A major seven-day agricultural festa. How many prize bulls, tattooed carnies and blue-singleted sheep shearers can you handle? (theshow.com.au)

⚒ Mahbilil Festival

Early in September, the Mahbilil Festival in Jabiru gets Kakadu rocking with local bands, performances and plenty of bush tucker – magpie goose anyone? (p170)

October

Everyone in the Top End scans the horizon waiting for rain as the build-up to the Wet brings sweltering humidity. Many tours take last orders. Down south, the weather avoids extremes everywhere.

🍷 Riverland Wine & Food Festival

Sample Riverland food and drink in Berri, on the banks of the mighty, meandering Murray River (Australia's Mississippi). (p113)

⚒ Malandarri Festival

Way out near the Gulf of Carpentaria, Borroloola hosts the Malandarri Festival, a memorable two-day spectacle with traditional dance and artistic

creativity at the heart of everything. (p194)

November

The rains have arrived in the north – rivers swell, tourist businesses close and much of Arnhem Land becomes inaccessible. Warm spring South Australian days tease city workers with a hint of summer.

⚒ Feast Festival

Annual gay-and-lesbian festival in Adelaide, with film, cabaret, music, forums, theatre and literature (and a few feasts). (p259)

🏃 Barra Fishing

The best months to go fishing for barramundi tend to be either side of the Wet and Dry – November is nearly guaranteed to be good, but there's also March, April and October in case you miss out. (p164)

December

Ring the bell, school's out! Holidays begin two weeks before Christmas. Darwin, Alice and Adelaide fill with shoppers and the weather is hot. Up north it's low season and monsoon season: afternoon thunderstorms bring pelting rain.

👁 Lights of Lobethal

Get a wholesome dose of Christmas with a dusk drive through Lobethal, a Germanic Adelaide Hills' town festooned with fairy lights. (p80)

Itineraries

The Best of SA & NT

To cover such vast terrain in two weeks might be bordering on insanity, but if you've only got two weeks to spare and a passion to explore the Australian outback, this is the way to do it. To make it work, you'll need to take an internal flight.

Begin in **Adelaide** (p53), one of Australia's coolest and most culturally rich cities, and spend two nights here. Pick up a car and head north, pausing overnight in **Port Augusta** (p124) – long enough to visit the Wadlata Outback Centre and Australian Arid Lands Botanic Garden. The next morning drive on to **Coober Pedy** (p138), precisely the sort of disconcerting remote outpost you'd expect to find at the end of a long outback drive. The next morning, buckle up for the longest drive of your trip, a nine-hour paved-road desert traverse to **Yulara** (p218), your base for exploring Uluru-Kata Tjuta National Park (p217). After three nights, drive to **Watarrka National Park** (p216) for a night, then on to **Alice Springs** (p198) the following day. From Alice, fly to **Darwin** (p143) from where you could take a whirlwind three- or (better) four-day tour that takes in **Kakadu National Park** (p166) and **Litchfield National Park** (p163). Return to Darwin for a great meal, art galleries and your flight home.

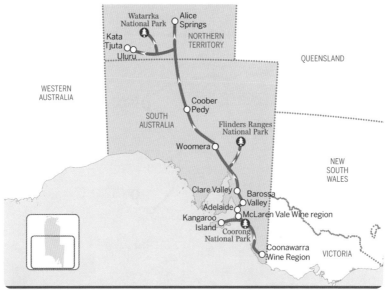

4 WEEKS Southeastern SA to Alice Springs

This month-long epic is like traversing the soul of a continent, from the verdant green vineyards of South Australia's wine regions to the searing red heart of the outback. You'll need your own wheels to take this one on.

Begin your journey in the **Coonawarra wine region** (p119). From here explore the dunes and lagoons of **Coorong National Park** (p116), sip your way through **McLaren Vale wine region** (p81), hop over to **Kangaroo Island** (p89) for a few days of wildlife watching, then roll into festival-frenzied **Adelaide** (p53). Don't miss a trip to Adelaide Central Market for lunch, and a night eating and drinking on Rundle St.

More wine! About an hour north of Adelaide is the old-school **Barossa Valley** (p102) (big reds); and about two hours north is the boutiquey **Clare Valley** (p106) with its world-class riesling, cottagey B&Bs and old stone mining towns.

You're a couple of weeks in already – time to put some serious kilometres under your belt. Continuing north, raggedy **Flinders Ranges National Park** (p135) jags up from the semi-desert like a rust-coloured mirage. Rich in Indigenous culture, the Flinders – the heart of which is the amazing Ikara (Wilpena Pound) – will sear itself into your memory. Hit the Stuart Hwy and journey north to the mildly spooky rocket-testing town **Woomera** (p138) and the opal-tinged dugouts of **Coober Pedy** (p138).

Trucking north, you'll enter the Simpson Desert and cross into the Northern Territory. The Lasseter Hwy turn-off takes you to peerless **Uluru** (p222) and the mesmerising **Kata Tjuta** (p224) rock formations. No matter how many times you've seen a photo, there's nothing quite like seeing an Uluru sunset firsthand.

About 300km north of Uluru, the spectacular, vertigo-inducing **Kings Canyon**, in **Watarrka National Park** (p216), rewards intrepid travellers with scenic walks into and around the rim of the gaping desert chasm. Finish up in the desert oasis of **Alice Springs** (p198), in the heart of the steep-sided MacDonnell Ranges. Alice has plenty to keep you busy for a few days: the excellent Alice Springs Desert Park, some classy restaurants or just a soak in a swimming pool as you gear up for the next leg of your journey.

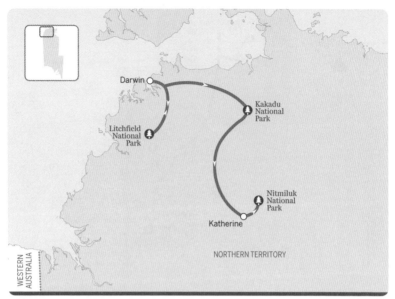

10 DAYS Darwin, Kakadu & Nitmiluk

This route gets you to the heart of the Top End, from multicultural Darwin to the great national parks of the north – visit some of these and you've seen some of Australia's most beautiful wild places.

Gone are the days when **Darwin** (p143) was a brawling frontier town full of fishermen, miners and truck drivers blowing off steam. These days it's all about outstanding museums, galleries of Indigenous art and great food.

A few hours south on the Stuart Hwy you'll run into some superb national parks. **Litchfield National Park** (p163) is famous for its plummeting waterfalls, bushwalks and cooling swimming holes, and is worthy of at least two days. From here, backtrack 50km north then head east into World Heritage–listed **Kakadu National Park** (p166), a wetland of international significance with amazing rock outcrops adorned with equally amazing, millennia-old Aboriginal rock art as well as a full suite of native Australian wildlife. Spend four days here and make sure you pop across the croc-rich East Alligator River to Gunbalanya (Oenpelli; p176) for great Aboriginal art.

Further south, spend a day in **Katherine** (p181), the regional 'big smoke' (make sure you have a meal at Marksies Camp Tucker; p183) before ending up in **Nitmiluk (Katherine Gorge) National Park** (p184), where the Katherine River cuts its way through 13 jagged ravines.

Top: Kangaroo Island rocks (p89)

Bottom: Red collared lorikeet at Litchfield National Park (p163)

BILDAGENTUR ZOONAR GMBH/SHUTTERSTOCK ©

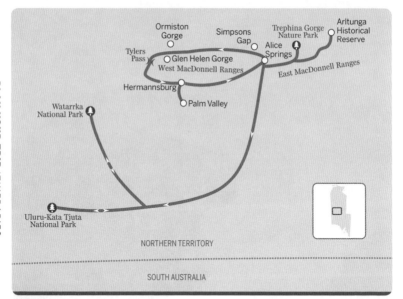

NORTHERN TERRITORY

SOUTH AUSTRALIA

The Red Centre

Exploring Australia's Red Centre is the essence of the outback: rocky outcrops, remote and red; fascinating wildlife; and a horizon seemingly without end. It's a journey you'll never forget. You'll need your own wheels (preferably a 4WD) to make this journey.

Alice Springs (p196; 'Alice' to her friends), at once frontier town in the middle of nowhere and a place to enjoy the trappings of civilisation, is the ideal starting point. Once you've sampled her charms, plan on two trips, one a day trip, the other an overnight loop from Alice.

Begin with a half- or full-day excursion along the East MacDonnell Ranges to **Trephina Gorge Nature Park** (p208) and **Arltunga Historical Reserve** (p208). Next head in the opposite direction from Alice to explore the West MacDonnells, visiting Simpsons Gap, **Ormiston Gorge** (p211) and **Glen Helen Gorge** (p212; overnight here). The next morning, get an early start and make for **Tylers Pass** (p212) for vast views, then continue on a loop back to Alice Springs, detouring to **Hermannsburg** (p213) and **Palm Valley** (p213) along the way.

Track south down the Stuart Hwy then west on the Lasseter to oasis-like **Watarrka National Park** (p216) to see **Kings Canyon**. Saving the best until last, make your pilgrimage to **Uluru-Kata Tjuta National Park** (p217).

Plan Your Trip

South Australian Food & Wine

The wine and food of SA are its greatest achievement, its allure and its saving grace. Adelaide packs the culinary and viticultural punch of a heavyweight. Beyond the city you'll find fresher seafood, smoother shiraz, tastier cheddar and fatter strawberries than anywhere else in this hemisphere – and that's just for lunch!

Where to Go

Barossa & Clare Valleys

Close enough to be kissing cousins but far enough apart to conjure up very different wine-region experiences, these two valleys are probably the first regions that spring to mind when anyone mentions South Australian wine. Just an hour from Adelaide, the **Barossa Valley** (p102) represents SA's old-school Germanic establishment, with day trippers galore and iconic names such as Penfolds and Henschke ruling the roost (actually, Henschke is 10km over the hill in Eden Valley, but close enough). Big, ballsy Australian red wine is what you're here for.

A further hour north, the **Clare Valley** (p106) is a more intimate, cloistered overnighter, with myriad stone B&Bs dating from the late 1800s and cool-climate valley folds producing world-class riesling. The Riesling Trail (p108) is an easy-does-it bike track meandering through the vineyards.

McLaren Vale

Just an hour south of Adelaide, **McLaren Vale** (p81) is an agrarian patchwork landscape, with vineyards and almond groves patterning the sun-baked slopes of the Willunga Escarpment as it levels

Best Wineries

Deviation Road (p79) Unpretentious Adelaide Hills winery doing cool climate drops to warm your heart.

Alpha Box & Dice (p84) McLaren Vale outfit bottling luscious blends and small-release shiraz.

Majella Wines (p115) Classy Coonawarra cabernet made by fourth-generation locals.

Rockford Wines (p103) Gorgeous old stone cellar door off the beaten path in the well-beaten Barossa.

Pikes (p108) A big angry fish? Hard to imagine as you sip into a summery riesling in the Clare Valley.

Best Places to Eat

Central Market (p53) Fill your Adelaide picnic hamper with cheese, salami, pasta, seafood, yoghurt, nuts, mushrooms, pickles, bratwursts ...

Peel Street (p66) Cutting-edge cafe ... or is it a top-notch bistro, or perhaps a slick wine bar? All of the above!

Russell's Pizza (p84) Showcasing Fleurieu Peninsula produce on big rustic pizzas. In Willunga.

Flying Fish Cafe (p87) The best of SA seafood right on the Encounter Coast. In Port Elliot.

Ferment Asian (p104) If you prefer red duck curry to bratwursts, this Barossa Valley food room will be your saviour.

out down to shimmering Gulf St Vincent. This gorgeous place – a kind of fantastical new-world Tuscany – produces some of the best shiraz you'll ever smack across your lips, and has a progressive vibe. You won't find much that's quaint or cottagey here – the mood is more celebratory, decadent and contemporary, with some fab restaurants, cafes and markets in among the rows of vines.

Coonawarra

Practical, no-fuss **Coonawarra** (p119) is far enough from both Adelaide and Melbourne to rule it out as a day trip or easy overnighter. People live here rather than pass through: the resultant wine trade is hard-working, utilitarian and often family-run, exploiting the area's fertile *terra rossa* soils and producing supersilky cabernet sauvignon. Penola is the region's service town. It's an affable country hamlet, with a decent pub, a couple of good eateries and Australia's only saint – one-time resident school teacher St Mary MacKillop – presiding over the grape business with benevolence.

Lesser-Known Wine Regions

Ever heard of wines from Padthaway, Kangaroo Island, the Adelaide Hills, the Riverland, Currency Creek or Langhorne Creek? Maybe not. The wine industries in these regions veer between nascent and surprisingly well-established, producing everything from chardonnay to sparking shiraz.

➡ **Padthaway** (www.padthawaywineregion. com) It isn't far from the Coonawarra, but with a tad more altitude and frosty nights it does a mean there's chardonnay to go with the local cab sav. There are a lot of vineyards here, but not many cellar doors.

➡ **Kangaroo Island** (kangarooislandwineries. com.au) There are six wineries on 'KI', the oldest of which dates from the distant 1990s. But that means they're free from the binds of expectation! Expect flinty sauvignon blanc and sunny chardonnay.

➡ **Adelaide Hills** (www.adelaidehillswine.com. au) Actually, you might have heard of wines from the Adelaide Hills: awesome cool-climate chardonnay, pinot noir, shiraz, sauvignon blanc and more interesting pinot grigio, pinot gris and

Cheeses at Adelaide Central Market (p53)

viognier vintages. Plenty of classy cellar doors, and just 20 minutes up the hill from Adelaide.

➡ **Riverland** (www.riverlandwine.org.au) Around Renmark and Barmera is one of Australia's largest wine-growing regions, but one with almost no hype or wine-tourism trade. It's all about volume here, with endless acres of vines irrigated by the Murray River. Not many cellar doors, but some great bargains to be had.

➡ **Currency & Langhorne Creeks** Inland from Goolwa on the Fleurieu Peninsula, Currency Creek (www.currencycreekwineregion.com.au) is one of South Australia's oldest wine regions, but it still feels like a well-kept secret. The same applies to nearby Langhorne Creek (www. langhornecreek.com): both areas are compact and accessible, yet remarkably untouristy. Swing through midweek and you'll have them all to yourself. Impressive shiraz, to say the least.

Where to Stay

➡ **For festivals** The Barossa Valley seems to have a major event of one kind or another every month. Lots of music and German heritage on display.

Wynns Coonawarra Estate (p115)

➡ **For romantic B&Bs** Cuddle up in an 1880s stone cottage in the Clare Valley, with DIY bacon and eggs for breakfast.

➡ **For foodie culture** McLaren Vale brings the foodies down from Adelaide: farmers markets, winery restaurants and cafes conspire to keep them sober.

➡ **For a day trip from Adelaide** Head for the Adelaide Hills, just 20 minutes up the freeway from the city. Old German towns, savvy wineries, cafes and cosy pubs.

➡ **For winery work** The Coonawarra is gritty, dirt-under-the-fingernails wine country, with seasonal pruning and picking work aplenty.

When to Go

➡ **For crowd-free cellar doors** Winter (June to August) is the right time for empty cellar doors with attentive vignerons.

➡ **For festivals** Summer (December to February) sees plenty of crooners among the vines.

➡ **For vineyard photos** Autumn vine colours (April and May) are hard to beat, but in winter (June to August) mists creeping along vine rows paint a compelling picture.

➡ **For winery work** Grape-picking season is autumn (March to May); pruning season is early winter (June and July).

What to Eat

From oysters to honey and blueberries to brie, tasting the local fare is one of the true pleasures of travel in SA.

Cheese

Cheese, glorious cheese! There's plenty of the good stuff (at great prices) at **Adelaide Central Market** (p53), or head for the Adelaide Hills where the **Woodside Cheese Wrights** (☑08 8389 7877; www.woodsidecheese.com.au; Heritage Park, 22 Henry St, Woodside; tastings free, cheeses from $5; ⊗11am-4pm) specialises in delightfully gloopy soft cheeses. Nearby in Hahndorf, **Udder Delights** (☑08 8388 1588; www.udderdelights.com.au; 91a Main St; meals $13-25; ⊗9am-5pm; ☑) (ha-ha) is a cool cafe with a dedicated cheese-tasting

Oysters, Kangaroo Island (p89)

counter. In picture-perfect Angaston in the Barossa Valley, follow your nose to the marvellous **Barossa Valley Cheese Company** (p106), where sublime feta, brie and even haloumi vie for your affections. In McLaren Vale township you'll find **Blessed Cheese** (p82), purveyor of all things cheesy. Inland from here near Mt Compass, **Alexandrina Cheese Company** (p87) is an old-fashioned cheesemaker with individually named Jersey cows (and super cheddar).

Seafood

Love seafood? Love SA. Kangaroo Island (being an island) is one of the best places to try the local product. King George whiting is the best of the sea's bounty – not a big fish, but succulent and flavoursome, best served simply with parsley and lemon. To the southeast, Robe, Kingston SE and Port MacDonnell have large fishing fleets heading out from shore for crayfish (aka lobster). If you're into oysters, head straight for the Eyre Peninsula: the calm, shallow waters off Coffin Bay and Ceduna are bivalve hotbeds. **Oysterfest** (p128) happens every September in Ceduna. Back towards Adelaide, Port Lincoln has a big rep for big tuna and the big tuna-fishing fleet that lines the town's coffers; they host the annual **Tunarama Festival** (p125) in January.

Honey

An anomaly of natural quarantine, Kangaroo Island is home to the purest strain of Ligurian bees in the world (purer, even, than the busy bees in Liguria itself). Imported for their hard-working ways and passive temperament, they've survived here for decades without generic interference from mainland Australian bees. The honey they produce, sourced from native wildflowers and eucalyptus blooms, is divine. Try some at the low-key **Clifford's Honey Farm** (p96) (which also does honey ice cream), or the more touristy **Island Beehive** (p94). Further afield, try **Buzz Honey** (p81) in the Adelaide Hills.

PREFER BEER?

Of course, not everyone is into wine, and given South Australia's long hot summers it's no surprise that beer is big business here. For such a successful mainstream brand, Coopers (p59), the all-conquering Adelaide brewery, bottles surprisingly interesting and largely preservative-free beers. Take a tour of the shiny brewery vats and pipes (with tastings afterwards) or rock into pretty much any pub in Adelaide for a cold Pale Ale.

Beyond Adelaide there are some brilliant microbreweries, studded belligerently in the middle of wine regions and in unexpected small-town locations. A few of our faves:

➡ **Prancing Pony** (p81) Adelaide Hills outfit and new kid on the block with great amber ale and a real buzz on weekends.

➡ **Barossa Valley Brewing** (p104) All sorts of lovely beers on the fringes of Tanunda in the Barossa.

➡ **Lobethal Bierhaus** (p80) Backed by Lobethal's long-standing German heritage, this cool factory conversion in the Adelaide Hills is a beaut spot for a beer. Work your way through from the pilsner to yeasty *hefeweizen* and hearty Red Truck porter.

➡ **Goodieson Brewery** (p81) Run by a beer-loving couple, Goodieson flies in the face of McLaren Vale's endless shiraz with a citrusy pilsner, thick stout, light pale ale and nutty seasonal Christmas ale.

➡ **Woolshed Brewery** (p114) Near Renmark in the Riverland, newcomer Woolshed – a zero-waste brewer – has been making a splash with its Amazon Ale, an easy-drinking pale ale.

➡ **Steam Exchange Brewery** (p88) Down on the wharf in Goolwa, these guys have been making seaworthy brews for a while now: stout, dark ale, pale ale and a rather astonishing double-chocolate vanilla-bourbon porter.

Fruit & Nuts

Need a bit of a health infusion? Tee up a bowlful of plump Adelaide Hills strawberries. At **Beerenberg Strawberry Farm** (p78) in Hahndorf you can pick your own between November and May. While we're talking vitamin C, it would be simply remiss to venture along the Murray River without sampling some Riverland citrus fruit. Berri is the orange-juice capital of the known universe. Further south on the peaty plateaus of the Fleurieu Peninsula, load up on blueberries at the **Blueberry Patch** (☑08 8556 9100; www.blueberrypatch.com.au; Nangkita Rd, Mt Compass; ⊙by appointment) (December to February). In nearby Willunga, the prevailing passion is for almonds. The **Almond Blossom Festival** (www.almondblossomfestival.com.au; ⊙Jul) happens here in the last week of July. Willunga is also home to the best farmers market in SA, the logically named **Willunga Farmers Market** (p83).

Outback Delicacies

Competing with truck stop burgers and steaks, offbeat tucker has found a foothold in the outback. At pubs and diners along the way you'll find camel schnitzels, emu patties, kangaroo sausages and fillets (which are delicious cooked rare, and served with a red wine and pepper glaze), and even crocodile (imported from the Northern Territory). A one-stop-shop for all of the above is the famed **Prairie Hotel** (p136) in Parachilna in the northern Flinders Ranges. And while you're in the Flinders, make sure you try a quandong pie – the preferred format for consuming these bittersweet native bush cherries (which taste a bit like rhubarb). Head for the **Quandong Café** (☑08 8648 6155; www.facebook.com/quandongcafe; 31 First St; mains $5-15; ⊙8.30am-3.30pm Tue-Sun, reduced summer hours) in Quorn, or the identically named **Quandong Cafe** (p137) at Copley Caravan Park.

Plan Your Trip

Your Outback Trip

Exactly where Australia's outback starts and ends is hard to pin down on a map. But you'll know you're there when the sky yawns enormously wide, the horizon is unnervingly empty, and the sparse inhabitants you encounter are incomparably resilient and distinctively Australian. Out here, enduring Indigenous culture, unique wildlife and intriguing landscapes await the modern-day adventurer.

Best...

For Indigenous Culture
Kakadu National Park in the tropical Top End wilderness offers ancient rock art and cultural tours run by Indigenous guides.

Outback National Park
Iconic Uluru in Uluru-Kata Tjuta National Park is simply unmissable, while nearby Kata Tjuta is less well known but just as impressive.

Outback Track
Oodnadatta Track: 620km of red dust, emus, lizards, salt lakes and historic railroad remnants

Outback Road Trip
The Stuart Hwy from Darwin to Port Augusta is an epic journey from the tropical north to the parched central deserts.

Season to Visit
June to October, with mild temperatures and generally dry weather early in the season, and wildflowers in spring.

Things to Pack
Sunscreen, sunglasses, a hat, insect repellent, plenty of water and some good tunes for the car stereo.

About the Outback

The Australian outback is a vast region, radiating out from the centre of the continent. While most Australians live on the coast, that thin green fringe is hardly typical of this enormous land mass. Inland is the desert soul of Australia.

Weather patterns vary from region to region – from sandy arid desert to semi-arid scrubland to tropical savannah – but you can generally rely on hot sunny days, starry nights and kilometre after kilometre of unbroken horizon.

When to Go
Best Times

Winter June through August is when southeastern Australia (where most of the population lives) is sniffling through rainy and cloudy winter days, and the outback comes into its own. Rain isn't unheard of in outback Australia – in fact there's been a whole lot of it over recent years, including in December 2016 when they had to briefly close Uluru-Kata Tjuta National Park to visitors and several outback communities flooded. But moderate daytime temperatures, cold nights and good driving conditions are the norm. Winter is also the best time to visit the tropical Top End, with low humidity, dry days and mild temperatures.

Spring September and October is springtime, and prime time to head into the outback, especially if you're into wildflowers. The MacDonnell Ranges near Alice Springs and the Flinders Ranges in northern South Australia erupt with colourful blooms, all the more dazzling in contrast with red-orange desert sands.

Avoid

Summer Central Australia heats up over summer (December through February) – temperatures approaching 50°C have been recorded in some desert towns – but that's just part of the picture. With the heat comes dusty roads, overheating cars, driver fatigue, irritating flies and the need to carry extra water everywhere you go. In the Top End the build-up to the wet season is uncomfortably humid, and the eventual monsoon can see many a road cut and dirt roads made impassable for weeks at a time.

Planes, Trains or Automobiles

Air If you want to access the outback without a long drive, the major airlines fly into Alice Springs and Yulara (for the central deserts) and Darwin (for the tropical Top End), departing from Perth, Adelaide and the major east-coast cities. From Darwin or Alice you can join a guided tour or hire a 4WD and off you go.

Train Unlike much of the world, train travel in Australia is neither affordable nor expedient. It's something you do for a special occasion or for the sheer romance of trains, not if you want to get anywhere in a hurry. That said, travelling on the *Indian Pacific* between Perth and Sydney or the legendary *Ghan* between Adelaide and Darwin takes you through parts of the country you wouldn't see otherwise, and it certainly makes for a leisurely holiday. Train travel is also a good way to beat the heat if you're travelling in summer. So if you have time on your side and you can afford it, train travel could be perfect for you.

Car You can drive through the Red Centre from Darwin to Adelaide with detours to Uluru and Kakadu and more without ever leaving sealed roads. However, if you really want to see outback Australia, there are plenty of side routes that breathe new life into the phrase 'off the beaten track' (bring a 4WD). Driving in the outback has its challenges – immense distances and occasionally difficult terrain – but it's ultimately the most rewarding and intimate way to experience Australia's 'dead heart' (rest assured, it's alive and kicking!).

Essential Outback

The Red Centre: Alice Springs, Uluru & Kings Canyon

Alice is a surprising oasis: big enough to have some great places to eat and stay, as well as some social problems. Nearby, the East and West MacDonnell Ranges are classic outback landforms: red rocks, dramatic canyons and plenty of wildlife. Palm Valley in Finke National Park is one of the outback's least-known gems. Uluru is to tourists what half a watermelon is to ants at a picnic: people from all over the globe swarm to and from this monolith at all times of the day. But it's still a remarkable find. The local Anangu people would prefer that you didn't climb it. Kings Canyon, in Watarrka National Park about 300km north of Uluru, is a spectacular chasm carved into the rugged landscape.

The Stuart Highway: Adelaide to Darwin

In either direction, from the north or south, the paved Stuart Hwy is one of Australia's greatest road trips: 2834km of red desert sand, flat scrubland and galloping roadside emus. Heading north, make sure you stop at spookily pock-marked Coober Pedy – the opal-mining capital of the world – and detour to Uluru on your way to the Alice. Nitmiluk (Katherine Gorge) National Park is also en route, a photogenic series of sheer rocky gorges and waterholes. Kakadu National Park is next, with World Heritage-listed tropical wetlands. When you get to Darwin, reward yourself with a cold beer and some nocturnal high jinks on Mitchell St.

The Tropics: Darwin, Kakadu & Katherine

The outback in the tropical Top End is a different experience to the deserts further south. Here, the wet and dry seasons determine how easy it is to get from A to B. In the Wet, roads become impassable and crocodiles move freely through the wetlands. But before you cancel your plans, this is also a time of abundance and great natural beauty in the national parks – plus Kakadu resorts can go down to half the price! Darwin isn't technically in the outback, but it still feels like a frontier town, especially in the Dry when backpackers from around the world fill the bars and Mindil Beach market. Katherine, three hours to the south, is much more 'country', and the jumping-off point for the astonishing Nitmiluk (Katherine Gorge) National Park.

The Victoria Highway: Katherine to the Kimberley

The Victoria Hwy is a significant section of the epic Savannah Way from Cairns to Broome, the classic 'across-the-top' route. Leaving Katherine it winds through classic cattle country, where farms can be as big as small European countries. It also passes some lovely river-and-escarpment country around Victoria River Crossing and there are 4WD and hiking opportunities, outback camp sites, rock art, national parks, red gorges and crocodiles. And this region boasts some of the Top End's best barramundi fishing. The immense Gregory National Park, a former cattle station, is best explored with a 4WD (some tracks may be accessible in a 2WD in the Dry), while Keep River

On the Oodnadatta Track (p140)

National Park is also worth exploring. Exploring the Kimberley requires a 4WD to tackle trails like the epic Gibb River road.

OUTBACK CYCLING

Pedalling your way through the outback is certainly not something to tackle lightly, and certainly not something you'd even consider in summer. But you do see the odd wiry, suntanned soul pushing their panniers along the Stuart Hwy between Adelaide and Darwin. Availability of drinking water is the main concern: isolated water sources (bores, tanks, creeks etc) shown on maps may be dry or undrinkable. Make sure you've got the necessary spare parts and bike-repair knowledge. Check with locals if you're heading into remote areas, and always tell someone where you're headed. And if you make it through, try for a book deal – this is intrepid travel defined.

Facilities

Outback roadhouses emerge from the desert-heat haze with surprising regularity. It always pays to calculate the distance to the next fuel stop, but even on the remote Oodnadatta Track or Tanami Road you'll find petrol and cold beer every few hundred kilometres. Most roadhouses (many of them open 24 hours) sell fuel and have attached restaurants where you can get a decent steak and a fry-up feed. Just don't expect an epicurean experience. There's often accommodation for road-weary drivers out the back, including camp sites, air-conditioned motel-style rooms, often with shared bathrooms, and basic cabins.

ROAD TRAINS

On many outback highways you'll see thundering road trains: huge trucks (a prime mover plus two, three or four trailers), some more than 50m long. These things don't move over for anyone: it's like a scene from *Mad Max* having one bear down on you at 120km/h.

A few tips: when you see a road train approaching on a narrow bitumen road, slow down and pull over – if the truck has to put its wheels off the road to pass you, the resulting barrage of stones will almost certainly smash your windscreen. When trying to overtake one, allow plenty of room (about a kilometre) to complete the manoeuvre. Road trains throw up a lot of dust on dirt roads, so if you see one coming it's best to just pull over and stop until it's gone past.

And while you're on outback roads, don't forget to give the standard bush greeting to oncoming drivers – it's simply a matter of lifting the index finger off the steering wheel to acknowledge your fellow explorer.

Resources

Department of Environment, Water & Natural Resources (www.environment.sa.gov.au/parks/Home) South Australian national parks info.

Bureau of Meteorology (www.bom.gov.au) Weather forecasts and warnings.

Parks & Wildlife (www.nt.gov.au/leisure/parks-reserves) NT national parks info; click through to fact-sheet PDFs for each park.

Parks Australia (www.environment.gov.au/topics/national-parks) Extensive information about the federally administered Kakadu and Uluru-Kata Tjuta National Parks.

South Australian Tourism Commission (www.southaustralia.com) Accommodation, activities, events, tours and transport.

Travel NT (www.northernterritory.com) NT travel guide with excellent high-level coverage.

Organised Tours

If you don't feel like doing all the planning and driving, a guided tour is a great way to experience the Aussie outback. These range from beery backpacker jaunts between outback pubs, to Indigenous cultural tours and multiday bushwalking treks into remote wilderness.

Outback Tracks

The Australian outback is criss-crossed by sealed highways, but one of the more interesting ways to get from A to B is by taking a detour along historic cattle and rail routes. While you may not necessarily need a 4WD to tackle some of these roads, the rugged construction of these vehicles makes for a much more comfortable drive. But whatever your wheels of choice, you will need to be prepared for the isolation and lack of facilities.

Don't attempt the tougher routes during the hottest part of the year (December to February, inclusive); apart from the risk of heat exhaustion, simple mishaps can lead to tragedy in these conditions. There's also no point going anywhere on outback dirt roads if there has been recent flooding.

Unpaved Tracks

Most outback tracks are unsealed, although there may be some sections paved with tarmac.

Mereenie Loop Road

Starting in Alice Springs this well-used track is an alternative route to the big attractions of the Red Centre. The route initially follows the sealed Larapinta and Namatjira Drives skirting the magnificent MacDonnell Ranges to Glen Helen Gorge. Beyond Glen Helen the route meets the Mereenie Loop Rd. This is where things get interesting. The Mereenie Loop Rd requires a permit ($5) and is usually so heavily corrugated that it will rattle a conventional 2WD until it finds its weak spot. This is the rugged short cut to Watarrka National Park; from Watarrka the sealed Luritja Rd

Outback Tracks

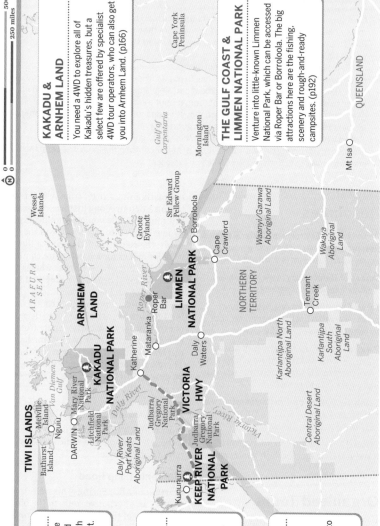

TIWI ISLANDS

Leave the car far behind and venture across the waters to Bathurst Island to experience Tiwi Island culture with its fascinating history and unique art. (p157)

KEEP RIVER NATIONAL PARK

A little-visited yet rewarding detour on the way to northern WA. Keep River National Park features Aboriginal art, wildlife, short walks and stunning sandstone formations. (p187)

VICTORIA HWY

The Victoria Hwy travels through legendary cattle country, much of it returning to nature as national park. Detours lead off the highway and onto 4WD tracks boasting remote camps under big skies. (p186)

KAKADU & ARNHEM LAND

You need a 4WD to explore all of Kakadu's hidden treasures, but a select few are offered by specialist 4WD tour operators, who can also get you into Arnhem Land. (p166)

THE GULF COAST & LIMMEN NATIONAL PARK

Venture into little-known Limmen National Park, which can be accessed via Roper Bar or Borroloola. The big attractions here are the fishing, scenery and rough-and-ready campsites. (p192)

DESERT TRACKS

The famous cross-desert routes – the Birdsville, Oodnadatta and Strzelecki Tracks – should not be taken lightly. Well-prepared travellers are rewarded with pioneering history, big skies and unparalleled solitude. (p140-1)

FLINDERS RANGES

Getting off the tarmac is the best way to explore the Flinders and the only way to get into the Gammon Ranges. Experience Aboriginal heritage, mining relics and magnificent scenery. (p132)

RED CENTRE WAY

Link iconic central Australia – the gorges of the MacDonnell Ranges, the gape of Kings Canyon, and the splendor of Uluru and Kata Tjuta – by taking this road less travelled. (p214)

Map labels

WESTERN AUSTRALIA

Lake Mackay Aboriginal Land

Lake Mackay

Gibson Desert

Haasts Bluff Aboriginal Land

MacDonnell Ranges

Alice Springs

Finke Gorge National Park

RED CENTRE WAY

Kings Canyon

Petermann Aboriginal Land

Uluru-Kata Tjuta National Park

Atnetye Aboriginal Land

Pmere Nyente Aboriginal Land

Pmer Ulperre Ingwemirne Aboriginal Land

Simpson Desert

Simpson Desert Regional Reserve

Birdsville

BIRDSVILLE TRACK

Innamincka Regional Reserve

STRZELECKI TRACK

Strzelecki Regional Reserve

OODNADATTA TRACK

SOUTH AUSTRALIA

Coober Pedy

Marla

Pitjantjatjara Aboriginal Land

Conservation Park

Tallaringa Conservation Park

Maralinga Tjarutja Aboriginal Land

Yellabinna Regional Reserve

Yalata Aboriginal Land

Nullarbor Regional Reserve

Nullarbor National Park

Nullarbor Plain

Great Victoria Desert

Eucla

Ceduna

Lake Eyre North

Lake Eyre South

Lake Eyre National Park

Marree

Vulkathunha-Gammon Ranges National Park

FLINDERS RANGES

Lake Torrens

Port Augusta

Lake Gairdner

Great Australian Bight

OUTBACK DRIVING & SAFETY CHECKLIST

Due to the lack of water, long distances between fuel stops and isolation, you need to be particularly organised and vigilant when travelling in the outback, especially on remote sandy tracks.

Communication

➡ Report your route and schedule to the police, a friend or relative.

➡ Mobile phones are useless if you go off the highway. Consider hiring a satellite phone, high-frequency (HF) radio transceiver equipped to pick up the Royal Flying Doctor Service bases, or emergency position-indicating radio beacon (EPIRB).

➡ In an emergency, stay with your vehicle; it's easier to spot than you are, and you won't be able to carry a heavy load of water very far.

➡ If you do become stranded, consider setting fire to a spare tyre (let the air out first). The pall of smoke will be visible for kilometres.

Your Vehicle

➡ Have your vehicle serviced and checked before you leave.

➡ Load your vehicle evenly, with heavy items inside and light items on the roof rack.

➡ Consider carrying spare fuel in an appropriate container.

➡ Carry essential tools: a spare tyre (two is preferable), fan belt, radiator hose, tyre-pressure gauge and air pump, and a shovel.

➡ An off-road jack might come in handy, as will a snatch strap or tow rope for quick extraction when you're stuck (useful if there's another vehicle to pull you out).

Supplies & Equipment

➡ Carry plenty of water: in warm weather allow 5L per person per day and an extra amount for the radiator, carried in several containers.

➡ Bring plenty of food in case of a breakdown.

➡ Carry a first-aid kit, a torch with spare batteries, a compass and a GPS.

Weather & Road Conditions

➡ Check road conditions before travelling: roads that are passable in the Dry (March to October) can disappear beneath water during the Wet.

➡ Don't attempt to cross flooded bridges or causeways unless you're sure of the depth, and of any road damage hidden underwater.

Dirt-Road Driving

➡ Inflate your tyres to the recommended levels for the terrain you're travelling on; on desert sand, deflate your tyres to 20–25psi to avoid getting bogged. Don't forget to re-inflate them when you leave the sand.

➡ Reduce speed on unsealed roads, as braking distances increase.

➡ Dirt roads are often corrugated: keeping an even speed is the best approach.

➡ Dust on outback roads can obscure your vision, so stop and wait for it to settle.

➡ Choose a low gear for steep inclines and the lowest gear for steep declines. Use the brake sparingly and don't turn sideways on a hill.

Road Hazards

➡ Take a rest every few hours: driver fatigue is an all-too-common problem.

➡ Wandering cattle, sheep, emus, kangaroos, camels etc make driving fast a dangerous prospect. Take care and avoid nocturnal driving, as this is often when native animals come out. Many car-hire companies prohibit night-time driving.

➡ Road trains are an ever-present menace on the main highways and even on some unsealed roads. Give them a wide berth – they're much bigger than you!

Outback road signs

connects to the Lasseter Hwy and Uluru-Kata Tjuta National Park. There has been talk for years of sealing this track, but it remains just talk.

Oodnadatta Track

Mostly running parallel to the old *Ghan* railway line through outback SA, this iconic track is fully bypassed by the sealed Stuart Hwy to the west. Using this track, it's 429km from Marree in the northern Flinders Ranges, to Oodnadatta, then another 216km to the Stuart Hwy at Marla. As long as there is no rain, any well-prepared conventional vehicle should be able to manage this fascinating route, but a 4WD will do it in style.

Birdsville Track

Spanning 517km from Marree in SA to Birdsville just across the border of Queensland, this old droving trail is one of Australia's best-known outback routes – although it's not known for spectacular and varying scenery. It's often feasible to travel it in a well-prepared, conventional vehicle but not recommended.

Strzelecki Track

This track covers much of the same territory through SA as the Birdsville Track. Starting south of Marree at Lyndhurst, it reaches Innamincka 460km northeast and close to the Queensland border. It was close to Innamincka that the hapless explorers Burke and Wills died. A 4WD is a safe bet, even though this route has been much improved due to work on the Moomba gas fields.

Nathan River Road

This road, which resembles a farm track in parts, is a scenic section of the Savannah Way, a cobbled-together route which winds all the way from Cairns to Broome. This particular section traverses some remote country along the western edge of the Gulf of Carpentaria between Roper Bar and Borroloola, much of it protected within Limmen National Park. A high-clearance vehicle is a must and carrying two spare tyres is recommended because of the frequent sharp rocks. Excellent camping beside barramundi- and crocodile-filled streams and waterholes is the main attraction here.

Tanami Track

Turning off the Stuart Hwy just north of Alice Springs, this 1055km route runs northwest across the Tanami Desert to Halls Creek in Western Australia. The road has received extensive work so conventional vehicles are often OK, although there are sandy stretches on the WA side and it can be very corrugated if it hasn't been graded recently. Get advice on road conditions in Alice Springs.

Plenty & Sandover Highways

These remote routes run east from the Stuart Hwy, north of Alice Springs, to Boulia or Mt Isa in Queensland. The Plenty Hwy skirts the northern fringe of the Simpson Desert and offers the chance of gem fossicking in the Harts Range. The Sandover Hwy offers a memorable if monotonous experience in remote touring. It is a novelty to see another vehicle. Both roads are not to be taken lightly; they are often very rough going with little water and with sections that are very infrequently used. Signs of human habitation are rare and facilities are few and far between.

Finke & Old Andado Tracks

The Finke Track (the first part of which is the Old South Rd) follows the route of the old *Ghan* railway (long since dismantled) between Alice Springs and the Aboriginal settlement of Finke (Aputula). Along the

way you can call into Chambers Pillar Historical Reserve to view the colourful sandstone tower. From Finke the road heads east along the Goyder Creek, a tributary of the Finke River, before turning north towards Andado Station and, 18km further, the homestead. At Old Andado the track swings north for the 321km trip to Alice. The Old Andado Track winds its way through the Simpson Desert to link the Homestead with Alice Springs. On the way you pass the Mac Clark Conservation Reserve, which protects a stand of rare waddy trees. A high-clearance 4WD is definitely recommended and you should be equipped with high-frequency (HF) radio or emergency position-indicating radio beacon (EPIRB).

Simpson Desert

The route crossing the Simpson Desert from Mt Dare, near Finke, to Birdsville is a real test of both driver and vehicle. A 4WD is definitely required on the unmaintained tracks and you should be in a party of at least three vehicles equipped with sat phones, HF radio and/or EPIRB.

Paved Roads

Stuart Highway

The Stuart Hwy is one of the world's truly epic road trips, covering 2834km from Darwin in the north to Port Augusta. It's paved all the way, offering gateways to the outback's major attractions, and punctuated by roadhouses at regular intervals like outback opals on a chain.

Lasseter Highway

From Alice Springs it's a six-hour drive to Uluru-Kata Tjuta National Park along the paved Stuart and then Lasseter Hwys. The road is also paved from Lasseter Hwy up to Kings Canyon, in Watarrka National Park, along the Luritja Rd.

Victoria Highway

The Victoria Hwy runs from Katherine to Kununurra (515km). It's the only paved road connecting the NT with WA and passes through Victoria River and Timber Creek en route.

PERMITS FOR ABORIGINAL LANDS

➡ In the outback, if you plan on driving through pastoral stations and Aboriginal communities you may need to get permission first. This is for your safety; many travellers have tackled this rugged landscape on their own and required complicated rescues after getting lost or breaking down.

➡ Permits (p270) are issued by various Aboriginal land-management authorities. Processing applications can take anywhere from a few minutes to a few days.

Plan Your Trip
Travel with Children

Travelling with children in outback Australia can be joyous – camping, bushwalks, stargazing, swimming, wildlife spotting...Only extreme temperatures, humidity and distances conspire to spoil the party. But if you can beat the heat, this isn't a place where you'll encounter much urban menace, pollution or tedious queuing.

South Australia & Northern Territory for Kids

➡ You'll find public toilets with family rooms where you can go to feed babies or change nappies in most shopping centres. As anywhere, children should be accompanied in all public toilets, including shopping centres.

➡ Motels and some caravan parks often have playgrounds and swimming pools, and can supply cots and baby baths. Top-end hotels and some (but not all) midrange hotels often accommodate children for free, but B&Bs are often child-free zones.

➡ For babysitting, check under Baby Sitters and Child Care Centres in the local *Yellow Pages*, or phone the local council for a list. **Dial-an-Angel** (☑1300 721 111, 08 8338 3433; www.dialanangel.com.au; 6/202-208 Glen Osmond Rd, Fullarton) provides nannies and babysitters in Adelaide.

➡ Child prices (and family rates) apply for most tours, sight admission fees, and air, bus and train transport, with some discounts as high as 50% off. However, the definition of 'child' can vary from under 12 to under 18 years.

➡ Heat is a problem while travelling in central Australia, especially in summer, with relentless desert sun and high humidity in the Top End. Time your visit for winter (which is high season!),

Best Regions for Kids

Kangaroo Island
Yes, there are roos here. Plus wild goannas, echidnas, seals, dolphins, cockatoos and eagles.

Kakadu National Park
One word: crocodiles. Plus jabirus, turtles, lizards and twittering flocks of birds.

Fleurieu Peninsula
Fantastic swimming beaches, farmers markets and fresh fish-and-chip dinners.

Uluru-Kata Tjuta National Park
Aboriginal culture and excellent short walks around Uluru and through the monumental boulders of Kata Tjuta.

Adelaide
Playgrounds, parklands, safe-swimming beaches, food markets, Adelaide Zoo and dinosaur bones in the South Australian Museum.

Darwin
Fish-feeding, tropical wildlife parks, an outdoor cinema and satay sticks at Mindil Beach Sunset Market.

or make sure the kids are enshrouded in big floppy hats, SPF 30+ sunscreen and sunglasses. Always carry plenty of water and drink regularly.

➡ Medical services here are of a high standard, with items such as baby-food formula and nappies widely available from pharmacies and supermarkets (plan ahead if heading to remote regions).

➡ Major hire-car companies can supply booster seats, for which you'll be charged around $25 for up to three days' use, with an additional daily fee for longer periods.

On the Road

As anyone with kids knows, getting from A to B is the biggest threat to having a good time. Both A and B are fine once you get there, but the long road-tripping hours in between can be hell on wheels.

For babies and toddlers, time your drives with established sleep times: once they're asleep the hypnotic lull of tyres-on-asphalt can keep them that way for hours. For older kids, there's something to be said for technological distractions in the back seat: portable DVD players or Play Station–type games (with headphones!) can help pass the kilometres, and audio-books (available at ABC Shops) are suited to long drives. Factor in regular pit stops, and bring plenty of snacks, colouring books and crayons, sticker albums, drink bottles … And a good game of 'I Spy With My Little Eye' never goes astray.

Have a read of Lonely Planet's *Travel With Children* (2015) for some more ideas.

At the Hotel

When you're knee-high to a grasshopper, staying at a hotel is an adventure. Kids aren't fussed about interior design, fluffy bathrobes, Italian tapware or the dated tropical-flower print on the bed linen. The key requirements are facilities-based: swimming pools, playgrounds, games rooms, in-house movies, children's menus and the presence of other kids top the list of priorities. If it means your kids will be happier, try to suspend any ingrained hotel snobberies and stay somewhere where the little ones will be well catered for.

CHILDREN'S HIGHLIGHTS

Best Wildlife Encounters

➡ **Alice Springs Desert Park** (p199) Many desert species are nocturnal (too hot during the day!). This brilliant park offers a chance to see them in action.

➡ **Guluyambi Cultural Cruise** (p166) Cruise alongside countless crocs in Kakadu.

➡ **Seal Bay Conservation Park** (p96) An up-close encounter with Australian sea lions on a tour or self-guided boardwalk stroll on Kangaroo Island.

➡ **Territory Wildlife Park** (p162) A really sophisticated park, with fantastic re-created environments. Don't miss the birds of prey.

➡ **Jumping Crocs** (p160) The kids will never forget seeing a 5m saltie propel itself out of the Adelaide River to chomp a dead chicken.

Best Swimming Spots

➡ **Litchfield National Park** (p163) Take a dip in a cool, clear tropical pool below a waterfall – the stuff of fantasy.

➡ **Port Willunga Beach** (p84) Safe swimming an hour south of Adelaide, with a fish-and-chip kiosk for lunch.

➡ **Glenelg Beach** (p59) Adelaide's biggest and busiest beach is on one end of the city's only tram line: make a day trip of it!

➡ **Wave Lagoon** (p143) You can't swim in the sea around Darwin (stingers and crocs), so hit the surf at this waterfront wave pool.

➡ **Mataranka Thermal Pools** (p190) Free thermal swimming holes bubbling up an hour south of Katherine.

Regions at a Glance

Central Australia is vast and utterly diverse: it's hard to carve it into bite-sized regions for travel consumption. But here goes!

Adelaide is festival-addicted and riddled with fab places to eat and drink. Fanning out from here you'll find impressive wine regions, brilliant beaches and wildlife-spotting opportunities. In the South Australian outback are desolate desert tracks, quirky towns and astonishing national parks.

In the tropical Top End, Darwin is a hip hub with great markets, breezy restaurants and kooky festivals. Don't miss adventures, wildlife encounters and Aboriginal cultural experiences on the Tiwi Islands, in Arnhem Land and in Kakadu and Nitmiluk (Katherine Gorge) National Parks. Further south in the desert is arty/festive Alice Springs, a launch pad for visits to iconic Uluru, Kata Tjuta and Kings Canyon.

Adelaide & Around

Festivals
Wine Regions
Wildlife

Mad March

Every March Adelaide erupts with festivals: visual arts, music, theatre, busking and the growl of V8 engines. The question is, why do it all at once?

McLaren Vale

An hour south of Adelaide, the McLaren Vale wine region produces SA's most quaffable shiraz. A vine-striped patchwork adjacent to some sheltered, pretty beaches, the region is dotted with top-quality cellar doors and eateries.

Kangaroo Island Critters

Kangaroo Island is overrun with goannas, cockatoos, snakes, koalas, echidnas and (predictably) kangaroos. Offshore are whales, seals and dolphins, and King George whiting on the end of your hook.

p52

Southeastern SA

Wine Regions
River Life
National Parks

Barossa & Clare Valleys

Big-time wine regions are just north of Adelaide. Meander between historic German towns in the Barossa; get on your bike and scoot between cellar doors around the pretty Clare Valley.

Houseboats on the Murray

Get some friends together and hire a houseboat for a slow-boat weekend of fishing, drifting and shunting around Murray River bends, stopping at river towns for pub dinners and coffee shots.

Coorong & Naracoorte

Paddle a kayak through the salty Coorong dunescape, where the Murray River meets the sea; or go underground near Naracoorte to see age-old limestone formations.

p99

Western SA

Food
National Parks
Wildlife

Eyre Peninsula Seafood

Enormous fresh oysters, line-caught whiting, freshest tuna...this is one of the best places in the world to sample excellent seafood.

Superb Coastal Landscapes

Innes National Park on the bottom of the Yorke Peninsula boot, and Coffin Bay and Lincoln National Parks on the Eyre Peninsula are remote, fabulously wild and photogenic. Trek in and camp.

Whale Watching

Make the epic trip to the dramatic Head of Bight cliffs to see pods of southern right whales surfacing in giant swells, between May and October.

p120

Outback SA

National Parks
Outback Towns
Desert Tracks

Flinders Ranges

The Flinders Ranges loom large in russet, purple and brown: super-scenic, desert-edge ridgelines awash with arid scrub and native pines. Don't miss incredible Ikara (Wilpena Pound).

Coober Pedy

Locals in opal-crazed Coober Pedy beat the desert heat in underground houses, dreaming of deposits of the 'fire in the stone' that will one day make them rich.

Oodnadatta Track

Belting across 615km of desert between the Flinders Ranges and the Stuart Hwy is the historic Oodnadatta Track: red dust, emus, skittering lizards and last-gasp towns remembering the railway that once ran through here.

p129

Darwin & the Top End

City Life
Aboriginal Culture
Wildlife

Darwin at Dusk

Tropical Darwin wakes up at sunset: don't miss the outdoor bars and restaurants at Cullen Bay Marina and Stokes Hill Wharf, and famous Mindil Beach Sunset Market.

Rock Art & Festivals

Tour Kakadu National Park's ancient rock-art galleries with an Aboriginal guide, or take a bush-tucker tour. From Darwin, hop over to the Tiwi Islands for the legendary Tiwi Grand Final and Art Show.

Crocs & Birds

Cruise Top End rivers and billabongs where crocs lurk and see massive flocks of waterbirds, colourful parrots and stately jabirus. You can even feed a wild jumping croc on the Adelaide River.

p142

Uluru & Outback NT

National Parks
Culture
Aquatic Adventures

Australian Icons

It's a long haul to get here, but it's worth it! Visit stupendous Uluru and Kata Tjuta, or explore the awesome gorge of Kings Canyon in Watarrka National Park.

Indigenous Arts

The Red Centre is home to the renowned Desert Art Movement: learn the stories behind these dazzling paintings and make an informed purchase in Alice Springs.

Gorges & Waterholes

Paddle a canoe through the gorgeous gorges of Nitmiluk (Katherine Gorge) National Park, or cool off in the thermal pools at Mataranka.

p179

On the Road

Adelaide & Around

Best Places to Eat

➜ Peel Street (p66)
➜ Gin Long Canteen (p67)
➜ Fred Eatery (p80)
➜ Flying Fish Cafe (p87)

Best Places to Sleep

➜ Mayfair Hotel (p64)
➜ Largs Pier Hotel (p66)
➜ Stirling Hotel (p79)
➜ Port Elliot Beach House YHA (p87)
➜ Southern Ocean Lodge (p97)

Why Go?

Escape the frenzy of Australia's east coast in gracious, relaxed Adelaide. Capital of the driest state on the driest inhabited continent, Adelaide beats the heat by celebrating life's finer things: fine landscapes, fine festivals, fine food, and (...OK, forget the other three) fine wine. This is a musical town, too, recently dubbed a Unesco 'City of Music' – catch some live tunes while you're here. And don't miss Adelaide Central Market and the Adelaide Oval – two truly world-class Adelaide experiences.

Inland, Adelaide's plains rise into the Adelaide Hills, just up the freeway. The Hills' gorgeous valley folds, old-fangled towns and cool-climate vineyards are all close at hand.

A day trip away, the Fleurieu Peninsula is Adelaide's favourite naughty-weekender, with surf and safe-swimming beaches, historic towns and the fabulous McLaren Vale wine region (love that shiraz). Further afield, Kangaroo Island's wildlife, forests and seafood await just offshore.

When to Go
Adelaide

Feb–Mar Festival season in Adelaide: arts, offbeat entertainment and fast cars.

Apr–May Autumn: the McLaren Vale vines would make Van Gogh reach for his tube of vermilion.

Jun–Aug Empty beaches, affordable accommodation and open fires.

ADELAIDE

POP 1.34 MILLION

Sophisticated, cultured, neat-casual – the self-image Adelaide projects, a nod to the days of free colonisation without the 'penal colony' taint. Adelaidians may remind you of their convict-free status, but the stuffy, affluent origins of the 'City of Churches' did more to inhibit development than promote it. Bogged down in the old-school doldrums and painfully short on charisma, this was a pious, introspective place.

But these days things are different. Multicultural flavours infuse Adelaide's restaurants; there's a pumping arts and live-music scene; and the city's festival calendar has vanquished dull Saturday nights. There are still plenty of church spires here, but they're hopelessly outnumbered by pubs and a growing number of hip bars tucked away in lanes.

Just down the tram tracks is beachy Glenelg: Adelaide with its guard down and boardshorts up. Nearby Port Adelaide is slowly gentrifying but remains a raffish harbour 'hood with buckets of soul.

History

South Australia was declared a province on 28 December 1836, when the first British colonists landed at Holdfast Bay (current-day Glenelg). The first governor, Captain John Hindmarsh, named the state capital Adelaide, after the wife of the British monarch, William IV. While the eastern states struggled with the stigma of convict society, Adelaidians were free citizens – a fact to which many South Australians will happily draw your attention.

Adelaide has maintained a socially progressive creed: trade unions were legalised here in 1876; women were permitted to stand for parliament in 1894; and SA was one of the first places in the world to give women the vote, and the first state in Australia to outlaw racial and gender discrimination, legalise abortion and decriminalise gay sex.

◉ Sights

◉ Central Adelaide

★ **Adelaide Central Market**   MARKET
(Map p62; ☑08 8203 7494; www.adelaide centralmarket.com.au; Gouger St; ⊙7am-5.30pm Tue, 9am-5.30pm Wed & Thu, 7am-9pm Fri, 7am-3pm Sat) A tourist sight, or a shopping op? Either way, satisfy your deepest culinary cravings at the 250-odd stalls in superb Adelaide Central Market. A sliver of salami from the Mettwurst Shop, a crumb of English Stilton from the Smelly Cheese Shop, a tub of blueberry yoghurt from the Yoghurt Shop – you name it, it's here. Good luck making it out without eating anything. Adelaide's Chinatown is right next door. **Adelaide's Top Food & Wine Tours** (☑08 8386 0888; www.topfoodandwinetours.com.au) offers guided tours.

★ **Art Gallery of South Australia**   GALLERY
(Map p62; ☑08 8207 7000; www.artgallery.sa.gov. au; North Tce; ⊙10am-5pm) **FREE** Spend a few hushed hours in the vaulted, parquetry-floored gallery that represents the big names in Australian art. Permanent exhibitions include Australian, Aboriginal and Torres Strait Islander, Asian, European and North American art (20 bronze Rodins!) Progressive visiting exhibitions occupy the basement. There are free guided tours (11am and 2pm daily) and lunchtime talks (12.30pm every day except Tuesday). There's a lovely cafe out the back too.

South Australian Museum   MUSEUM
(Map p62; ☑08 8207 7500; www.samuseum. sa.gov.au; North Tce; ⊙10am-5pm) **FREE** Dig into Australia's natural history with the museum's special exhibits on whales and Antarctic explorer Sir Douglas Mawson. An Aboriginal Cultures Gallery displays artefacts of the Ngarrindjeri people of the Coorong and lower Murray. Elsewhere, the giant squid and the lion with the twitchy tail are definite highlights. Free tours depart 11am weekdays and 2pm and 3pm weekends. The cafe here is a handy spot for lunch/recaffeination.

Adelaide Botanic Gardens   GARDENS
(Map p62; ☑08 8222 9311; www.botanic gardens.sa.gov.au; cnr North Tce & East Tce; ⊙7.15am-sunset Mon-Fri, from 9am Sat & Sun) **FREE** Meander, jog or chew through your trashy airport novel in these lush city-fringe gardens. Highlights include a restored 1877 palm house, the water-lily pavilion (housing the gigantic *Victoria amazonica*), the First Creek wetlands, the engrossing **Museum of Economic Botany** and the fabulous steel-and-glass arc of the **Bicentennial Conservatory** (10am to 4pm), which re-creates a tropical rainforest. Free

N

0 —————————— 40 km
0 —————————— 20 miles

Spencer Gulf

Minlaton

Port Vincent

Corny Point

Corny Point

Yorke Peninsula

Stansbury

Warooka

Yorketown

Yorke Peninsula

Edithburgh

West Cape

Innes National Park

Marion Bay

Troubridge Point

Cape Spencer

Investigator Strait

Cape Cassini

Point Marsden

Stokes Bay

Emu Bay

Emu Bay

Middle River

Cygnet River

Kingscote

Cape Forbin

Western River Conservation Park

Cygnet River

Nepean Bay

Cape Borda

Parndana

American River

Kangaroo Island

Timber Creek

Rocky River

Kangaroo Island Wilderness Trail

Karatta

Cape Gantheaume Conservation Park

Cape Bedout

Snake Lagoon

Flinders Chase National Park

⑧

Kelly Hills Conservation Park

Vivonne Bay

Cape du Couedic

Cape Bouguer

Cape Gantheaume

Adelaide & Around Highlights

① **Central Market** (p53) Roaming the delicious-smelling aisles at Adelaide's world-class food market.

② **Pubs & Bars** (p66) Joining Adelaide's after-work booze hounds on Peel St, Leigh St or at Rundle St's Exeter Hotel.

③ **Adelaide Oval** (p58) Watching the cricket or footy, or taking a behind-the-scenes tour of Adelaide's excellent stadium.

④ **Live Music** (p72) Tuning in to some local jazz, funk or rock in this Unesco 'City of Music'.

⑤ **Adelaide Hills wineries** (p76) Cooling your boots with

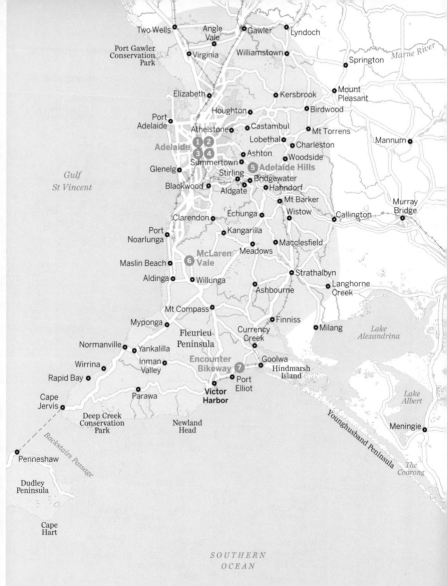

some vino at an excellent Hills winery.

6 McLaren Vale wineries (p84) Swirling, nosing and quaffing your way through some fine McLaren Vale

shiraz, with a top-notch winery restaurant meal afterwards.

7 Encounter Bikeway (p86) Cycling along the wave-battered coast, keeping an eye out for whales.

8 Kangaroo Island Wilderness Trail (p98) Hiking through 61km of KI's wildest wilds over five days. Camp en route, or sleep off-trail in accommodated comfort.

Adelaide

1½-hour guided walks depart the Schomburgk Pavilion at 10.30am daily. The classy **Botanic Gardens Restaurant** (Map p62; ☑08 8223 3526; www.botanicgardensrestaurant. com.au; off Plane Tree Dr, Adelaide Botanic Gardens; 2-/3-courses $55/72; ⊗noon-2.30pm Tue-Sun, 6.30-9pm Fri & Sat) is here too.

National Wine Centre of Australia   WINERY
(Map p62; ☑08 8313 3355; www.wineaustralia. com.au; cnr Botanic & Hackney Rds; ⊗8am-6pm Mon-Thu, to 9pm Fri, 9am-9am Sat, to 6pm Sun) **FREE** Check out the free self-guided, interactive Wine Discovery Journey exhibition at this very sexy wine centre (actually a

research facility for the University of Adelaide, rather than a visitor centre per se). You will gain an insight into the issues winemakers contend with, and can even have your own virtual vintage rated. 'Uncorked' drinks every second Friday night happen at

4.30pm, or you can explore the Cellar Door and get stuck into some cleverly automated tastings (from $2.50).

Adelaide Zoo ZOO
(Map p68; ☑08 8267 3255; www.zoossa.com. au/adelaide-zoo; Frome Rd; adult/child/family $34.50/19/88.50; ☺9.30am-5pm) Around 1800 exotic and native mammals, birds and reptiles roar, growl and screech at Adelaide's wonderful zoo, dating from 1883. There are free walking tours half-hourly (plus a slew of longer and overnight tours), feeding sessions and a children's zoo. Wang Wang and Fu Ni are Australia's only giant pandas and always draw a crowd (panda-monium!) Other highlights include the nocturnal and reptile houses. You can take a river cruise to the zoo on Popeye (p60).

West Terrace Cemetery CEMETERY
(Map p62; ☑08 8139 7400; www.aca.sa.gov.au; West Tce; ☺6.30am-6pm Nov-Apr, to 8.30pm May-Oct) FREE Driven-by and overlooked by most Adelaidians, this amazing old cemetery (established in 1837, and now with 150,000 residents) makes a serene and fascinating detour. One of five self-guided tours, the 2km Heritage Highlights Interpretive Trail passes 29 key sites; pick up a brochure at the West Terrace gates. Guided tours run at 10.30am Tuesday and Sunday ($10/5 per adult/child). Night tours ($25/15) run twice every Friday, at varying times throughout the year; check the website. Call for tour bookings.

⊙ North Adelaide

★**Adelaide Oval** LANDMARK
(Map p68; ☑08 8205 4700; www.adelaideoval. com.au; King William Rd, North Adelaide; tours adult/child $22/12; ☺tours 10am, 11am & 2pm daily, plus 1pm Sat & Sun) Hailed as the world's prettiest cricket ground, the Adelaide Oval hosts interstate and international cricket matches in summer, plus national AFL football and state football matches in winter. A wholesale redevelopment has boosted seating capacity to 50,000 – when they're all yelling, it's a serious home-town advantage! Guided 90-minute tours run on nongame days, departing from the Riverbank Stand (south entrance), off War Memorial Dr: call for bookings or book online.

Also here is the Bradman Collection (Map p68; ☑08 8211 1100; www.adelaideoval. com.au; Adelaide Oval, War Memorial Dr, North Adelaide; ☺9am-4pm non-playing days) FREE, where devotees of Don Bradman, cricket's greatest batsman, can pore over the minutiae of his legend, on loan from the State Library of South Australia. Check out the bronze statue of 'the Don' cracking a cover drive out the front of the stadium. Also here is Roofclimb Adelaide Oval (p61), where you scale the giant roof scallops above the hallowed turf (amazing views!)

ADELAIDE IN ...

Two Days
If you're here at Festival, WOMADelaide or Fringe time ('Mad March') lap it up. Otherwise, kick-start your day at the Central Market (p53) then wander through the Adelaide Botanic Gardens (p53), finishing up at the National Wine Centre (p56). After a few bohemian beers at the Exeter Hotel (p70), have a ritzy dinner on Rundle St (p66). Next day, visit the Art Gallery of South Australia (p53) and then wander down to the revamped Adelaide Oval (p58) to check out the Bradman Collection (p58). Grab a cab out to Coopers Brewery (p59) for a beer-tinged tour, then ride the tram to Glenelg (p59) for an evening swim and fish and chips on the sand.

Four Days
Follow the two-day itinerary – perhaps slotting in the South Australian Museum (p53) and Jam Factory Contemporary Craft & Design Centre (Map p62; ☑08 8231 0005; www.jamfactory.com.au; 19 Morphett St; ☺10am-5pm Mon-Sat, noon-4pm Sun) FREE – then pack a picnic basket of Central Market produce and take a day trip to the nearby Adelaide Hills (p76), McLaren Vale (p81) or Barossa Valley (p102) wine regions. Next day, truck out to the museums and historic pubs of Port Adelaide (p59), then catch a live band at the Grace Emily Hotel (p70) back in the city, before dinner on Gouger St (p66).

Inner Suburbs

Coopers Brewery BREWERY
(Map p56; ☑ 08 8440 1800; www.coopers.com.au; 461 South Rd, Regency Park; 1hr tours per person $27.50; ☻ tours 1pm Tue-Fri) You can't possibly come to Adelaide without entertaining thoughts of touring Coopers Brewery. Tours take you through the brewhouse, bottling hall and history museum, where you can get stuck into samples of stouts, ales and lagers. Bookings required; minimum age 18. The brewery is in the northern suburbs; grab a cab, or walk 1km from Islington train station.

Penfolds Magill Estate Winery WINERY
(Map p56; ☑ 08 8301 5569; www.penfolds.com; 78 Penfolds Rd, Magill; tastings from $10; ☻ 9am-6pm) This 100-year-old winery is home to Australia's best-known wine – the legendary Grange. Taste the product at the cellar door; dine at the fab restaurant or bistro; take the Heritage Tour ($20); or steel your wallet for the Great Grange Tour ($150). Tour bookings essential.

Glenelg

Glenelg, or 'the Bay' – the site of SA's colonial landing – is Adelaide at its most LA. Glenelg's beach faces towards the west, and as the sun sinks into the sea, the pubs and bars burgeon with surfies, backpackers and sun-damaged sexagenarians. The tram rumbles in from the city, past the Jetty Rd shopping strip to the alfresco cafes around Moseley Sq.

The **Glenelg Visitor Information Centre** (Map p56; ☑ 08 8294 5833; www.glenelgsa.com.au; Glenelg Town Hall, Moseley Sq, Glenelg; ☻ 9am-5pm Mon-Fri, 10am-2pm Sat & Sun, reduced winter hours) has the local low-down, including information on diving and sailing opportunities. Pick up the *Kaurna yarta-ana* cultural map for some insights into Aboriginal heritage in the area.

From the city, take the tram or bus 167, 168 or 190 to get to Glenelg.

Bay Discovery Centre MUSEUM
(Map p56; ☑ 08 8179 9508; www.glenelgsa.com.au/baydiscover; Town Hall, Moseley Sq, Glenelg; admission by donation; ☻ 10am-5pm Oct-Mar, to 4pm Apr-Sep) This low-key museum in Glenelg's 1887 Town Hall building depicts the social history of Glenelg from colonisation to today, and addresses the plight of

the local Kaurna people, who lost both their land and voice. Don't miss the relics dredged up from the original pier, and the spooky old sideshow machines.

Port Adelaide

Mired in the economic doldrums for decades, Port Adelaide – 15km northwest of the city – is slowly gentrifying, morphing its old redbrick warehouses into art spaces and museums, and its brawl-house pubs into boutique beer emporia. There's even an organic food market here now: the place has soul!

The helpful **Port Adelaide Visitor Information Centre** (Map p56; ☑ 08 8405 6560, 1800 629 888; www.portenf.sa.gov.au; 66 Commercial Rd, Port Adelaide; ☻ 9am-5pm; ☎) stocks brochures on self-guided history, heritage-pub and dolphin-spotting walks and drives, plus the enticements of neighbouring Semaphore, a very bohemian beach burb. Activities include dolphin cruises and kayaking, plus downloadable walking-tour apps.

Adelaide's solitary tram line is rumoured to be extending to Port Adelaide at some stage. Until then, bus 150 will get you here from North Tce, or take the train.

South Australian Maritime Museum MUSEUM
(Map p56; www.samaritimemuseum.com.au; 126 Lipson St, Port Adelaide; adult/child/family $10/5/25; ☻ 10am-5pm daily, lighthouse 10am-2pm Sun-Fri) This salty cache is the oldest of its kind in Australia. Highlights include the iconic **Port Adelaide Lighthouse** ($1 on its own, or included in museum admission), busty figureheads made everywhere from Londonderry to Quebec, shipwreck and explorer displays, and a computer register of early migrants. Ask about tours to the nearby Torrens Island Quarantine Station.

🏃 Activities

On the Land

Adelaide is a pancake-flat town – perfect for cycling and walking (if it's not too hot!) You can take your bike on trains if there's room (you'll need to buy a ticket for your bike), but not on buses or the tram.

Trails SA (www.southaustraliantrails.com) offers loads of cycling- and hiking-trail info: pick up its *40 Great South Australian Short Walks* brochure, or download it from the website.

There are free guided walks in the Adelaide Botanic Gardens (p53). The riverside Linear Park Trail is a 40km walking/cycling path running from Glenelg to the foot of the Adelaide Hills, mainly along the River Torrens: pick up the two brochures covering the route from city to the hills, and the city to the beach, or download maps from www.southaustraliantrails.com. Another popular hiking trail is the steep Waterfall Gully Track (three hours return) up to Mt Lofty Summit and back.

To pick up an Adelaide Free Bike to explore for a day, contact Bicycle SA (p75).

Eagle Mountain Bike Park   MOUNTAIN BIKING
(Map p56; www.bikesa.asn.au/ridemapslist; Mt Barker Rd, Leawood Gardens; ☺dawn-dusk) FREE Mountain bikers should wheel themselves to the Eagle Mountain Bike Park in the Adelaide Hills, pronto; it has 21km of gnarly trails. Check the website for directions.

Adelaide Bowling Club   BOWLING
(Map p62; ☑08 8223 5516; www.adelaidebowlingclub.com.au; 58 Dequetteville Tce; per person $15; ☺noon-late Sun Oct-Mar) Trundle over for a few lawn bowls on Sunday Superbowlz sessions at this old club, just east of the CBD. Show up early for lunch and a few lubricative ales in the clubhouse.

Mega Adventure   ADVENTURE SPORTS
(Map p56; ☑1300 634 269; www.megaadventure.com.au; 4 Hamra Ave, West Beach; adult/child $55/48; ☺11am-6pm Mon-Fri, 10am-6pm Sat & Sun, last entry 4pm) Behind the West Beach dunes you'll find this imposing steel-frame structure, festooned with ropes, ramps, swings, platforms and other precipitous mechanisms from which to dangle yourself at dangerous altitude. Fun for the fearless!

On & In the Water

Adelaide gets *really* hot in summer. Hit the beach at Glenelg, or try any other activity that gets you out on the water. Away from the beach, check out Popeye (Map p62; ☑0400 596 065; www.thepopeye.com.au; return adult/child $15/8, one-way $10/5; ☺10am-4pm, reduced winter hours) cruises on the River Torrens and the little Paddle Boats (Map p62; ☑0400 596 065; www.facebook.com/popeyeadelaide; Elder Park; hire per 30min $15; ☺10am-5pm, reduced winter hours) nearby, run by the same folks. Rymill Park Rowboats (Map p62; ☑08 8232 2814; Rymill Park, East Tce; boats per 30min $10; ☺8am-4.30pm Sat & Sun) on the east side of the CBD are another cool-down option.

ADELAIDE FOR CHILDREN

There are few kids who won't love the tram ride from the city down to Glenelg (p59) (kids under five ride for free!) You may have trouble getting them off the tram – the lure of a splash at the beach then some fish and chips on the lawn should do the trick.

During school holidays, the South Australian Museum (p53), State Library of South Australia (p74), Art Gallery of South Australia (p53), Adelaide Zoo (p58) and Adelaide Botanic Gardens (p53) run inspired kid- and family-oriented programs with accessible and interactive general displays. The Art Gallery also runs a START at the Gallery kids' program (tours, music, activities) from 11am to 3pm on the first Sunday of the month.

Down on the River Torrens there are Popeye (p60) river cruises and Paddle Boats (p60), which make a satisfying splash. Rymill Park Rowboats (p60) are along similar nautical lines.

In Port Adelaide, you can check out the Maritime Museum (p59), National Railway Museum (Map p56; www.natrailmuseum.org.au; 76 Lipson St, Port Adelaide; adult/child/family $12/6/32; ☺10am-4.30pm) or South Australian Aviation Museum (Map p56; www.saam.org.au; 66 Lipson St, Port Adelaide; adult/child/family $10/5/25; ☺10.30am-4.30pm), or set sail on a dolphin-spotting cruise.

The free monthly paper *Child* (www.childmags.com.au), available at cafes and libraries, is largely advertorial, but does contain comprehensive events listings.

Getting around town, Adelaide's buses and trains are straightforward to navigate with kids (through the tram is your best bet if you're pushing a pram). The city is 'flat as a tack', as they say – so getting around the streets with a pusher is easy. Baby-change facilities are available in some public toilets and large department stores: David Jones on Rundle Mall has a good one. For babysitters, try Dial-an-Angel (p47).

Adventure Kayaking SA KAYAKING
(☑08 8295 8812; www.adventurekayak.com.au;
tours adult/child from $50/25, kayak hire per 3hr
1-/2-/3-seater $40/60/80) ✦ Family-friendly
guided kayak tours around the Port River
estuary (dolphins, mangroves, shipwrecks).
Also offers kayak and stand-up paddle-board
hire, plus self-guided tours.

Adelaide Aquatic Centre SWIMMING
(Map p68; ☑08 8203 7665; www.adelaide
aquaticcentre.com.au; Jeffcott Rd, North Adelaide;
adult/child/family $8.50/6.50/23; ⊙6am-9pm
Mon-Fri, 7am-7pm Sat & Sun) The closest pool to
the city, with indoor swimming and diving
pools, and the usual gym, sauna, spa and
coffee-afterwards stuff.

Adelaide Scuba DIVING
(Map p56; ☑08 8294 7744; www.adelaidescuba.
com.au; Patawalonga Frontage, Glenelg North;
⊙9am-5.30pm Mon-Fri, 8am-5pm Sat & Sun)
Hires out snorkelling gear (per day $30)
and runs local dives (single/double dive
$50/100). There are also two-weekend learn-
to-dive courses for $399.

🗝 Tours

★ **Adelaide City Explorer** TOURS
(www.adelaidecityexplorer.com.au) Excellent
new downloadable walking tours around
the city, cosponsored by the Adelaide City
Council and the National Trust (there's a
definite architectural bias here…which we
like!) There are 15 themed trails in all – art
deco, pubs, North Tce, outdoor art, trees
etc – get 'em on your phone and get walking.

RoofClimb Adelaide Oval CLIMBING
(Map p68; ☑08 8331 5222; www.roofclimb.com.au;
Adelaide Oval, King William Rd, North Adelaide; adult
day/twilight $99/109, child $69/79) As per the
Sydney Harbour Bridge and Brisbane's Story
Bridge, you can now scale the lofty rooftops
of the Adelaide Oval (p58). And the views
are astonishing! Kids can climb too, but all
climbers must be at least 120cm tall, and at
most 136kg. Better yet, watch Port Adelaide
play a quarter of AFL football from the roof
for $225!

Escapegoat MOUNTAIN BIKING
(☑0422 916 289; www.escapegoat.com.au) ✦
Careen down the slopes of 727m Mt Lofty
into Adelaide below ($99), or take a day
trip through McLaren Vale by bike ($129).
Extended Flinders Ranges MTB trips also
available.

Bookabee Tours CULTURAL
(☑08 8235 9954; www.bookabee.com.au) ✦
Indigenous-run half-/full-day city tours
($180/255) focusing on Tandanya National
Aboriginal Cultural Institute, the South Australian Museum and bush foods in the Adelaide Botanic Gardens. A great insight into
Kaurna culture.

Haunted Horizons TOURS
(☑0407 715 866; www.adelaidehauntedhorizons.
com.au; per adult $35) Get spooked on these
two-hour, adults-only nocturnal tours of the
old Adelaide Arcade, or a walking tour of the
East End, digging up the dirt on Adelaide's
macabre, murderous and mysterious past.

🎭 Festivals & Events

Tour Down Under SPORTS
(www.tourdownunder.com.au; ⊙Jan) The world's
best cyclists sweating in their lycra: six races
through SA towns, with the grand finale in
downtown Adelaide.

Adelaide Fringe PERFORMING ARTS
(www.adelaidefringe.com.au; ⊙Feb/Mar) This
annual independent arts festival in February
and March is second only to the Edinburgh
Fringe. Funky, unpredictable and downright
hilarious. Get into it!

Adelaide Festival PERFORMING ARTS
(www.adelaidefestival.com.au; ⊙Mar) Top-flight
international and Australian dance, drama,
opera, literature and theatre performances
in March. Don't miss the Northern Lights
along North Tce – old sandstone buildings
ablaze with lights – and the hedonistic late-
night club.

WOMADelaide MUSIC
(www.womadelaide.com.au; ⊙Mar) One of the
world's best live-music events, with more
than 300 musicians and performers from
around the globe. Perfect for families and
those with a new-age bent.

Clipsal 500 SPORTS
(www.clipsal500.com.au; ⊙Mar) Rev-heads
preen their mullets as Adelaide's streets
become a four-day Holden-versus-Ford racing track in March. A massive rock gig coincides (past performers include Kiss, Cold
Chisel and Mötley Crüe).

Tasting Australia FOOD & DRINK
(www.tastingaustralia.com.au; ⊙May) SA
foodie experiences around the city and its
encircling wine regions. Expect classes,

Central Adelaide

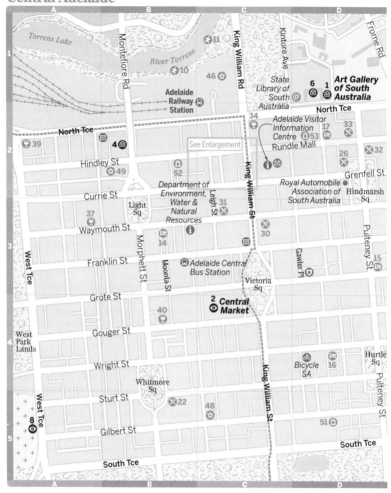

demonstrations, talks and plenty to put in your mouth. First week of May.

Adelaide Cabaret Festival PERFORMING ARTS
(www.adelaidecabaretfestival.com; ☺ Jun) The only one of its kind in the country. A bright, uplifting tonic in the deep and dark Adelaide winter (June).

Adelaide Guitar Festival MUSIC
(www.adelaideguitarfestival.com.au; ☺ Aug)
Annual axefest with a whole lotta rock, classical, country, blues and jazz goin' on. Held in August (when there's not much else to do).

South Australian Living Artists Festival ART
(SALA; www.salafestival.com.au; ☺ Aug) Progressive exhibitions and displays across town in August (expired artists not allowed).

City to Bay SPORTS
(www.city-bay.org.au; ☺ Sep) In September there's an annual 12km fun run from the city to Glenelg (aka 'the Bay'): much sweat and cardiac duress.

OzAsia Festival CULTURAL
(www.ozasiafestival.com.au; ☺ Sep/Oct)
Food, arts, conversation, music and the

🛏 Sleeping

🛏 Central Adelaide

Adelaide Central YHA
HOSTEL $

(Map p62; ☎08 8414 3010; www.yha.com.au; 135 Waymouth St; dm from $31, d without/with bathroom $90/110, f from $121; 🅿❄@🛜) The YHA isn't known for its gregariousness – you'll get plenty of sleep in the spacious and comfortable rooms here. This is a seriously schmick hostel with great security, a roomy kitchen and lounge area, and immaculate bathrooms. A real step up from the average backpacker places around town. Parking is around $10 per day…but the pancakes (Tuesday and Friday) are free!

Backpack Oz
HOSTEL $

(Map p62; ☎08 8223 3551, 1800 633 307; www.backpackoz.com.au; cnr Wakefield & Pulteney Sts; dm $24-30, s/d/tw/tr $65/75/80/96; ❄🛜) It doesn't look flash externally, but this converted pub (the old Orient Hotel) strikes the right balance between party and placid. There are spacious dorms and an additional no-frills guesthouse over the road (good for couples; add $10 to these prices). Get a coldie and shoot some pool in the bar. Free breakfast, wi-fi, bikes, linen and Wednesday-night BBQ.

Hostel 109
HOSTEL $

(Map p62; ☎1800 099 318, 08 8223 1771; www.hostel109.com; 109 Carrington St; dm/s/tw/d/tr $30/65/75/90/105; ❄@🛜) A small, well-managed hostel in a quiet corner of town, with a couple of little balconies over the street and a cosy kitchen/communal area. Clean and super-friendly, with lockers, good security and gas cooking. The only negative: rooms open onto light wells rather than the outside world. Free on-street parking after 5pm.

★Adabco Boutique Hotel
BOUTIQUE HOTEL $$

(Map p62; ☎08 8100 7500; www.adabcohotel.com.au; 223 Wakefield St; d/f from $140/185; ❄🛜) This excellent, stone-clad boutique hotel – built in 1894 in high Venetian Gothic style – has at various times been an Aboriginal education facility, a roller-skating rink and an abseiling venue! These days you can expect three levels of lovely rooms with interesting art and quality linen, plus complimentary breakfast, free wi-fi and smiling staff.

mesmerising Moon Lantern Festival. Two weeks in September/October.

Feast Festival
LGBT

(www.feast.org.au; ☺Oct/Nov) Adelaide's big-ticket gay-and-lesbian festival happens over two weeks in October/November, with a carnival, theatre, dialogue and dance.

Christmas Pageant
CULTURAL

(www.cupageant.com.au; ☺Nov) An Adelaide institution for 70-plus years – kitschy old floats, bands and cheesy marching troupes occupy city streets for a day in (oddly) November.

Central Adelaide

Soho Hotel   HOTEL $$

(Map p62; ☏08 8412 5600; www.thesohohotel.
com.au; 264 Flinders St; d from $159; [P][❄][🔊][🏊]) Attempting to conjure up the vibe of London's Soho district, these plush suites in Adelaide's East End (some with spas, most with balconies) are complemented by sumptuous linen, 24-hour room service, Italian-marble bathrooms, a rooftop jet pool and a fab restaurant. Rates take a tumble midweek. Parking from $20; free wi-fi.

Roof Garden Hotel   HOTEL $$

(Map p62; ☏1800 008 499, 08 8100 4400; www.
majestichotels.com.au; 55 Frome St; d from $162; [P][❄][@][🔊]) Everything looks new in this central, Japanese-toned place. Book a room facing Frome St for a balcony and the best views (Rundle St is metres away), or take a bottle of wine up to the namesake rooftop garden to watch the sunset. Free wif-fi and good walk-in and last-minute rates. Parking from $20 per day.

Hotel Richmond   HOTEL $$

(Map p62; ☏08 8215 4444; www.hotelrichmond.
com.au; 128 Rundle Mall; d from $165; [P][❄][🔊]) This opulent hotel in a grand 1920s building in the middle of Rundle Mall has mod-minimalist rooms with king-sized beds, marble bathrooms, and American oak and Italian furnishings. Oh, and that hotel rarity – opening windows. Rates include movies and newspapers. Parking from $20 per day.

★**Mayfair Hotel**   HOTEL $$$

(Map p62; ☏08 8210 8888; www.mayfairhotel.
com.au; 45 King William St; d from $215; [P][❄][@][🔊]) The gargoyles on Adelaide's 1934

Colonial Mutual Life insurance building guarded a whole lot of empty rooms for decades (has the money gone out of insurance?), but the old dame has been reborn as the very luxe Mayfair Hotel. It's a fabulous fit-out, with myriad bars, eateries and smiling, good-looking staff all over the place. Enjoy! Parking $20.

North Adelaide

Greenways Apartments　　　　APARTMENT $$

(Map p68; ☎08 8267 5903; www.greenways apartments.com.au; 41-45 King William Rd, North Adelaide; 1-/2-/3-bedroom apt $132/175/250; P❄☎) These 1938 apartments ain't flash, but if you have a pathological hatred of slick, 21st-century open-plan 'lifestyles', then Greenways is for you! And where else can you stay in apartments so close to town at these rates? A must for cricket fans, with the Adelaide Oval just a lofted hook shot away – book early for Test matches. New bathrooms.

Minima Hotel　　　　HOTEL $$

(Map p68; ☎08 8334 7766; www.majestichotels. com.au; 146 Melbourne St, North Adelaide; d from $100; P❄@☎) The mural-clad Minima offers compact but stylish rooms, each decorated by a different SA artist, in a prize-winning Melbourne St location (wake up and smell the coffee). Limited parking from $10 per night.

O'Connell Inn　　　　MOTEL $$

(Map p68; ☎08 8239 0766; www.oconnellinn. com.au; 197 O'Connell St, North Adelaide; d/f from $175/200; P❄☎) It's absurdly difficult to find a decent motel in Adelaide (most are mired in the '90s), but this one makes a reasonable fist of the new century, helped along by new bathrooms and vivid Aboriginal art. It's smallish, friendly, affordable and in a beaut location – handy for forays north to the Barossa, Clare, Flinders etc. Apartments also available.

Inner Suburbs

Adelaide Caravan Park　　　　CARAVAN PARK $

(Map p68; ☎08 8363 1566; www.aspenholiday parks.com.au/our-parks/adelaide-caravan-park; 46 Richmond St, Hackney; powered sites from $39, cabins & units from $112; P❄☎❄) A compact, no-frills park on the River Torrens, rather surprisingly slotted in on a quiet street 2km northeast of the city centre. It's clean and well run, with a bit of

green grass if it's not too far into summer (and a pool if it is).

Watson　　　　BOUTIQUE HOTEL $$

(Map p56; ☎08 7087 9666, 1800 278 468; www. artserieshotels.com.au/watson; 33 Warwick St, Walkerville; d from $165, 1-/2-bedroom ste from $216/280, B&B from $275; P❄☎❄) The Watson (named after indigenous artist Tommy Watson, whose works dazzle here) is a sassy, multilevel 115-unit complex 4km north of the CBD in Walkerville (an easy commute). Once upon a time these rooms were government Department of Infrastructure offices. There's a gym, a lap pool, 24-hour concierge, free bikes, free parking, car hire... Nice one!

Glenelg, Port Adelaide & Around

Glenelg Beach Hostel　　　　HOSTEL $

(Map p56; ☎08 8376 0007, 1800 359 181; www. glenelgbeachhostel.com.au; 1-7 Moseley St, Glenelg; dm/s/d/f from $25/60/70/110; ☎) A couple of streets back from the beach, this beaut old terrace (1878) is Adelaide's budget golden child. Fan-cooled rooms maintain period details and are mostly bunk-free. There's cold Coopers in the basement bar (live music on weekends), open fireplaces, lofty ceilings, girls-only dorms, free on-street parking and a courtyard beer garden. Book *waaay* in advance in summer.

BIG4 Adelaide Shores　　　　CARAVAN PARK $

(Map p56; ☎08 8355 7320, 1800 444 567; www. adelaideshores.com.au; 1 Military Rd, West Beach; powered sites $40-55, eco-tents $109, 1-/2-bed cabins from $109/159; P❄☎❄) Hunkered down behind the West Beach dunes, with a walking/cycling track extending to Glenelg (3.4km) in one direction and Henley Beach (3.5km) in the other, this vast holiday park is a choice spot in summer. There are lush sites, permanent 'eco-tents', snappy-looking cabins and passing dolphins.

Port Adelaide Backpackers　　　　HOSTEL $

(Map p56; ☎08 8447 6267; www.portadelaide backpacker.com.au; 24 Nile St, Port Adelaide; dm/s/d without bathroom from $20/60/60, f with bathroom from $130; P❄☎) We're unashamed fans of Port Adelaide, and it gladdens the heart to see this backpackers making a (rather casual) stand here. It's a reimagined brick seaman's lodge in Port Adelaide's historic hub. New bathrooms and laundry; free wi-fi and on-street parking.

★ Largs Pier Hotel
HOTEL **$$**

(Map p56; ☑08 8449 5666; www.largspierhotel.com.au; 198 Esplanade, Largs Bay; d/f/apt from $164/184/199; [P][✿][🖝]) Surprise! In the snoozy beach 'burb of Largs Bay, 5km north of Port Adelaide, is this gorgeous, 130-year-old, three-storey wedding-cake hotel with sky-high ceilings, big beds, taupe-and-chocolate colours and beach views. There's a low-slung wing of motel rooms off to one side; apartments are across the street. Pub trivia: AC/DC and Cold Chisel often played here in the bad old days.

Adelaide Luxury Beach House
RENTAL HOUSE **$$$**

(Map p56; ☑0418 675 339; www.adelaideluxurybeachhouse.com.au; 163 Esplanade, Henley Beach; 3-/4-bedrooms $590/630; [P][✿][🖝]) Do you like to be beside the seaside? Adelaide's beaches face west, so there are brilliant sunsets. Sit on the terrace at this mod beach house with a sundowner and watch the big orange orb descend. It's a plush, three-tier, four-bedroom affair, with room for 12 bods. Pricey, but very lovely – and something different on the Adelaide accommodation scene.

✖ Eating

Foodies flock to West End hot spots like Gouger St (goo-jer), Chinatown and the food-filled Central Market. There are some great pubs here too. Arty/alternative Hindley St – Adelaide's dirty little secret – also has a smattering of good eateries. In the East End, Rundle St and Hutt St offer alfresco cafes and people watching. North Adelaide's Melbourne and O'Connell Sts have a healthy spread of bistros, cafes and pubs.

✖ Central Adelaide

★ Central Market
MARKET **$**

(Map p62; ☑08 8203 7494; www.adelaidecentralmarket.com.au; Gouger St; ⏰7am-5.30pm Tue, 9am-5.30pm Wed & Thu, 7am-9pm Fri, to 3pm Sat) This place is an exercise in sensory bombardment: a barrage of smells, colours and cacophonous stallholders selling fresh vegetables, breads, cheeses, seafood and gourmet produce. Cafes, hectic food courts, a supermarket and Adelaide's Chinatown are here too. Just brilliant.

Café Troppo
CAFE **$**

(Map p62; ☑08 8211 8812; www.cafetroppoadelaide.com; 42 Whitmore Sq; mains $10-17;

⏰7.30am-4pm Tue-Thu, to late Fri, 9am-late Sat, to 4pm Sun; 🖝✿) ✦ Breathing vigour into Whitmore Sq, the least utilised of central Adelaide's five squares, corner-cafe Troppo has jaunty exposed timberwork and a sustainable outlook (local ingredients, recycling, organic milk, ecofriendly cleaning products etc). The coffee is fab, and so is the breakfast pizza and the black lentil, almond, cauliflower and tahini salad. Sandals, noserings, dreadlocks...

Zen Kitchen
VIETNAMESE **$**

(Map p62; ☑08 8232 3542; www.facebook.com/zenkitchenadelaide; unit 7, tenancy 2, Renaissance Arcade; mains $5-14; ⏰10.30am-4.30pm Mon-Thu, to 5pm Fri, 11am-3pm Sat) Superb, freshly constructed rice paper rolls, *pho* and super-crunchy barbecue-pork bahn mi, eat-in or take away. Wash it all down with a cold coconut milk or a teeth-grindingly strong Vietnamese coffee with sugary condensed milk. Authentic, affordable and absolutely delicious.

★ Peel Street
MODERN AUSTRALIAN, ASIAN **$$**

(Map p62; ☑08 8231 8887; www.peelst.com.au; 9 Peel St; mains $20-35; ⏰7:30am-10:30pm Mon & Wed-Fri, 7.30am-4:30pm Tues, 6-10:30pm Sat) Peel St itself – a long-neglected service lane in Adelaide's West End – is now Adelaide's after-dark epicentre, lined with hip bars and eateries, the best of which is this one. It's a super cool café/bistro/wine bar that just keeps packing 'em in: glam city girls sit at window seats nibbling parmesan-crumbed parsnips and turkey meatballs with preserved lemon. Killer wine list.

Pizza e Mozzarella Bar
ITALIAN **$$**

(Map p62; ☑08 8164 1003; www.pizzaemozzarellabar.com.au; 33 Pirie St; mains $18-32; ⏰noon-3pm Mon-Thu, to 9pm Fri, 5.30-9.30pm Sat) Everything at this split-level, rustic Italian eatery – adorned with breadbaskets and beautified by Italian staff – is cooked in the wood oven you see when you walk in the door. Pizzas are thin-based (Roma style); mozzarella plates come with wood-oven bread and meats (octopus, tuna, *salumi*). Super Italian/SA wine and beer list. Cooking classes monthly.

Jasmin Indian Restaurant
INDIAN **$$**

(Map p62; ☑08 8223 7837; www.jasmin.com.au; Basement level, 31 Hindmarsh Sq; mains $17-29; ⏰noon-2.30pm Thu & Fri, 5.30-9pm Tue-Sat) Enter this basement wonderland for magical north Indian curries and consummately professional staff (they might remember your name from when you ate here in 2011). There's nothing too surprising about the menu, but it's done to absolute perfection. Bookings essential.

Gondola Gondola
ASIAN $$

(Map p62; ☑08 8123 3877; www.gondola gondola.com.au; 1 Peel St; small plates $9-18, big plates $19-32; ☺noon-2.30pm Mon-Fri, 6-10pm Mon-Sat) When the late-night food attack hits, duck out of the bar and into Gondola Gondola – a bright, buzzy, fishbowl diner on the corner of Peel St and Hindley St. Go the salt-and-pepper eggplant, or the red steak: chargrilled sirloin with mixed herbs, heaps of chilli and peanuts. Then back to the bar.

Good Life
PIZZA $$

(Map p62; ☑08 8223 2618; www.goodlifepizza.com; 170 Hutt St; pizzas $20-39; ☺noon-2.30pm Mon-Fri, 6pm-late daily; ☑) ☞ At this brilliant organic pizzeria, thin crusts are stacked with tasty toppings like free-range roast duck, Spencer Gulf prawns and spicy Hahndorf salami. Ahhh, life is good… Also has a branch in Glenelg (Map p56; ☑08 8376 5900; www.goodlifepizza.com; level 1, cnr Jetty Rd & Moseley St, Glenelg; pizzas $20-39; ☺noon-2.30pm Tue-Fri & Sun, 6pm-late daily; ☑) ☞.

Sukhumvit Soi.38
THAI $$

(Map p62; ☑08 8223 5472; www.soi38.com.au; 54 Pulteney St; mains $14-25; ☺11.30am-2.30pm Mon-Fri, 5.30-9.30pm Mon-Sat) ☞ As the after-work brigades trudge between the East End pubs and the West End bars, some-times they get hungry. That's where this street-food joint enters the fray: rapid-fire Thai snacks, soups, curries and stir-fries, take away or woofed down in the lavish black-and-gold dining room. Sustainable ingredients all the way.

★Press
MODERN AUSTRALIAN $$$

(Map p62; ☑08 8211 8048; www.pressfood andwine.com.au; 40 Waymouth St; mains $16-46; ☺noon-late Mon-Sat) The pick of the restaurants on office-heavy Waymouth St. Super stylish (brick, glass, lemon-coloured chairs) and not afraid of offal (pan-fried lamb's brains, sweetbreads, grilled calf's tongue) or things raw (beef carpaccio, grav-lax salmon). Tasting menu $68 per person. Book a table upstairs, or they'll fit you in downstairs near the bar, alongside journos from the *Advertiser* across the street.

Chianti
ITALIAN $$$

(Map p62; ☑08 8232 7955; www.chianti.net.au; 160 Hutt St; mains $34-44; ☺7.30am-late Mon-Fri, 8am-late Sat & Sun) Classy Chianti has been around since the '80s, but remains a fixture in the upper echelon of Adelaide fine dining. Step inside the welcoming, shady dining room in high summer and permit yourself some culinary respite: the house-made potato gnocchi with slow-cooked free-range goose and caramelised onion is a stunner. Breakfast too.

Orana
MODERN AUSTRALIAN $$$

(Map p62; ☑08 8232 3444; www.restaurant orana.com; upstairs, 285 Rundle St; tasting menus lunch/dinner $80/175, wine extra $75/150) Rack-ing up plenty of 'Adelaide's Best Restaurant' awards, Orana is a secretive beast, with minimal signage and access via a black staircase at the back of Blackwood restau-rant on Rundle St. Upstairs a fab tasting menu awaits: at least seven courses for lunch, and 18 for dinner (18!) Add wine to the experience to fully immerse yourself in SA's best offerings.

✕ North Adelaide

Bakery on O'Connell
BAKERY $

(Map p68; ☑08 8361 7377; www.bakeryon oconnell.com.au; 128-130 O'Connell St, North Adelaide; items $4-8; ☺24hr) Hunger pangs at 3am? Roll on into the Bakery on O'Con-nell for pizza slices, cakes, buns, pies, past-ies and doughnuts as big as your face. Or perhaps a classic SA 'pie floater' is more to your taste (a meat pie floating in a bowl of pea soup, smothered in tomato sauce – awesome!)

★Gin Long Canteen
ASIAN $$

(Map p68; ☑08 7120 2897; www.ginlongcanteen. com.au; 42 O'Connell St, North Adelaide; small plates $9-15, mains $18-45; ☺noon-2.30pm Tue-Fri, 5.30pm-late Tue-Sat) This energetic food room is a winner. Chipper staff allocate you a space at the communal tables (bookings only for six or more) and take your order pronto. The food arrives just as fast: fab cur-ries, slow-braised Thai beef and pork, net-ted spring rolls, Malay curry puffs… It's a pan-Asian vibe, bolstered by jumbo bottles of Vietnamese beer and smiles all round.

Ruby Red Flamingo
ITALIAN $$

(Map p68; ☑08 8267 5769; www.rubyred flamingo.com; 142 Tynte St, North Adelaide; mains $22-30; ☺noon-2.30pm Wed-Fri, 5.30-9.30pm

North Adelaide

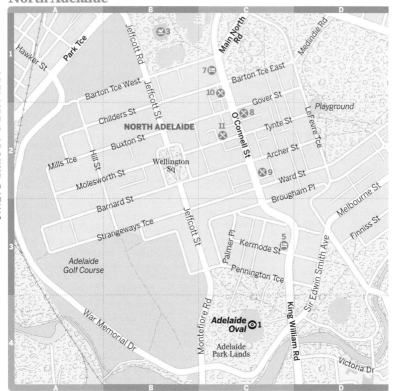

Wed-Sat) Fancy Italian on a North Adelaide side street, seated either in old-cottage confines, or out by the babbling fountain (a very Tuscan scene). The calamari-and-pea arancini balls and octopus carpaccio are utterly memorable. No bookings.

Lucky Lupitas   MEXICAN **$$**
(Map p68; ☑08 8267 3082; www.luckylupitas. com; Shop 1, 163 O'Connell St, North Adelaide; tacos $6-9, mains $17-25; ☺noon-2pm Sun, 5.30-9pm Mon-Thur & Sun, to 10pm Fri, 5-10pm Sat) Lucky Lupitas was holed-up in a humble southern-suburbs shopfront for years, before a wrecking crew arrived to expand the adjacent highway. But now they're back in North Adelaide! Nifty plywood panelling, stacks of hot-sauce boxes by the door and unbelievably good spicy King George whiting tacos and beef brisket nachos. Cold *cerveza* by the gallon.

✕ Inner Suburbs

★ **Argo on the Parade**   CAFE **$**
(Map p56; ☑08 8431 1387; www.facebook.com/ argoespresso; 212 The Parade, Norwood; mains $8-22; ☺7am-5.30pm Sat & Sun) The best cafe in affluent, eastern-suburbs Norwood is arguably the best cafe in Adelaide, too. It *is* in Norwood, so by default it's a bit thin on soul. But the food, coffee, service and quirky design all take the cake. As does the breakfast burrito. And the marinated tuna bowl. And the sweet potato fries...

Jarmer's Kitchen   CAFE **$$**
(Map p56; ☑08 8340 1055; www.jarmerskitchen. com.au; 18 Park Tce, Bowden; mains $12-36; ☺7.30am-4pm Mon, to 9pm Tue-Fri, 8am-9pm Sat, to 4pm Sun) Jarmer's is a mainstay of rapidly redeveloping Bowden, a city-edge suburb once an industrial wasteland, now home to hundreds of hip new town houses with hip

urbanites inside them. It's a fancy day/night affair in an old pub building, serving savvy sandwiches, pastas, burgers and substantial mains: try the pork-and-fennel sausages. Terrific wine list too.

Parwana Afghan Kitchen AFGHANI **$$**
(Map p56; ☑ 08 8443 9001; www.parwana.com. au; 124b Henley Beach Rd, Torrensville; mains $14-25; ⊙ 6-10pm Tue-Thu & Sun, to 10.30pm Fri & Sat) Nutty, spicy, slippery and a little bit funky: Afghan food is unique, and this authentic restaurant, west of the CBD across the parklands, is a great place to try it. The signature *banjaan borani* eggplant dish is a knock-out. There's also a lunchtime branch just off Rundle St in the city called **Kutchi Deli Parwana** (Map p62; ☑ 08 7225 8586; www.parwana. com.au; 7 Ebenezer Pl; ⊙ 11.30am-3pm Mon-Sat). BYO; cash only.

✘ Glenelg, Port Adelaide & Around

Zest Cafe Gallery CAFE **$**
(Map p56; ☑ 08 8295 3599; www.zestcafegallery. com.au; 2a Sussex St, Glenelg; meals $9-17; ⊙ 7.30am-6pm Mon-Sat, 8.30am-5pm Sun; 🖐) Little sidestreet Zest has a laid-back vibe and brilliant breakfasts – more than enough compensation for any shortcomings in size. Baguettes and bagels are crammed with creative combos, or you can banish your hangover with some 'Hell's Eggs': baked in a ramekin with rosemary, tomato salsa, cheese and Tabasco sauce. Great coffee, arty staff and regular vegetarian specials.

Zucca GREEK **$$**
(Map p56; ☑ 08 8376 8222; www.zucca.com.au; shop 5, Marina Pier, Holdfast Shores, Glenelg; meze $11-25, mains $24-29; ⊙ noon-3pm & 6pm-late) Multicoloured tables, marina views, super service and a contemporary menu of mezze plates – you'd struggle to find anything this appealing on Santorini. The grilled Hindmarsh Valley halloumi with spiced raisins and the seared scallops with feta and pistachio are sublime.

Mestizo
PERUVIAN $$

(Map p56; ✆ 08 8294 0295; www.mestizo cocinaperuana.com.au; 114 Partridge St, Glenelg South; mains $12-32; ⊙ 12.30-3pm Fri, 5.30pm-late Tue-Fri, 1pm-late Sat & Sun) This endearing little plum-coloured eatery in the Glenelg South back blocks is Adelaide's best (only) Peruvian restaurant. The hard-working kitchen turns out fabulous pork ribs with spicy green *huacatay* sauce and *chimichurri*; or go on an Andean journey via the 'chef's selection' menu ($60 per person). Terrific South American wines too.

Low & Slow American BBQ
AMERICAN $$

(Map p56; ✆ 0402 589 722; www.lowandslow americanbbq.com; 17 Commercial Rd, Port Adelaide; meals $10-29; ⊙ noon-2.30pm Fri, 6-9pm Wed-Sun) Give your arteries something to do: this woody food room plates up succulent US-style BBQ meats, with a slew of slaws, beans, greens and grits on the side. Wash it all down with a Brooklyn Lager and a couple of Wild Turkey shots. Hip!

🍸 Drinking & Nightlife

Rundle St has a few iconic pubs, while in the West End, Hindley St's red-light sleaze collides with the hip bars on Leigh and Peel Sts. Cover charges at clubs can be anything from free to $15, depending on the night. Most clubs close Monday to Thursday.

🍷 Central Adelaide

★ **Exeter Hotel**
PUB

(Map p62; ✆ 08 8223 2623; www.theexeter.com. au; 246 Rundle St; ⊙ 11am-late) Adelaide's best pub, this legendary boozer attracts an eclectic brew of postwork, punk and uni drinkers, shaking the day off their backs. Pull up a bar stool or nab a table in the grungy beer garden and settle in for the evening. Original music nightly (indie, electronica, acoustic); no pokies. Book for curry nights in the upstairs restaurant (usually Wednesdays).

★ **Maybe Mae**
BAR

(Map p62; ✆ 0421 405 039; www.maybemae. com; 15 Peel St; ⊙ 5pm-late Mon-Fri, 6pm-late Sat & Sun) Down some stairs down an alleyway off a laneway, Maybe Mae doesn't proclaim its virtues loudly to the world. In fact, if you can't find the door, you won't be the first thirsty punter to wander back upstairs looking confused. But once you're inside, let the good times roll: classic rock, cool staff, booth seats and brilliant beers. Love it!

★ **Grace Emily Hotel**
PUB

(Map p62; ✆ 08 8231 5500; www.graceemily hotel.com.au; 232 Waymouth St; ⊙ 4pm-late) Duking it out with the Exeter Hotel (p70) for the title of 'Adelaide's Best Pub' (it pains us to separate the two), the 'Gracie' has live music most nights (alt-rock, country, acoustic, open-mic nights), kooky '50s-meets-voodoo decor, open fires and great beers. Regular cult cinema; no pokies. Are the Bastard Sons of Ruination playing tonight?

★ **Nola**
BAR

(Map p62; www.nolaadelaide.com; 28 Vardon Ave; ⊙ 4pm-midnight Tue-Thu, noon-2am Fri & Sat, 11am-midnight Sun) This hidden back-lane space was once the stables for the adjacent Stag Hotel. Out with the horse poo, in with 16 craft beers on tap, American and Australian whiskies (no Scotch!), Cajun cooking (gumbo, oysters, jambalaya, fried chicken) and regular live jazz. A saucy bit of Deep South in the East End.

Pink Moon Saloon
BAR

(Map p62; www.pinkmoonsaloon.com.au; 21 Leigh St; ⊙ 4pm-late Sat-Thu, noon-late Fri) Now this place is hip! Wedged into an impossibly tight alleyway space off Leigh St (seriously, it's only a couple of metres wide), Pink Moon Saloon has a bar in its front room, a little courtyard behind it, then a neat BBQ shack out the back. Cocktails and craft beer are why you're here. The same folks run Clever Little Taylor (p70).

Hains & Co
BAR

(Map p62; ✆ 08 8410 7088; www.hainsco.com.au; 23 Gilbert Pl; ⊙ 4pm-late Tue-Fri & Sun, 6pm-late Sat) The nautical vibe might seem incongruous on a hot Adelaide night this far from the ocean (diving helmets, barometers, anchors etc) – but somehow it works. A really clever fit-out of a tight laneway space, with the focus on all things gin and rum. Get a few under your belt and belt out a sea shanty or three.

Clever Little Taylor
BAR

(Map p62; ✆ 0407 111 857; www.cleverlittletailor. com.au; 19 Peel St; ⊙ 4pm-late Mon-Sat) CLT was one of the vanguard which ushered in the new brigade of small bars in Adelaide's laneways. Good liquor is the thrust here, along with fine SA wines and a hip brick-and-stone renovation (no prizes for guessing what this space used to be). Zippy bar food too.

Udaberri
BAR

(Map p62; 📞 08 8410 5733; www.udaberri.com.
au; 11-13 Leigh St; ⏰ 4pm-late Tue-Fri, 6pm-late
Sat & Sun) Laneway boozing at its best (in
fact, this was one of Adelaide's first laneway
bars), nouveau-industrial Udaberri is a compact bar on Leigh St, serving Spanish wines
by the glass, good beers on tap and *pintxos*
(Basque bar snacks) like oysters, cheeses,
jamón and tortillas. The after-work crowd is
cashed-up and city-savvy.

2KW
ROOFTOP BAR

(Map p62; 📞 08 8212 5511; www.2kwbar.com.au; 2
King William St; ⏰ 10am-late Mon-Fri, noon-late Sat
& Sun) K2 on the China–Pakistan border is
8611m tall. 2KW is eight floors high – not
quite as lofty, but it's an upmarket spot
for a cocktail and eye-popping views out
towards North Adelaide nonetheless. If you
pass aesthetic muster (no running shoes; no
logo-spangled T-shirts), access is via a *Get
Smart*-like series of elevators.

Zhivago
CLUB

(Map p62; 📞 08 8212 0569; www.zhivago.com.au;
54 Currie St; ⏰ 9pm-late Fri-Sun) The pick of the
West End clubs, Zhivago is all muscles and
manscaping vs high heels and short skirts,
with DJs pumping out everything from reggae and dub to quality house. Popular with
the 18 to 25 dawn patrol.

Mars Bar
CLUB

(Map p62; 📞 08 8231 9639; www.themarsbar.
com.au; 120 Gouger St; ⏰ 9pm-late Fri & Sat) The
lynchpin of Adelaide's nocturnal gay and lesbian scene, always-busy Mars Bar features
glitzy decor, flashy clientele and OTT drag
shows.

HQ Complex
CLUB

(Map p62; 📞 08 7221 1245; www.hqcomplex.com.
au; 1 North Tce; ⏰ 8pm-late Wed, Fri & Sat) Adelaide's heftiest club fills five big rooms with
shimmering sound and light. Night-time is
the right time on Saturdays – the biggest
(and trashiest) club night in town. Retro
Wednesdays; live acts Fridays. Check the
website for other gig listings.

🍷 North Adelaide

Kentish Hotel
PUB

(Map p68; 📞 08 8267 1173; www.thekentish.com.
au; 23 Stanley St, North Adelaide; ⏰ 11.30am-11pm
Mon-Thu, to midnight Fri & Sat, to 10pm Sun) They
don't make 'em like they used to. Actually,
these days, when it comes to handsome

ℹ️ PINT OF COOPERS PLEASE!

Things can get confusing at the bar in
Adelaide. Aside from the 200ml (7oz)
'butchers' – the choice of old men in
dim, sticky-carpet pubs – there are
three main beer sizes: 285ml (10oz)
'schooners' (pots or middies elsewhere
in Australia), 425ml (15oz) 'pints'
(schooners elsewhere) and 568ml
(20oz) 'imperial pints' (traditional English pints). Now go forth and order with
confidence!

---

two-storey sandstone pubs, they don't make
'em at all. This backstreet beauty is great
for a cold one on a hot afternoon, or gastro-
nomic delights including a funky fish stew
and a 'Memphis Burger' with fried chicken
and smoked bourbon barbecue sauce.

🍴 Inner Suburbs

★ Wheatsheaf
PUB

(Map p56; 📞 08 8443 4546; www.wheatsheaf
hotel.com.au; 39 George St, Thebarton; ⏰ 1pm-mid-
night Mon-Fri, noon-midnight Sat, to 9pm Sun;
📶) A hidden gem under the flight path in
industrial Thebarton, with an arty crowd of
students, jazz musos, lesbians, punks and
rockers. Tidy beer garden, eclectic live music
out the back (acoustic, blues, country), open
fires and food trucks parked out the front.
Kick-ass craft beers to boot.

Earl of Leicester
PUB

(Map p56; 📞 08 8271 5700; www.earl.com.au; 85
Leicester St, Parkside; ⏰ 11am-late) Hidden in
the suburban Parkside backstreets is this
atmospheric old bluestone pub, serving a
winning combo of abundant craft beers
and the biggest schnitzels you're ever likely
to bite into (mains $14 to $35). A mere 150
beers will see your name added to the 'Beer
Legends' (dis)honour board.

🍷 Glenelg, Port Adelaide
& Around

The Moseley
PUB

(Map p56; 📞 08 8295 3966; www.themoseley.
com.au; Moseley Sq, Glenelg; ⏰ 11am-late Mon-
Fri, 8am-late Sat & Sun) This old boozer was
an Irish pub for years, but that's just *sooo*
2001… Reborn as the Moseley, a fancy refit
has purged all the dark wood and replaced
it with wicker. The upstairs balcony is where

you want to be, sipping a G&T as the tram rumbles into Moseley Sq from the city. Classy pub mains $18 to $36.

Lighthouse Wharf Hotel   PUB
(Map p56; ☑08 8447 1580; www.thelighthouse wharfhotel.com.au; 1 Commercial Rd, Port Adelaide; ☺10am-late Mon-Sat, 9am-11pm Sun) There are more raffish old pubs in Port Adelaide than hours in your afternoon. But if you're dry, swing into the 1935 Lighthouse Wharf Hotel for a quick Coopers, some whiting-and-chips or a bargain $11 weekday lunch. Kitchen open all day on weekends.

☆ Entertainment

Arty Adelaide has a rich cultural life that stacks up favourably with much larger cities. For listings and reviews see *Adelaide Now* (www.adelaidenow.com.au) and *Adelaide Review* (www.adelaidereview.com.au). Agencies for big-ticket event bookings include BASS (☑13 12 46; www.bass.net.au) and Moshtix (☑1300 438 849; www.moshtix.com.au).

Live Music

Adelaide knows how to kick out the jams! Top pub venues around town include the Wheatsheaf (p71), Grace Emily Hotel (p70) and Exeter Hotel (p70). For gig listings check out the following:

➡ *Adelaide Review* (www.adelaide review.com.au/guides)

➡ *Music SA* (www.musicsa.com.au)

➡ *Jazz Adelaide* (www.jazz.adelaide.onau.net)

★ Governor Hindmarsh Hotel   LIVE MUSIC
(Map p56; ☑08 8340 0744; www.thegov.com.au; 59 Port Rd, Hindmarsh; ☺11am-late) Ground zero for live music in Adelaide, 'The Gov' hosts some legendary local and international acts. The odd Irish band fiddles around in the bar, while the main venue features rock, folk, jazz, blues, salsa, reggae and dance. A huge place with an inexplicably personal vibe. Good food too.

★ Thebarton Theatre   LIVE MUSIC
(Map p56; ☑08 8443 5255; www.thebarton theatre.com.au; 112 Henley Beach Rd, Torrensville) Now this old stager has got soul! Vaguely art deco, the 'Thebby' is an iconic Adelaide live-music venue with great acoustics and buckets of charm. Midsize acts like Rodriguez, Morrissey and the Black Crowes make the grade.

Gilbert Street Hotel   JAZZ
(Map p62; ☑08 8231 9909; www.gilbertsthotel.com.au; 88 Gilbert St; ☺11am-late) The best place in Adelaide to catch some live jazz (on Tuesday nights, at any rate) the Gilbert is a renovated old pub but continues to ooze soul. Order a *vin rouge* at the bar and dig the scene with the goatee-d regulars. Soul and acoustic acts Thursday and Sunday.

Jive   LIVE MUSIC
(Map p62; ☑08 8211 6683; www.jivevenue.com; 181 Hindley St) In a converted theatre spangled with a brilliant mural, Jive caters to an off-beat crowd of student types who like their tunes funky, left-field and removed from the mainstream. A sunken dance floor = great atmosphere. Top marks for endurance in an ever-changing world.

Adelaide
Entertainment Centre   CONCERT VENUE
(Map p56; ☑08 8208 2222; www.theaec.net; 98 Port Rd, Hindmarsh; ☺box office 9am-5pm Mon-Fri) Around 12,000 bums on seats for everyone from the Wiggles to Keith Urban to Stevie Wonder.

Adelaide
Symphony Orchestra   CLASSICAL MUSIC
(ASO; Map p62; ☑08 8233 6233; www.aso.com.au; 91 Hindley St; ☺box office 9am-4.30pm Mon-Fri) The estimable ASO, with gigs at various venues including the Grainger Studio on Hindley St, the Festival Theatre and Adelaide Town Hall. Check the website for performance info.

Cinemas

For cinema 'what's-on' listings: www.yourmovies.com.au/cinemas/city/adelaide and www.my247.com.au/adelaide/cinemas.

Palace Nova Eastend Cinemas   CINEMA
(Map p62; ☑08 8232 3434; www.palacecinemas.com.au; 250-51 Rundle St; tickets adult/child $19.50/15.50; ☺10am-late) Facing-off across Rundle St, both these cinema complexes screen 'sophisticated cinema': new-release art-house, foreign-language and independent films as well as some mainstream flicks. Fully licensed too.

Moonlight Cinema   CINEMA
(Map p68; ☑1300 551 908; www.moonlight.com.au/adelaide; Botanic Park, Hackney Rd; tickets adult/child $20/15; ☺7pm daily Dec-Feb) In summer pack a picnic and mosquito repellent, and sprawl out on the lawn to watch old and new classics under the stars. 'Gold

Grass' tickets, which cost a little more, secure you a prime-viewing beanbag.

Theatre & Comedy

See *Adelaide Theatre Guide* (www.theatre guide.com.au) for booking details, venues and reviews for comedy, drama and musicals.

At the time of writing, Adelaide's long-running comedy club the Rhino Room was scheduled to relocate to a new venue; check online to see if it's back in action.

Adelaide Festival Centre   PERFORMING ARTS
(Map p62; ☑08 8216 8600; www.adelaide festivalcentre.com.au; King William Rd; ☺box office 9am-6pm Mon-Fri) The hub of performing arts in SA, this crystalline white Festival Centre opened in June 1973, four proud months before the Sydney Opera House! The *State Theatre Company* (www. statetheatrecompany.com.au) is based here. Is it just us, or does the old dame need a bit of a spruce-up?

Sport

As most Australian cities do, Adelaide hangs its hat on the successes of its sporting teams. In the **Australian Football League** (www.afl.com.au), the Adelaide Crows and Port Adelaide Power have sporadic success and play at the Adelaide Oval. Suburban Adelaide teams compete in the confusingly named **South Australian National Football League** (www.sanfl.com.au). The football season runs from March to September.

In the **National Basketball League** (www.nbl.com.au), the Adelaide 36ers have been a force for decades (lately, not so much). In netball, the Adelaide Thunderbirds play in the **ANZ Championship** (www.anz-championship.com) with regular success. In soccer's **A League** (www.a-league.com.au), Adelaide United ('the Reds') won the championship in 2016.

In summer, under the auspices of **Cricket SA** (www.cricketsa.com.au), the Redbacks play one-day and multiday state matches at the Adelaide Oval. The Redbacks rebrand as the Adelaide Strikers in the national **T20 Big Bash** (www.bigbash. com.au) competition. International cricket also happens at the Adelaide Oval (www. cricketaustralia.com.au).

🔒 Shopping

Shops and department stores line Rundle Mall. The beautiful old arcades running between the mall and Grenfell St retain their original splendour, and house eclectic little shops. Rundle St and the adjunct Ebenezer Pl are home to boutique and retro clothing shops.

★**Streetlight**   BOOKS, MUSIC
(Map p62; ☑08 8227 0667; www.facebook.com/ streetlightadelaide; 2/15 Vaughan Pl; ☺10am-6pm Mon-Thu & Sat, to 9pm Fri, noon-5pm Sun) Lefty, arty and subversive in the best possible way, Streetlight is the place to find that elusive Miles Davis disc or Charles Bukowski poetry compilation.

★**Imprints Booksellers**   BOOKS
(Map p62; ☑08 8231 4454; www.imprints.com. au; 107 Hindley St; ☺9am-6pm Mon-Wed, to 9pm Thu & Fri, to 5pm Sat, 11am-5pm Sun) The best bookshop in Adelaide is in the worst location (in the thick of the Hindley St strip-club fray). Still, don't let it bug you: jazz, floorboards, Persian rugs and occasional live readings and book launches more than compensate. And a bit of sleaze has always been solid literary fuel.

Midwest Trader   FASHION & ACCESSORIES
(Map p62; ☑08 8223 6606; www.facebook.com/ Midwest-Trader; Shop 1 & 2 Ebenezer Pl; ☺10am-6pm Mon-Thu & Sat, to 9pm Fri, noon-5pm Sun) Stocks a snarling range of punk, skate, vintage, biker and rockabilly gear, plus second-hand cowboy boots. Rock on! Check out its Facebook page for its latest wares.

Miss Gladys Sym Choon   FASHION & ACCESSORIES
(Map p62; ☑08 8223 1500; www. missgladyssymchoon.com.au; 235a Rundle St; ☺9.30am-6pm Mon-Thu, to 9pm Fri, 10am-5.30pm Sat, 11am-5.30pm Sun) Named after a famed Rundle St trader from the 1920s (the first woman in SA to incorporate a business) this hip shop is the place for fab frocks, rockin' boots, street-beating sneakers, jewellery, watches and hats.

Adelaide Farmers Market   MARKET
(Map p56; ☑08 8231 8155; www.adelaide farmersmarket.com; Adelaide Showground, Leader St, Wayville; ☺9am-1pm Sun) 🌱 Don't mind dragging yourself out of bed too early on a Sunday and paying $8 for an organic parsnip? The Adelaide Farmers Market is for you! Actually, ignore our cynicism – the food offerings here are fabulous: fresh, organic, local and sustainable, take home or cooked into delicious things you can eat on the spot.

Gilles Street Market
MARKET
(Map p62; www.gillesstreetmarket.com.au; Gilles Street Primary School, 91 Gilles St; ⊙10am-4pm 3rd Sun of the month, plus 1st Sun Oct-May) Kids' clothes, fashion, arts, crafts, buskers and general commercial hubbub consume an East End Adelaide school grounds.

Jurlique
COSMETICS
(Map p62; ☑08 8410 7180; www.jurlique.com.au; 50 Rundle Mall; ⊙9am-6pm Mon-Thu, to 9pm Fri, to 5pm Sat, 11am-5pm Sun) An international success story, SA's own Jurlique sells fragrant skincare products (some Rosewater Balancing Mist, anyone?) that are pricey but worth every cent.

ℹ Information

EMERGENCY

AMBULANCE, FIRE, POLICE	☑000
RAA EMERGENCY ROADSIDE ASSISTANCE	☑13 11 11

INTERNET ACCESS
State Library of South Australia (Map p62; ☑08 8207 7250; www.slsa.sa.gov.au; 1st fl, cnr North Tce & Kintore Ave; ⊙10am-8pm Mon-Wed, to 6pm Thu & Fri, to 5pm Sat & Sun) Free internet access (book ahead), and kids' school-holiday programs.

MEDIA
Adelaide's daily tabloid is the parochial *Advertiser*, though the *Age*, *Australian* and *Financial Review* are also widely available.

➡ **Adelaide Review** (www.adelaidereview.com.au) Highbrow articles, culture and arts. Free monthly.

➡ **Blaze** (www.gaynewsnetwork.com.au) Gay-and-lesbian street press; free fortnightly.

➡ **CityMag** (www.citymag.indaily.com.au) Food reviews, culture and urban happenings. Free quarterly.

➡ **Scenestr** (www.scenestr.com.au/adelaide) Free monthly street press: music, fashion, clubbing and arts.

MEDICAL SERVICES
Emergency Dental Service (☑08 8222 8222; www.sadental.sa.gov.au) Sore tooth?

Midnight Pharmacy (Map p62; ☑08 8232 4445; 192-198 Wakefield St; ⊙7am-midnight Mon-Sat, 9am-midnight Sun) Late-night presciptions.

Royal Adelaide Hospital (Map p62; ☑08 8222 4000; www.rah.sa.gov.au; 275 North Tce; ⊙24hr) Emergency department (not for blisters!) and STD clinic.

Women's & Children's Hospital (☑08 8161 7000; www.cywhs.sa.gov.au; 72 King William Rd, North Adelaide; ⊙24hr) Emergency and sexual-assault services.

MONEY
Travelex (Map p62; ☑08 8231 6977; www.travelex.com.au; shop 4, Beehive Corner, Rundle Mall; ⊙8.30am-6pm Mon-Fri, 9am-3pm Sat, noon-5pm Sun) Foreign currency exchange.

POST
Adelaide General Post Office (GPO; Map p62; ☑13 13 18; www.auspost.com.au; 141 King William St; ⊙9am-5.30pm Mon-Fri, to 12.30pm Sat) Adelaide's main (and rather stately) post office. There are also post offices just off **Rundle Mall** (Map p62; ☑13 13 18; www.auspost.com.au; 59 City Cross Arc; ⊙8.30am-5pm Mon-Fri, 9am-12.30pm Sat, 11am-4pm Sun) and another on the **UniSA campus** (Map p62; ☑13 13 18; www.auspost.com.au; 61 North Tce; ⊙9am-5pm Mon-Fri).

TOURIST INFORMATION
Adelaide Visitor Information Centre (Map p62; ☑1300 588 140; www.adelaidecitycouncil.com; 9 James Pl, off Rundle Mall; ⊙9am-5pm Mon-Fri, 10am-4pm Sat & Sun, 11am-3pm public holidays) Adelaide-specific information, plus abundant info on SA including fab regional booklets.

Department of Environment, Water & Natural Resources (DEWNR; Map p62; ☑08 8204 1910; www.environment.sa.gov.au; ground fl, 81-95 Waymouth St; ⊙9am-5pm Mon-Fri) National parks information and bookings.

There are also helpful visitors centres in **Glenelg** (p59) and **Port Adelaide** (p59).

ℹ Getting There & Away

AIR
International, interstate and regional flights via a number of airlines service **Adelaide Airport** (ADL; Map p56; ☑08 8308 9211; www.adelaideairport.com.au; 1 James Schofield Dr; 7km west of the city centre. Domestic services include:

➡ **Jetstar** (www.jetstar.com.au) Direct flights between Adelaide and Perth, Darwin, Cairns, Brisbane, Gold Coast, Sydney and Melbourne.

➡ **Qantas** (www.qantas.com.au) Direct flights between Adelaide and Perth, Alice Springs, Darwin, Cairns, Brisbane, Sydney, Canberra and Melbourne.

➡ **Regional Express** (Rex; www.regionalexpress.com.au) Flies from Adelaide to regional centres around SA – Kingscote, Coober Pedy, Ceduna, Mount Gambier, Port Lincoln and Whyalla – plus Broken Hill in NSW and Mildura in Victoria.

⇒ **Tiger Airways** (www.tigerairways.com.au) Direct flights between Adelaide and Melbourne, Sydney and Brisbane.

⇒ **Virgin Australia** (www.virginaustralia.com. au) Direct flights between Adelaide and Perth, Alice Springs, Brisbane, Gold Coast, Sydney, Canberra and Melbourne.

BUS

Adelaide Central Bus Station (Map p62; ☑ 08 8221 5080; www.adelaidemetro.com.au/bussa; 85 Franklin St; ⊙ 6am-9.30pm) is the hub for all major interstate and statewide bus services; see the website for route and time-table info. Note: there is no Adelaide–Perth bus service.

⇒ **Firefly Express** (☑ 1300 730 740; www.fireflyexpress.com.au) Runs between Sydney, Melbourne and Adelaide.

⇒ **Greyhound Australia** (☑ 1300 473 946; www.greyhound.com.au) Australia's main long-distance player, with services between Adelaide and Melbourne, Canberra, Sydney, Alice Springs and Darwin.

⇒ **Premier Stateliner** (p269) Statewide bus services.

⇒ **V/Line** (p266) Bus and bus/train services between Adelaide and Melbourne.

CAR & MOTORCYCLE

The major international car-rental companies have offices at Adelaide Airport and in the city. There's also a crew of local operators, including the following. Note that some companies don't allow vehicles to be taken to Kangaroo Island.

Acacia Car Rentals (☑ 08 8234 0911; www.acaciacarrentals.com.au; 91 Sir Donald Bradman Dr, Hilton; ⊙ 8am-5pm Mon-Fri, to noon Sat) Cheap rentals for travel within a 100km radius of Adelaide; scooter hire available.

Access Rent-a-Car (☑ 08 8340 0400, 1800 812 580; www.accessrentacar.com; 464 Port Rd, West Hindmarsh; ⊙ 8am-6pm Mon-Fri, to noon Sat & Sun) Kangaroo Island travel permitted; 4WDs available.

Cut Price Car & Truck Rentals (☑ 08 8443 7788; www.cutprice.com.au; cnr Sir Donald Bradman Dr & South Rd, Mile End; ⊙ 7.30am-5pm Mon-Fri, to 3pm Sat & Sun) 4WDs available.

Koala Car Rentals (☑ 08 8352 7299; www.koalarentals.com.au; 41 Sir Donald Bradman Dr, Mile End; ⊙ 7.30am-5pm Mon-Fri, 8am-3pm Sat & Sun)

Smile Rent-a-Car (☑ 08 8234 0655, 1800 891 002; www.smilerentacar.com.au; 315

Sir Donald Bradman Dr, Brooklyn Park; ⊙ 8am-6pm)

The **Royal Automobile Association of South Australia** (p259) provides auto advice (including road conditions in outback areas) and plenty of maps.

TRAIN

Interstate trains run by **Great Southern Rail** (p267) grind into the **Adelaide Parklands Terminal** (Railway Tce, Keswick; ⊙ 6am-5pm Mon & Fri, 6.30am-5.30pm Tue, 9am-5pm Wed, to 7pm Thu, 8.30am-1pm Sun), 1km southwest of the city centre. The following trains depart Adelaide regularly; backpacker discounts apply:

⇒ **The Ghan to Alice** Springs (from $799, 19 hours)

⇒ **The Ghan to Darwin** (from $1499, 47 hours)

⇒ **The Indian Pacific to Perth** (from $1189, 39 hours)

⇒ **The Indian Pacific to Sydney** (from $589, 25 hours)

⇒ **The Overland to Melbourne** (from $149, 11 hours)

❶ Getting Around

TO/FROM THE AIRPORT & TRAIN STATION

Prebooked private **Adelaide Airport Flyer** (☑ 08 8353 5233, 1300 856 444; www.adelaideairportflyer.com) minibuses run door-to-door between the airport and anywhere around Adelaide; get a quote and book online (into the city from the airport for one person costs $35). Public Adelaide Metro **JetExpress** (www.adelaidemetro.com.au/timetables-maps/special-services; $3.20-5.10; ⊙ 6.30am-11pm Mon-Fri, 7.15am-11pm Sat & Sun) and **JetBus** (www.adelaidemetro.com.au/timetables-maps/special-services; $3.20-5.10; ⊙ 6.30am-11pm Mon-Fri, 7.15am-11pm Sat & Sun) bus services – routes J1, J1X, J3, J7 and J8 – connect the airport with Glenelg and the CBD; standard Metro fares apply.

Taxis charge around $30 into the city from the airport (15 minutes); or about $15 from Adelaide Parklands Terminal (10 minutes). Many hostels will pick you up and drop you off if you're staying with them. **Adelaide Transport** (p76) also offers shuttle transfers.

BICYCLE

Adelaide is pizza-flat: great for cycling! With a valid passport or driver's licence you can borrow an **Adelaide Free Bike** from **Bicycle SA** (Map p62; ☑ 08 8168 9999; www.bikesa.asn.au; 53 Carrington St; ⊙ 9am-5pm Mon-Fri, 8am-5pm Sat & Sun); helmet and lock provided. There are a couple of dozen locations around town: you can collect a bike at any of them, provided you return it to the same place. Multiday hires also available.

Down at the beach, hire a bike from **Glenelg Bicycle Hire** (Map p56; ☑ 08 8376 1934; www.glenelgbicyclehire.com.au; Norfolk Motel, 71 Broadway, Glenelg South; bikes per day $25, tandems per hour/day $25/50).

PUBLIC TRANSPORT

Adelaide Metro (Map p62; ☑ 1300 311 108; www.adelaidemetro.com.au; cnr King William & Currie Sts; ☺ 8am-6pm Mon-Fri, 9am-5pm Sat, 11am-4pm Sun) runs Adelaide's decent and integrated bus, train and tram network.

Tickets can be purchased on board, at staffed train stations and in delis and newsagents across the city. Ticket types include day trip ($10), two-hour peak ($5.30) and two-hour off-peak ($3.40) tickets. Peak travel time is before 9am and after 3pm. Kids under five ride free! There's also a three-day, unlimited-travel visitor pass ($26). If you're here for longer, save at least $1 per trip with a rechargable multitrip Metrocard.

Bus

Adelaide's buses are clean and reliable. Most services start around 6am and run until midnight.

Every 30 minutes daily, Adelaide Metro's **Free City Loop buses** (☑ 1300 311 108; www.adelaidemetro.com.au/timetables-maps/special-services; ☺ 9am-7.15pm Sat-Thu, to 9.15pm Fri) – routes 98A and 98C – run clockwise and anticlockwise around the CBD fringe, passing North Tce, Victoria Sq, Hutt St, the Central Market and winding through North Adelaide en route. The 99A and 99C buses ply the same route (minus North Adelaide), Monday to Friday – the net effect is a free bus every 15 minutes Monday to Friday.

Adelaide Metro's **After Midnight buses** (www.adelaidemetro.com.au/timetables-maps/special-services; ☺ midnight-5am Sat) run select standard routes but have an 'N' preceding the route number on their displays. Standard ticket prices apply.

Train

Adelaide's hokey old diesel trains are slowly being electrified. Trains depart from **Adelaide Station** (www.railmaps.com.au/adelaide.htm; North Tce), plying five suburban routes (Belair, Gawler, Grange, Noarlunga and Outer Harbour). Trains generally run between 6am and midnight (some services start at 4.30am).

Tram

Adelaide's state-of-the-art trams rumble to/from Moseley Sq in Glenelg, through Victoria Sq in the city and along North Tce to the Adelaide Entertainment Centre. Trams run approximately every 10 minutes on weekdays (every 15 minutes on weekends) from 6am to midnight daily. Standard Metro ticket prices apply, but the section between South Tce and the Adelaide Entertainment Centre is free. New route extensions are being discussed!

TAXI

Adelaide Independent Taxis (☑ 13 22 11; www.aitaxis.com.au) Regular and wheelchair-access cabs.

Adelaide Transport (☑ 08 8212 1861; www.adelaidetransport.com.au) Minibus taxis for four or more people, plus airport-to-city transfers.

Suburban Taxis (☑ 13 10 08; www.suburbantaxis.com.au) Taxis, all suburbs.

Yellow Cabs (☑ 13 22 27; www.yellowcabgroup.com.au) Regular cabs (most of which are white!)

ADELAIDE HILLS

When the Adelaide plains are desert-hot in the summer months, the Adelaide Hills (technically the Mt Lofty Ranges) are always a few degrees cooler, with crisp air, woodland shade and labyrinthine valleys. Early colonists built stately summer houses around Stirling and Aldgate, and German settlers escaping religious persecution also arrived, infusing towns like Hahndorf and Lobethal with European values and architecture.

The Hills make a brilliant day trip from Adelaide: hop from town to town (all with at least one pub), passing carts of fresh produce for sale, stone cottages, olive groves and wineries along the way.

☞ Tours

Ambler Touring　　　　　　　　　　　TOURS
(☑ 0414 447 134; www.ambler.net.au; half-/full-day tours per person $99/155) See the Hills in style with these personalised, locally run tours taking in Hahndorf, Mt Lofty Summit, Beerenberg Farm and plenty of other sights. Lots of wine, cheese, chocolate and arts.

✵ Festivals & Events

Crush　　　　　　　　　　　　　　　　WINE
(www.crushfestival.com.au; ☺ Jan) Celebrating all things good about life in the Adelaide Hills, with food and wine at the fore. Lots of cellar-door events and tastings.

Winter Reds　　　　　　　　　　　　WINE
(www.winterreds.com.au; ☺ Jul) 'Brrr, it's chilly. Pour me another shiraz.' Winter Reds

Adelaide Hills

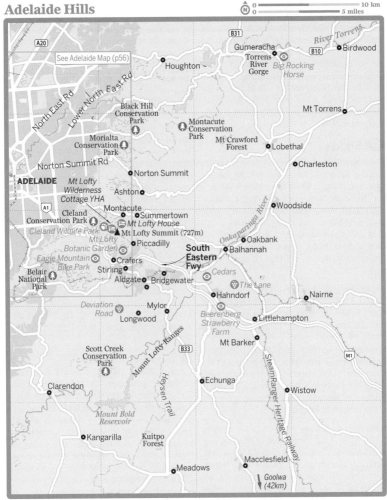

celebrates the cold season in the Adelaide Hills, with winery tastings, hearty food and lots of open fires.

ℹ Getting There & Away

To best explore the Hills, BYO wheels. Alternatively, **Adelaide Metro** (www.adelaidemetro.com.au) runs buses between the city and most Hills towns. The 864 and 864F city–Mt Barker buses stop at Stirling, Aldgate and Hahndorf. The 823 runs from Crafers to Mt Lofty Summit and Cleland Wildlife Park; the 830F runs from the city to Oakbank, Woodside and Lobethal. Buses 835 and 835A connect Lobethal with Mt Barker. Standard Metro fares apply (one-way from $3.40).

Hahndorf

POP 2550

Like the Rocks in Sydney, and Richmond near Hobart, Hahndorf is a 'ye olde worlde' colonial enclave that trades ruthlessly on its history: it's something of a kitsch parody of itself.

That said, Hahndorf is undeniably pretty, with Teutonic sandstone architecture, European trees, and flowers overflowing from half wine barrels. And it *is* interesting: Australia's oldest surviving German settlement (1839), founded by 50 Lutheran families fleeing religious persecution in Prussia. Hahndorf was placed under martial law during WWI, and its name changed to 'Ambleside' (renamed Hahndorf in 1935). It's also slowly becoming less kitsch, more cool: there are a few good cafes here now, and on a sunny day the main street is positively pumping.

⊙ Sights

The Lane
WINERY
(☑08 8388 1250; www.thelane.com.au; Ravenswood La; ☉10am-4pm) Wow! What a cool building, and what a setting. Camera-conducive views and contemporary varietals (viognier, pinot grigio, pinot gris), plus an outstanding restaurant (book for lunch: two/three courses $59/70, serving noon to 3pm). Tastings of entry-level wines free.

Beerenberg Strawberry Farm
FARM
(☑08 8388 7272; www.beerenberg.com.au; Mount Barker Rd; strawberry picking per adult/child $4/free, strawberries per kg $10; ☉9am-5pm) ✐ Pick your own strawberries between November and April from this famous, family-run farm, also big-noted for its myriad jams, chutneys and sauces. Last entry for picking 4.15pm; open til 8.30pm Fridays in December and January. Strawberry ice cream to go.

Hahndorf Academy
MUSEUM
(☑08 8388 7250; www.hahndorfacademy.org.au; 68 Main St; ☉10am-5pm) FREE This 1857 building houses an art gallery with rotating exhibitions and original sketches by Sir Hans Heysen, famed landscape artist and Hahndorf homeboy (ask about tours of his nearby former studio, The Cedars (☑08 8388 7277; www.hansheysen.com.au; Heysen Rd; tours adult/child $10/free; ☉10am-4.30pm Tue-Sun, tours 11am, 1pm & 3pm Sep-May, 11am & 2pm Jun-Aug)). The museum depicts the lives of early German settlers, with churchy paraphernalia, dour dresses and farm equipment. The Adelaide Hills Visitor Information Centre (p78) is here too.

⟲ Tours

Hahndorf Walking Tours
WALKING
(☑0477 288 011; www.facebook.com/hahndorfwalkingtours; tours per person $33; ☉tours 2pm Sat & Sat, plus 6pm daily Oct-Mar)

Short on distance but big on insight, these history-soaked, 90-minute walks are a great way to get a feel for the old town. Bookings essential; tours depart Hahndorf Academy (p78).

🛏 Sleeping & Eating

Manna
MOTEL, APARTMENTS $$
(☑08 8388 1000; www.themanna.com.au; 25 & 35a Main St; d/ste from $149/199; ❇ 🛜 ☒) The Manna is a stylish, contemporary maze of motel suites on the main street, spread over several buildings. There are also older units nearby at the affiliated, refurbished Hahndorf Motor Lodge, an exposed-brick complex set back from the street (cheaper rates... and where the pool is).

Billy's Cottage
RENTAL HOUSE, B&B $$$
(☑0417 833 665; www.facebook.com/billyscottagehahndorf; 59 Auricht Rd; up to 4 people $250, extra person $60; ❇) Just far enough from the main drag for you to enjoy the walk, Billy's is an eccentric, renovated, self-contained stone cottage sleeping up to six, with plenty of beds and a weird stage platform in case an impromptu performance urge grabs you. Great value for groups or families.

★ Seasonal Garden Cafe
CAFE $$
(☑08 8388 7714; www.facebook.com/theseasonalgardencafe; 100 Main St; mains $10-25; ☉7.30am-4.30pm Mon-Fri, to 5.30pm Sat & Sun; ☒) ✐ Swimming against Hahndorf's mainstream currents – although slightly less earthy than it was, in its snappy new shopfront – this zero-waste cafe is adorned with wreaths, piles of pumpkins and strings of chubby chillies. Food-wise it's good coffee, grass-green smoothies and lots of local, seasonal and organic ingredients (try the potted baked eggs with house-made beans).

❶ Information

Adelaide Hills Visitor Information Centre
(☑1800 353 323, 08 8388 1185; www.adelaidehills.org.au; 68 Main St; ☉9am-5pm Mon-Fri, 10am-4pm Sat & Sun) The usual barrage of brochures, plus accommodation bookings. The Hahndorf Academy (p78) is here too.

Stirling Area

The photogenic little villages of old-school **Stirling** (population 2950) and one-horse **Aldgate** (population 3350) are famed for their bedazzling autumn colours, thanks to the deciduous trees the early residents saw fit to plant. Oddly, Aldgate has also been home to both Bon Scott and Mel Gibson over the years. On a less rock 'n' roll tack, the 6km **Aldgate Valley Nature Walk** runs from Aldgate to nearby Mylor; follow the bandicoot signs from the little park across the road from the Aldgate shops (map from www.ahc.sa.gov.au).

Towards the city from Stirling, **Crafers** (population 1970) has a drive-through vibe but a seriously good pub...and access to lofty Mt Lofty Summit!

⊙ Sights

Mt Lofty Summit   VIEWPOINT
(Map p56; ☑ 08 8370 1054; www.environment. sa.gov.au/parks; Mt Lofty Summit Rd, Crafers; ⊙24hr) FREE From Cleland Wildlife Park (p79) you can bushwalk (2km) or drive up to Mt Lofty Summit (a surprising 727m), which has show-stopping views across Adelaide. **Mt Lofty Summit Visitor Information Centre** (☑ 08 8370 1054; www.mtloftysummit.com; Mt Lofty Summit Rd, Crafers; ⊙9am-5pm) has info on local attractions and walking tracks, including the steep Waterfall Gully Track (8km return, 2½ hours) and Mt Lofty Botanic Gardens Loop Trail (7km loop, two hours). The video of the Ash Wednesday bushfires of 16 February 1983 is harrowing. There's a snazzy **cafe/restaurant** (mains lunch $9-20, dinner $37-42; ⊙cafe 9am-5pm Mon-Fri, 8.30am-5pm Sat & Sun, restaurant 6pm-late Wed-Sat) here too.

Deviation Road   WINERY
(☑ 08 8339 2633; www.deviationroad.com; 207 Scott Creek Rd, Longwood; ⊙10am-5pm; ⊕) Nothing deviant about the wines here: sublime pinot noir, substantial shiraz, zingy pinot gris and a very decent bubbly, too. Grab a cheese platter and wind down in the afternoon in the sun. Unpretentious and lovely.

Mt Lofty Botanic Garden   GARDENS
(Map p56; ☑ 08 8222 9311; www.botanic gardens.sa.gov.au; gates on Mawson Dr & Lampert Rd, Crafers; ⊙8.30am-4pm Mon-Fri, 10am-5pm Sat & Sun) FREE From Mt Lofty, truck south 1.5km to the cool-climate slopes of the botanic garden. Nature trails wind past a lake, exotic temperate plants, native stringybark forest and eye-popping ranks of rhododendron blooms. Free guided walks depart the lower Lampert Rd car park at 10.30am every Thursday.

Cleland Wildlife Park   WILDLIFE RESERVE
(Map p56; ☑ 08 8339 2444; www.clelandwildlife park.sa.gov.au; 365 Mt Lofty Summit Rd, Crafers; adult/child/family $25/12/56; ⊙9.30am-5pm, last entry 4.30pm) Within the steep **Cleland Conservation Park** (Map p56; ☑ 08 8278 5477; www.environment.sa.gov.au/parks; Mt Lofty Summit Rd, Crafers; ⊙24hr) FREE, this place lets you interact with all kinds of Australian beasts. There are keeper talks and feeding sessions throughout the day, plus occasional Night Walks (adult/child $50/40) and you can have your mugshot taken with a koala ($30; 2pm to 3.30pm daily, plus 11am to noon Sundays). There's a **cafe** (meals $5-15; ⊙9.30am-5pm) here too. From the city, take bus 864 or 864F from Grenfell St to Crafers for connecting bus 823 to the park.

🛏 Sleeping & Eating

Crafers Hotel   BOUTIQUE HOTEL, PUB $$
(Map p56; ☑ 08 8339 2050; www.crafershotel. com.au; 8 Main St, Crafers; d from $180; ❄ 🖙) How marvellous: the seedy old Crafers Inn has been sandblasted, painted, gutted and refitted and has morphed from a sticky-carpet old-man's boozer into a boisterous craft-beer pub with seven stylish ensuite rooms upstairs. Crafers itself remains a loose affiliation of buildings with no civic heart...but perhaps this lovely old pub now fills this void.

Mt Lofty YHA   CABIN $$
(Map p56; ☑ 08 8414 3000; www.yha.com.au; Gate 25, Mt Lofty Summit Rd, Crafers; per night from $160) And now, for something completely different: a short detour off the road on the steep flanks of Mt Lofty, this 1880 stone cottage was originally a shepherd's hut. Today it's a simple, self-contained, three-bedroom cabin sleeping 10, with peek-a-boo views of Adelaide through the eucalyptuses. Pick up the keys from Adelaide Central YHA (p63) in the city.

★ Stirling Hotel   BOUTIQUE HOTEL, PUB $$$
(Map p56; ☑ 08 8339 2345; www.stirlinghotel. com.au; 52 Mt Barker Rd, Stirling; d from $280; ❄ 🖙) The owners spent so much money tarting up this gorgeous old dame, it's a wonder they can pay the staff. Upstairs are five guest suites: plush, contemporary and stylish. Downstairs is a free-flowing,

all-day bistro (classy pub grub and pizzas) and a romantic restaurant (upmarket regional cuisine). The whole shebang is a runaway success story.

★ **Fred Eatery** CAFE $$
(☑08 8339 1899; www.fredeatery.com.au; 220 Mt Barker Rd, Aldgate; mains $11-26; ⊙7.30am-4pm Tue-Sun, plus 6-9pm Fri; 🐾) Build it, and they will come... For decades Aldgate eked-out a cafe lifestyle with no quality offerings. Then along came Fred, a rather urbane fellow, decked out in green, black and white, with a savvy cityside menu, killer coffee and great staff. The house bircher muesli makes a solid start to the day, while the bodacious Reuben sandwich is calorific heaven.

 Shopping

Stirling Markets MARKET
(Map p56; ☑0488 770 166; www.stirlingmarket. com.au; Druid Ave, Stirling; ⊙10am-4pm 4th Sun of the month, 3rd Sun in Dec) 'Bustling' is such a corny, overused adjective...but in this case it applies! Market stalls fill oak-lined Druid Ave: much plant-life, busking, pies, cakes, affluent locals with dogs and Hills knick-knackery (not many druids...).

Gumeracha, Birdwood & Lobethal

A scenic drive from Adelaide to Birdwood leads through the Torrens River Gorge to Gumeracha (gum-er-ack-a; population 1020), a hardy hillside town with a pub at the bottom (making it hard to roll home). Nearby Birdwood (population 1300) marks the finishing line for September's Bay to Birdwood classic-car rally. The rest of the year it makes a perfectly soporific Hills detour, with an excellent automotive musuem.

Back towards Woodside, Lobethal (population 2350), was established by Lutheran Pastor Fritzsche and his followers in 1842. Like Hahndorf, Lobethal was renamed during WWI – 'Tweedale' was the unfortunate choice. It's still a pious sort of town: church life plays a leading role in many locals' day-to-day lives, though the local craft-beer brewery and some excellent wineries in the surrounding hills demand reverence of a different kind.

◉ **Sights**

Pike & Joyce WINERY
(☑08 8389 8102; www.pikeandjoyce.com.au; 730 Mawson Rd, Lenswood; ⊙11am-5pm, to 4pm Jun-Aug) High on a hill behind Lenswood (itself behind Lobethal), Pike & Joyce is an architectural doozy, with rammed-earth walls, jaunty corrugated-iron roof pitches and mesmerising views over the vine-striped hillsides and apple orchards below. Sip some chardonnay or interesting Austrian gruner veltliner. There's a fancy restaurant here too (mains $28 to $32, serving noon to 3pm Thursday to Sunday).

National Motor Museum MUSEUM
(☑08 8568 4000; www.nationalmotormuseum. com.au; Shannon St, Birdwood; adult/child/family $15.50/6.50/35; ⊙10am-5pm) Behind an impressive 1852 flour mill in Birdwood, the National Motor Museum has a collection of 300-plus immaculate vintage, modern and classic cars (check out the DeLorean!) and motorcycles.

Big Rocking Horse MONUMENT
(☑08 8389 1085; www.thetoyfactory.com.au; 452 Torrens Rd, Gumeracha; $2; ⊙9am-5pm) Gumeracha's main attraction is climbing the 18.3m-high Big Rocking Horse, which doesn't actually rock, but is unusually tasteful as far as Australia's 'big' tourist attractions go. You can buy nifty wooden kids' toys at the shop below.

 Festivals & Events

Bay to Birdwood SPORTS
(www.baytobirdwood.com.au; ⊙Sep) Come September, a convoy of classic cars chugs its way up from Adelaide to Birdwood in the Adelaide Hills, crossing the finishing line at the National Motor Museum.

Lights of Lobethal CHRISTMAS
(www.lightsoflobethal.com.au; ⊙Dec) Dazzling Christmas lights festival, lighting up Lobethal's front yards. In December (naturally). Expect bumper-to-bumper traffic.

🍺 **Drinking & Nightlife**

Lobethal Bierhaus BREWERY
(☑08 8389 5570; www.bierhaus.com.au; 3a Main St, Lobethal; ⊙noon-10pm Fri & Sat, to 6pm Sun) Repair to the quasi-industrial Lobethal Bierhaus for some serious craft-brewed concoctions (the Red Truck Porter will put hairs on your chest).

Mt Barker

POP 11,810

The biggest town in the Adelaide Hills and just a 35-minute commute to the city, Mt Barker began life as a small rural village. But these days it's booming, with 20,000 new residents predicted in the coming years as paddocks are subdivided apace. Mt Barker CBD can barely keep up, with shopping centres and new services being knocked together at a furious pace. There's still some small-town charm to be found on Gawler St, though, and some fab local businesses are keeping the new residents fed and watered.

◎ Sights

★ **Prancing Pony**   BREWERY

(☑ 08 8398 3881; www.prancingponybrewery.com. au; 42 Mt Barker Rd, Totness; ☉ 10am-6pm Mon-Thu, to 10pm Fri & Sat, to 8pm Sun) Prize-winning craft beers, burgers, platters, bar snacks and live troubadours all make an appearance at this funky beer shed, on the road out of Mt Barker heading for Hahndorf. Something other than a pub or a winery in the Adelaide Hills was so long overdue it wasn't funny. But now we can all laugh, kicking back with an Amber Ale or three.

🛍 Shopping

Buzz Honey   FOOD

(☑ 08 8388 0274; www.buzzhoney.com.au; 42 Mount Barker Rd, Totness; ☉ 8.30am-4.30pm Mon-Fri, 9.30am-4.30pm Sat) In Mt Barker's industrial backblocks, Buzz Honey has been generating quite a buzz of late, selling superb Adelaide Hills honey from its non-descript shopfront. Learn about the process, taste some, then buy some to go (the local Blue Gum is a classic).

FLEURIEU PENINSULA

Patterned with vineyards, olive groves and almond plantations running down to the sea, the Fleurieu (*floo*-ree-oh) is Adelaide's weekend playground. The McLaren Vale wine region is booming, producing gutsy reds (salubrious shiraz) to rival those from the Barossa Valley (actually, we think McLaren Vale wins hands down). Further east, the Fleurieu's Encounter Coast is an engaging mix of surf beaches, historic towns and whales cavorting offshore.

❶ Getting There & Away

Your own vehicle is the best way to explore the Fleurieu, but several bus companies service the towns here.

➔ **Adelaide Metro** (www.adelaidemetro.com. au) suburban trains run between Adelaide and Seaford (one hour). From here, bus 751 runs to McLaren Vale and Willunga (45 minutes). Regular Adelaide Metro ticket prices apply (from $3.40). **Southlink** (☑ 08 8186 2888; www.southlink.com.au) buses also service the Fleurieu Peninsula, working in conjunction with Adelaide Metro service.

➔ **LinkSA** (www.linksa.com.au) runs daily buses from Adelaide to Victor Harbor ($26, one hour), continuing on to Port Elliot and Goolwa for the same fare.

➔ On the Gulf St Vincent coast, the Kangaroo Island ferry company **SeaLink** (www.sealink.com. au) runs daily buses between Adelaide and Cape Jervis on the Fleurieu, from where the ferry departs. The bus can drop you off in Yankalilla or Normanville en route ($19, 1¼ hours).

SteamRanger Heritage Railway (☑ 08 8263 5621, 1300 655 991; www.steamranger.org. au) On the first and third Sundays from June to November inclusive, SteamRanger Heritage Railway operates the *Southern Encounter* (adult/child return $71/37) tourist train from Mt Barker in the Adelaide Hills to Victor Harbor via Strathalbyn, Goolwa and Port Elliot. The *Cockle Train* (adult/child return $29/15) runs along the Encounter Coast between Victor Harbor and Goolwa via Port Elliot every Sunday and Wednesday, and daily during school holidays.

McLaren Vale

POP 3870

Flanked by the wheat-coloured Willunga Scarp and striated with vines, McLaren Vale is just 40 minutes south of Adelaide. Servicing the wine industry, it's an energetic, utilitarian town that's not much to look at – but it has some great eateries and offers easy access to some truly excellent winery cellar doors.

◎ Sights & Activities

Most people come to McLaren Vale to cruise the 80-plus wineries here: you could spend days doing nothing else! Pick up a winery map at the visitor information centre (p83).

Goodieson Brewery   BREWERY

(☑ 0409 676 542; www.goodiesonbrewery.com.au; 194 Sand Rd, McLaren Vale; tastings $5; ☉ 11am-5.30pm) There sure are a lot of wineries around here... Anyone for a beer? This family-run outfit brews a pale ale, pilsner, wheat beer and brown ale, plus brilliant seasonal beers. Sip a few on the sunny terrace.

Shiraz Trail　　　　　CYCLING, WALKING

(www.walkingsa.org.au; ⊙ 24hr) Get the McLaren Vale vibe on this 8km walking/cycling track, along an old railway line between McLaren Vale and Willunga. If you're up for it, the trail continues another 29km to Marino Rocks as the **Coast to Vines Rail Trail**. Hire a bike from **Oxygen Cycles** (✆ 08 8323 7345; www. oxygencycles.com.au; 143 Main Rd; bike hire per half-day/full day/overnight $15/25/40; ⊙ 10am-6pm Tue-Fri, 9am-5pm Sat, plus Sun & Mon Dec-Feb); ask the visitor information centre for a map.

Tours

Off Piste 4WD Tours　　　　　TOURS

(✆ 0423 725 409; www.offpistetours.com.au; half-/ full-day tours $199/299) Full- or half-day 4WD adventure tours around the Fleurieu for two to 10 folks, with lots of wilderness, wine, beer and beaches. A really great insight into the region, away from the well-trodden trail.

Adelaide's Top Food & Wine Tours　　　　　FOOD & DRINK

(✆ 08 8386 0888; www.topfoodandwinetours.com. au) Either a full-day winery tour ex-Adelaide ($160 per person), or a more detailed cheese-and-wine trail through the Vale ($320).

Chook's Little Winery Tours　　　　　TOURS

(✆ 0414 922 200; www.chookslittlewinerytours. com.au; per person from $100) Small-group tours visiting some of the lesser-known boutique McLaren Vale wineries, ex-Adelaide, run by the irrepressible Chook McCoy.

Festivals & Events

Sea & Vines Festival　　　　　FOOD & DRINK

(www.seaandvines.com.au; ⊙ Jun) It seems like most of Adelaide gets tizzed-up and buses down to the annual Sea & Vines Festival over the June long weekend. Local wineries cook up seafood, splash wine around and host live bands. Can get messy later in the evening.

Sleeping

McLaren Vale Backpackers　　　　　HOSTEL $

(✆ 08 8323 0916; www.mclarenvalebackpackers. com.au; 106 Main Rd; dm $28, s & d from $70; ❄@🖢) McLaren Vale's boisterous backpackers fills an old heath club on the main street, with winery workers' beds in the old

squash courts and regular dorms and private rooms out the front. Plus there's a sauna, spa and plunge pool! Good weekly rates.

★ **Bethany Chapel B&B**　　　　　B&B $$

(✆ 0416 342 470; www.bethanychapelbnb.com; 219 Strout Rd; d $155-195; ❄) Rest in peace in this lovely split-level conversion of an 1854 Wesleyan chapel, with honey-coloured floorboards, a sunny rear deck and wide views across the vines (and the old cemetery – the residents therein also resting in peace). Terrific value for your own private, self-contained church (worship your complimentary bottle of Wirra Wirra on arrival).

Red Poles　　　　　B&B $$

(✆ 08 8323 8994; www.redpoles.com.au; 190 McMurtrie Rd; d with/without bathroom $125/115; ❄🖢) Bushy, eccentric Red Poles is a great place to stay (and eat!) Aim for the rustic ensuite room (bigger than its two counterparts). Order some gnocchi with goats curd (mains from $10 to $30, serving 9am to 4.30pm), and check out some local artwork while you wait. Live music Sunday afternoons, and tastings of McLaren Vale Beer Company (www.mvbeer.com) ales.

McLaren Eye　　　　　RENTAL HOUSE $$$

(✆ 08 8383 7122; www.mclareneye.com.au; 36a Peters Creek Rd, Kangarilla; 1-/2-bedroom $450/800; ❄) Super-luxe hillside architectural splendour with an outlook from here to eternity, McLaren Eye has everything you need for a decadent stay – and every room has a view, even the bathroom (slip into the fancy two-person bath). In Kangarilla, 13km from McLaren Vale township. Two-night minimum.

Eating

★ **Blessed Cheese**　　　　　CAFE, DELI $

(✆ 08 8323 7958; www.blessedcheese.com.au; 150 Main Rd; mains $11-18; ⊙ 8am-4pm Mon-Fri, to 5pm Sat, 9am-4pm Sun) The staff at this blessed cafe crank out great coffee, croissants, wraps, salads, tarts, burgers, cheese platters, massive cakes and funky sausage rolls. The menu changes every couple of days, always with an emphasis on local produce. Sniff the aromas emanating from the cheese counter – deliciously stinky! Love the lime citrus tarts and Spanish baked eggs.

Salopian Inn　　　　　MODERN AUSTRALIAN $$$

(✆ 08 8323 8769; www.salopian.com.au; cnr Main & McMurtrie Rds; mains $30-33; ⊙ noon-3.30pm daily, 6pm-late Thu-Sat) This old vine-covered

Fleurieu Peninsula

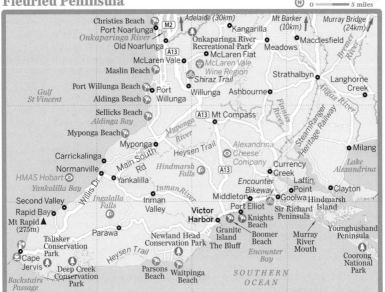

inn has been here since 1851 (!) Its latest incarnation features super Mod Oz offerings with an Asian twist: launch into the Berkshire pork buns or blue swimmer crab and prawn dumplings, with a bottle of something local which you can hand-select from the cellar. And there are 170 gins with which to construct your G&T!

ℹ️ Information

McLaren Vale & Fleurieu Visitor Information Centre (☑1800 628 410, 08 8323 9944; www.mclarenvale.info; 796 Main Rd; ⊙9am-5pm Mon-Fri, 10am-4pm Sat & Sun) At the northern end of McLaren Vale's main strip. Winery info, plus accommodation assistance and Sealink bus/ferry bookings for Kangaroo Island. Pick up the *McLaren Vale Heritage Trail* brochure for an historic walk around the main street.

Willunga

POP 2420

A one-horse town with three pubs (a winning combo!), arty Willunga took off in 1840 when high-quality slate was discovered nearby and exported across Australia (used for everything from flagstones to billiard tables). Today, the town's early buildings along sloping High St are occupied by some terrific eateries, B&B accommodation and galleries. The Kidman Trail (www.kidmantrail.org.au) kicks off here, winding north to beyond the Barossa Valley.

👁️ Sights

⭐**Willunga Farmers Market**   MARKET
(☑08 8556 4297; www.willungafarmersmarket.com; Willunga Town Sq; ⊙8am-12.30pm Sat) Heavy on the organic, the bespoke and the locally sourced, Willunga Farmers Market happens every Saturday morning, on the corner of High St and Main Rd. Buskers, coffee, breakfast and hamper-filling goodies. Brilliant.

🎉 Festivals & Events

Fleurieu Folk Festival   MUSIC
(www.fleurieufolkfestival.com.au; ⊙Oct) Willunga Recreation Park hosts the annual FFF over a hyperactive weekend in October: more acoustic guitars than you've ever seen in one town before.

🛏️ Sleeping & Eating

Willunga House B&B   B&B $$
(☑08 8556 2467; www.willungahouse.com.au; 1 St Peters Tce; d incl breakfast from $200; ❄️🐕🏠) If you're looking for a real treat, this graceful,

DON'T MISS

MCLAREN VALE WINERIES

If the Barossa Valley is SA wine's old school, then McLaren Vale is the upstart teenager smoking cigarettes behind the shed and stealing nips from mum's sherry bottle. The luscious vineyards around here have a Tuscan haze in summer, rippling down to a calm coastline that's similarly Ligurian. This is shiraz country – solid, punchy and seriously good. Quaff some at five of the region's best:

Alpha Box & Dice (☎08 8323 7750; www.alphaboxdice.com; 8 Olivers Rd, McLaren Vale; ⏰11am-5pm Mon-Fri, 10am-6pm Sat & Sun) One out of the box, this refreshing little gambler wins top billing for interesting blends, funky retro furnishings, quirky labels and laid-back staff.

Coriole (☎08 8323 8305; www.coriole.com; Chaffeys Rd, McLaren Vale; ⏰10am-5pm Mon-Fri, 11am-5pm Sat & Sun) Take your regional tasting platter out into the garden of this beautiful cottage cellar door (1860) to share kalamata olives, homemade breads and Adelaide Hills' Woodside cheeses, made lovelier by a swill of the Redstone shiraz or the flagship chenin blanc.

d'Arenberg (☎08 8329 4888; www.darenberg.com.au; Osborn Rd, McLaren Vale; ⏰10am-5pm) 'd'Arry's' relaxes atop a hillside with mighty fine views. The wine labels are part of the character of this place: the Dead Arm shiraz and the Broken Fishplate sauvignon blanc are our faves. Book for lunch at the excellent d'Arry's Verandah restaurant (mains $34 to $40).

Wirra Wirra (☎08 8323 8414; www.wirrawirra.com; cnr McMurtrie & Strout Rds, McLaren Vale; ⏰10am-5pm Mon-Sat, 11am-5pm Sun) Fancy some *pétanque* with your plonk? This barn-like, 1894 cellar door has a grassy picnic area, and there's a roaring fire inside in winter. Sample reasonably priced stickies (dessert wines) and the super-popular Church Block blend. Whites include a citrusy viognier and an aromatic riesling.

SC Pannell (☎08 8323 8000; www.pannell.com.au; 60 Olivers Rd, McLaren Vale; ⏰11am-5pm) With one of the best views in the business, SC Pannell (Steve, to his mates) produces excellent reds you can drink young. Cellar them if you want, but really, life's too short. Kitchen open noon to 4pm Thursday to Sunday.

two-storey 1850 mansion off the main street is for you: Baltic-pine floorboards, Italian cherrywood beds, open fires, Indigenous art and a swimming pool. Breakfast is a feast of organic muesli, fruit salad and poached pears, followed by cooked delights.

The Farm B&B $$$
(☎08 8328 2140, 0434 125 172; www.thefarm willunga.com.au; 11 Martin Rd; d from $290; ❄🐾) High on the hill behind Willunga (great views!), The Farm is a cafe/providore and working organic farm, with two ritzy accommodation suites out the back, one atop the other. You'll pay a bit more to be upstairs, but really, both suites are stylish, contemporary and utterly comfortable. DIY breakfast from the fridge, or have it cooked in the cafe.

Russell's Pizza PIZZA $$
(☎08 8556 2571; 13 High St; pizzas from $24; ⏰6-11.30pm Fri & Sat) It may look like a rustic, ramshackle chicken coop, but Russell's is the place to be on weekends for sensational wood-fired pizza. No one minds the wait for a meal (which could be an hour) – it's all about the atmosphere. It's super popular, so book way ahead.

Gulf St Vincent Beaches

There are some ace swimming beaches (but no surf) along the Gulf St Vincent coastline from suburban **Christies Beach** onto **Maslin Beach**, the southern end of which is a nudist and gay hang-out. Maslin is 45 minutes from Adelaide by car – just far enough to escape the sprawling shopping centres and new housing developments trickling south from the city.

Port Willunga is the closest sand to McLaren Vale and is the best swimming spot along this stretch of coast. There's a superb cafe on the clifftops here, with the remnant piers of what once was a 145m-long jetty down below.

Keep trucking south to cute little **Myponga** (population 540), where the craft beers at **Smiling Samoyed Brewery** (☑08 8558 6166; www.facebook.com/mypongabrewery; 46 Main South Rd, via Hansen St, Myponga; ☺11am-6pm Fri-Sun) will have you smiling like a hound. There are four main brews to try – a kolsch, an APA, IPA and a dark ale – plus seasonal efforts.

Further south is soporific **Yankalilla** (population 1020), which has the regional **Yankalilla Bay Visitor Information Centre** (☑08 8558 0240, 1300 965 842; www.yankalilla.sa.gov.au; 163 Main South Rd, Yankalilla; ☺9am-5pm Mon-Fri, 10am-4pm Sat & Sun; ☎). There's a small local history **museum** (☑1300 965 842; www.yankalilla.sa.gov.au; 169 Main South Rd, Yankalilla; museum adult/child/family $5/1/12; ☺9am-5pm Mon-Fri, 10am-4pm Sat & Sun) out the back; look for the radar antenna from the scuttled *HMAS Hobart* (www.exhmashobart.com.au), now a nearby dive site offshore.

About 60km south of Adelaide is **Carrickalinga** (population 290), which has a gorgeous arc of white sandy beach: it's a very chilled spot with no shops. For supplies and accommodation, head to neighbouring **Normanville** (population 1360). Here you'll find a rambling pub, a supermarket and a couple of caravan parks. About 10km out of Normanville along Hay Flat Rd are the picturesque little **Ingalalla Falls** (follow the signs from the Yankalilla side of town). Along similar lines, the **Hindmarsh Falls** are off Hindmarsh Tiers Rd, inland from Myponga.

About 14km south of Normanville is little **Second Valley** (population 500). The beach here is good for a sheltered swim. Another 5km south is the turn-off to **Rapid Bay**, an eerie semi-ghost-town with a *looong* fishing jetty.

There's not much at **Cape Jervis**, 107km from Adelaide, other than the Kangaroo Island ferry terminal, and the start point for the **Heysen Trail** (www.heysentrail.asn.au). Nearby, **Deep Creek Conservation Park** (☑08 8598 0263; www.environment.sa.gov.au; via Main South Rd, Deep Creek; per car $10; ☺24hr) has sweeping coastal views, man-size yakkas *(Xanthorrhoea semiplana tateana)*, sandy beaches, kangaroos, kookaburras and popular bush-camping areas (per car $9 to $25).

Tours

Adventure Kayaking SA KAYAKING
(☑08 8295 8812; www.adventurekayak.com.au; tours from $180) 🚣 Runs six-hour paddling trips around the Rapid Bay coastline, checking out sea caves, beaches and wildlife.

🛏 Sleeping & Eating

Jetty Carvan Park CARAVAN PARK $
(☑08 8558 2038; www.jettycaravanpark normanville.com.au; 34 Jetty Rd, Normanville; unpowered/powered sites $34/42, cabins with/without bathroom from $121/82; ❇☎) The pick of the two caravan parks in 'Normy', split into two sections either side of the Bungala River, Jetty CP has grassy sites, towering Norfolk Island pines and trim cabins. The beachfront kiosk across the car park does a mean fish and chips.

Ridgetop Retreats COTTAGE $$
(☑08 8598 4169; www.southernoceanretreats.com.au; Tanappa Rd, Deep Creek; d $225, extra adult/child $35/25) Off the road to Deep Creek Conservation Park are the curved roofs of the superb Ridgetop Retreats, designed by estimable SA architect Max Pritchard: three corrugated iron-clad, self-contained luxury units in the bush, with wood heaters, leather lounges and stainless-steel benchtops. See the website for less-pricey local options.

Victory Hotel PUB FOOD $$
(☑08 8556 3083; www.victoryhotel.com.au; Main South Rd, Sellicks Beach; mains $17-33; ☺noon-2.30pm & 6-8.30pm) On the highway near Sellicks Beach is a rowdy, 1858 pub, the Victory. There are awesome views of the silvery gulf, a cheery, laid-back vibe and a beaut beer garden. Factor in inspired meals, an impressive cellar and wines by the glass and you'll be feeling victorious. Three cabins available too (doubles $150, or $165 including breakfast).

⭐**Star of Greece** MODERN AUSTRALIAN $$$
(☑08 8557 7420; www.starofgreececafe.com.au; 1 The Esplanade, Port Willunga; mains $29-38; ☺noon-3pm Wed-Sun, 6pm-late Fri & Sat, daily Jan) Port Willunga hosts the eternally busy, cliff-top seafood shack the Star of Greece, named after a shipwreck; it has funky decor, great staff and a sunny patio. We asked the waiter where the whiting was caught: he gazed across the bay and said, 'See that boat out there?'. There's a takeaway kiosk too (snacks $7 to $15, open weekends and school holidays).

Victor Harbor

POP 15,200

The biggest town on the Encounter Coast is Victor Harbor (yes, that's the correct spelling: blame one of SA's poorly schooled early Surveyor Generals). It's a raggedy, brawling holiday destination with three huge pubs and migrating whales offshore. 'Another day in paradise,' says a pony tailed pensioner to no-one in particular, as he shuffles along Ocean St in the sun.

⊙ Sights

South Australian Whale Centre MUSEUM
(☑08 8551 0750; www.sawhalecentre.com; 2 Railway Tce; adult/child/family $9/4.50/24; ⊙10.30am-5pm) Victor Harbor is on the migratory path of southern right whales (May to October). The multilevel South Australian Whale Centre has impressive whale displays (including a big stinky skull) and can give you the low-down on where to see them. Not whale season? Check out the big mammals in the 3D-cinema, and the new exhibit on Aboriginal whale stories. For whale sightings info, call the Whale Information Hotline (☑1900 942 537).

Encounter Coast Discovery Centre & Museum MUSEUM
(☑08 8552 4440; www.nationaltrust.org.au/sa; 2 Flinders Pde; adult/child/family $6/4/16; ⊙1-4pm) Inside Victor's 1866 Customs House on the foreshore, this National Trust museum has interesting local-history displays from pre-European times to around 1900: whaling, railways, shipping and local Aboriginal culture. Good for a rainy day.

🏃 Activities

Horse-Drawn Tram OUTDOORS
(☑08 8551 0720; www.horsedrawntram.com.au; Foreshore; return adult/child/family $9/7/25; ⊙hourly 10.30am-3.30pm) Just offshore is the boulder-strewn Granite Island, connected to the mainland by a 632m causeway built in 1875. You can walk to the island, but it's much more fun to take the 1894 double-decker tram pulled by a big Clydesdale. It's the definitive Victor Harbor experience. Tickets are available from the driver or visitor information centre.

Encounter Bikeway CYCLING
(☑08 8551 0777; www.victor.sa.gov.au/webdata/resources/files/bikeway.pdf) The much-wheeled Encounter Bikeway extends 30km from Victor Harbor to Laffin Point beyond Goolwa, past beaches, lookouts and the odd visiting whale. The visitors centre stocks maps (or download one); hire a bike from **Victor Harbor Cycle Skate Bay Rubber** (☑08 8552 1417; www.victorharborcycles.com; 73 Victoria St; bike hire per 4/8hr $30/40; ⊙9am-5pm Mon-Fri, 10am-3pm Sat, 11am-3pm Sun).

👉 Tours

Big Duck BOATING
(☑08 8555 2203; www.thebigduck.com.au; Granite Island Causeway; 45min tour adult/child/family $35/25/110, 90min $60/50/195) Do a lap of Granite Island and cruise along the coast to check out seals, dolphins and whales (in season) on the rigid inflatable Big Duck boat. Call or go online for times and bookings. Strict guidelines about proximity to whales are adhered to.

⭐ Festivals & Events

Schoolies Festival MUSIC
(www.encounteryouth.com.au/schoolies-festival; ⊙Nov) In November, Victor Harbor's grassy foreshore runs rampant with teenage school-leavers blowing off steam. Accommodation dries up.

🛌 Sleeping & Eating

Anchorage GUESTHOUSE $
(☑08 8552 5970; www.anchorageseafronthotel.com; 21 Flinders Pde; s/d/tr/apt from $65/90/135/260; ❄🌐) This grand old guesthouse exudes seaside charm. Immaculately maintained, great-value rooms open off long corridors. Most rooms face the beach, and some have a balcony (you'd pay through the nose for this in Sydney!) The cheapest rooms are view-free and share bathrooms. The cafe-bar (breakfast mains $5-17, lunch & dinner $12-30; ⊙8am-late) downstairs is a winner.

Victor Harbor City Inn MOTEL $$
(☑08 8552 2455; www.victorharborcityinn.com.au; 51 Ocean St; d/2-bedroom unit from $115/135; ❄🌐) Smack dab in the middle of town, this old '70s motel has been on the receiving end of much renovation recently: new beds, new linen, new bathrooms, new paint... It's a modest, 15-room affair – great value for money and brilliantly located.

Nino's CAFE, ITALIAN $$
(☑08 8552 3501; www.ninoscafe.com.au; 17 Albert Pl; mains $19-38; ⊙9.30am-late) Nino's cafe has been here since 1974 (and the

building a lot longer) but it manages to put a contemporary sheen on downtown VH. Hip young staff and a mod interior set the scene for gourmet pizzas, burgers, pasta, salads, risottos and meaty Italian mains. Good coffee, cakes and takeaways, too.

Shopping

Alexandrina Cheese Company CHEESE
(☑08 8554 9666; www.alexandrinacheese. com.au; Sneyd Rd, Mt Jagged; tastings free, cheese platters from $15; ⊙noon-5pm Mon-Fri, 10am-4.30pm Sat & Sun) On the road to Mt Compass, 18km north of Victor Harbor, this Fleurieu success story opens its doors to cheese fans and milkshake mavens. Taste the gouda, the edam and the feta, then buy a block of the powerful vintage cheddar to go.

Information

Victor Harbor Visitor Information Centre
(☑08 8551 0777; www.tourismvictorharbor. com.au; Foreshore; ⊙9am-5pm) Handles tour and accommodation bookings. Stocks the *Beaches on the South Coast* brochure for when you feel like a swim, and when you don't, the *Victor Harbor Historic Markers Discovery Trail* walking-tour brochure.

Port Elliot

POP 3100

About 8km east of Victor Harbor, historic (and today, rather affluent) Port Elliot is set back from **Horseshoe Bay**, a gorgeous orange-sand arc with gentle surf and good swimming. Norfolk Island pines reach for the sky, and there are whale-spotting updates posted on the pub wall. If there are whales around, wander out to **Freemans Knob** lookout at the end of the Strand and peer through the free telescope.

Activities

Port Elliot Bike & Leisure Hire CYCLING
(☑0448 370 007; www.portelliotbikeleisurehire. myob.net; 85-87 Hill St; per day from $40; ⊙9am-5pm Mon-Sat, from 10.30am Sun) Pick up a mountain bike and hit the Encounter Bikeway (p86), running through Port Elliot to Goolwa (15km east) and Victor Harbor (7km west).

Surfing

Commodore Point, at the eastern end of Horseshoe Bay, and nearby **Boomer Beach** and **Knights Beach**, have reliable waves

for experienced surfers, with swells often holding around 2m. The beach at otherwise-missable **Middleton**, the next town towards Goolwa, also has solid breaks. Further afield, try wild **Waitpinga Beach** and **Parsons Beach**, 12km southwest of Victor Harbor.

The best surfing season is March to June, when the northerlies doth blow. See www. southaustralia.com for info, and www. surfsouthoz.com for surf reports. There are a few good surfing schools in Middleton.

Surf & Sun SURFING
(☑1800 786 386; www.surfandsun.com.au; 44 Victor Harbor-Goolwa Rd, Middleton; ♿) Offers board/wetsuit hire (per half-day $20/10), and surfing lessons ($55 for a two-hour lesson, including gear). Very kid friendly (two-hour family lessons $240).

Sleeping & Eating

★ **Port Elliot Beach House YHA** HOSTEL $
(☑08 8554 1885; www.yha.com.au; 13 The Strand; dm/tw/d/f from $30/91/110/125; ❄@ 🛜) Built in 1910 (the old Arcadia Hotel), this sandstone beauty has sweeping views across the Port Elliot coastline. Drag your eyes away from the scenery and you'll find polished floorboards, new ensuite rooms, nice linen and contemporary colour schemes: a million-dollar fit-out. Surf lessons are almost mandatory, and the fab Flying Fish Cafe is 200m away.

BIG4 Port Elliot Holiday Park CARAVAN PARK $
(☑1800 008 480, 08 8554 2134; www.portelliot holidaypark.com.au; Victor Harbor-Goolwa Rd; powered sites/cabins/units/cottages from $35/90/115/145; ❄🛜) In an unbeatable position behind the Horseshoe Bay dunes (it can be a touch windy), this grassy, 5-hectare park has all the requisite facilities, including a shiny camp kitchen and all-weather barbecue area. Lush grass and healthy-looking trees. Prices plummet in winter.

★ **Flying Fish Cafe** MODERN AUSTRALIAN $$
(☑08 8554 3504; www.flyingfishcafe.com.au; 1 The Foreshore; mains cafe $6-20, restaurant $28-45; ⊙cafe 9am-4pm daily, restaurant noon-3pm daily & 6-8pm Fri & Sat; ♿) Sit down for a cafe breakfast and you'll be here all day – the views of Horseshoe Bay are sublime. Otherwise, grab some takeaway Coopers-battered flathead and chips and head for the sand. At night things get classy,

ADELAIDE & AROUND PORT ELLIOT

with à la carte mains focusing on independent SA producers. One of SA's must-visit foodie haunts.

Goolwa

POP 2200

Much more low-key and elegant than kissing-cousin Victor Harbor, historic Goolwa is an unassuming river port where the rejuvenated Murray River empties into the sea. Beyond the dunes is a fantastic beach with ranks of breakers rolling in from the ocean, same as it ever was…

◎ Sights & Activities

Steam Exchange Brewery BREWERY
(☑08 8555 3406; www.steamexchange.com.au; 1 Cutting Rd, Goolwa Wharf; ◎11.30am-5pm Wed-Sun) Down on the wharf, the Steam Exchange Brewery is a locally run brewery, turning out stouts and ales. Sip a Southerly Buster Dark Ale and look out over the rippling river. And SA's only single malt whiskey distillery is here! Small tasting fee; group tours by arrangement.

☞ Tours

Canoe the Coorong CANOEING
(☑0424 826 008; www.canoethecoorong.com; tours adult/child $135/85) ⏺ Full-day paddles around the Coorong and Murray River mouth, departing Goolwa. Includes lunch and a bush-tucker walk through the dunes. Three-hour sunset tours and overnight expeditions also available.

Spirit of the Coorong CRUISE
(☑08 8555 2203, 1800 442 203; www.coorongcruises.com.au; Goolwa Wharf) ⏺ Eco-cruises on the Murray and into the Coorong National Park, including lunch and guided walks. The four-hour Coorong Discovery Cruise (adult/child $95/69) runs on Thursdays all year, plus Mondays from October to May. The six-hour Coorong Adventure Cruise ($110/76) runs on Sundays all year, plus Wednesdays from October to May. Bookings essential.

Cruise the Coorong CRUISE
(☑0410 488 779; www.cruisethecoorong.com.au; Goolwa Wharf; adult/child $130/100) Small-boat, 6½-hour Coorong Ultimate cruises with walks, bush tucker, seal spotting and digging for *pipis* (shellfish) on the beach. Lunch and snacks included. Shorter Coorong Highlights tours also

available during school holidays (adult/child $60/50).

★♥ Festivals & Events

**South Australian
Wooden Boat Festival** SPORTS
(www.woodenboatfestival.com.au; ◎Apr) Wooden boats of all sizes, configurations and degrees of quaintness make a splash in the Murray in April in odd-numbered years.

🛏 Sleeping & Eating

Captains Quarters B&B $$
(☑0402 254 742; www.facebook.com/captainsquartersgoolwa; 15 Wildman St; d from $150) It looks like an oldie, but it's actually a newie. Built in 2010, Captains Quarters is a super cute cottage in the Goolwa backstreets, just a short walk from the shops and cafes. Sleeps six in three bedrooms – a very clever use of space on a tight block of land.

★**Boathouse Retreat** B&B $$$
(☑08 8555 0338; www.birksharbour.com.au/stay/boathouse; 138 Liverpool Rd; d from $325; ❄🐾) Around the riverfront from downtown Goolwa, the Boathouse is a photogenic, woody boat shed (minus the boat), with a sunny deck and private marina out the front full of bobbing boats. It's a private, two-person affair, angled towards the romantically inclined. DIY breakfast goodies in the fridge.

Australasian BOUTIQUE HOTEL $$$
(☑08 8555 1088; www.australasian1858.com; 1 Porter St; d incl breakfast from $395; ❄🐾) This gorgeous 1858 stone hotel at the head of Goolwa's main street has been reborn as a sassy B&B, with a sequence of Japanese-inspired decks and glazed extensions, and an upmarket dining room. The five plush suites all have views, and the breakfast will make you want to wake up here again. Two-night minimum.

Bombora CAFE $$
(☑08 8555 5396; www.bomboragoolwa.com; Goolwa Beach Car Park, Beach Rd; mains $10-28; ◎8am-5pm Fri-Mon, closed mid-May–mid-Jul) Down at the Goolwa surf beach, this modest little brick bunker has a big rep, serving baguettes, burgers, salads, brilliant bacon-and-egg damper with homemade chutney and Goolwa cockles. Sit in the adjunct raised pavilion for surf views, or just grab an ice cream to go. Open daily during school holidays, and for dinner in summer.

Motherduck CAFE

(☑ 08 8555 1462; www.motherduckcafe.com.au; 1/13 Cadell St; mains breakfast $8-21, lunch $13-27; ☺ 8am-4pm Tue-Sun; ♠) A buzzy highlight of the Goolwa shopping strip is this crafty little cafe, which always seems busier than anywhere else in Goolwa. Exposed stone walls, bravely strong coffee, Spanish-style baked eggs, Langhorne Creek wines, curries, pancakes and Jack Johnson on the stereo – the perfect small-town cafe?

ℹ Information

Goolwa Visitor Information Centre (☑ 1300 466 592, bike hire 0402 814 541; www.visit alexandrina.com; 4 Goolwa Tce; ☺ 9am-5pm Mon-Fri, 10am-4pm Sat & Sun) Inside an 1857 post office, with detailed local info (including accommodation). Bike hire also available, if you feel like tackling the Encounter Bikeway (☑ 1300 466 592; www.victor.sa.gov.au/webdata/resources/files/bikeway.pdf).

KANGAROO ISLAND

From Cape Jervis, car ferries chug across the swells of the Backstairs Passage to Kangaroo Island (KI). Long devoid of tourist trappings, the island these days is a booming destination for wilderness and wildlife fans – it's a veritable zoo of seals, birds, dolphins, echidnas and (of course) kangaroos. Still, the island remains rurally paced and underdeveloped – the kind of place where kids ride bikes to school and farmers advertise for wives on noticeboards. Island wine and produce is a highlight.

History

Many KI place names are French, attributable to Gallic explorer Nicholas Baudin who surveyed the coast in 1802 and 1803. Baudin's English rival, Matthew Flinders, named the island in 1802 after his crew feasted on kangaroo meat here. By this stage the island was uninhabited, but archaeologists think Indigenous Australians lived here as recently as 2000 years ago. Why they deserted KI is a matter of conjecture, though the answer is hinted at in the Indigenous name for KI: Karta (Land of the Dead). In the early 1800s an Indigenous presence (albeit a tragically displaced one) was re-established on KI when whalers and sealers abducted Aboriginal women from Tasmania and brought them here.

⚡ Activities

The safest swimming is along the north coast, where the water is warmer and there are fewer rips than down south. Try Emu Bay, Stokes Bay, Snelling Beach or Western River Cove.

For surfing, hit the uncrowded swells along the south coast. Pennington Bay has strong, reliable breaks; Vivonne Bay and Hanson Bay in the southwest also serve up some tasty waves. Pick up the *Kangaroo Island Surfing Guide* brochure from visitor information centres, or do a web search for 'Kangaroo Island Surfing Guide' and follow the download link on www.tourkangarooisland.com.au.

There's plenty to see under your own steam on KI, including bushwalking trails ranging from 1km to the epic 61km, five-day Kangaroo Island Wilderness Trail (p98). Check out www.tourkangarooisland.com.au/experiences for more trail info.

The waters around KI are home to 230 species of fish, plus coral and around 60 shipwrecks – great snorkelling and diving! Kangaroo Island Dive & Adventures (☑ 08 8346 3422) runs diving trips and offers gear and kayak hire; call for current prices.

There's plenty of good fishing around the island, including jetties at Kingscote, Penneshaw, Emu Bay and Vivonne Bay. Fishing charter tours (half-/full day per person from $150/250) include tackle and refreshments, and you keep what you catch. Try KI Fishing Charters (☑ 0401 727 234; www.kiboathire.com.au; 5 people per half-/full-day $550/950) or Kangaroo Island Fishing Adventures (☑ 08 8559 3232; www.kangarooislandadventures.com.au).

☞ Tours

Groovy Grape TOURS

(☑ 08 8440 1640, 1800 059 490; www.groovygrape.com.au) Two-day, all-inclusive, small-group wildlife safaris ($435, or $390 in winter) ex-Adelaide, with sandboarding, swimming, campfires and all the main sights.

Adventures Beyond ADVENTURE

(☑ 1300 736 014; www.adventuresbeyond.com.au; 1-/2-day tours $275/435) All-inclusive two-day island wildlife tours (small backpacker groups), departing Adelaide, with lots of activities (sandboarding, snorkelling, hiking and farm-stay accommodation…). One-day tours also available.

ADELAIDE & AROUND KANGAROO ISLAND

Kangaroo Island

20 km
10 miles
0

Rapid Head

Victor Harbor (50km);
McLaren Vale (75km)

Cape Jervis

Backstairs Passage

Hog Bay

27

Antechamber Bay

15

2 Cape Willoughby

Pennshaw
21

25

Eastern Cove

Baudin Beach

Dudley Peninsula

Browns Beach

Dudley Conservation Park

SOUTHERN OCEAN

Napean Bay

American River

Island Beach

Pelican Lagoon

29

Pennington Bay

Point Marsden

Bay of Shoals

32 20
13 Kingscote
Brownlow

Western Cove

6 Cygnet River

5

Kingscote Airport

3

Hog Bay Rd

D'Estrees Bay

Emu Bay

Emu Bay

17

4

North Coast Rd

Cape Cassini

Cape Gantheaume Conservation Park

Cape Gantheaume

Investigator Strait

Stokes Bay

Cygnet River

Pardana

Timber Creek

Eleanor River

8

10

Snelling Beach

11
28

Middle River

Little Sahara

Vivonne

Vivonne Bay

24 12

Vivonne Bay Conservation Park

Playford Hwy

30

14

South Coast Rd

Snug Cove

Western River Conservation Park

West End Hwy

Karatta

7

Hanson Bay

23

18

Harvey's Return

1
19

Cape Borda

Ravine des Casoars

Flinders Chase National Park

9 31

22

16

Cape du Couedic Lighthouse

Cape du Couedic

Remarkable Rocks

Admirals Arch

West Bay

26

Snake Lagoon

Maupertius Bay

Kangaroo Island

Kangaroo Island Adventure Tours TOURS (☑08 8202 8678; www.kiadventuretours.com.au) Two-day, all-inclusive tours ex-Adelaide (from $445 with dorm accommodation, a little bit more for private rooms – both at Vivonne Bay Lodge) with a backpacker bent and plenty of activities.

🛏 Sleeping

KI accommodation is expensive, adding insult to your wallet's injury after the pricey ferry ride. Self-contained cottages, B&Bs and beach houses start at around $160 per night per double (usually with a two-night minimum stay). There are, however, some great camp sites around the island, plus a few midrange motels and unsophisticated hostels. Quality caravan parks are scarce.

There are a few agencies which can help book accommodation on the island:

Gateway Visitor Information Centre (☑1800 811 080; www.tourkangarooisland.com.au/accommodation), **Kangaroo Island Holiday Accommodation** (☑08 8553 9007; www.kangarooislandholidayaccommodation.com.au) and **SeaLink** (☑13 13 01; www.sealink.com.au/kangaroo-island-accommodation).

ℹ Information

Kangaroo Island Hospital (☑08 8553 4200; www.countryhealthsa.sa.gov.au; 3 Esplanade; ⊘24hr) is in Kingscote.

There are ATMs in Kingscote and Penneshaw.

Island mobile phone reception can be patchy outside the main towns (reception is best with Telstra).

The main **Gateway Visitor Information Centre** (p93) is in Penneshaw.

ℹ Getting There & Away

AIR

Kingscote Airport (☑13 17 13; www.kangarooisland.sa.gov.au/airport) is 14km from Kingscote. **Regional Express** (Rex; www.regionalexpress.com.au) flies daily between Adelaide and Kingscote (return from $280).

Car-hire companies and some accommodation providers will meet you when you land. **Kangaroo Island Transfers** (☑0427 887 575; www.kitransfers.com.au) connects the airport with Kingscote (per person $25), American River ($70 for one or two people) and Penneshaw ($90 for one or two people). Bookings essential.

BUS

SeaLink (p268) runs daily buses (return adult/child $48/24, 2¼ hours one way) between Adelaide and Cape Jervis on the Fleurieu Peninsula, where the ferry departs.

FERRY

SeaLink (p268) operates the car ferry between **Cape Jervis** (p85) and Penneshaw on KI, with at least three ferries each way daily (return adult/child from $98/50, bicycles/motorcycles/cars $22/66/282, 45 minutes one-way). One driver is included with the vehicle price (cars only, not bikes).

ⓘ Getting Around

Forget public transport: you're gonna need some wheels. The island's main roads are sealed, but the rest are gravel, including those to Cape Willoughby, Cape Borda and the North Coast Rd (take it slowly, especially at night). There's **petrol** at Kingscote, Penneshaw, American River, Parndana and Vivonne Bay.

BUS

Once they roll off the ferry, **SeaLink** (p268) coaches run from Penneshaw to American River and Kingscote (one-way adult/child $16.50/9 and $19.50/11 respectively). Call for times and booking.

Rockhopper (☑ 08 8553 4500; www.kangarooisland.sa.gov.au/rockhopper) is a community bus service traversing eastern and western routes from Kingscote. The eastern service runs three times each way on Wednesdays, stopping at American River and Penneshaw; the western service runs twice daily on Tuesdays and Fridays, visiting Cygnet River, Parndana and Vivonne Bay. Flat-rate fares are one-way adult/child $10/5. Call for bookings.

CAR HIRE

Not all Adelaide car-rental companies will let you take their cars onto KI. **Budget** (www.budget.com.au) and **Hertz** (www.hertz.com.au) supply cars to Penneshaw, Kingscote and Kingscote Airport.

Penneshaw & Dudley Peninsula

Looking across Backstairs Passage to the Fleurieu Peninsula, Penneshaw (population 300), on the north shore of the Dudley Peninsula, is the ferry arrival point and KI's second-biggest town. The passing tourist trade lends a certain transience to the businesses here, but the pub and the backpacker joints remain authentically grounded.

⊙ Sights

Kangaroo Island Farmers Market MARKET
(☑08 8553 1237; www.facebook.com/pg/kangarooislandfarmersmarket; Lloyd Collins Reserve, 99 Middle Tce, Penneshaw; ⊙9am-1pm 1st Sun of the month) Baked goods, chutneys, seafood, olive oil, honey, eggs, cheese, yoghurt…and of course buskers and wine! SeaLink (p268) offers dedicated passenger-only return tickets (adult/child $41/31) from the mainland if you'd just like to visit the market for the day.

Cape Willoughby Lightstation LIGHTHOUSE
(☑ accommodation 08 8553 4410; www.environment.sa.gov.au/parks; Cape Willoughby Rd, Cape Willoughby; tours adult/child/family $16/10/42, self-guided tour not incl lighthouse $3; ⊙guided tours 11.30am, 12.30pm & 2pm) About 28km southeast of Penneshaw (unsealed road) on a treeless headland, this tidy white turret started shining out in 1852 (SA's first lighthouse) and is now used as a weather station. Inside is lots of shipwreck info, with basic cottage accommodation adjacent (doubles from $170, extra person $30). Extra tours at 3pm and 4pm during school holidays.

☞ Tours

Nocturnal Tour WILDLIFE
(☑0448 575 801; www.kiwildlifesafari.net; tours adult/child $65/50) Two-hour after-dark tours ex-Penneshaw, looking for kangaroos, possums and wallabies under a great spangle of southern stars.

Kangaroo Island Ocean Safari ADVENTURE
(☑0419 772 175; www.kangarooislandoceansafari.com.au; tours adult/child $77/55) Hop aboard this buoyant 12-seater for a 75-minute nautical tour ex-Penneshaw, spying seals, dolphins, birds and (sometimes) whales.

🛏 Sleeping

Antechamber Bay South Campground CAMPGROUND $
(☑08 8204 1910; www.environment.sa.gov.au/parks; off Creek Bay Rd, Antechamber Bay; unpowered sites per person/car $9/15) Within Lashmar Conservation Park where the Chapman River runs into Antechamber Bay, these dozen refreshingly low-key camp sites are right on the riverbank, with fire pits, a BBQ hut and silvery bream on the end of your fishing line. There are more sites on the north bank of the river.

Kangaroo Island Backpackers HOSTEL $

(☑ 0439 750 727; www.kangarooislandbackpackers.
com; 43 North Tce, Penneshaw; dm/s/tw/d/f from
$28/38/55/80/130; ❄) A tidy, affable inde-
pendent hostel a short wander from both
the pub and the ferry dock – proximity is
the main asset here. It's a simple, compact
set-up, but hey, you're on holiday on an
island – who needs interior design? Dangle
a line off the jetty instead.

Wallaby Beach House RENTAL HOUSE $$

(☑ 08 8362 5293; www.wallabybeachhouse.com.
au; off Hog Bay Rd, Browns Beach; d from $180,
extra person $25) A secluded, self-contained
three-bedroom beach house, 13km west of
Penneshaw on unpeopled Browns Beach.
Simple beachy decor, with broad sunset
views and passing seals, dolphins and pen-
guins to keep you company. Sleeps six.

✖ Eating

★ **Dudley Wines Cellar Door** CAFE $$

(☑ 08 8553 1333; www.dudleywines.com.au; 1153
Cape Willoughby Rd, Cuttlefish Bay; mains $15-32;
⊙ 10am-5pm) About 12km east of Penneshaw,
KI's pioneering winery has a superb cellar
door (doubling in size when we visited). It's
a fancy corrugated-iron shed, with astonishing views back to the mainland and serving
superb pizzas (try the King George whiting
version), oysters and buckets of prawns –
perfect with a bottle of chardonnay on the
deck.

Fish SEAFOOD $$

(☑ 0439 803 843; www.2birds1squid.com; 43
North Tce, Penneshaw; mains $13-24; ⊙ 4.30-8pm
mid-Oct–Apr) Takeaway fish and chips like
you ain't never had before – grilled, beer-
battered or crumbed whiting and garfish –
plus giant KI scallops, marron (freshwater
crayfish), lobster medallions, prawns and
oysters. Dunk them in an array of excellent
homemade sauces. Hours can vary; call in
advance.

❶ Information

Gateway Visitor Information Centre

(☑ 1800 811 080, 08 8553 1185; www.
tourkangarooisland.com.au; 3 Howard Dr, Pen-
neshaw; ⊙ 9am-5pm Mon-Fri, 10am-4pm Sat &
Sun; 🛜) Just outside Penneshaw on the road to
Kingscote, this centre is brimming with bro-
chures and maps. Also books accommodation,
and sells park entry tickets and the **Kangaroo
Island Tour Pass** (p94).

American River

POP 230

Between Penneshaw and Kingscote, on the
way to nowhere in particular, American
River squats redundantly by the glassy **Pel-
ican Lagoon**. The town was named after a
crew of American sealers who built a trad-
ing schooner here in 1804. There's no such
industriousness here today, just a general
store and a pod of pelicans.

🛏 Sleeping & Eating

**American River
Camping Ground** CAMPGROUND $

(☑ 08 8553 4500; www.kangarooisland.sa.gov.
au/camping; Tangara Dr; unpowered/powered
sites per 2 people $15/25, extra person $5)
Shady, council-run camping by the lagoon,
with fire pits, showers, toilets and a nifty
BBQ hut. Pay via self-registration.

Mercure Kangaroo Island Lodge LODGE $$

(☑ 1800 355 581, 08 8553 7053; www.kilodge.
com.au; 201-216 Scenic Dr; d from $160;
❄🛜🏊) Up-to-scratch motel-style suites
overlooking either the pool or lagoon (the
rammed-earth wing has the best rooms).
The restaurant plates up buffet breakfasts

**ALL CREATURES
GREAT & SMALL**

You bump into a lot of wildlife on KI
(sometimes literally). Kangaroos,
wallabies, bandicoots and possums
come out at night, especially in wilderness areas such as Flinders Chase
National Park. Koalas and platypuses
were introduced to Flinders Chase
in the 1920s when it was feared they
would become extinct on the mainland. Echidnas mooch around in the
undergrowth, while goannas and tiger
snakes keep KI suitably scaly.

Of the island's 267 bird species,
several are rare or endangered. One
notable species – the dwarf emu – has
gone the way of the dodo. Glossy black
cockatoos may soon follow it out the
door due to habitat depletion.

Offshore, dolphins and southern
right whales are often seen cavorting,
and there are colonies of little penguins, New Zealand fur seals and Australian sea lions here too.

ⓘ KANGAROO ISLAND TOUR PASS

If you plan on seeing most of the main sights, save some cash with a Kangaroo Island Tour Pass (☑08 8553 4444; www.environment.sa.gov.au/parks/entry-fees/parks-passes; adult/child/family $70/43/191), which covers all KI park and conservation area entry fees, plus ranger-guided tours at Seal Bay, Kelly Hill Caves, Cape Borda and Cape Willoughby. Available online, at visitor centres or at most sights.

and dinners featuring lots of local seafood (mains $28 to $36, serving 7.30am to 9am and 6pm to 8pm).

Oyster Farm Shop   SEAFOOD $

(☑08 8553 7122; www.facebook.com/oyster farmshop; 486 Tangara Dr, American River; meals $5-20; ☺11am-3pm) Run by a local oyster farm, this little shack acts as an outlet for sustainable seafood producers from all over KI. Oysters, marron, abalone, King George whiting...even barramundi, cooked into meals (nothing is deep-fried) or take away uncooked. Get change from $10 for a dozen fresh unshucked oysters.

★ KI Tru Thai   THAI $$

(☑0408 848 211; Willowbrook, 148 Old Salt Lake Rd, Haines; mains $9-18, four dishes $30; ☺5.30-8.30pm Thu) Hungry? Thursday night? If it's 'affirmative' to all of the above, wander over to this big steel farm shed (a couple of kilometers down a dirt road across from the American River turn-off) for some brilliant home-cooked Thai curries and stir-fries. Live music, kitsch Thai paintings, bark-chip floor – it's a great fun night!

Kingscote

POP 2040

Once slated as the future capital city of the South Australian colony, snoozy seaside Kingscote (kings-coat) is the main settlement on KI, and the hub of island life. It's a photogenic town with swaying Norfolk Island pines, a couple of pubs and some decent eateries.

◉ Sights

Kangaroo Island Brewery   BREWERY

(☑0409 264 817; www.kangarooislandbrewery.com.au; 61 North Coast Rd; ☺11am-7pm Sat & Sun) Here a brewery, there a brewery... Seems you can't go anywhere in Australia these days without being tempted by craft beer, and KI is no exception. This neat, black roadside shack pours some tasty drops, including a ginger wheat bear and Sheoak Stout. Retro/rustic interiors; tasting paddles $10.

Kangaroo Island Spirits   DISTILLERY

(KIS; ☑08 8553 9211; www.kispirits.com.au; 856 Playford Hwy, Cygnet River; tastings free, bottles from $42; ☺11am-5pm Wed-Mon, daily during school holidays) This fiesty little moonshiner makes small-batch gin with KI native juniper berries, plus vodka, brandy and liqueurs (pray the organic honey-and-walnut version hasn't sold out).

Island Pure Sheep Dairy   DAIRY

(☑08 8553 9110; www.islandpure.com.au; 127 Gum Creek Rd, Cygnet River; tours adult/child/family $6.50/5.50/22; ☺11am-4pm) Near Cygnet River, 12km from Kingscote, this dairy features 1500 sheep lining up to be milked (from 2pm daily). Take a tour of the factory, which includes yoghurt and cheese tastings (the halloumi is magic).

Island Beehive   FARM

(☑08 8553 0080; www.island-beehive.com.au; 59 Playford Hwy; tours adult/child/family $5/4/15; ☺9am-5pm, tours every 30min 9.30am-3.30pm) Runs 20-minute factory tours where you can study up on passive, hard-working Ligurian bees and bee-keeping, then stock up on by-products (bee-products?) including delicious organic honey and honeycomb ice cream.

⚐ Activities

Pelican Feeding   BIRDWATCHING

(☑08 8553 3112; www.kipenguincentre.com.au/pelican-feeding.php; Kingscote Wharf; adult/child $5/3; ☺5pm) Pull up a pew and watch the daily feeding frenzy of 20-something ravenous pelicans at Kingscote Wharf. The host is well protected – hatted, gloved and booted – and mic'd-up so you can hear the spiel above the voraciously snapping beaks.

☞ Tours

**Kangaroo Island
Marine Adventures** TOURS
(☑0427 315 286, 08 8553 3227; www.
kimarineadventures.com) One-hour north coast
boat tours (adult/child $60/45) and longer
three-hour jaunts (adult/child $190/110),
spotting dolphins, seal colonies and eagles
and visiting remote areas of KI. You can
swim with the dolphins – and these guys
adhere to a rigorous marine-mammal interaction policy – but be aware that natural
behaviours and breeding patterns may be
affected by such interactions.

🛏 Sleeping & Eating

**Kangaroo Island Central
Backpackers** HOSTEL **$**
(☑08 8553 2787; www.kicentralbackpackers.com;
19 Murray St; dm/s/d/cabins from $27/65/65/80;
❄🛜) Just a couple of blocks from
Kingscote's main strip, this small, innocuous
hostel is clean and affordable, and has a cosy
lounge, lush lawns and a beaut ensuite double cabin out the back. It feels like staying at
someone's house – good or bad, depending
on how sociable you're feeling.

Haven Cottage RENTAL HOUSE **$$**
(☑0447 062 867; www.sealink.com.au/kangaroo-
island-accommodation/487-haven-cottage; cnr
Ayliffe St & Telegraph Rd; f from $180, extra person
$25; 🛜) Fronted by standard roses, a lush
patch of lawn and a wisteria-hung arbour,
Haven Cottage is an old iron-clad house
with a refreshing dearth of lace and 'ye
olde' affectation (cast-iron beds are about as
twee as things get). Three bedrooms; sleeps
six (bunk beds for the kids). Two-night
minimum.

Aurora Ozone Hotel HOTEL **$$**
(☑08 8553 2011; www.ozonehotelki.com.au; 67
Chapman Tce; d $170-220, 1-/2-bedroom apt from
$250/420; ❄🛜🏊) Opposite the foreshore
with killer views, the 100-year-old Ozone
pub has quality pub rooms upstairs, motel
rooms, and stylish deluxe apartments in a
new wing across the street. The eternally
busy bistro (mains $18 to $42) serves meaty
grills and seafood, and you can pickle yourself on KI wines at the bar.

Bella ITALIAN **$$**
(☑08 8553 0400; 54 Dauncey St; pizzas
$14-41, mains lunch $11-25, dinner $29-34;
⊘10am-8.30pm Mon-Sat, 4-8pm Sun) Sit inside
or on the pavement, al fresco, at Bella, a
cheery Italian cafe/restaurant/pizza bar. Piz-
zas start around lunchtime (eat in or take
away); dinner is à la carte (or pizzas), fea-
turing American River oysters, Island Pure
halloumi, local juniper-spiced roo and KI
whiting.

North Coast Road

Exquisite beaches (calmer than the south
coast), bushland and undulating pastures
dapple the North Coast Rd, running from
Kingscote along the coast to the Playford
Hwy 85km west. There's not a whole lot
to do here other than swan around on the
beach – sounds good!

⊙ Sights

About 18km from Kingscote, **Emu Bay** is
a holiday hamlet with a 5km-long, white-
sand beach flanked by dunes – one of KI's
best swimming spots. Around 36km further
west, **Stokes Bay** has a penguin rookery
and broad rock pool, accessible by scram-
bling through a 20m tunnel in the cliffs at
the bay's eastern end (mind your head!)
Beware the rip outside the pool.

Further west along North Coast Rd, the
view as you look back over Snelling Beach
from atop Constitution Hill is awesome!
Continue 7km west and you'll hit the turn-
off to **Western River Cove**, where a small
beach is crowded in by sombre basalt cliffs.
The ridge-top road in is utterly scenic (and
steep).

Snelling Beach BEACH
(off North Coast Rd, Middle River) The best swim-
ming beach on the north coast, with a lovely
arc of powdery white sand and sheltered
shallows. There's not much else at Snelling
by way of facilities but that's all part of its
charm.

Emu Bay Lavender FARM
(☑08 8553 5338; www.emubaylavender.com.au;
75 Emu Bay Rd, Wisanger; ⊘10am-4.30pm Wed-
Sun mid-Sep–mid-May, daily during school holidays)
FREE Lavender is yet another species that
thrives in KI's Mediterranean climate. Fol-
low the purple haze to this cute little road-
side farm, where you can sniff out some gifts
(oils, soaps, fumigating lavender bags) or
grab a coffee and a lavender-infused snack.

🛏 Sleeping & Eating

Discovery Lagoon Caravan & Camping Grounds
CARAVAN PARK **$**

(☑08 8553 5220; www.discoverycamping.com.au; 948 North Coast Rd, Emu Bay; unpowered sites $23-28, cabins $65) Not far along the road into Emu Bay after you turn off the North Coast Rd, this simple lakeside campground has lots of grass and shade, a neat camp kitchen and toilets, and the lake itself (or rather, lagoon) to look at, with ghostly white trunks emerging from the waters. Check in at 948 North Coast Rd.

Lifetime Private Rentals
RENTAL HOUSE **$$$**

(www.life-time.com.au; North Coast Rd, Snelling Beach, Middle River; d from $430, extra person $25; ❄) Pricey but worth every penny, these four gorgeous self-contained stone-and-timber houses dot the hillsides above beautiful Snelling Beach (...actually, they're not that pricey if there's a few of you: from $570 for six people in three bedrooms). Expect decks, big windows, quirky artworks and knock-out views. Food-and-accommodation packages also available, including lunch with Hannaford & Sachs (p96).

Rockpool Café
CAFE **$$**

(☑08 8559 2277; www.facebook.com/therockpoolcafe; off North Coast Rd, Stokes Bay; mains $15-28; ☺11am-5pm mid-Sep–mid-May) Don't worry about sandy feet at this casual, al fresco joint by the beach in Stokes Bay. 'What's the house special?', we asked. 'Whatever I feel like doin'!', said the chef (usually seafood, washed down with local wines and decent espresso). Closed Mondays outside of school holidays; occasionally open Friday nights.

★ Hannaford & Sachs
MODERN AUSTRALIAN **$$$**

(☑08 8559 2236; www.hannafordandsachs.com.au; 5997 North Coast Rd, Middle River; lunch $115; ☺noon-3pm Tue-Sun Dec-Mar) Beneath the sun-dappled boughs of a 150-year-old fig tree, Rachel Hannaford and Sasha Sachs deliver a unique gourmet lunch experience: canapes, entrees, mains, desserts and accompaniments, with global influences from Lebanon and India to Thailand and Mexico. And of course, fine wine. Bookings essential.

South Coast Road

Tracking from Kingscote to Flinders Chase National Park, the South Coast Rd doesn't often come close to the coast (at it's eastern end, at any rate). But if it did,

you'd see that the wave-swept shores here are much less sheltered than those on the northern side of KI. This is wild country, and a great place to meet some island wildlife. And don't miss Vivonne Bay, one of SA's most beautiful beaches.

⊙ Sights

Clifford's Honey Farm
FARM

(☑08 8553 8295; www.cliffordshoney.com.au; 1157 Elsegood Rd, Haines; ☺9am-5pm) **FREE** It's almost worth swimming the Backstairs Passage for the honey ice cream (sourced from a colony of rare Ligurian bees) at this charming, uncommercial farm, which is a bit off the tourist radar (again, charming). Honey-infused drinks, biscuits, mead, cosmetics and candles are also available in the cute shop. Look for the queen bee in the glass-fronted beehive.

Seal Bay Conservation Park
NATURE RESERVE

(☑08 8553 4463; www.sealbay.sa.gov.au; Seal Bay Rd, Seal Bay; guided tours adult/child/family $35/20/85; ☺tours 9am-4pm plus twilight year-round, extra tours Dec-Feb) 🖉 'Observation, not interaction' is the mentality here. Guided tours stroll along the beach (or boardwalk on self-guided tours; adult/child/family $16/10/42) to a colony of (mostly sleeping) Australian sea lions: book in advance for both. Twilight beach tours (adult/child/family $60/38/165) run year-round on Monday, Wednesday and Friday; call for departure times and bookings.

Raptor Domain
ZOO

(☑08 8559 5108; www.kangarooislandbirdsofprey.com.au; cnr South Coast & Seal Bay Rds, Seal Bay; adult/child/family birds of prey $18/12/55, reptiles $12/10/35; ☺10am-4pm) Check out some KI wedge-tailed eagles, barn owls and kookaburras at a one-hour birds-of-prey display (11.30am and 2.30pm), or go scaly at a one-hour lizards and snakes show (1pm).

Little Sahara
NATURE RESERVE

(off South Coast Rd, Vivonne Bay; ☺24hr) **FREE** A turn-off 6km west of Seal Bay Rd leads to a rolling white dunescape looming above the surrounding scrub. Amazing! You can hire sandboards from Kangaroo Island Outdoor Action (☑08 8559 4296; www.kioutdooraction.com.au; 188 Jetty Rd, Vivonne Bay).

**Kelly Hill
Conservation Park**   NATURE RESERVE

(📞 08 8553 4464; www.environment.sa.gov.
au/parks; South Coast Rd, Hanson Bay; tours
adult/child/family $18/10/45, adventure caving
adult/child $70/40; ⏱10.15am-4.30pm) This
series of dry limestone caves was 'discovered' in the 1880s by a horse named Kelly,
who fell into them through a hole. Take the
standard show cave tour (10.30am, then
hourly 11am to 4pm), or add on an adventure
caving tour (2.15pm; bookings essential). The
Hanson Bay Walk (9km one-way) runs
from the caves past freshwater wetlands.
There are extra show cave tours during
school holidays.

🏃 Activities

Tiger Trails   HORSE RIDING

(📞 0427 392 030; www.tiger-trails-kangarooisland.
com; 2492 East West Two Hwy, Newland;
30min/1hr/2hr rides per person $30/60/100)
Horse and pony rides long and short, along
the Harriet River at Newland in the middle
of the island. Bookings essential.

🛏 Sleeping & Eating

Flinders Chase Farm   HOSTEL, CABINS $

(📞 0447 021 494; www.flinderschasefarm.com.au;
1561 West End Hwy, Karatta; dm/cabins/d/f from
$28/80/110/120) A working farm with charm,
a short drive from Flinders Chase National
Park. Accommodation includes tidy dorms,
a couple of cosy cabins and ensuite rooms in
a lodge. There's also a terrific camp kitchen,
fire pits and 'tropical' outdoor showers.

SupaShak   RENTAL HOUSE $$

(📞 08 8410 4557; www.sealink.com.au/kangaroo-
island-accommodation/470-supashak; Flinders
St, Vivonne Bay; d $190-310, extra person $25)
Oh look – a lunar landing pod has touched
down in the Vivonne Bay dunes… This
angular architectural craft is future-fantas-
tic, responding to the bushfire-prone locale
with steel and fibre-cement construction
and lots of water storage. Geared towards
longer stays (minimum three nights), with
room for six bods. The wood fire cranks in
winter; ceiling fans spin in summer.

⭐ **Southern Ocean Lodge**   LUXURY HOTEL $$$

(📞 08 8559 7347; www.southernoceanlodge.com.
au; Hanson Bay Rd, Hanson Bay; d per night from
$1100; ❄ @ 🛜 🏊) Looking for a place to your
woo your sweetheart? The shining star in
the SA tourism galaxy is Southern Ocean
Lodge, a sexy, low-profile snake tracing the

Hanson Bay cliff-top – a really lovely piece
of architecture, and an utterly lovely place
to stay. Two-night minimum; prices include
airport transfers, all meals and drinks, and
guided tours of KI.

Marron Café   MODERN AUSTRALIAN $$

(📞 08 8559 4114; www.andermel.com.au; 804
Harriet Rd, Central Kangaroo Island; mains $18-
46; ⏱11am-4.30pm Sep-Apr, noon-3.30pm
May-Aug) Around 15km north of Vivonne
Bay you can check out marron in breeding
tanks, then eat some! It's a subtle taste,
not always enhanced by the heavy sauces
issued by the kitchen… There are salads,
steak and chicken dishes too, for the crus-
tacean-shy. Last orders 30 minutes before
closing. Two Wheeler Creek winery cellar
door is here too.

Flinders Chase National Park

Occupying the western end of the island,
Flinders Chase National Park is one of
SA's top national parks. Much of the park
is mallee scrub, and there are also some
beautiful, tall sugar-gum forests, particu-
larly around Rocky River and the Ravine
des Casoars, 5km south of Cape Borda.
Sadly, around 100,000 acres of bush were
burned out by bushfires in 2007, but the
park is making a steady recovery. Kooky
rock formations and brilliant bushwalks
are the highlights. Pay your park entry
fees at the Flinders Chase Visitor Infor-
mation Centre (p98).

◉ Sights

Once a farm, Rocky River, the area around
the visitor centre, is now a rampant hotbed
of wildlife, with kangaroos, wallabies and
Cape Barren geese competing for your affec-
tions. A slew of good walks launch from
behind the visitors centre, including the
Rocky River Hike (9km loop, three hours),
on which you might spy a platypus. There's
also camping and accommodation here.

From Rocky River, a road runs south to a
remote 1906 lighthouse atop wild Cape du
Couedic (de *coo*-dick). You can't access the
lighthouse, but it's nice to look at! There's
cottage accommodation here too. Not far
away, a boardwalk weaves down to Admi-
rals Arch, a huge archway ground out by
heavy seas, and passes a colony of New Zea-
land fur seals (sweet smelling they ain't…).

At Kirkpatrick Point, a few kilometres east of Cape du Couedic, the much-photographed Remarkable Rocks are a cluster of hefty, weather-gouged granite boulders atop a rocky dome that arcs 75m down to the sea. Remarkable!

On the northwestern corner of the island, the square 1858 Cape Borda Lightstation (☑08 8559 3257; www.environment.sa.gov.au/parks; tours adult/child/family $16/10/42, self-guided tour $3; ⊙9am-5pm, tours 11am, 12.30pm & 2pm) stands tall above the rippling iron surface of the Southern Ocean. There are walks here from 1.5km to 9km, and extra tours at 3.15pm and 4pm during summer holidays. The cannon is fired at 12.30pm! There's accommodation here too.

At nearby Harvey's Return a cemetery speaks poignant volumes about the reality of isolation in the early days. From here you can drive to Ravine des Casoars (literally 'Ravine of the Cassowaries', referring to the now-extinct dwarf emus seen here by Baudin's expedition). The challenging Ravine des Casoars Hike (8km return, four hours) tracks through the ravine to the coast.

🏃 Activities

⭐ Kangaroo Island Wilderness Trail   HIKING
(☑08 8553 4410; www.kangarooislandwildernesstrail.sa.gov.au/home; Flinders Chase Visitor Information Centre, South Coast Rd, Flinders Chase; adult/child $161/96) The big-ticket bushwalk in Flinders Chase NP is this five-day, four-night wilderness trail – an excellent 61km adventure through the park wilds, with dedicated campsites or beds off-trail if you're in need of some comfort. The trail starts at the park visitors centre and ends at Kelly Hill Conservation Park on the south coast. Maximum numbers apply; book online.

🛏 Sleeping

Within the park there are campgrounds at Rocky River (per vehicle $30), Snake Lagoon (per vehicle $15), West Bay (per vehicle $15) and Harvey's Return (per vehicle $15). You'll need a 4WD to get to Harvey's Return and West Bay.

There's also refurbished cottage accommodation at Rocky River – the budget Postman's Cottage (d $75, extra person $26) and family-friendly May's Homestead (d $176, extra adult/child $30/15) – and lightkeepers' cottages at Cape du Couedic (d $225, extra adult/child $30/15) and Cape Borda (d $50-225, extra adult/child $30/15).

For all park accommodation, book online before you go at www.environment.sa.gov.au/parks/booking, through the Flinders Chase Visitor Information Centre, or at the Natural Resources Centre (☑08 8553 4444; www.naturalresources.sa.gov.au/kangarooisland; 37 Dauncey St; ⊙9am-5pm Mon-Fri) in Kingscote.

🍴 Eating

Chase Cafe   CAFE $$
(☑08 8559 7339; www.thechasecafe.net; 442 Cape du Couedic Rd, Flinders Chase National Park; meals $7-30; ⊙9am-5pm) On the food front, if you're not self-catering the only option within Flinders Chase National Park is the buzzy, daytime Chase Cafe at the visitor centre, serving burgers, wraps, soup, pizzas, big salads, coffee and wines by the glass.

ℹ Information

Flinders Chase Visitor Information Centre (☑08 8553 4470, accommodation ☑08 8553 4410, camping 08 8553 4471; www.environment.sa.gov.au/parks; Cape du Couedic Rd, Flinders Chase; park entry adult/child/family $11/6/28; ⊙9am-5pm) Info, park passes, maps and camping/accommodation bookings, plus the Chase Cafe and displays on island ecology.

Barossa Valley & Southeastern South Australia

Best Places to Eat

➡ Fino Seppeltsfield (p104)
➡ Red Door Espresso (p103)
➡ Skillogalee (p108)
➡ Union Cafe (p116)
➡ Banrock Station (p111)

Best Places to Sleep

➡ Kirche @ Charles Melton (p103)
➡ Reilly's (p107)
➡ Dalton on the Lake (p117)
➡ Caledonian Inn (p116)
➡ Wigley Retreat (p110)

Why Go?

From legendary wine regions north of Adelaide, around the undulating bends of the Murray River, and down along the Limestone Coast, this vast swathe of South Australia demands your undivided attention.

You can tackle the Barossa and Clare Valleys as day trips from Adelaide but why not sip a few excellent local wines and sleep in? Cycling trails weave between the vines and fabulous restaurants complement the liquid offerings. These compact SA valleys and their historic towns are custom-built holiday haunts.

Conversely, the Murray River is enormous, curling across the entire state. Towns here are utilitarian with country sensibility at the helm. Silently sliding by, the big river is undeniable in its beauty and grace.

Tracking southeast from Adelaide to Mount Gambier, SA's second-biggest city, you'll pass the dunescapes and lagoons of Coorong National Park, super-charming beach towns and the cab-sauv vines of the Coonawarra wine region.

When to Go
Tanunda

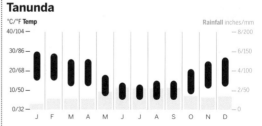

Jan–Feb School's out, the sun is high and the Limestone Coast beaches are the place to be.

Mar–May Low autumn sunsets and russet-red grapevines: harvest is in the air.

Jun–Aug Winter is quiet on the Murray: gorgeous clear mornings, affordable accommodation..

Barossa
Valley &
Southeastern
South
Australia
Highlights

1 **Barossa Valley Wineries** (p103) Spending a day bouncing between winery cellar doors in SA's quintessential wine region.

2 **Barossa Farmers Market** (p106) Sourcing fine regional produce at this Saturday morning market.

3 **Riesling Trail** (p109) Cycling between old towns and cellar doors, from one end of the Clare Valley to the other, following the course of an old railway line.

4 **Coorong National Park** (p116) Trundling past pelicans, dunes and briny lagoons.

NEW SOUTH WALES

Murray River

Paringa
Renmark
Berri
Loxton
Kingston on Murray
Barmera
Pinnaroo
Lameroo
Coonalpyn
Karoonda
B12
Meningie
Tailem Bend
Murray Bridge
Mannum
Swan Reach
Blanchetown
Morgan
Murray River
8 Murray River
Walkerie
Eudunda
Kapunda
Greenock
Nuriootpa
Angaston
Tanunda
Barossa Farmers Market
Lyndoch
Williamstown
Mount Pleasant
Birdwood
Mount Torrens
1 2 Barossa Valley Wineries
Freeling
Gawler
Callington
Strathalbyn
Lake Alexandrina
Lake Albert
Milang
Goolwa
Victor Harbor
Normanville
Cape Jervis
Kangaroo Island
Fleurieu Peninsula
Mount Compass
Sellicks Beach
Willunga
McLaren Vale
Macclesfield
Echunga
Mount Barker
Adelaide
Port Adelaide
Virginia
Two Wells
Mallala
Port Wakefield
Ardrossan
Port Vincent
Gulf St Vincent
Owen
Balaklava
Riverton
Saddleworth
Auburn
Mintaro
Clare Valley
Clare
Blyth
Snowtown
Bute
Burra
32
3 Riesling Trail
Murray River

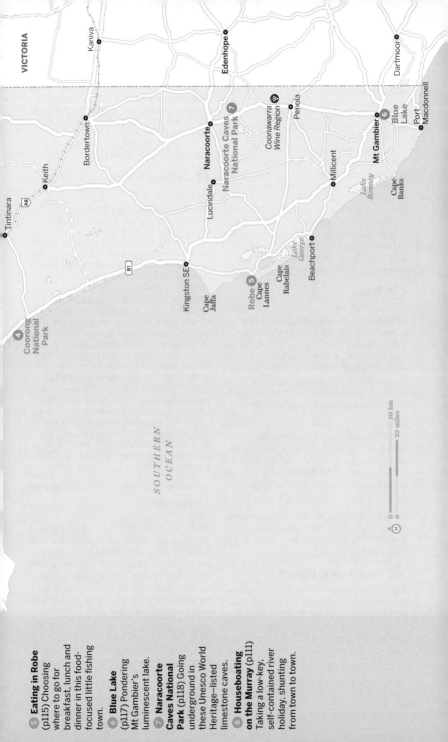

VICTORIA

Kaniva

Bordertown

Keith

Tintinara

A8

B1

Edenhope

Dartmoor

Naracoorte

Naracoorte Caves
National Park ⑦

Coonawarra
Wine Region

Penola

Lucindale

Mt Gambier

Blue ⑥
Lake

Port
Macdonnell

Millicent

Lake
Bonney

Cape
Banks

Kingston SE

Cape
Jaffa

Robe ⑤
Cape
Lannes

Cape
Rabelais

Lake
George

Beachport

Coorong ④
National
Park

SOUTHERN
OCEAN

50 km
25 miles

N

⑤ **Eating in Robe**
(p115) Choosing
where to go for
breakfast, lunch and
dinner in this food-
focused little fishing
town.

⑥ **Blue Lake**
(p117) Pondering
Mt Gambier's
luminescent lake.

⑦ **Naracoorte
Caves National
Park** (p118) Going
underground in
these Unesco World
Heritage–listed
limestone caves.

⑧ **Houseboating
on the Murray** (p111)
Taking a low-key,
self-contained river
holiday, shunting
from town to town.

BAROSSA VALLEY

With hot, dry summers and cool, moderate winters, the Barossa is one of the world's great wine regions – an absolute must for anyone with even the slightest interest in a good drop. It's a compact valley – just 25km long – yet it manages to produce 21% of Australia's wine, and it makes a no-fuss day trip from Adelaide, which is 65km southwest of the region.

The local towns have a distinctly German heritage, dating back to 1842. Fleeing religious persecution in Prussia and Silesia, settlers (bringing their vine cuttings with them) created a Lutheran heartland where German traditions endure today. The physical remnants of colonisation – Gothic church steeples and stone cottages – are everywhere. Cultural legacies of the early days include a dubious passion for oom-pah bands, and an appetite for wurst, pretzels and sauerkraut.

Tours

Barossa Explorer　　　　　　　　TOURS
(☑ 0423 376 155; www.barossaexplorer.com; per person/family $30/100; ◷ 10am-5pm Thu-Sun) Jump aboard this hop-on/hop-off tourist bus, which loops past nine handy Barossa sites, including the Barossa Valley Brewery, Maggie Beer's Farm Shop and the visitor centre in Tanunda. Do the whole loop in an hour, or take your own sweet time about it.

Uber Cycle Adventures　　　　　CYCLING
(☑ 08 8563 1148; www.ubercycle.com.au; 2hr/half-day/full-day tours $95/145/195) Get on your bike and see the Barossa on two wheels, with lots of native flora and fauna en route (oh, and some wine!)

Groovy Grape　　　　　　　　　TOURS
(☑ 1800 059 490, 08 8440 1640; www.groovygrape.com.au; full-day tours $99) Backpacker-centric day tours ex-Adelaide with a pizza lunch: good value, good fun.

Festivals & Events

Barossa Gourmet Weekend　　FOOD & DRINK
(www.barossagourmet.com; ◷ Sep) Fab food matched with winning wines at select wineries; usually happens in September. The number-one event in the valley (book your beds way in advance).

Barossa Vintage Festival　　　FOOD & DRINK
(www.barossavintagefestival.com.au) A week long festival with music, maypole dancing, tug-of-war etc; around Easter (harvest time – very atmospheric) in odd-numbered years.

Getting There & Away

The Barossa Valley makes an easy day-trip from Adelaide, just 65km southwest of the region. If you're driving, consider the slightly longer route through the Adelaide Hills, which is super-scenic.

Adelaide Metro (www.adelaidemetro.com.au) runs regular daily trains from Adelaide to Gawler ($5.30, one hour), from where **LinkSA** (www.linksa.com.au) buses run to Tanunda ($10.10, 45 minutes), Nuriootpa ($12.80, one hour) and Angaston ($15.60, 1¼ hours).

Getting Around

BICYCLE

The 27km **Jack Brobridge Track** runs from Gawler to Tanunda, with a 14km **rail trail** continuing through Nuriootpa to Angaston, passing plenty of wineries. It's part of the longer (40km) north–south **Barossa Trail**. Pick up the *Barossa by Bike* brochure at the **Barossa Visitor Information Centre** (p105) in Tanunda, or download one from its website.

Based in Nuriootpa, **Barossa Bike Hire** (☑ 0400 537 770; www.barossabikehire.com; 5 South Tce; ◷ 9am-5pm) rents out quality cycles/tandems from $40/70 per day (pick-up price: bikes can be delivered for $10/20 extra). Electric bikes, foodie hampers and guided half-day bike tours also available. In Tanunda, run by the visitor centre, the **Barossa Cycle Hub** (☑ 08 8563 0600, 1300 852 982; www.barossa.com; 70 Murray St; ◷ 9am-5pm Mon-Fri, to 4pm Sat, 10am-4pm Sun) has bikes per half-/full-day for $30/44. **Angaston Hardware** (☑ 08 8564 2055; www.angastonhardware.com.au; 5 Sturt St; ◷ 8.30am-5.30pm Mon-Fri, 9am-4pm Sat, 10am-4pm Sun) also rents out bikes for $25/35 per half-/full day.

Tanunda
POP 4680

At the centre of the valley both geographically and socially, Tanunda is the Barossa's main tourist town. Tanunda manages to morph the practicality of Nuriootpa with the charm of Angaston without a sniff of self-importance. There are some great eateries around town, but the wineries are what you're here for – sip, sip, sip!

Sights

Mengler's Hill Lookout　　　　　VIEWPOINT
(Map p104; Menglers Hill Rd) From Tanunda, take the scenic route to Angaston via Bethany for hazy valley views (just ignore the naff sculptures in the foreground). The road tracks through beautiful rural country, studded with huge eucalyptuses.

Keg Factory
FACTORY

(Map p104; ☑08 8563 3012; www.thekegfactory.com.au; 25 St Hallett Rd; ☺8am-4pm Mon-Fri, 11am-4pm Sat & Sun) **FREE** Watch honest-to-goodness coopers make and repair wine barrels, 4km south of town. Amazing!

🛏 Sleeping

Discover Holiday Parks
Barossa Valley
CARAVAN PARK $

(Map p104; ☑ 08 8563 2784, 1800 991 590; www.discoveryholidayparks.com.au; Barossa Valley Way; unpowered/powered sites from $30/38, cabins with/without bathroom from $145/110, villas from $240; ❋☎☲) This spacious park just south of town is dotted with mature trees offering a little shade to ease your hangover. Facilities include a playground, barbecues, a laundry and bike hire for guests (per day $35). The flashy villas sleep up to six and have a two-night minimum stay.

Barossa Backpackers
HOSTEL $

(Map p104; ☑08 8563 0198; www.barossaback packers.com.au; 9 Basedow Rd; dm/s/d from $28/80/80; @☎) Occupying a converted, U-shaped winery office building 500m from Tanunda's main street, Barossa Backpackers is a clean, secure and shipshape affair (if a little soulless) with good weekly rates. Management can help you find picking/pruning work.

★**The Kirche @ Charles Melton**
B&B $$$

(Map p104; ☑08 8563 3606, 0409 838 802; www.thekirche.com.au; 192 Krondorf Rd; d $515, extra adult/child $75/40; ❋☎) Knocked together in 1964, this old stone Lutheran church – the Zum Kripplein Christi church, in fact – is now a fabulous boutique B&B. It's a few minutes' drive south of central Tanunda, on the same road as a string of good wineries. Inside you'll find black leather couches, a marble-tiled bathroom, two bedrooms and a cranking winter wood-heater. Two-night minimum.

🍴 Eating

★**Red Door Espresso**
CAFE $$

(Map p104; ☑08 8563 1181; www.reddoorespresso.com; 79 Murray St; mains breakfast $8-26, lunch $12-30; ☺7.30am-4pm Mon, to 5pm Wed-Sat, 9.30am-4pm Sun; ☎👪) A decent cafe shouldn't be hard to create, but it's rare in the Barossa for good food, coffee, staff, music and atmosphere to come together this well. The avocado

DON'T MISS

BAROSSA VALLEY WINERIES

The Barossa is best known for shiraz, with riesling the dominant white. There are around 80 vineyards here and 60 cellar doors, ranging from boutique wine rooms to monstrous complexes. The long-established 'Barossa Barons' hold sway – big, ballsy and brassy – while spritely young boutique wineries are harder to sniff out. The pick of the bunch:

Henschke (☑08 8564 8223; www.henschke.com.au; 1428 Keyneton Rd, Keyneton; ☺9am-4.30pm Mon-Fri, to noon Sat) Detour about 10km southeast of Angaston to the Eden Valley, where old-school Henschke is known for its iconic Hill of Grace red ... but most of the wines here are classics.

Rockford Wines (Map p104; ☑08 8563 2720; www.rockfordwines.com.au; 131 Krondorf Rd, Tanunda; ☺11am-5pm) One of our favourite boutique Barossa wineries, this 1850s cellar door sells traditionally made, small-range wines, including sparkling reds. The Black Shiraz is a sparkling, spicy killer.

Penfolds (Map p104; ☑08 8568 8408; www.penfolds.com; 30 Tanunda Rd, Nuriootpa; ☺9am-5pm) You know the name: Penfolds is a Barossa legend. Book ahead for the Make Your Own Blend tour ($65), or the Taste of Grange tour ($150), which allows you to slide some luscious Grange Hermitage across your lips.

Peter Lehmann Wines (Map p104; ☑08 8565 9555; www.peterlehmannwines.com.au; Para Rd, Tanunda; ☺9.30am-5pm Mon-Fri, 10.30am-4.30pm Sat & Sun) The shiraz and riesling vintages here (oh, and the semillon) are probably the most consistent, affordable and widely distributed wines in the Barossa.

St Hallett (Map p104; ☑08 8563 7070; www.sthallett.com.au; St Hallett Rd, Tanunda; ☺10am-5pm) Using only Barossa grapes, improving St Hallett produces reasonably priced but consistently good whites (try the Poacher's Blend) and the excellent Old Block Shiraz. Unpretentious and great value for money.

Barossa Valley

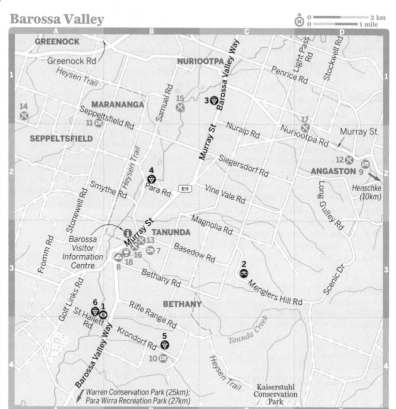

and basil-infused eggs Benedict is a winner, best consumed with an eye-opening coffee in the pot-planted courtyard. Live music over weekend brunch; wine, cheese and antipasto in the afternoons.

Ferment Asian   SOUTHEAST ASIAN **$$**
(Map p104; 08 8563 0765; www.fermentasian. com.au; 90 Murray St; mains $26-34; noon-2pm Thu-Sun, 6-8.30pm Wed-Sat) In a lovely old stone villa fronting onto Tanunda's main street at a jaunty angle, Ferment always does things a little differently. What sounds exotic is actually refreshingly simple: *cari rau* (yellow vegetable curry); *tom nuong va boi* (citrus and prawn salad). Chef Tuoi Do really knows how to put it all together.

⭐**Fino Seppeltsfield**   MODERN AUSTRALIAN **$$$**
(Map p104; 08 8562 8528; www.fino.net.au; 730 Seppeltsfield Rd, Seppeltsfield; small/large plates from $22/46; noon-3pm daily, 6-8.30pm Fri & Sat) From humble beginnings in a little stone cottage on the Fleurieu Peninsula, Fino has evolved into one of Australia's best restaurants, now ensconced in the gorgeous 1851 Seppeltsfield estate west of Tanunda. Food from the understated, deceptively simple menu highlights local ingredients, and is designed to be shared. Try the braised lamb with sherry, fennel, orange and chilli.

🍷 Drinking & Nightlife

Barossa Valley Brewing   CRAFT BEER
(Map p104; 08 8563 0696; www.bvbeer.com.au; 2a Murray St; noon-9pm Sun, Mon & Thu, to 6pm Tue & Wed, to 10pm Fri & Sat) Beer! Real beer, here amongst all the wine! If only for variety, pay a visit to BVB on the southern fringes of Tanunda – there's a paved terrace beneath some astoundingly big eucalypts, just made for an afternoon with a few easy-drinking IPAs. You can also peer at the stout steel tanks in the brewery, or grab a bite to eat.

ⓘ Information

Barossa Visitor Information Centre (Map p104; ☑1300 852 982, 08 8563 0600; www.barossa.com; 66-68 Murray St; ⊙9am-5pm Mon-Fri, to 4pm Sat, 10am-4pm Sun; ☎) The low-down on the valley, plus internet access, bike hire and accommodation and tour bookings. Stocks the *A Town Walk of Tanunda* brochure.

Nuriootpa

POP 5705

Along an endless main street at the northern end of the valley, Nuriootpa is the Barossa's commercial centre. It's not as endearing as Tanunda or Angaston, but has a certain agrarian simplicity. Lutheran spirit runs deep in 'Nuri': a sign says, 'God has invested in you – are you showing any interest?'.

🛏 Sleeping & Eating

The Louise   BOUTIQUE HOTEL **$$$**
(Map p104; ☑08 8562 2722; www.thelouise.com.au; 375 Seppeltsfield Rd, Marananga; d from $600; ❋@☎☎) Top of the accommodation tree in the BV, the Louise does everything with

consummate style, from the architecture and the linen to the in-house restaurant Appellation and the smile at the front desk. Louise might stretch your wallet, but is worth every penny. Marananga (less a town, more an area) is equidistant from Nuriootpa and Tanunda.

Maggie Beer's Farm Shop   DELI **$**
(Map p104; ☑08 8562 4477; www.maggiebeer.com.au; 50 Pheasant Farm Rd; items $5-20, picnic baskets from $16; ⊙10.30am-5pm) Celebrity SA gourmet Maggie Beer has been hugely successful with her range of condiments, preserves and pâtés (and TV appearances!) The vibe here isn't as relaxed as it used to be, but stop by for some gourmet tastings, a cooking demo (2pm daily) or a takeaway hamper of delicious bites. Off Samuel Rd.

🍷 Drinking & Nightlife

★**Stein's Taphouse**   CRAFT BEER, BAR
(Map p104; ☑08 8562 2899; www.steinstaphouse.com.au; 18-28 Barossa Valley Way; ⊙noon-late) Inside the old Provenance Building in the Penfolds complex is this excellent craft beer bar (sacrilege?), also serving artisan spirits, small-production SA wines and food that pairs up nicely with all three (burgers, pork ribs, chilli con carne). There are a dozen beer taps: study the blackboard behind the bar and see what takes your fancy. Live music occasionally, too.

Angaston

POP 1910

Photo-worthy Angaston was named after George Fife Angas, a pioneering Barossa pastoralist. An agricultural vibe persists, as there are relatively few wineries on the town doorstep: cows graze in paddocks at end of the town's streets, and there's a vague whiff of fertiliser in the air. Along the photogenic main drag are two pubs and some terrific cafes and eateries.

🛏 Sleeping & Eating

Marble Lodge   B&B **$$$**
(Map p104; ☑08 8564 2478; www.marblelodge.com.au; 21 Dean St; d $225-250; ❋☎) A grandiose 1915 Federation-style villa on the (reasonably steep!) hill behind the town, built from local pink and white granite. Accommodation is in two plush suites behind the house (high-colonial or high-kitsch, depending on your world view). Breakfast is served in the main house – a candlelit, buffet-style experience.

Casa Carboni ITALIAN $$

(Map p104; ☑ 0415 157 669; www.casacarboni.com.au; 67 Murray St; meals from $25; ⊙ 9am-3pm Thu-Sun, 6pm-late Fri, closed Jul) Part Italian cooking school, part *enoteca*, Casa Carboni is run by real-life Italian Matteo Carboni, who visited the Barossa for a month in 2012 and has been here ever since. Sign up for a pasta master class, or just enjoy the spoils of the kitchen and some fine Italian wine (if you've had enough big, ballsy Barossa red).

Vintners Bar & Grill MODERN AUSTRALIAN $$$

(Map p104; ☑ 08 8564 2488; www.vintners.com.au; cnr Stockwell & Nuriootpa Rds; mains $36-40; ⊙ noon-2.30pm daily, 6.30-9pm Mon-Sat) One of the Barossa's landmark restaurants, Vintners stresses simple elegance in both food and atmosphere. The dining room has an open fire, vineyard views and bolts of crisp white linen; menus concentrate on local produce (the seared chicken livers with potato, muscat and burnt onion is a flavour sensation).

🛍 Shopping

Barossa Farmers Market MARKET

(Map p104; ☑ 0402 026 882; www.barossafarmersmarket.com; cnr Stockwell & Nuriootpa Rds; ⊙ 7.30-11.30am Sat) Happens in the big farm shed behind Vintners Bar & Grill every Saturday. Expect hearty offerings, coffee, flowers, lots of local produce and questionable buskers.

Barossa Valley Cheese Company CHEESE

(Map p104; ☑ 08 8564 3636; www.barossacheese.com.au; 67b Murray St; ⊙ 10am-5pm Mon-Fri, to 4pm Sat, 11am-3pm Sun) The Barossa Valley Cheese Company is a fabulously stinky room, selling handmade cheeses from the milk of local cows and goats. Tastings are free, but it's unlikely you'll leave without buying a wedge of the Washington Washed Rind. Plenty of tourist brochures and maps, too.

CLARE VALLEY

At the centre of the fertile midnorth agricultural district, two hours north of Adelaide, the slender Clare Valley produces world-class, sweet scented rieslings and mineral-rich reds. This is gorgeous countryside, with open skies, rounded hills, stands of large gums and wind rippling over wheat fields. Towns here date from the 1840s; many were built to service the Burra copper mines.

You can tackle the Clare Valley as a day trip from Adelaide, but when the wine and food are this good, why rush? Spend a few days exploring old-fangled towns, cycling between cellar doors, eating and revelling in general hedonism.

👣 Tours

Clare Valley Tours TOURS

(☑ 0418 832 812; www.clarevalleytours.com; tours from $145) Interesting valley tours with a local guide, 'Mr Wilson', taking you along the back roads and delivering some indigenous Ngadjuri insights along with all the wine and colonial history. Ex-Clare Valley.

Clare Valley Grape Express TOURS

(☑ 08 8842 3098, 0428 055 590; david@clare-valleytaxis.com.au; tours $85) Quick-fire (four hour), affordable winery tours for those short on time, run by a local taxi company.

✯ Festivals & Events

**Clare Valley
Gourmet Weekend** FOOD & DRINK

(www.clarevalley.com.au; ⊙ May) A fab frenzy of Clare Valley wine, food and music in May. LinkSA (www.linksa.com.au) buses get involved, with shuttles to/from Adelaide.

❶ Getting There & Around

In Auburn and Clare you can hire a bike to pelt around the wineries. Rates around $40 per day.

Clare Valley Taxis (☑ 08 8842 1400, 13 10 08; www.131008.com) will drop-off/pick-up anywhere along the Riesling Trail.

Yorke Peninsula Coaches (☑ 08 8821 2755; www.ypcoaches.com.au) Runs Adelaide to Auburn ($34, 2¼ hours) and Clare ($42, 2¾ hours) on Monday, Wednesday, Friday and Sunday (also running in the opposite direction on these days). Services extend to Burra ($42, 3¼ hours) on Wednesday only.

Auburn

POP 600

Sleepy Auburn (1849) – the Clare Valley's southernmost village – is a leave-the-back-door-open-and-the-keys-in-the-ignition kinda town, with a time-warp vibe that makes you feel like you're in an old black-and-white photograph. The streets are defined by beautifully preserved, hand-built stone buildings; cottage gardens overflow with untidy blooms. Pick up a copy of the *Walk with History at Auburn* brochure from the Clare Valley Visitor Information Centre (p108).

Now on the main route to the valley's wineries, Auburn initially serviced bullock drivers and South American muleteers whose wagons – up to 100 a day – trundled between Burra's copper mines and Port Wakefield.

🛏 Sleeping

Bed in a Shed   APARTMENT, B&B $$
(☎ 0418 346 836; www.vineartstudio.com; cnr Leasingham Rd & Blocks Rd, Leasingham; d from $200; ❄ ☎) Around 7km north of Auburn in little Leasingham, Bed in a Shed puts a different spin on the Clare Valley B&B: a rustic (but very well insulated) corrugated-iron farm shed decked out with cool art, woody built-in shelves, recycled timbers, quirky furnishings and a fridge full of breakfast stuff. Not a floral bedspread or lace curtain in sight! Nice one.

The Loft at Cobbler's Rest   APARTMENT $$
(☎ 0424 784 572; www.theloftclarevalley.com.au; 24 Horrocks Hwy; d/q from $170/290; ❄) Upstairs in a beautiful stone building in the heart of Auburn, the Loft is a compact apartment comprising two double bedrooms, kitchen/dining and a big bathroom. There's just enough of a 'cottage' vibe for the whole set-up to feel authentic, without overdoing it. Sleeps four; breakfast provisions provided.

🍴 Eating

Rising Sun Hotel   PUB FOOD $$
(☎ 08 8849 2015; www.therisingsunhotel.com.au; 19 Horrocks Hwy; mains $18-33; ⊙ noon-2pm & 6-8pm, bar open 11am; ☎) This classic 1850 pub has a huge rep for its atmosphere, food and accommodation. The seasonal pub food is inventive with plenty of local wines to try. Accommodation takes the form of ensuite pub rooms and cottage mews rooms out the back (doubles including breakfast $100 to $160).

⭐ Terroir   MODERN AUSTRALIAN $$$
(☎ 08 8849 2509; www.terroirauburn.com.au; 21 Horrocks Hwy; mains from $35; ⊙ 2-5.30pm Fri & Sat, noon-4pm Sun, 6-8.30pm Wed-Sat; ☎) 🍷 'Terroir' – a word often associated with the wine trade – defines the nature of a place: its altitude, its soil, its climate, its vibe. At this excellent rest–aurant it applies to ingredients, sourced seasonally from within 100 miles, and cooked with contemporary savvy. The menu changes weekly. Love the Mintaro-slate floor.

Mintaro

POP 370

Heritage-listed Mintaro (min-*tair*-oh; founded 1849) is a lovely village that could have been lifted out of the Cotswolds and plonked into the Australian bush. There are few architectural intrusions from the 1900s – the whole place seems to have been largely left to its own devices. A fact for your next trivia night: Mintaro slate is used internationally in the manufacture of billiard tables.

Pick up the *Historic Mintaro* pamphlet around the valley.

◉ Sights & Activities

⭐ Martindale Hall   HISTORIC BUILDING
(☎ 08 8843 9088; www.martindalehall.com; 1 Manoora Rd, Mintaro; adult/child $12/8; ⊙ 11am-4pm Wed-Mon, daily during school holidays) Martindale Hall is an astonishing 1880 manor 3km from Mintaro. Built for young pastoralist Edmund Bowman Jnr, who subsequently partied away the family fortune (OK, so drought and plummeting wool prices played a part…but it was mostly the partying), the manor features original furnishings, a magnificent blackwood staircase, Mintaro-slate billiard table and an opulent, museum-like smoking room. The hall starred as Appleyard College in the 1975 film *Picnic at Hanging Rock,* directed by Peter Weir. 'Mirandaaa…'

Mintaro Maze   OUTDOORS
(☎ 08 8843 9012; www.mintaromaze.com.au; Jacka Rd; adult/child $12/6; ⊙ 10am-4pm Wed-Mon, daily school holidays, closed Feb) Hedge your bets at the Mintaro Maze as you try to find your way into the middle and back out again. There's a little cafe here too.

🛏 Sleeping & Eating

⭐ Reilly's   MODERN AUSTRALIAN $$
(☎ 08 8843 9013; www.reillyswines.com.au; cnr Hill St & Leasingham Rd; mains $24-30; ⊙ 10am-4pm) Reilly's started life as a cobbler's shop in 1856. An organic veggie garden out the back supplies the current restaurant, which is decorated with local art and serves creative, seasonal Mod Oz food (antipasto, rabbit terrine, platters) and Reilly's wines. The owners also rent out four gorgeous old stone cottages on Hill St (doubles from $175, including cook-your-own breakfast).

Clare

POP 3280

Named after County Clare in Ireland, this town was founded in 1842 and is the biggest in the valley. Strung out along the Horrocks Hwy, it's more practical than charming. All the requisite services are here (post,

DON'T MISS

CLARE VALLEY WINERIES

The Clare Valley's cool microclimate, cool airs circulating around rivers, creeks and gullies, noticeably affect the local wines, enabling whites to be laid down for long periods and still be brilliant. The valley produces some of the world's best riesling, plus grand semillon and shiraz. Five of our favourites:

Skillogalee (☑ 08 8843 4311; www.skillogalee.com.au; 23 Trevarrick Rd, Sevenhill; ⊙ 7.30am-5pm) Skillogalee is a small family outfit known for its spicy shiraz, fabulous food and top-notch riesling (a glass of which is like kissing someone gorgeous on a summer afternoon). Kick back with a long, lazy lunch on the verandah (breakfast mains $17 to $19, lunch $24 to $49; book ahead). This place just might be heaven.

Pikes (☑ 08 8843 4370; www.pikeswines.com.au; Polish Hill River Rd, Sevenhill; ⊙ 10am-4pm) The industrious Pike family set up shop in the Polish Hill River sub-region of the Clare Valley in 1984, and have been producing show-stopping riesling ever since (and shiraz, sangiovese, pinot grigio, viognier ...). It also bottles up the zingy Oakbank Pilsener, if you're parched.

Knappstein (☑ 08 8841 2100; www.knappstein.com.au; 2 Pioneer Ave, Clare; ⊙ 9am-5pm Mon-Fri, 11am-5pm Sat, to 4pm Sun) Taking a minimal-intervention approach to wine making, Knappstein has built quite a name for itself. Shiraz and riesling steal the show, but they also make a mighty fine semillon-sauvignon blanc blend (and beer!)

Sevenhill Cellars (☑ 08 8843 4222; www.sevenhill.com.au; 111c College Rd, Sevenhill; ⊙ 10am-5pm) Like a little religion with your drink? This place was established by Jesuits in 1851, making it the oldest winery in the Clare Valley (check out the incredible 1866 St Aloysius Church). Oh, and the wine is mighty fine too!

Shut The Gate (☑ 08 8843 0111; www.shutthegate.com.au; 2 Horrocks Hwy, Watervale; ⊙ 10am-4.30pm) Across a little creek and through a white gate (no need to shut it), this upbeat little cellar door has been making a few 'Best New Wineries' lists of late. Taste some of their good stuff inside the old duck-your-head cottage, or outside at the rather abstract collection of tables. Winning riesling.

supermarket, fuel, pubs), but you'll have a more interesting Clare Valley experience sleeping out of town.

🛏️ Sleeping & Eating

Bungaree Station FARMSTAY **$**
(☑ 08 8842 2677; www.bungareestation.com.au; 431 Bungaree Rd; per person per night $59-99; ☰) About 12km north of Clare is this beautiful, 175-year-old homestead – once with 50 staff, a church and a school! It's still a 3000-acre working farm, with accommodation in renovated heritage buildings, sleeping two to 10, some with shared bathrooms. You can also feed farm animals, walk a history trail (per adult/child $15/7.50) or have a dip in the pool.

Riesling Trail & Clare Valley Cottages B&B **$$**
(☑ 0427 842 232; www.rtcvcottages.com.au; 9 Warenda Rd; 1-/2-/3-bedroom cottage incl breakfast from $160/195/390; ☰) A well-managed outfit offering seven contemporary cottages, encircled by country gardens and right on the

Riesling Trail (Riesling Trail Bike Hire (p109) is across the street). The biggest cottage sleeps six; there are good deals on multinight and midweek stays.

★**Little Red Grape** BAKERY **$**
(☑ 08 8843 4088; www.thelittleredgrape.info; 148 Horrocks Hwy, Sevenhill; items $3-6; ⊙ 7am-5pm) There's a cellar door here, focusing on small-production local vineyards, but most folks are here for the bakery, serving excellent pies, cakes, big donuts, toasted bacon-and-egg Turkish bread sandwiches and wake-you-up coffee. The saltbush-lamb and rosemary pie is hard to top. It's at Sevenhill, 7km south of Clare.

ℹ️ Information

Clare Valley Visitor Information Centre (☑ 1800 242 131, 08 8842 2131; www.clarevalley.com.au; cnr Horrocks Hwy & Spring Gully Rd; ⊙ 9am-5pm Sat-Thu, to 7pm Fri; 🛜) Local info, valley-wide accommodation bookings and the *Clare History Walk* brochure. Local produce for sale too.

MURRAY RIVER

On the lowest gradient of any Australian river, the slow-flowing Murray hooks through 650 South Australian kilometres. Tamed by weirs and locks, it irrigates the fruit trees and vines of the sandy Riverland district to the north, and winds through the dairy country of the Murraylands district to the south. Raucous flocks of white corellas and pink galahs launch from cliffs and river red gums, darting across lush vineyards and orchards.

Prior to European colonisation, the Murray was home to Meru communities. Then came shallow-draught paddle-steamers, carrying wool, wheat and supplies from Murray Bridge as far as central Queensland along the Darling River. With the advent of railways, river transport declined. These days, waterskiers, jet skis and houseboats crowd the river, especially during summer. If your concept of riverine serenity doesn't include the roar of V8 inboards, then sidestep the major towns and caravan parks during holidays and weekends.

❶ Getting There & Away

As with most places in regional SA, having your own vehicle will give you the most flexibility when exploring the Murray River towns. But if you are bussing it, there are a couple of options.

LinkSA (p269) runs several daily bus services between Adelaide and Murray Bridge ($22.50, 1¼ hours) sometimes via a bus change at Mt Barker in the Adelaide Hills; plus Murray Bridge to Mannum ($7.50, 30 minutes) from Monday to Friday.

Premier Stateliner (www.premierstateliner. com.au) runs daily Riverland buses from Adelaide, stopping in Waikerie ($47.50, 2½ hours), Barmera ($59, 3¼ hours), Berri ($59, 3½ hours) and Renmark ($59, four hours). Change at Kingston-on-Murray for buses to Loxton ($59, 3¾ hours).

Murray Bridge

POP 17,920

SA's largest river town and a rambling regional hub (the fifth-biggest town in SA), Murray Bridge has lots of old pubs, an underutilised riverfront, a huge prison and charms more subtle than obvious.

◉ Sights

Monarto Zoo   ZOO
(✆08 8534 4100; www.monartozoo.com.au; Old Princes Hwy, Monarto South; adult/child/family $34.50/19/88.50; ⊙9.30am-5pm, last entry 3pm)

About 14km west of Murray Bridge, this excellent open-range zoo is home to Australian and African beasts including cheetahs, meerkats, rhino, zebras and giraffe (and the photogenic offspring thereof). A hop-on/hop-off bus tour is included in the price; keeper talks happen throughout the day. There's a cafe here too, if you forget your sandwiches/thermos.

Murray Bridge Regional Gallery   GALLERY
(✆08 8539 1420; www.murraybridgegallery.com. au; 27 Sixth St; ⊙10am-4pm Tue-Sat, 11-4pm Sun) **FREE** This is the town's cultural epicentre, a great little space housing touring and local exhibitions: paintings, ceramics, gorgeous glassware, jewellery and prints. A terrific diversion on a rainy river afternoon.

❶ Information

Murray Bridge Visitor Information Centre
(✆08 8339 1142, 1800 442 784; www.murray bridge.sa.gov.au; 3 South Tce; ⊙9am-5pm Mon-Fri, 10am-4pm Sat & Sun) Stocks the Murray Bridge *Accommodation Guide* and *Dining Guide* brochures, and history walk and drive pamphlets. Also has information on river-cruise operators.

THE RIESLING TRAIL

Following the course of a disused railway line between Auburn and Barinia, north of Clare, the fabulous Riesling Trail is 33km of wines, wheels and wonderment. It's primarily a cycling trail, but the gentle gradient means you can walk or push a pram along it just as easily. It's a two-hour dash end to end on a bike, but why hurry? There are three loop track detours and extensions to explore, and dozens of cellar doors to tempt you along the way. The Rattler Trail continues for another 19km south of Auburn to Riverton.

For bike hire, check out Clare Valley Cycle Hire (✆0418 802 077; www. clarevalleycyclehire.com.au; 32 Victoria Rd; bike hire per half-/full day $20/30; ⊙9am-5pm) or Riesling Trail Bike Hire (✆0418 777 318; www.rieslingtrailbikehire. com.au; 10 Warenda Rd; bike hire per half-/full day $25/40, tandems $40/60; ⊙8am-6pm Fri-Mon, other times by appointment) in Clare, or Cogwebs Hub Cafe (✆08 8849 2380, 0400 290 687; www.cogwebs. com.au; 30 Horrocks Hwy; bike hire per half-/full day $25/40, tandems $35/60; ⊙10am-5pm; 🛜) in Auburn.

Mannum

POP 2570

About 30km upstream from Murray Bridge, clinging to a narrow strip of riverbank, improbably cute Mannum is the unofficial houseboat capital of the world! The *Mary Ann,* Australia's first riverboat, was knocked together here in 1853 and made the first paddle-steamer trip up the Murray.

◉ Sights

Mannum itself, clinging to the crumbling riverbanks, is quite a sight! The Mannum Visitor Information Centre incorporates the Mannum Dock Museum of River History (☑ 08 8569 1303, 1300 626 686; www.psmarion. com; 6 Randell St; adult/child/family $7.50/4/20; ◑ 9am-5pm Mon-Fri, 10am-4pm Sat & Sun), featuring info on local Ngarrindjeri Aboriginal communities, an 1876 dry dock and the restored 1897 paddle steamer *PS Marion,* on which you can occasionally chug around the river.

About 9km out of Mannum on the way to Murray Bridge, Mannum Waterfalls (off Cascade Rd; ◑ 24hr) FREE surge impressively over granite boulders after it's been raining (not much action in February). Head to the top car park for the best access.

From Mannum heading north to Swan Reach, the eastern riverside road often tracks a fair way east of the river, but various lookouts en route help you scan the scene. Around 9km south of Swan Reach, the Murray takes a tight meander called Big Bend, a sweeping river curve with pock-marked, ochre-coloured cliffs.

Sedentary old Swan Reach (population 850), about 80km north of Mannum, is a bit of a misnomer: there's an old pub, a museum and plenty of pelicans here, but not many swans.

🏃 Activities

Breeze Holiday Hire   CANOEING
(☑ 0439 829 964; www.murrayriver.com.au/ breeze-holiday-hire-1052) Hires out canoes and kayaks (per day $75), dinghies with outboards (per day $95) and fishing gear (per day $15), and can get you waterskiing too. Based in Mannum.

🛏 Sleeping & Eating

River Shack Rentals   ACCOMMODATION SERVICES
(☑ 0447 263 549, 08 8569 1958; www. rivershackrentals.com.au) Offers a raft of riverside properties (doubles from $100) to rent from Murray Bridge, Mannum and further upstream. Most of them are right on the water: 36 River Lane is a solid Mannum-centric option with room for 10 (from $450). Houseboats also available.

Pretoria Hotel   PUB FOOD $$
(☑ 08 8569 1109; www.pretoriahotel.com.au; 50 Randell St; mains $20-34; ◑ 11.30am-2.30pm & 5.30-8.30pm) The family-friendly Pretoria (built 1900) has a vast bistro and deck fronting the river, and plates up big steaks and salads, king prawn linguine and impressive parmas (amongst other things). When the 1956 flood swamped the town they kept pouring beer from the 1st-floor balcony!

ℹ Information

Mannum Visitor Information Centre (☑ 08 8569 1303, 1300 626 686; www.psmarion.com/ visitor-centre; 6 Randell St; ◑ 9am-5pm Mon-Fri, 10am-4pm Sat & Sun) This is the place for cruise and houseboat bookings, the *Mannum Historic Walks* brochure and the Mannum Dock Museum of River History (p110). Bike hire also available (per half-/full-day $25/40).

Waikerie

POP 2720

A citrus-growing centre oddly festooned with TV antennas, Waikerie takes its name from the Aboriginal phrase for 'anything that flies'. Indeed, there's plenty of bird life around here, plus houseboats gliding past on the river. The Waikerie vibe is utilitarian and workaday – tourism runs a distant second to fruit.

◉ Sights

Nippy's   FACTORY
(☑ 08 8541 0600; www.nippys.com.au; 2 Ian Oliver Dr; ◑ 8am-noon & 12.30-4pm Mon-Fri) A long-running local fruit-juice company with factory-front sales. Its lip-nipping lemon juice is ace on a hot river afternoon.

🛏 Sleeping & Eating

★ Wigley Retreat   B&B $$
(☑ 0417 186 364; www.facebook.com/wigleyretreat; Wigley Flat Rd, Wigley Flat; d from $190; ❄) Some 27km east of Waikerie and a couple of kilometres off the Sturt Hwy, Wigley Retreat is a simple but stylish stone cottage right on the riverbank. It's a one-bedroom arrangement,

with a well-stocked fridge and a table for two by the water. Super-private, super-scenic. The perfect spot to destress for a couple of days.

★**Waikerie Hotel Motel**   HOTEL, MOTEL **$$**
(☎08 8541 2999; www.waikeriehotel.com; 2 McCoy St; d from $120; 🅿️❄️🛜) Much of this huge pub burnt down in 2012, two days shy of its 100th birthday! The 19 rebuilt ensuite pub rooms upstairs are awesome: fancy linen, glowing bar fridges and big TVs, with leather and granite everywhere. The bistro does pub-grub classics (mains $14 to $27). Slightly cheaper are the updated motel rooms out the back. Bike hire available.

Waikerie Bakery   BAKERY **$**
(☎08 8541 2142; 3 Peake Tce; items $4-8; ⊙8.30am-5.30pm Mon-Fri, to 1pm Sat) Hey, that rhymes! This simple little bakehouse does fabulous pumpkin-and-feta pasties, apricot chicken pies, jam tarts, pecan pies and bags of biscuits. Consume them on the sunny deck off to one side.

ℹ️ Information

Waikerie Visitor Information Centre (☎08 8541 0708; www.waikerie.com; Strangman Rd; ⊙9am-5pm Mon-Fri, 10am-4pm Sat & Sun) The modest little Waikerie Visitor Information Centre is on the big roundabout on the way into town. Old-building fans should look for the *Waikerie Heritage Walk* brochure.

Barmera & Around

On the shallow shores of Lake Bonney (upon which world land-speed record holder Donald Campbell unsuccessfully attempted to break his water-speed record in 1964), snoozy Barmera (population 3020) was once a key town on the overland stock route from NSW. These days the local passion for both kinds of music (country *and* western) lends a simple optimism to proceedings. **Kingston-On-Murray** (population 260; aka Kingston OM) is a tiny town nearby, en route to Waikerie.

👁️ Sights

★**Banrock Station**   WINERY
(☎08 8583 0299; www.banrockstation.com.au; Holmes Rd, Kingston OM; tastings free, wetland walks by gold-coin donation; ⊙9am-4pm Mon-Fri, to 5pm Sat & Sun) 🌿 Overlooking regenerated wetlands off the Sturt Hwy at Kingston OM, carbon-neutral Banrock Station Wine & Wetland Centre is a stylish, rammed-earth wine-tasting centre (love the tempranillo). The jazzy lunchtime **restaurant** (mains $25 to $33 – try the slow-cooked pork belly with Riverland fennel) uses ingredients sourced locally. There are three **wetland walks** here too: 2.5km, 4.5km and 8km.

**Rocky's Hall of Fame
Pioneers Museum**   MUSEUM
(☎0407 720 560; www.facebook.com/rockyscountrymusicmuseum; 4 Pascoe Tce, Barmera; $2; ⊙8.30am-noon Mon & Thu, 9am-4pm Tue & Wed, to 12.30pm Fri) Named after Dean 'Rocky' Page, local radio legend, Rocky's blares sincere rural twangings down the main street from outdoor speakers. Inside is a wealth of country-and-western ephemera. Don't miss the 35m Botanical Garden Guitar out the back, inlaid with the handprints of 160 country musos: Slim Dusty to Kasey Chambers and everyone in between.

🎭 Festivals & Events

**South Australian
Country Music Festival**   MUSIC
(www.riverlandcountrymusic.com; ⊙Jun) Country music is a big deal in Barmera, with the South Australian Country Music Festival held in June. Bring your hat, your horse and your dusty old acoustic guitar and get into it.

HOUSEBOATING ON THE MURRAY
....

Houseboating is big business on the Murray. Meandering along the river is great fun – you just need to be over 18 with a current driving licence. Boats depart most riverside towns; book ahead, especially between October and April.

The **Houseboat Hirers Association** (☎1300 665 122, 08 8346 6655; www.houseboatbookings.com) is a reputable booking service, with boats in most Murray River towns. For a three-night weekend, expect to pay anywhere from $750 for two people to $2700 for a luxury 10-bed boat. Most boats sleep at least two couples and there's generally a bond involved (starting at $200). Many provide linen – just bring food and wine. See also SA Tourism's *Houseboat Holidays* booklet for detailed houseboat listings.

🛏 Sleeping

Discovery Holiday Parks Lake Bonney
CARAVAN PARK $

(☑08 8588 2234; www.discoveryholidayparks. com.au; Lakeside Dr, Barmera; unpowered/powered sites from $23/34, cabins from $99; ❄🔊🐾) This keenly managed, facility-rich lakeside park has small beaches (safe swimming), electric barbecues, a camp kitchen, a laundry and plenty of room for kids to run amok. Lots of trees and waterfront camp sites too, plus tandems, canoes and paddle boats for hire.

🍴 Eating

Backyard Bread
CAFE $

(☑08 8588 2159; www.backyardbread.com.au; cnr Sturt Hwy & McKenzie Rd, Barmera; items $5-15; ⏰10am-4pm Fri-Mon) A rusty, iron-clad shopfront on the Waikerie side of Barmera, Backyard Bread is a deli/cafe baking 'bread bites': mouth-sized bits of flavour-packed bread, infused with local ingredients (red wine, olive oil, pumpkin, lemon myrtle etc). Try some on a tasting platter, or just duck in for a coffee and a slice of cake.

Overland Corner Hotel
PUB FOOD $$

(☑08 8588 7021; www.overlandcornerhotel.com. au; 205 Old Coach Rd, via Barmera; mains $17-28; ⏰noon-2pm Tue-Sun, 6-8pm Thu-Sat) About 19km northwest of Barmera, this moody 1859 boozer is named after a Murray River bend where drovers used to camp. The pub walls ooze character and the meals are drover sized, plus there's a museum, resident ghosts, a beaut beer garden and four walking trails leading down to the river (pick up the *Historic Overland Corner* brochure in Barmera).

ℹ Information

Barmera Visitor Information Centre (☑08 8588 2289; www.barmeratourism.com.au; Barwell Ave, Barmera; ⏰9am-4pm Mon-Fri, 10am-1pm Sat & Sun) Can help with transport and accommodation bookings. Pick up the *Historic Overland Corner* and *Heritage Walk Barmera* walking trail brochures.

Loxton

POP 3780

Sitting above a broad loop of the slow-roaming Murray, Loxton proclaims itself the 'Garden City of the Riverland'. The vibe here is low-key, agricultural and untouristy, with more tyre distributors, hardware shops and irrigation supply outlets than anything else.

It's perhaps telling that the two most interesting things in town are ancient trees.

👁 Sights

Tree of Knowledge
LANDMARK

(Grant Schubert Dr) Down by the river near the caravan park, the Tree of Knowledge is marked with flood levels from previous years. The flows of 1931, '73, '74, '75, and 2011 were totally outclassed by the flood-to-end-all-floods of 1956, marked about 4m up the trunk.

Loxton Pepper Tree
LANDMARK

(Allen Hosking Dr) This gnarled, weather-split, termite-ravaged old pepper tree dates back to 1878, allegedly planted by boundary rider William Charles Loxton, after whom the town was named. He lived near here in a little pine hut from 1878 to 1881.

🛏 Sleeping

Mill Cottage
B&B $$

(☑0439 866 990; www.millcottage.com.au; 2 Mill Rd; d from $177, extra person $35; ❄🔊) In an unlikely locale down a dead-end street in Loxton's industrial back streets, Mill Cottage is a dignified, genteel 1924 B&B option. Breakfast provisions (terrific eggs!) are included for your first two nights. The decor is a bit cottagey, but hey, it's a cottage. Sleeps six; two-night minimum.

Loxton Hotel
HOTEL, MOTEL $$

(☑1800 656 686, 08 8584 7266; www.loxtonhotel. com.au; 45 East Tce; d hotel/motel from $110/170; ❄🔊🐾) With all profits siphoned back into the Loxton community, this large complex offers immaculate rooms with tasty weekend packages. The original pub dates from 1908, and it has been relentlessly extended. Bistro meals available for breakfast, lunch and dinner (mains $15 to $35).

🍷 Drinking & Nightlife

Here's Your Beer
BAR

(☑0472 688 012; www.facebook.com/heresyour beer; 2 Mill Rd; ⏰5-10pm Wed & Thu, 11am-10pm Fri, 10am-8pm Sun) In a big tin shed in Loxton's back blocks, this hipster haven pours craft beers and plates up beaut burgers to anyone who doesn't want to go to the local pub. The vibe is 'urbanish', says the owner. Closed Saturdays (somewhat irritatingly).

ℹ Information

Loxton Visitor Information Centre (☑1300 869 990, 08 8584 8071; www.loxtontourism.

com.au; Bookpurnong Tce; ⊘9am-5pm Mon-Fri, to 4pm Sat, 10am-4pm Sun) A friendly place for accommodation, transport and national-park info, plus there's an art gallery and local dried fruits for sale (oh those peaches!) Has the *History Walk of Loxton* brochure been reprinted yet?

Berri

POP 4110

The name Berri derives from the Aboriginal term *berri berri,* meaning 'big bend in the river', and it was once a busy refuelling stop for wood-burning paddle steamers. These days Berri is an affluent regional hub for both state government and agricultural casual-labour agencies; it's one of the best places to chase down casual harvest jobs. The 'Big Orange' – one of Australia's iconic 'big' roadside tourist lures – awaits resuscitation on the edge of town.

◎ Sights

Riverland Farmers Market   MARKET
(☑0417 824 648; www.riverlandfarmersmarket. org.au; Senior Citizens Hall, Crawford Tce; ⊘7.30-11.30am Sat) All the good stuff that grows around here in one place. A bacon-and-egg roll and some freshly squeezed orange juice will right your rudder.

☞ Tours

Canoe Adventures   CANOEING
(☑0421 167 645; www.canoeadventure.com.au; canoe hire per half-/full-day from $35/45, tours per adult/child half-day $95/60, full day $140/90) ⚑ Canoe hire, guided half- and full day canoe trips and camping expeditions ahoy! This outfit conducts all of the above from its Berri base, and can also deliver to most Riverland towns.

⋆⋆ Festivals & Events

Riverland Wine
& Food Festival   FOOD & DRINK
(RWFF; www.riverlandwineandfood.com; ⊘Oct) Get festive on the banks of the Murray at the annual Riverland Wine & Food Festival, highlighting local produce and booze. It's a reasonably classy event – buy tickets in advance and dress up.

⛏ Sleeping & Eating

Berri Backpackers   HOSTEL $
(☑08 8582 3144; www.berribackpackers.com.au; 1081 Old Sturt Hwy; dm per night/week $35/160; ✳☎⛱) This eclectic hostel is destination

numero uno for work-seeking travellers, who chill out in quirky new-age surrounds after a hard day's manual toil. Rooms range from messy dorms to doubles, share houses, a tepee and a yurt – all for the same price. The managers can hook you up with harvest work (call in advance).

Sprouts Café   CAFE $
(☑08 8582 1228; www.sproutscafe.com.au; 28 Wilson St; mains $7-13; ⊘8.30am-4pm Mon-Fri, 9.30am-1pm Sat) A cheery cafe on the hill a few blocks back from the river, with a natty lime-green colour scheme. Serves soups, quiches, burgers, pasta, curries, wraps and mighty fine coffee. Homemade cakes, scones and chocolate pecan pudding too.

ⓘ Information

Berri Visitor Information Centre (☑08 8582 5511, 1300 768 582; www.berribarmera.sa.gov. au; Riverview Dr; ⊘9am-5pm Mon-Fri, to 2pm Sat, 10am-2pm Sun) Right by the river, with brochures, maps, waterproof canoeing guides ($10) and clued-up staff.

Renmark & Paringa

Renmark (population 7500) is the first major river town across from the Victorian border; about 254km from Adelaide. It's not a pumping tourist destination by any means, but has a relaxed vibe and a grassy waterfront, where you can pick up a houseboat. This is also the hub of the Riverland wine region: lurid signs on the roads into town scream 'Buy 6 Get 1 Free!' and 'Bulk port $5/litre!'.

On the other side of the river, 4km upstream, is Renmark's low-key satellite town, Paringa (population 950).

◎ Sights

⭐**Twenty Third**
Street Distillery   DISTILLERY
(☑08 8586 8500; www.23rdstreetdistillery.com.au; cnr 23rd St & Renmark Ave, Renmark; tour/tasting $15/15, combined $25; ⊘10am-4pm) Sip your way into some heady Riverland spirits at this fabulously renovated, art-deco factory on the road into Renmark. The old distillery here closed in 2002, buckling under market pressures, but it's made one helluva comeback. Gin, whisky and brandy are the headliners: do a tasting, take a tour of the century-old copper stills, or both.

👉 Tours

Murray River Walk   HIKING
(☑0418 808 475; www.murrayriverwalk.com.au;
per person from $2300) 🏊 Step out into the
Murray River wilderness on this four-day,
three-night guided hike, traversing private
land through redgum forests and flood plain
wetlands. Prices include all meals and houseboat accommodation, and a full day of river
cruising on the final day. Ex-Renmark.

Canoe the Riverland   CANOEING
(☑0475 754 222; www.canoetheriverland.com;
835 Murtho Rd, Paringa; full-day tours adult/child
$125/75) 🏊 Slow-paced guided canoe tours
on the Murray, departing Paringa, across the
river from Renmark, with a picnic lunch of
regional produce. Canoe/kayak hire (per day
from $60/35) and sunset, moonlight and
overnight camping tours also available.

🛏 Sleeping & Eating

BIG4 Renmark
Riverfront Holiday Park   CARAVAN PARK $
(☑1300 664 612, 08 8586 8111; www.big4renmark.
com.au; cnr Sturt Hwy & Patey Dr, Renmark; unpow-
ered/powered sites from $41/48, cabins/villas from
$115/155; 🌋🏡🏊) Highlights of this spiffy
riverfront park, 1km east of town, include
a camp kitchen, canoe and paddleboat
hire, splashy water park for kids and absolute waterfront cabins and powered sites.
The newish corrugated-iron cabins are top
notch, and look a little 'Riviera' surrounded
by scraggy palms. The waterskiing fraternity
swarms here during holidays.

Paringa Backpackers Resort   HOSTEL $
(☑0400 659 659; www.paringabackpackersresort.
com.au; 11 Hughes Ave, Paringa; dm per night/week
$35/130, d per week $300; 🌋🏡🏊) Not a rancid
laundry, dank bathroom or crummy kitchen
in sight, Paringa's sparkling highway-side
hostel really is a resort, with tidy ranks of
bright ensuite dorms (8 or 10-bed maximum), palm trees, a gym, pool, games room,
BBQ terrace… What's the catch? An almost
complete absence of soul.

Renmark Hotel   HOTEL, MOTEL $$
(☑08 8586 6755, 1800 736 627; www.renmarkhotel.
com.au; cnr Para St & Murray Ave, Renmark; d from
$100; 🌋🏡🏊) The sexy art deco curves of
Renmark's humongous pub are looking good.
Choose from older-style hotel rooms and
upmarket motel rooms. On a sultry evening
it's hard to beat a cold beer and some grilled
barramundi on the balcony at **Nanya Bistro**

(mains $16 to $32, serving noon to 2.30pm
and 5.30pm to 8.30pm).

Renmark Club   PUB FOOD $$
(☑08 8586 6611; www.renmarkclub.com.au; 160
Murray Ave, Renmark; mains $18-37; ☉noon-
2.30pm & 6-8.30pm; 🍴) Right on the river, this
old pub/club has been reborn as a shiny mod
bistro, serving upmarket pub food (rustic
shank pie, seared Lyrup kangaroo with bush
spices and quandong jus) with unbeatable
water views.

🍷 Drinking & Nightlife

★**Woolshed Brewery**   BREWERY
(☑08 8595 8188; www.aboverenmark.com.au;
Wilkinson Rd, Murtho, via Paringa; ☉11am-5pm)
Amid the grapevines and orchards, 15km
north of Renmark on a Murray River kink,
the Woolshed is doing marvellous things.
Part of the historic Wilkadene Homestead,
the 100-year-old shed is now a craft-beer
brewery, its broad riverside deck built from
floorboards from Adelaide's demolished Centennial Hall (The Beatles stood here!) Dive
into a tasting paddle and enjoy. Live weekend music.

❶ Information

**Renmark Paringa Visitor Information Cen-
tre** (☑08 8586 6704, 1300 661 704; www.
visitrenmark.com; 84 Murray Ave, Renmark;
☉9am-5pm Mon-Fri, 10am-2pm Sat & Sun) Has
the usual local info, brochures and contacts for
backpacker accommodation around town, plus
an interpretive centre and bike hire (per half-/
full day $25/40). The adjacent recommissioned
1911 paddle steamer *PS Industry* goes for a
90-minute chug on the first Sunday of the
month (adult/child $20/10).

LIMESTONE COAST

The Limestone Coast – strung out along
southeastern SA between the flat, olive span
of the lower Murray River and the Victorian
border – is a curiously engaging place. On the
highways you can blow across these flatlands
in under a day, no sweat – but around here
the delight is in the detail. Detour off-road
to check out the area's lagoons, surf beaches
and sequestered bays. Also on offer are wine
regions, photogenic fishing ports and snoozy
agricultural towns. And what's *below* the
road is even more amazing: a bizarre subterranean landscape of limestone caves, sink-
holes and bottomless crater lakes – a broad,

DON'T MISS

COONAWARRA WINERIES

When it comes to spicy cabernet sauvignon, it's just plain foolish to dispute the virtues of the Coonawarra wine region (www.coonawarra.org). The *terra rossa* (red earth) soils here also produce irresistible shiraz and chardonnay. Five of the Coonawarra's best:

Majella Wines (☑ 08 8736 3055; www.majellawines.com.au; Lynn Rd, Coonawarra; ☺ 10am-4.30pm) The family that runs Majella are fourth-generation Coonawarrans, so they know a thing or two about gutsy reds (love 'The Musician' shiraz-cabernet).

Rymill Coonawarra (☑ 08 8736 5001; www.rymill.com.au; Riddoch Hwy, Coonawarra; ☺ 11am-5pm Mon-Sat, noon-5pm Sun) Rymill rocks the local boat by turning out some of the best sauvignon blanc you'll ever taste. The cellar door is fronted by a statue of two duelling steeds – appropriately rebellious.

Wynns Coonawarra Estate (☑ 08 8736 2225; www.wynns.com.au; 1 Memorial Dr, Coonawarra; ☺ 10am-5pm) The oldest Coonawarra winery, Wynns' cellar door dates from 1896 and was built by Penola pioneer John Riddoch. Top-quality shiraz, fragrant riesling and golden chardonnay are the mainstays.

Zema Estate (☑ 08 8736 3219; www.zema.com.au; Riddoch Hwy, Coonawarra; ☺ 9am-5pm Mon-Fri, 10am-4pm Sat & Sun) A steadfast, traditional winery started by the Zema family in the early '80s. It's a low-key affair with a handmade vibe infusing the shiraz and cab sav.

Balnaves of Coonawarra (☑ 08 8737 2946; www.balnaves.com.au; 15517 Riddoch Hwy, Coonawarra; ☺ 9am-5pm Mon-Fri, noon-5pm Sat & Sun) The tasting notes here ooze florid wine speak (dark seaweed, anyone?), but even if your nosing skills aren't that subtle, you'll enjoy the cab sav and chardonnay.

formerly volcanic area that's known as the Kanawinka Geopark.

Heading southeast, trace the Limestone Coast through the sea-salty Coorong, past beachy holiday towns to Mount Gambier, SA's second city. And, if you haven't already overdosed on wine in SA, the Coonawarra wine region awaits.

❶ Getting There & Away

The Dukes Hwy (A8) is the most direct route between Adelaide and Melbourne (729km), but the coastal Princes Hwy (B1; about 900km), adjacent to the Coorong National Park, is infinitely more scenic.

AIR

Regional Express (Rex; www.regionalexpress.com.au) flies daily between Adelaide and Mount Gambier (one-way from $176, 1¼ hours).

BUS

Premier Stateliner (www.premierstateliner.com.au) runs two bus routes – coastal and inland – between Adelaide and Mount Gambier ($83, six hours). From Adelaide along the coast (Wednesday, Friday and Sunday) via the Coorong, you can stop at Meningie ($42, two hours), Robe ($75, 4½ hours) and Beachport ($79, five hours). The inland bus runs Tuesday to Sunday via Naracoorte ($79, five hours) and Penola ($81, 5¾ hours).

Robe

POP 1020

Robe is a cherubic little fishing port that's become a holiday hotspot for Adelaidians and Melburnians alike. The sign saying 'Drain L Outlet' as you roll into town doesn't promise much, but along the main street you'll find quality eateries and boundless accommodation, and there are some magic beaches and lakes around town. Over Christmas and Easter, Robe is packed to the heavens – book *waaay* in advance.

◉ Sights

Robe Town Brewery　　　　　BREWERY
(☑ 0415 993 693; www.robetownbrewery.com; 97 Millicent Rd; ☺ noon-5pm Tue-Sun) Riding the crest of Australia's craft beer wave, Robe Town uses old-fangled methods to produce its hearty Shipwreck Stout and an excellent amber ale (among other creative brews). The brewery occupies a low-key shed in the eastern outskirts of town. Is the Robe Beer Festival on here this September?

🏃 Activities

Steve's Place　　　　　SURFING
(☑ 08　8768　2094; www.facebook.com/steves.place.66; 26 Victoria St; ☺ 9.30am-5pm Mon-Fri,

to 1pm Sat, 10am-1pm Sun) Steve's Place has been here for 50 years (!) and rents out boards (per day $40), bodyboards ($20), paddleboards ($50) and wetsuits ($20). It's also the place for info on surfing lessons and the annual Robe Easter Classic in April, SA's longest-running surf comp (since 1968).

🛏 Sleeping

Local rental agents with properties from as low as $100 per night in the off season include **Happyshack** (☑ 08 8768 2341, 0403 578 382; www.happyshack.com.au), **SAL Coastal Holidays** (☑ 08 8768 2737; www.bookrobe accommodation.com.au; 25 Victoria St; ⊙ 9am-5pm Mon-Fri), **Ottson Holidays** (☑ 08 8768 2600; www.robeholidayrentals.com.au) and **Robe Lifestyle** (☑ 1300 760 629; www.robelifestyle.com.au).

Lakeside Tourist Park   CARAVAN PARK **$**
(☑ 08 8768 2193; www.lakesiderobe.com.au; 24 Main Rd; unpowered/powered sites from $36/37, cabins/villas from $80/140; ❄ 🐾) Right on Lake Fellmongery (a 'fellmonger' is a wool washer, don't you know) this abstractly laid-out, rather boutique park has heritage-listed pine trees and reception building (130-year-old former stables), plenty of grass, basic cabins and flashy villas. The closest camping to the town centre.

⭐ **Caledonian Inn**   HOTEL **$$**
(☑ 08 8768 2029; www.caledonianinnrobe.com. au; 1 Victoria St; s/d without bathroom from $55/90, cottages/houses from $200/400; ❄ 🐾) This historic inn (1859) has a half-dozen bright and cosy upstairs pub rooms: shared bathrooms and no air-con, but great value. Out the back, 'tween pub and sea, are a row of lovely two-tier cottages and a three-bedroom rental house called Splash. The pub grub is classy too (mains $23 to $35, serving noon to 2pm and 6pm to 8pm).

Robe Harbour View Motel   MOTEL **$$**
(☑ 08 8768 2155; www.robeharbourview.com. au; 2 Sturt St; d/f from $120/175; ❄ 🐾) At the quiet end of town (and a five-minute walk from the action), this tidy, well-run motel has namesake harbour views from the best half-dozen rooms at the front. The standard rooms out the back don't have views but are perfectly decent (who needs views when you're asleep?). Expect nice linen, subtle colours and vamped-up bathrooms.

✕ Eating

⭐ **Union Cafe**   CAFE **$**
(☑ 08 8768 2627; 4/17-19 Victoria St; mains $7-18; ⊙ 8am-4pm; 🐾) Always busy, this curiously angled corner cafe has polished-glass fragments in the floor and surf art on the walls. Unionise your hangover with a big cooked breakfast, lashed with locally made hot sauce. Good coffee, pancakes, curries, salads and wraps. Hard to beat!

Vic St Pizza Project   PIZZA **$$**
(☑ 08 8768 2081; www.facebook.com/ pizzaprojectrobesa; 6 Victoria St; mains $17-25; ⊙ 11.30am-2pm & 5-8pm; 🪑) Go for something trad (Hawaiian, margarita, pepperoni) or something more daring (lamb souvlaki, squid and chorizo) – either way, the pizzas at this bright, roomy room are sure-fire crowd pleasers. Pastas, risottos and salads too. Open early for dinner when you've got hungry familiars in tow.

Sails   MODERN AUSTRALIAN **$$$**
(☑ 08 8768 1954; www.sailsatrobe.com.au; 2 Victoria St; mains $28-44; ⊙ noon-2.30pm & 6-9pm) Sails is Robe's classiest restaurant, and comes with a big rep for seafood (oh that Sicilian seafood stew!) Not in an undersea mood? Try the kangaroo fillets with beetroot fritters and horseradish, or the warm beetroot salad with roasted shallots and pecorino cheese. Lovely ambience; smooth service.

ℹ Information

Robe Visitor Information Centre (☑ 1300 367 144, 08 8768 2465; Public Library, cnr Mundy Tce & Smillie St; ⊙ 9am-5pm Mon-Fri, 10am-1pm Sat & Sun) History displays, brochures and free internet. Look for the *Scenic Drive, Heritage Drive* and *A Walk Through History* pamphlets.

Meningie & Coorong National Park

The amazing **Coorong National Park** (☑ 08 8204 1910, 08 8575 1200; www.environment. sa.gov.au/parks; ⊙ 24hr) **FREE** is a fecund lagoon landscape curving along the coast for 145km from Lake Alexandrina towards Kingston SE. A complex series of soaks and salt pans, it's separated from the sea by the chunky dunes of the **Younghusband Peninsula**. More than 200 waterbird species live here. *Storm Boy*, an endearing film about a young boy's friendship with a pelican (based on the novel by Colin Thiele), was filmed here.

In the 1860s when white settlers started to arrive, the bountiful resources of the Coorong were supporting a large Ngarrindjeri population. The Ngarrindjeri are still closely connected to the Coorong, and many still live here.

Bordering the Coorong on **Lake Albert** (a large arm of Lake Alexandrina), Meningie (population 940) was established as a minor port in 1866. These 'lower lakes' were soupy puddles for many years before returning to life after the 2011 Murray River floods. A momentary reprieve from climate change? Time will tell…

🏃 Activities

For a watery perspective, try Spirit of the Coorong (p88) or Cruise the Coorong (p88) cruises, or Canoe the Coorong (p88), all based in Goolwa on the Fleurieu Peninsula.

🛏 Sleeping

Coorong National Park Camp Sites   CAMPGROUND **$**
(☑ 08 8575 1200, 08 8204 1910; www.environment. sa.gov.au/parks; per vehicle $15) There are 18 bush/beach camp sites in Coorong National Park; you need a permit from the Department of Environment, Water & National Resources (DEWNR), available online.

★ **Dalton on the Lake**   B&B **$$**
(☑ 0428 737 161; www.facebook.com/dalton onthelake; 30 Narrung Rd, Meningie; d from $150; 🌀) Generous in spirit and unfailingly clean, this lakeside B&B goes to great lengths to ensure your stay is comfortable. There'll be fresh bread baking when you arrive, jars of homemade biscuits, and bountiful bacon and eggs for breakfast. There's a modern self-contained studio off to one side, and a renovated stone cottage – book either, or both.

Coorong Cabins   RENTAL HOUSE **$$**
(☑ 0407 412 857; www.coorongcabins.com.au; 436 Seven Mile Rd, Meningie; d from $170, extra person $50; 🌀) Two mod, self-contained rental houses – Pelican and Wren, sleeping four and two respectively – about 14km south of town, but right on the waterfront within the national park. Decor is beachy-chi-chi, and there are bikes and kayaks available so you can explore the Coorong beyond where the road may take you.

🍴 Eating

Cheese Factory Restaurant   PUB FOOD **$$**
(☑ 08 8575 1914; www.meningie.com.au; 3 Fiebig Rd, Meningie; mains $15-33; ⊙ noon-2pm daily, 6-8pm Wed-Sat) Lean on the front bar with the locals, or munch into steaks, schnitzels, Coorong mullet or a Coorong wrap (with mullet!) in the cavernous dining room of this converted cheese factory (you might have guessed). The very lo-fi **Meningie Cheese Factory Museum** (www.meningie cheesefactorymuseum.com; $5; ⊙ 8.30am-5pm) is here too (butter churns, old typewriters, domestic knick-knackery).

ℹ️ Information

Meningie Visitor Information Centre (☑ 08 8575 1770; www.meningie.com.au; 14 Princes Hwy, Meningie; ⊙ 10am-4.30pm) The spot for local info, inside a craft shop.

Mount Gambier

POP 27,760

Strung out along the flatlands below an extinct volcano, Mount Gambier is the Limestone Coast's major town and service hub. 'The Mount' can sometimes seem a little short on urban virtues (though you can get a good coffee here these days!) But it's not what's above the streets that makes Mount Gambier special – it's the deep Blue Lake and the caves that worm their way though the limestone beneath the town. Amazing!

👁 Sights

Blue Lake   LAKE
(☑ 1800 087 187; www.mountgambierpoint.com. au/attractions/blue-lake; John Watson Dr; ⊙ 24hr) FREE Mount Gambier's big-ticket item is the luminous, 75m-deep lake, which turns an insane hue of blue during summer. Perplexed scientists think it has to do with calcite crystals suspended in the water, which form at a faster rate during the warmer months. Consequently, if you visit between April and November, the lake will look much like any other – a steely grey. But in February, WOW!

Aquifer Tours (☑ 08 8723 1199; www.aquifer tours.com; cnr Bay Rd & John Watson Dr; adult/ child/family $10/5/29; ⊙ tours hourly 9am-5pm Nov-Jan, to 2pm Feb-May & Sep-Oct, to noon Jun-Aug) runs hourly tours, taking you down near the lake shore in a glass-panelled lift. Or you can just wander around the rim of the lake along a 3.6km trail.

DON'T MISS

NARACOORTE CAVES NATIONAL PARK

About 10km southeast of Naracoorte is World Heritage–listed **Naracoorte Caves National Park** (☑08 8762 2340; www.environment.sa.gov.au/naracoorte; 89 Wonambi Rd, Naracoorte; tours from adult/child/family $9/5.50/25, Wonambi Fossil Centre $13/8/36; ☺9am-5pm). The discovery of an ancient fossilised marsupial in these limestone caves raised palaeontological eyebrows around the world, and featured in the BBC's David Attenborough series *Life on Earth*. The 26 limestone caves here, including **Alexandra Cave**, **Cathedral Cave** and **Victoria Fossil Cave**, have bizarre stalactite and stalagmite formations.

Prospective Bruce Waynes should check out the **Bat Cave**, from which thousands of endangered southern bentwing bats exit en masse at dusk during summer. You can see the **Wet Cave** by self-guided tour (adult/child/family $9/5.50/25), but the others require ranger-guided tours. The behind-the-scenes **World Heritage Tour** (per two people $280) gives you a scientific slant on the action. A new family-/wheelchair-friendly **walkway** is due to link the visitor centre with the main caves. There's also a self-registration **campground** (☑08 8760 1210; www.environment.sa.gov.au/naracoorte; Naracoorte Caves National Park, Wonambi Rd; unpowered/powered sites $29/31) here, just past the turn-off to the caves.

The visitor centre doubles as the **Wonambi Fossil Centre** – a re-creation of the rainforest that covered this area 200,000 years ago. Follow a ramp down past grunting, life-sized reconstructions of extinct animals, including a marsupial lion, a giant echidna, *Diprotodon australis* (koala meets grizzly bear), and *Megalania prisca* – 500kg of bad-ass goanna.

For more local info and tips on places to stay, contact **Naracoorte Visitor Information Centre** (☑1800 244 421, 08 8762 1399; www.naracoortelucindale.com; 36 MacDonnell St, Naracoorte; ☺9am-5pm Mon-Fri, 10am-4pm Sat & Sun) in Naracoorte.

Riddoch Art Gallery
GALLERY

(☑08 8723 9566; www.riddochartgallery.org.au; Main Corner, 1 Bay Rd; ☺10am-5pm Mon & Wed-Fri, to 3pm Sat & Sun) **FREE** If Mount Gambier's famed Blue Lake isn't blue, don't feel blue – cheer yourself up at one of Australia's best regional galleries. There are three galleries housing touring and permanent exhibitions, contemporary installations and community displays. In the same Main Corner complex are heritage exhibits and a cinema screening local history flicks (11am and 1pm).

Cave Gardens
CAVE

(☑1800 087 187; www.mountgambierpoint.com.au/attractions/cave-gardens; cnr Bay Rd & Watson Tce; ☺24hr) **FREE** A 50m-deep sinkhole right in the middle of town, with the odd suicidal shopping trolley at the bottom. You can walk down into it, and watch the nightly **Sound & Light Show** (from 8.30pm) telling local Aboriginal Dreaming stories.

🛏 Sleeping

Old Mount Gambier Gaol
HOSTEL $

(☑08 8723 0032; www.theoldmountgambiergaol.com.au; 25 Margaret St; dm $30, d with/without bathroom $100/90, f from $180; ☎) If you can forget that this place was a prison until 1995 (either that or embrace the fact),

these refurbished old buildings make for an atmospheric and comfortable stay. There are backpacker dorms available in old admin buildings, or you can up the spooky stakes and sleep in a former cell. There's a bar, too, in which to plot your next criminal exploit.

BIG4 Blue Lake Holiday Park
CARAVAN PARK $

(☑08 8725 9856; www.bluelakeholidaypark.com.au; 100 Bay Rd; unpowered/powered sites $35/41, cabins/units/bungalows from $99/129/162; ❄🛜☒) Adjacent to the Blue Lake, a golf course and walking and cycling tracks (but too far to walk into town), this amiable park has some natty grey-and-white cabins and well-weeded lawns. There are also spiffy contemporary, self-contained 'retreats' (from $199) that sleep four.

★Colhurst House
B&B $$

(☑08 8723 1309; www.colhursthouse.com.au; 3 Colhurst Pl; d from $170; ❄) Most locals don't know about Colhurst – it's up a laneway off a side street (Wyatt St), and you can't really see it from downtown Mount G. It's an 1878 mansion built by Welsh migrants, and manages to be old-fashioned without being overly twee. There's a gorgeous wraparound balcony upstairs with great views over the rooftops. Cooked breakfast. Nice.

Eating

★ **Metro Bakery & Cafe** CAFE **$$**
(☑ 08 8723 3179; www.metrobakeryandcafe.com.au; 13 Commercial St E; mains $8-34; ⊗ 8.30am-5pm Mon-Wed, to late Thu-Sat, 9am-3pm Sun) Ask a local where they go for coffee: chances are they'll say, 'the Metro, you fool!' On the main drag, it's an efficient cafe with natty black-and-white decor, serving omelettes, salads, sandwiches, pastries and meatier mains (try the twice-cooked lamb rump salad). There's a wine bar here too, brimming with Coonawarra cabernets. Book for dinner.

Macs Hotel PUB FOOD **$$**
(☑ 08 8725 2402; www.themacshotel.com.au; 21 Bay Rd; mains $17-35; ⊗ noon-2.30pm & 5.30-9pm) Char-grilled marinated calamari; pork belly with cauliflower puree and star anise glaze… Not your standard pub grub, but the old Macs is far from a standard pub. A super renovation has elevated it above the fray, attracting Mount Gambier's brightest young things by the dozen. Join them for a drink in the 'cider garden' before dinner.

ℹ Information

Mount Gambier Visitor Information Centre
(☑ 1800 087 187, 08 8724 9750; www.mountgambiertourism.com.au; 35 Jubilee Hwy E; ⊗ 9am-5pm Mon-Fri, 10am-4pm Sat & Sun) Has details on local sights, activities, transport and accommodation, plus *Heritage Walk* and *Historic Hotels* pamphlets and a town history movie. The Lady Nelson Discovery Centre (☑ 1800 087 187; www.mountgambier.sa.gov.au; Mount Gambier Visitor Information Centre, 35 Jubilee Hwy E; ⊗ as above) is here too. Bike hire available.

Penola & the Coonawarra Wine Region

A rural town on the way up, Penola is the kind of place where you walk down the main street and three people say 'Hello!' to you before you reach the pub. The town is famous for two things: first, for its association with the Sisters of St Joseph of the Sacred Heart, cofounded in 1867 by Australia's first saint, Mary MacKillop; and second, for being smack-bang in the middle of the Coonawarra wine region (killer cabernets).

◉ Sights

Mary MacKillop Interpretive Centre MUSEUM
(☑ 08 8737 2092; www.mackilloppenola.org.au; cnr Portland St & Petticoat Lane, Penola; adult/child $5/free; ⊗ 10am-4pm) The centre occupies a jaunty building with a gregarious entrance pergola (perhaps not as modest as St Mary might've liked!) There's oodles on Australia's first saint here, plus the Woods MacKillop Schoolhouse, the first school in Australia for children from lower socioeconomic backgrounds.

🛏 Sleeping

Penola Backpackers HOSTEL **$**
(☑ 08 8736 6170, 0428 866 700; www.penolabackpackers.com.au; 59 Church St, Penola; dm/s/d/f from $40/50/140/160; ⊛) In a Spanish Mission–style house on the main street, this five-bedroom backpackers has found its niche in the Limestone Coast accommodation scene. There's a clean kitchen, roses and daffodils out the front and a BBQ terrace out the back. Air-con in some rooms.

Alexander Cameron Suites MOTEL **$$**
(☑ 1800 217 011, 08 8737 2200; www.alexandercameronsuites.com.au; 23 Church St, Penola; s/d/tw/f from $145/145/160/190; ⊛⊛) Looking much less bleak now that some trees have matured around it, this newish motel on the Mount Gambier side of town offers stylish rooms and rural Australian architectural stylings. It's named after Penola's founder, a wiry Scottish pastoralist: check out his statue next to the pub. Three-bedroom house also available.

🍴 Eating

★ **Pipers of Penola** MODERN AUSTRALIAN **$$$**
(☑ 08 8737 3999; www.pipersofpenola.com.au; 58 Riddoch St, Penola; mains $35-40; ⊗ 6-9pm Tue-Sat) An intimate dining room tastefully constructed inside a 1908 Methodist church, with friendly staff and seasonal fare. The menu is studded with ingredients like truffled parsnip, mustard fruit and *labneh* (Lebanese yoghurt cheese) – serious gourmet indicators! The prices are lofty, but so is the quality. Superb wine list with lots of locals.

ℹ Information

Penola Visitor Information Centre (☑ 1300 045 373, 08 8737 2855; www.wattlerange.sa.gov.au/tourism; 27 Arthur St, Penola; ⊗ 9am-5pm Mon-Fri, 10am-4pm Sat & Sun) Services the Coonawarra region, with info about local cycling routes and winery tours. The John Riddoch Centre (☑ 08 8737 2855; www.wattlerange.sa.gov.au/tourism; 27 Arthur St, Penola; ⊗ as above) is also here. Pick up the *Walk With History* brochures, and the *Coonawarra Wineries Walking Trail* brochure detailing an easy 5km walk past five wineries.

Western South Australia

Why Go?

Within striking range of Adelaide, the Yorke Peninsula bills itself as 'Agriculturally Rich – Naturally Beautiful'. Indeed, the Yorke Peninsula is thin of urban hubbub, but it does exude agrarian beauty: deep azure summer skies and yellow barley fields spread across hazy rolling hills. The coastline here is gorgeous, with surf breaks, roaming emus and ospreys, and little beach towns, most of which have a pub and a fishing jetty.

Further west on the gargantuan Eyre Peninsula, wheat fields extend from horizon to horizon, while tuna, whiting and oysters abound offshore. Victoria's scenic Great Ocean Road gets all the press, but the Eyre Peninsula's west coast is just as spectacular, with craggy limestone cliffs, caves, wild surf and deep-orange-sand beaches. Towns here range from raggedy frontier outposts (Ceduna) to downright civilised centres (Port Lincoln).

Best Places to Eat

➡ Cornish Kitchen (p122)
➡ Ceduna Oyster Bar (p128)
➡ Fresh Fish Place (p126)
➡ Mocean

Best Places to Sleep

➡ Dawes Point Cottage (p127)
➡ Port Lincoln YHA (p126)
➡ Tanonga (p126)
➡ Yondah Beach House (p124)

When to Go
Ceduna

Dec–Feb Tourist season in full swing and it's warm enough to swim.

Mar–May Warm autumn days and cool nights: perfect beach, camping and fishing weather.

Sep–Nov The wheat heads are bobbing and the roads are empty.

YORKE PENINSULA

For history buffs, the northwestern end of boot-shaped 'Yorkes' – just under two hours northwest of Adelaide – has a trio of towns called the Copper Triangle: Moonta (the mine), Wallaroo (the smelter) and Kadina (the service town). Settled by Cornish miners, this area drove the regional economy following a copper boom in the early 1860s. In the big-sky peninsula country to the east and south, things are much more agricultural and laid-back, with sleepy holiday towns, isolated Innes National Park, remote surf breaks and empty coastline.

☞ Tours

Heading Bush OUTDOORS
(☑08 8356 5501; www.headingbush.com; 3-day tours from $695) ✎ Explore Yorkes – wildlife, cliffs, beaches, Aboriginal culture and even a winery – on a three-day tour ex-Adelaide. Price includes dorm accommodation; single, double or twin is available at extra cost.

❶ Information

Copper Coast Visitor Information Centre
(☑1800 654 991, 08 8821 2333; www. yorkepeninsula.com.au; 50 Mines Rd; ⊙9am-5pm Mon-Fri, 10am-4pm Sat & Sun) Yorke Peninsula's main visitor info centre, stocked to the rafters with brochures: look for the *Walk the Yorke* pamphlet detailing a dozen interesting trails, short and long, all around the peninsula; and the *Kadina Walking Trail* map. The **Farm Shed Museum** (☑08 8821 2333; www. farmshed.net.au; Copper Coast Visitor Information Centre, 50 Mines Rd; adult/child/family $10/5/23, railway per ride $2; ⊙9am-5pm Mon-Fri, 10am-4pm Sat & Sun, railway 1st & 3rd Sun of the month) is here too.

Yorke Peninsula Visitor Information Centre (☑08 8853 2600, 1800 202 445; www. visityorkepeninsula.com.au; 29 Main St, Minlaton; ⊙9am-5pm Mon-Fri) In agricultural Minlaton, right in the middle of the southern Yorke Peninsula. It's a good source of info on the lower half of the peninsula (including shipwrecks!)

❶ Getting There & Away

Yorke Peninsula Coaches (☑08 8821 2755; www.ypcoaches.com.au) Daily buses from Adelaide to Kadina ($40, 2¼ hours), Wallaroo ($40, 2½ hours) and Moonta ($40, three hours), with another route running down the peninsula's east coast daily except Tuesday and Thursday, stopping at Port Vincent ($52, 3¼ hours), Stansbury ($52, 3½ hours) and Edithburgh ($54, four hours).

West Coast

Fronting Spencer Gulf, the Yorke Peninsula's west coast has a string of shallow swimming beaches, plus the 'Copper Triangle' historic mining towns of Kadina, Wallaroo and Moonta, all a short drive from each other. Kernewek Lowender (www.kernewek. org; ⊙May), aka the Copper Coast Cornish Festival, happens around here in May of odd-numbered years. Further south, Point Turton is a magical little spot with a beaut caravan park and hillside tavern.

Wallaroo

POP 3230
Still a major wheat port and fishing town, Wallaroo is on the way up: there's a huge new subdivision north of town, a new shopping complex inserted in the middle of the old town, and the shiny new Copper Cove Marina is full of expensive boats. There are plenty of pubs here, and the pubs are full of folks.

That said, the old town area retains a romantically weathered 'seen-better-days' vibe: wander around the compact little streets and old cottages in the shadows of the huge grain silos and soak up the atmosphere (the place to pen your next novel?).

◎ Sights

Wallaroo Heritage & Nautical Museum MUSEUM
(☑08 8823 3015; www.nationaltrust.org.au; cnr Jetty Rd & Emu St; adult/child $6/3; ⊙10am-4pm) Down by the water, the stoic 1865 post office now houses the Wallaroo Heritage & Nautical Museum. There are several of these little National Trust museums around Yorkes: in Port Victoria, in Ardrossan, in Milaton, in Edithburgh… But this is the best of them, with tales of square-rigged English ships and George the pickled giant squid.

☷ Sleeping & Eating

Sonbern Lodge Motel HOTEL, MOTEL $
(☑08 8823 2291; www.sonbernlodgemotel.com. au; 18 John Tce; d/f from $85/100; ✳) The old Sonbern – a 100-year-old grand temperance hotel – is looking a bit weather-beaten these days, but it remains an old-fashioned charmer, right down to the old wooden balcony and antique wind-up phone. There are basic pub-style rooms in the main building (with bathrooms), and newish motel units out the back. Breakfast available.

Coopers Alehouse
PUB FOOD $$

(☑08 8823 2488; www.wallaroomarinahotel.com; 11 Heritage Dr; mains $15-39; ☉noon-2.30pm & 6-8.30pm) Head downstairs at the Wallaroo Marina Apartments (☑08 8823 4068; www. wallarooapartments.com.au; 11 Heritage Dr; d/ apt from $144/184; ❋☎) and you'll find cold Coopers ales, bistro meals (mixed grills, Spencer Gulf prawns and flathead), seductive marina views and regular live bands. Glowing in the corner, the pizza oven looks like Luke Skywalker's uncle's house in *Star Wars*. Try the 'Colossus' beef burger.

Moonta

POP 2670

In the late 19th century, the Moonta copper mine was the richest in Australia. These days the town, which calls itself 'Australia's Little Cornwall', maintains a faded glory and a couple of decent pubs.

◉ Sights

Moonta Mines Museum
MUSEUM

(☑08 8825 1891; www.moontatourism.org.au; Verran Tce; adult/child $8/4; ☉1-4pm, from 11am during school holidays) This impressive 1878 stone edifice was once the Moonta Mines Model School and had 1100 students. These days it's the centrepiece of the sprawling Moonta Heritage Site, and captures mining life – at work and at home – in intimately preserved detail. A little tourist train chugs out of the museum car park at 2pm on Wednesday, and 1pm, 2pm and 3pm on weekends (adult/child $8/4; daily during school holidays).

⌨ Sleeping & Eating

Cottage by Cornwall
B&B $$

(☑0438 313 952; www.cottagebycornwall.com.au; 24 Ryan St; d from $160, extra adult/child $20/free; ❋) The classiest accommodation in Moonta by a country mile, this tizzied-up 1863 cottage has three bedrooms (sleeping six), plus fancy bedding, mod furnishings and a claw-foot bath. It's just a short stroll to the pub and the Cornish Kitchen bakery. Two-night minimum stay. Cooked and continental provisions supplied.

Cornish Kitchen
BAKERY $

(☑08 8825 3030; 10-12 Ellen St; items $4-10; ☉9am-3pm Mon-Fri, to 2pm Sat) After a dirty day digging down the mine, swing your pick into the Cornish Kitchen for the ultimate Cornish pastie (the chunky steak and onion pies are pretty great too).

❶ Information

Moonta Visitor Information Centre (☑08 8825 1891; www.moontatourism.org.au; Old Railway Station, Blanche Tce; ☉9am-5pm) Stocks a smattering of history pamphlets including the *Moonta Walking Trail* map, and details on the Moonta Heritage Site 1.5km east of town.

East Coast

About 24km south of Ardrossan is magical little Black Point, a holiday hot spot with a long row of shacks built right on the dunes above a protected, north-facing beach (perfect if you've got kids).

Further south, unpretentious Port Vincent (population 480) is the happening-est town on the east coast, with lots of accommodation, a waterfront pub and a busy marina, from where yachts dart across to Adelaide. Continuing south, Stansbury (population 550; www.stansburysa.com) has a couple of motels and a beaut waterside pub.

Further south again, Edithburgh (population 400) has a free tidal swimming pool in a small cove. From the cliff tops here, views extend offshore to sandy Troubridge Island Conservation Park (☑08 8854 3200; www. environment.sa.gov.au/parks), home to much bird life including penguins, cormorants and terns. You can stay the night here at the old lighthouse (☑08 8852 6290; www. environment.sa.gov.au/parks; per adult/child incl transfers $120/60, min charge $480). The island is steadily eroding – what the sea wants, the sea will have…

South Coast & Innes National Park

At Innes National Park (☑08 8854 3200; www.environment.sa.gov.au/parks; via Stenhouse Bay Rd, Stenhouse Bay; per vehicle $10; ☉24hr) sheer cliffs plunge into indigo waters and rocky offshore islands hide small coves and sandy beaches. Marion Bay (www. marionbay.com.au), just outside the park, and Stenhouse Bay and Pondalowie Bay, both within the park, are the main local settlements. Pondalowie Bay has a bobbing lobster-fishing fleet and a gnarly surf beach. The rusty ribs of the 711-tonne steel barque *Ethel*, which foundered in 1904, arc forlornly from the sands just south of here.

Follow the sign past the Cape Spencer turn-off to the ghost-town ruins of Inneston, a mining community abandoned in 1930.

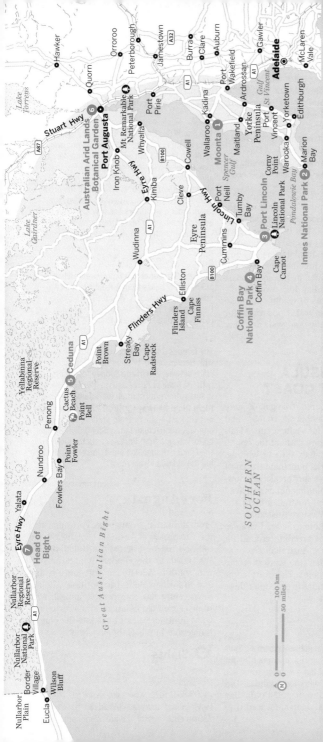

Western South Australia Highlights

1 Moonta (p122) Digging into Cornish copper-mining history.

2 Innes National Park (p122) Discovering industrial remnants, sparkling waters and remote surf breaks.

3 Port Lincoln seafood (p126) Seeing some seafood (or better still, eating it) in the tuna capital of Australia.

4 Coffin Bay National Park (p127) Exploring bays, dunes and remote walking tracks.

5 Ceduna (p128) Slurping down a dozen briny oysters au naturel in a roadside oyster shack.

6 Australian Arid Lands Botanic Garden (p124) Getting a feel for Australia's desert heart in Port Augusta

(here's your chance to see a Sturt's Desert Pea!)

7 Head of Bight (p128) Scanning the sea for migrating southern right whales.

🛏 Sleeping

⭐ Marion Bay Motel   MOTEL $$

(📞08 8854 4044; www.marionbaymotel.com.
au; Jetty Rd, Marion Bay; s/d/tr $120/150/170;
❄🛜) A highlight of tiny Marion Bay is this
wing of five spiffy motel rooms (white walls,
new TVs, nice linen) – a welcome surprise
if you've been camping or hanging out in
sandy-floor beach shacks and are in need of
a little sophistication. The Marion Bay tavern (📞08 8854 4141; www.marionbaytavern.com.
au; mains $16-38; ⊙bar 11am-late, meals noon-
2pm & 6-8pm) is just next door.

⭐ Yondah Beach House   RENTAL HOUSE $$$

(📞0417 829 010; www.yondah.com.au; off South
Coast Rd, Point Yorke; 1/2/3 bedrooms from
$300/380/440; ❄🛜🐾) 🌱 One of the stars of
the SA tourism scene, Yondah is a gorgeous,
architect-designed, three-bedroom beach
house, way over yonder in the south-coast
dunes east of Marion Bay. It's a wonderfully
isolated spot, with lots of wildlife and luxe
privacy by the bucketload. Good value for
a group or a big family. And you can bring
your dog!

EYRE PENINSULA & THE WEST COAST

The vast, straw-coloured triangle of Eyre
Peninsula is Australia's big-sky country, and
is the promised land for seafood fans. Meals
out here rarely transpire without the option
of trying the local oysters, tuna or whiting.
Sublime national parks punctuate the coast
along with world-class surf breaks and low-
key holiday towns, thinning out as you head
west towards the Great Australian Bight, the
Nullarbor Plain and Western Australia.

The peninsula's photogenic wild western
flank is an important breeding ground for
southern right whales, Australian sea lions
and great white sharks (the scariest scenes
in *Jaws* were shot here). There are some
memorable opportunities to encounter these
submariners along the way.

👉 Tours

Goin' Off Safaris   TOURS

(📞0428 877 488; www.goinoffsafaris.com.au; tours
from $185) Check the big-ticket items off your
Eyre Peninsula 'to-do' list – sharks, tuna, sea
lions and seafood – with local guides. Day
trips around Port Lincoln and Coffin Bay,
plus overnight jaunts, seafood-focused trips
and fishing expeditions.

ℹ Getting There & Away

AIR

Regional Express (Rex; www.regionalexpress.
com.au) operates daily flights from Adelaide to
Whyalla (one way from $128), Port Lincoln (from
$132) and Ceduna (from $189).

BOAT

The handy **SeaSA** (📞08 8823 0777; www.sea
sa.com.au; 1 Heritage Dr, Wallaroo; one-way per
adult/child/car from $35/10/140) car ferry run-
ning between Wallaroo on the Yorke Peninsula
and Lucky Bay near Cowell on the Eyre Peninsula
shaves 350km and several hours off the drive
from Adelaide via Port Augusta. The voyage
takes around two hours one way. Services have
been sporadic over recent years: book in advance to guarantee your passage, and reconfirm
a few days prior.

BUS

Premier Stateliner (www.premierstateliner.com.
au) has daily buses from Adelaide to Port Augusta ($63, 4¼ hours), Whyalla ($70, 5½ hours),
Port Lincoln ($126, 9¾ hours), Streaky Bay
($132, 10 hours) and Ceduna ($147, 11¼ hours).

TRAIN

The famous *Ghan* train connects Adelaide
with Darwin via Port Augusta; the *Indian Pacific* (between Perth and Sydney) connects
with the *Ghan* at Port Augusta. See www.
greatsouthernrail.com.au for details.

Pichi Richi Railway (📞1800 777 245; www.prr.
org.au; Port Augusta Train Station, Stirling Rd;
one-way adult/child/family $54/20/128) runs
historic trains from Port Augusta to Quorn in
the Flinders Ranges on most Saturdays, following the old *Ghan* train route.

Port Augusta

POP 13,900

From utilitarian, frontier-like Port Augusta –
the 'Crossroads of Australia' – highways and
railways roll west across the Nullarbor into
WA, north to the Flinders Ranges or Darwin, south to Adelaide or Port Lincoln, and
east to Sydney. Not a bad position! The old
town centre has considerable appeal, with
some elegant old buildings and a revitalised
waterfront: locals cast lines into the blue as
Indigenous kids backflip off jetties.

👁 Sights

Australian Arid Lands Botanic Garden   GARDENS

(📞08 8641 9116; www.aalbg.sa.gov.au; 144 Stuart
Hwy; guided tours adult/child $8/5; ⊙gardens
7.30am-dusk, visitor centre 9am-5pm Mon-Fri,

10am-4pm Sat & Sun) **FREE** Just north of town, the excellent (and free!) botanic garden has 250 hectares of sandhills, clay flats and desert fauna and flora (ever seen a Sturt's Desert Pea?). Explore on your own, or take a guided tour (10am Monday to Friday). There's a cafe here too.

Sleeping & Eating

Oasis Apartments   APARTMENT $$
(✐08 8648 9000; www.majestichotels.com.au; Marryatt St; d/f $160/260; ❄️🛜🅿️) Catering largely to conventioneers, this group of 75 luxury units (from studios to two-bedroom) with jaunty designs is right by the water. All rooms have washing machines, dryers, TVs, fridges, microwaves and flashy interior design. Fortress-like security might make you feel like you're in some sort of elitist compound…which you possibly are.

⭐**Archers' Table**   CAFE $
(✐08 7231 5657; www.archerstable.com.au; 11b Loudon Rd; mains $9-12; ⊙8am-4pm Mon-Fri, to 3pm Sat, to 2pm Sun) Beneath an attractive vine-hung awning across the gulf from downtown PA, Archers is an urbane cafe with small-town prices, serving interesting cafe fare (beef, pumpkin and spinach lasagne; spicy lentil and tomato soup; seafood salad with walnuts, feta and lemon tahini dressing). Great coffee, funky mural, open seven days. We have a winner!

ⓘ Information

Port Augusta Visitor Information Centre
(✐08 8641 9193, 1800 633 060; www.portaugusta.org.au; Wadlata Outback Centre, 41 Flinders Tce; ⊙9am-5.30pm Mon-Fri, 10am-4pm Sat & Sun) This is the major information outlet for the Eyre Peninsula, Flinders Ranges and outback. It's part of the **Wadlata Outback Centre** (✐08 8641 9193, 1800 633 060; www.wadlata.sa.gov.au; adult/child/family $21/12/46; ⊙9am-5.30pm Mon-Fri, 10am-4pm Sat & Sun).

Port Lincoln

POP 16,150

Prosperous Port Lincoln, the 'Tuna Capital of the World', overlooks broad Boston Bay on the southern end of Eyre Peninsula. It's a raffish fishing town a long way from anywhere, but the vibe here is energetic (dare we say progressive!)

If not for a lack of fresh water, Port Lincoln might have become the South Australian capital. These days it's salt water (and the tuna therein) that keeps the town ticking. The grassy foreshore is a busy promenade, and there are some good pubs, eateries and aquatic activities here to keep you out of trouble.

◎ Sights

Lincoln National Park   NATIONAL PARK
(✐08 8688 3111; www.environment.sa.gov.au/parks; via Proper Bay Rd; per vehicle $11; ⊙24hr) Lincoln National Park is 13km south of Port Lincoln. You'll find roaming emus, roos and brush-tailed bettongs, safe swimming coves, vast dunes and pounding surf beaches. Entry is via self-registration on the way in. The Port Lincoln Visitor Information Centre (p126) can advise on bush camping (per vehicle $12) and cottage accommodation (✐0419 302 300; www.visitportlincolnaccommodation.net.au/donington-cottage; Lincoln National Park; per night $100) within the park, including camping grounds at Fisherman's Point, Memory Cove, September Beach and Surfleet Cove.

⛵ Tours

Tasting Eyre   TOURS
(✐08 8687 0455; www.tastingeyre.com.au; adult/child $99/79) Scenery, wildlife and fishing are the names of the games on this well-planned day tour around Port Lincoln, including a walk in Lincoln National Park, a visit to Whalers Way and seafood tasting at the Fresh Fish Place.

Adventure Bay Charters   BOATING
(✐08 8682 2979; www.adventurebaycharters.com.au; 2 South Quay Blvd) Carbon-neutral Adventure Bay Charters takes you swimming with sea lions (adult/child $205/145) and cage diving with great white sharks (observer $395/285 – add $125 if you want to actually get in the water, or view through a submerged 'aqua sub'). Multiday ocean safaris also available. Note that research suggests that human interaction with sea mammals potentially alters their behavioural and breeding patterns.

☆☆ Festivals & Events

Tunarama Festival   CULTURAL
(www.tunarama.net; ⊙Jan) The annual Tunarama Festival on the Australia Day weekend in January celebrates every finny facet of the tuna-fishing industry (including the ethically questionable 'tuna toss').

Eyre Peninsula & Yorke Peninsula

🛏 Sleeping

⭐ Port Lincoln YHA   HOSTEL $

(☑ 08 8682 3605; www.yha.com.au; 26 London St; dm $24-35, tw/d/f from $80/100/125; ✳@🛜) This impressive 84-bed hostel occupies a former squash court complex. Thoughtful bonuses include chunky sprung mattresses, reading lights, a cafe/bar and power outlets in lockers. Outrageously clean, and with 300 movies for a rainy day (including *Jaws*). Staff can help with activities bookings too.

⭐ Tanonga   B&B $$$

(☑ 0427 277 417; www.tanonga.com.au; Pope Dr, Charlton Gully; d incl breakfast from $340; ✳) ✈ Two plush, solar-powered, architect-designed ecolodges, standing in stark-white modernist isolation in the hills behind Port Lincoln. They're both super-private and surrounded by native bush, bird life and walking trails. Roll into town for dinner, or order a DIY pack of local produce. Truly unique and absolutely glorious.

🍴 Eating

⭐ Fresh Fish Place   SEAFOOD $

(☑ 08 8682 2166; www.portlincolnseafood.com.au; 20 Proper Bay Rd; meals $9-20; ⊙8.30am-6pm Mon-Fri, to 2pm Sat) Check the 'fish of the day' on the blackboard out the front of this fabulous seafood shack. Inside you can buy fresh local seafood straight off the boats (King George whiting, tuna, kingfish, flathead, squid etc), plus Coffin Bay oysters for $12 a dozen and superb fish and chips. Not to be missed! Seafood tasting tours and cooking classes also available.

ℹ Information

Port Lincoln Visitor Information Centre
(☑1300 788 378, 08 8683 3544; www. visitportlincoln.net; 3 Adelaide Pl; ⊙9am-5pm Mon-Fri, 10am-4pm Sat & Sun) This

mega-helpful place books accommodation, has national-parks information and passes, and stocks the *Port Lincoln & District Cycling Guide*, and the *Parnkalla Walking Trail* map, tracing a course around the Port Lincoln coastline.

Coffin Bay

POP 650

Oyster lovers rejoice! Deathly sounding Coffin Bay (named in 1802 by English explorer Matthew Flinders after his buddy Sir Isaac Coffin) is a snoozy fishing village basking languidly in the warm sun...until a 4000-strong holiday horde arrives every January. Slippery, salty oysters from the nearby beds are exported worldwide – superb!

◉ Sights

Coffin Bay National Park   NATIONAL PARK
(☑ 08 8688 3111; www.environment.sa.gov.au/parks; via Coffin Bay Rd; per vehicle $10; ⊘ 24hr) Along the ocean side of Coffin Bay is wild, coastal Coffin Bay National Park, overrun with roos, emus and fat goannas. Access for conventional vehicles is limited: you can get to picturesque Point Avoid (coastal lookouts, rocky cliffs, good surf and whales passing between May and October) and Yangie Bay (arid-looking rocky landscapes and walking trails), but otherwise you'll need a 4WD. There are some isolated camp sites within the park (per vehicle $12), generally with dirt-road access.

⬛ Sleeping & Eating

★ **Dawes Point Cottage**   RENTAL HOUSE **$$**
(☑ 0427 844 568; www.coffinbayholidayrentals.com.au/properties/dawes-point; 5 Heron Ct; per night from $180; ❄) This old-fashioned fishing shack (Aussie author Tim Winton would call it 'fish deco') was won by the present owners in a card game! Now a million-dollar property, it maintains its modesty despite sitting right on the water. There are three bedrooms and a beaut little deck above the gin-clear bay. Sleeps six.

1802 Oyster Bar & Bistro   BISTRO **$$**
(☑ 08 8685 4626; www.1802oysterbar.com.au; 61 Esplanade; mains $18-33; ⊘ noon-2.30pm Tue-Sun, 6-8.30pm Thu-Sat) This snappy-looking place on the way into town, with its broad deck and rammed-earth walls, looks out across the boat-filled harbour. Order a bluefin tuna steak, some lamb cutlets with parsnip *skordalia,* or a bowl of seafood chowder to go with your crafty 1802 Cutters Dredge

Lager (on tap). Pizzas and (of course) oysters also available.

Streaky Bay & Around

POP 1630

This endearing little seasider (actually on Blanche Port) takes its name from the streaks of seaweed Matt Flinders spied in the bay as he sailed by. Visible at low tide, the seagrass attracts ocean critters and the bigger critters that eat them – first-class fishing.

The town itself has a terrific pub, plenty of accommodation and a couple of good eateries – a lovely spot to dream away a day or three.

◉ Sights

Murphy's Haystacks   LANDMARK
(www.nullarbornet.com.au/themes/murphyshaystacks.html; off Flinders Hwy, Point Labbatt; per person/family $2/5; ⊘ daylight hours) A few kilometres down the Point Labatt road are the globular Murphy's Haystacks, an improbable congregation of 'inselbergs' – colourful, weather-sculpted granite outcrops, which are an estimated 1500 million years old (not much chance of them eroding while you prep your camera – take your time).

⬛ Sleeping & Eating

Streaky Bay Motel & Villas   MOTEL **$$**
(☑ 08 8626 1126; www.streakybaymotelandvillas.com.au; 11-13 Alfred Tce; motel s/d/f from $110/130/160, villas $170-260; ❄ 🛜 🏊) A tidy row of bricky, older-style motel units (with a facelift), plus an ever-expanding complex of family-size villas that are much more 'now' (spiky pot plants, mushroom-hued render, lime-coloured outdoor furniture). Good off-season rates and three-bedroom houses also available. There's a pool, too, if you don't fancy the shark-proof swimming enclosure down at the jetty.

Bay Funktion   CAFE **$**
(☑ 0428 861 242; www.bayfunktion.com.au; cnr Wells St & Bay Rd; mains $7-12; ⊘ 8am-5pm Mon-Fri, to 2pm Sat) In a lovely old brick-and-stone shopfront on the main street, funky Bay Funktion is part cafe, part gift shop, part wedding planner (hence the slightly odd name). But as a cafe, it's great! Baguettes, pizzas, focaccias, breakfast wraps, slabs of cake and killer coffee, often served from the hip coffee van parked out the front. Also open Sundays during summer.

GULLIVER'S TRAVELS IN CEDUNA?

According to map coordinates in Jonathan Swift's famous 1726 novel *Gulliver's Travels*, the islands of St Peter and St Francis, a few kilometres off the coast of Ceduna in the Nuyts Archipelago, are where the tiny folk of Lilliput reside. While we can neither confirm nor deny this possibility, it's likely Swift drew inspiration from the adventures of the 158 Dutch sailors aboard the *Gulden Zeepaert*, which sailed through these waters in 1627.

ℹ Information

Streaky Bay Visitor Information Centre (✆08 8626 7033; www.streakybay.com.au; 21 Bay Rd; ◷9am-12.30pm & 1.30-5pm Mon-Fri) For the local low-down, swing by the visitor info centre.

Ceduna

POP 2290

Despite the locals' best intentions, Ceduna remains a raggedy fishing town that just can't shake its tag as a pit stop en route to WA (there are *five* caravan parks here). But the local oysters love it! And if you're heading west in whale season (May to October), Ceduna is the place for updates on sightings.

◉ Sights

Thevenard   AREA
(Thevenard Rd; 24hr) For a dose of weatherbeaten atmospheria, take a drive out to Thevenard, Ceduna's photogenic port suburb on the peninsula south of town. Boarded-up shops, a pub with barred windows, dusty old iron-clad shacks…If you're a painter or writer, this is fertile fuel for the imagination!

★✰ Festivals & Events

Oysterfest   FOOD
(www.ceduna.sa.gov.au/oysterfest; ◷Sep/Oct) If you're passing through Ceduna in late Sep/ early Oct, check out Oysterfest, the undisputed king of Australian oyster parties.

🛏 Sleeping & Eating

Ceduna Foreshore Hotel/Motel   MOTEL $$
(✆08 8625 2008; www.cedunahotel.com.au; 32 O'Loughlin Tce; d $150-195; ❋🐾) Clad in aquamarine tiles, this is the most luxurious option in town, with water views and a bistro (mains $18 to $38, serving 6.30am to 9am,

noon to 2pm and 6pm to 8.30pm) focused on west-coast seafood. The view from the outdoor terrace extends through Norfolk Island pines and out across the bay.

★**Ceduna Oyster Bar**   SEAFOOD $$
(✆08 8626 9086; www.facebook.com/ oysterbarceduna; Eyre Hwy; 12 oysters $12, meals $14-22; ◷10am-7.30pm) Pick up a box of freshly shucked molluscs and head for the foreshore, or sit up on the rooftop here under an umbrella and watch the road trains rumble in from WA. Fresh as can be.

ℹ Information

Ceduna Visitor Information Centre (✆1800 639 413, 08 8625 2780; www.cedunatourism. com.au; 58 Poynton St; ◷9am-5.30pm Mon-Fri, to 4pm Sat & Sun) The Ceduna Visitor Information Centre can help with local info and current whale-sighting stats.

Ceduna to the Western Australia Border

It's 480km from Ceduna to the WA border. Along this stretch you can get a bed and a beer at Penong (72km from Ceduna), Fowlers Bay (141km), Nundroo (151km), the Nullarbor Roadhouse (295km) near Head of Bight, and at Border Village on the border itself.

Wheat and sheep paddocks line the road to Nundroo, after which you're in mallee scrub for another 100km. Around 20km later, the trees thin to low bluebush as you enter the true Nullarbor (Latin for 'no trees'). Road trains, caravans and cyclists of questionable sanity are your only companions as you put your foot down and career towards the setting sun.

◉ Sights & Activities

Head of Bight   LANDMARK
(✆08 8625 6201; www.headofbight.com.au; off Eyre Hwy; adult/child/family Jun-Oct $15/6/35, Nov-May $7/5/14; ◷8am-5pm Jun-Oct, 8.30am-4pm Nov-May) The viewing platforms and boardwalks at Head of Bight overlook a major southern-right-whale breeding ground. Whales migrate here from Antarctica, and you can see them cavorting from May to October. The breeding area is protected by the **Great Australian Bight Commonwealth Marine Reserve** (✆1800 069 352; www.environment.gov. au), the world's second-largest marine park after the Great Barrier Reef. The info centre here has snacks.

Outback South Australia

Best Places to Eat

➡ Woolshed Restaurant (p136)

➡ Quorn Cafe (p134)

➡ Wilpena Pound Resort (p136)

➡ Outback Bar & Grill (p140)

Best Places to Sleep

➡ Rawnsley Park Station (p136)

➡ Quorn Caravan Park (p134)

➡ North Star Hotel (p133)

➡ Down to Erth B&B (p140)

➡ Marree Hotel (p141)

Why Go?

If you want to experience Australia's astoundingly large outback, wheeling into the Flinders Ranges in South Australia is a great way to start.

Approaching the Flinders Ranges from the south, the wheat fields and wineries of SA's midnorth district give way to arid cattle stations beneath ochre-coloured peaks. This is ancient country, imbued with the Dreaming stories of the Adnyamathanha people. Emus wander across roads; yellow-footed rock wallabies bound from boulder to boulder.

Trucking further north on the Stuart Hwy, the *real* desert shows its face: a sun-ravaged visage of red sand, spinifex and bullet-straight ribbons of tarmac, running for hundreds of kilometres between quirky outposts of civilisation like Coober Pedy, Woomera and Marree. And if the highway is still too 'city' for your tastes, the legendary Oodnadatta, Birdsville and Strzelecki Tracks stir up plenty of desert dirt.

When to Go
Quorn

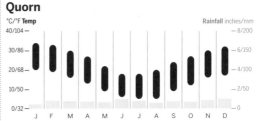

Apr–May Sunbaked desert colours shimmer as things cool at the end of autumn.

Jun–Aug Winter is peak season here: mild temperatures, clear skies.

Sep–Oct Native wildflowers bloom in the Flinders. Last chance to hit the outback before 35-degree days.

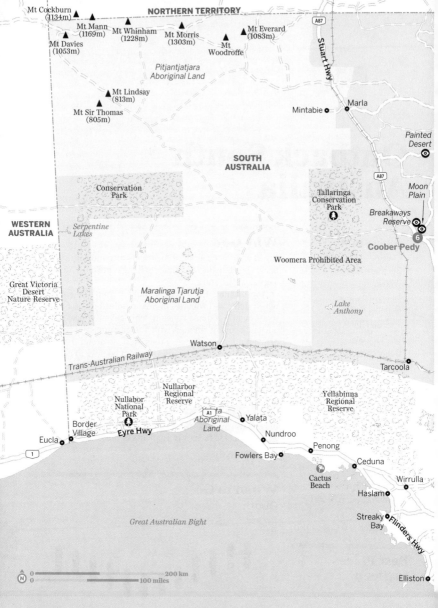

Outback South Australia Highlights

1 **Mt Remarkable National Park** (p133) Exploring gorgeous gorges and scenic slopes via meandering tracks.

2 **Melrose** (p133) Cycling single-track trails then sinking a cold beer at the North Star Hotel.

3 **Quorn** (p134) Checking out the Wild West vibes.

4 **Ikara (Wilpena Pound)** (p135) Hiking for knock-out views up at the Wangarra Lookout.

QUEENSLAND

Birdsville

Simpson
Desert

Witjira
National
Park

Simpson
Desert
Conservation
Park

Simpson
Desert
Regional
Reserve

Oodnadatta

Malkumba-
Coongie Lakes
National Park

Innamincka
Regional
Reserve

Innamincka

Moomba

Lake
Eyre
North

Lake Eyre
National Park

Strzelecki
Regional
Reserve

**Oodnadatta
Track** ⑤

William
Creek

Lake
Gregory

Lake
Blanche

Coward
Springs

Lake Eyre
South

Marree

Lake
Callabonna

Mt
Hopeless

B83

Lyndhurst

Arkaroola

Roxby
Downs

Copley

Vulkathunha-Gammon Ranges
National Park

Lake
Labyrinth

Lake
Torrens

Leigh
Creek

Glendambo

NEW
SOUTH
WALES

Mt Hack
(1086m)

Flinders Ranges

Lake
Frome

Woomera ⑦

Lake Torrens
National
Park

Pimba

Lake Gairdner
National Park

Island
Lagoon

B83

Flinders Ranges
National Park

Lake
Everard

Lake
Gairdner

A87

Lake
Acraman

Lake
Macfarlane

④ **Ikara
(Wilpena Pound)**

Hawker

Mundi
Mundi
Plain

Broken
Hill

Quorn

③

Barrier Hwy

Port Augusta

**Mt Remarkable
National Park**

A32

Iron Knob

① ②

Orroroo

Melrose

Wudinna

Peterborough

Danggali
Conservation
Park

A1

Kimba

Whyalla

Port
Pirie

Laura

Jamestown

Eyre
Peninsula

Lock

Cleve

Cowell

Crystal Brook

A32

Spalding

Port
Broughton

Burra

⑤ **Oodnadatta Track**
(p140) Jumping in a 4WD
and exploring this classic
Australian route.

⑥ **Coober Pedy** (p138)
Noodling for opals then
bunking down underground
for the night.

⑦ **Woomera** (p138)
Checking out amazing old
rocket remnants.

FLINDERS RANGES

Known simply as 'the Flinders', this ancient mountain range is an iconic South Australian environment. Jagged peaks and escarpments rise up north of Port Augusta and track 400km north to Mt Hopeless. The colours here are remarkable: as the day stretches out, the mountains shift from mauve mornings to midday chocolates and ochre-red sunsets.

Before Europeans arrived, the Flinders were prized by the Adnyamathanha peoples for their red ochre deposits, which had medicinal and ritual uses. Sacred caves, rock paintings and carvings abound throughout the region. In the wake of white exploration came villages, farms, country pubs and cattle stations, many of which failed under the unrelenting sun.

☞ Tours

Flinders Ranges By Bike MOUNTAIN BIKING
(☑08 8648 0048; www.flindersrangesbybike. com.au; per person 1/2/3/4 days $35/40/45/50) 🖉 Pedal your way along a 200km circuit through the best bits of the Flinders Ranges, starting (and ending) at Rawnsley Park Station (p136), south of Wilpena. Fees cover park entry and access to private properties

Flinders Ranges

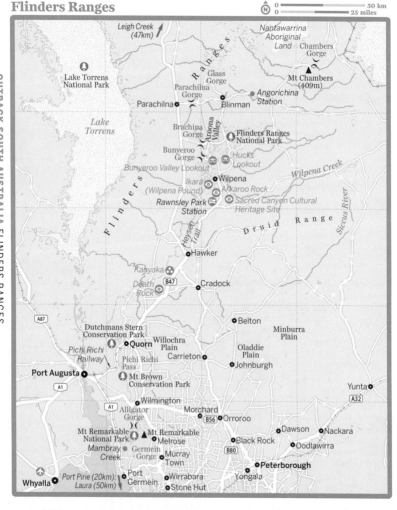

en route; book your own accommodation. Luggage transfers also available.

Arkaba Walk   WALKING
(☑02-9571 6399, 1300 790 561; www.arkabawalk. com; per person $2200; ☉mid-Mar–mid-Oct) Hike for four days through the Flinders in fine (guided) style. Prices include park entry fees, chef-cooked meals, luggage portage, deluxe camping and a night at the super-plush Arkaba Station (p135). A once-in-a-lifetime treat!

Groovy Grape Tours   OUTDOORS
(☑1800 661 177, 08 8440 1640; www.groovygrape. com.au) Small-group tours including a four-day Adelaide to Coober Pedy return trip via the Flinders Ranges ($445). Meals, camping and national-park entry fees are included.

❶ Getting There & Away

Exploring the Flinders on a tour or under your own steam is the only way to go (public transport is very limited).

Genesis Transport (☑08 8552 4000; www. genesistransport.com.au) runs an Adelaide-to-Copley bus on Thursdays, via Laura, Melrose, Quorn, Hawker, Parachilna and Leigh Creek, returning on Fridays in the other direction. Extensions to Wilpena and Blinman on demand. See the website for times and fares.

Pichi Richi Railway (☑1800 777 245; www. prr.org.au; Flinders Ranges Visitor Information Centre, Railway Tce, Quorn; one-way adult/child/family $54/20/128) runs historic trains from Port Augusta to Quorn in the Flinders Ranges on most Saturdays, following the old *Ghan* train route.

Southern Ranges

Port Pirie (population 14,050) is a big lead- and zinc-smelting town on the edge of the Southern Flinders Ranges; the Nyrstar smelter dominates the skyline. It's a good spot to stock up on supplies before heading north, and there are plenty of places to stay here too (motels, caravan parks).

You enter the Southern Ranges proper near **Laura** (population 800), which emerges from the wheat fields like Superman's Smallville (all civic pride and 1950s prosperity). The long, geranium-adorned main street has a supermarket, chemist, bakery, bank, post office…even a shoe shop!

The oldest town in the Flinders (1853) is photogenic **Melrose** (population 410), snug in the elbow of the 960m Mt Remarkable (which comprises most of Mt Remarkable National Park). Melrose has the perfect mix of well preserved architecture, a cracking good pub, quality accommodation and parks with actual grass. There are some great mountain-biking trails around here too. Pick up the *Melrose Historical Walk* brochure for a history tour.

Peterborough (population 1490), 87km inland from Melrose, is a characterful place: a former service town for SA Railways trains, with a time-tunnel main street lined with old shopfronts, rickety verandahs and huge stone pubs.

◉ Sights

Mt Remarkable National Park   NATIONAL PARK
(☑08 8841 3400; www.environment.sa.gov.au/parks; National Hwy 1, via Mambray Creek; per vehicle $10; ☉24hr) Bush boffins rave about the steep, jagged Mt Remarkable National Park, which straddles the Southern Flinders and rises above little Melrose like a protective overlord. Wildlife and bushwalking are the main lures, with various tracks (including part of the Heysen Trail) meandering through isolated gorges. Remarkable!

Steamtown Heritage Rail Centre   MUSEUM
(☑08 8651 3355; www.steamtown.com.au; 1 Telford Ave, Peterborough; adult/child/family $17.50/8/35, sound-and-light show per person $20; ☉9am-5pm) Inside Peterborough's original rail depot, this excellent museum takes you back to the days of steam power, when 100 trains a day were shunting through this little town. Guided tours (90 minutes) run all day, with the last one at 3.30pm. There's also a sound-and-light show at 8.30pm (7.30pm in winter).

🏃 Activities

Over The Edge   MOUNTAIN BIKING
(☑08 8666 2222; www.otesports.com.au; 6 Stuart St, Melrose; ☉9am-5pm Wed-Mon) Mountain biking is big in Melrose: Over The Edge has spares, repairs, bike rental ($45 to $100 per day) and a little cafe.

🛏 Sleeping

★North Star Hotel   PUB $$
(☑08 8666 2110; www.northstarhotel.com.au; 43 Nott St, Melrose; d/trucks from $110/160; ❄☎) As welcome as summer rain: the North Star is a noble 1854 pub renovated in city-meets-woolshed style. Sit under spinning ceiling fans at the bistro (mains $18 to $30) for lunch, dinner or just a cold beer. Accommodation comprises plush suites upstairs, Bundaleer

Cottage next door (sleeps 16) and quirky cabins atop two old trucks out the back.

Under The Mount RENTAL HOUSE **$**
(☎ 0409 093 649; www.underthemount.com.au; 9-11 Jacka St, Melrose; d/8-bed dm $110/180; ❄) Run by some mountain-biking doyens, casual Under The Mount features six ensuite doubles, two eight-bed dorms and a communal kitchen inside, and BBQs, fire areas, a bike workshop and hose-down areas outside. It's part share-house, part hostel, with a common love of mountain-biking good times uniting guests.

ℹ Information

Port Pirie Regional Tourism & Arts Centre
(☎ 08 8633 8700; www.pirie.sa.gov.au; 3 Mary Elie St, Port Pirie; ⊙ 9am-5pm Mon-Fri, to 4pm Sat, 10am-4pm Sun) Port Pirie's visitor centre also houses the excellent local art gallery, is chock-full of info on places to stay and proffers advice on where to get a good coffee. 'Outside the Gates' town tours leave from here at 12.30pm on Monday, Wednesday and Friday (adult/child/family $13/5/28).

Quorn
POP 1210

Is Quorn a film set after the crew has gone home? With more jeering crows than people, it's a cinematographic little outback town with a pub-lined main street. Wheat farming took off here in 1875, and the town prospered with the arrival of the Great Northern Railway from Port Augusta. Quorn (pronounced 'corn') remained an important railroad junction until trains into the Flinders were cut in 1970.

◎ Sights

Kanyaka RUINS
(off Quorn-Hawker Rd, via Kanyaka; ⊙ daylight hours) Out of town, derelict ruins litter the Quorn–Hawker Rd, the most impressive of which is Kanyaka, a once-thriving sheep station founded in 1851. From the ruins (41km from Quorn), it's a 20-minute walk to a waterhole loomed over by the massive **Death Rock**. The story goes that local Aboriginal people once placed their dying kinfolk here to see out their last hours.

⌂ Sleeping

★**Quorn Caravan Park** CARAVAN PARK **$**
(☎ 08 8648 6206; www.quorncaravanpark.com.au; 8 Silo Rd; unpowered/powered sites $28/25,

dm $40, van s/d $65/75, cabins $100-140; ❄) 🍃 Fully keyed-in to climate change, this passionately run park on Pinkerton Creek is hell bent on reducing emissions and restoring native habitat. Features include spotless cabins, a backpacker cabin (sleeps six), a camp kitchen made from recycled timbers, shady sites, rainwater tanks everywhere and a few lazy roos lounging about under the red gums. Discounts for walkers and cyclists.

Savings Bank of
South Australia RENTAL HOUSE **$$**
(SBSA; ☎ 0419 233 729, 0456 129 870; www.sbsa-quorn.com.au; 37 First St; up to 6 people $260; ❄) Bank on a good night's sleep at Quorn's lovely old red-brick bank, a two-storey, two-bathroom, three-bedroom conversion of this 1906 charmer. It's a terrific base for exploring the Flinders. Sleeps six; two-night minimum stay (good weekly rates).

✕ Eating

★**Quorn Cafe** CAFE **$**
(☎ 08 8648 6368; www.quorncafe.com.au; 43 First St; mains $10-25; ⊙ 8am-4pm Mon, 9am-3pm Tue & Wed, 7.30am-4pm Thu-Sun; ✐) The menu board at this unexpected, culturally displaced cafe is an old door hung on the wall, covered with brown-paper sandwich bags. Each bag has a menu item scribbled on it: vegetable frittata, warm chicken salad, egg and bacon sandwich… Everything is homemade and generous. Try the delicious goat curry. Quorn's best coffee, too.

ℹ Information

Flinders Ranges Visitor Information Centre
(☎ 08 8620 0510; www.flindersranges.com; Quorn Railway Station, Railway Tce; ⊙ 9am-5pm Mon-Fri, 10am-4pm Sat & Sun) Maps, brochures, internet access and advice – the main info hub for the Flinders Ranges. Check out the little history room out the back.

Hawker
POP 300

Hawker is the last outpost of civilisation before Ikara (Wilpena Pound), 59km to the north. Much like Quorn, Hawker has seen better days, most of which were when the old *Ghan* train stopped here. These days Hawker is a pancake-flat, pit-stop town with an ATM, a general store, a pub and the world's most helpful petrol station.

🛏 Sleeping

Arkaba Station   BOUTIQUE HOTEL $$$
(☑ 02 9571 6399, 1300 790 561; www.arkaba
station.com; Wilpena Rd, via Hawker; adult/child
from $465/930; ❄ 🛜 🏊) Flashy outback
station accommodation in an 1850s home-
stead, between Hawker and Wilpena: it's
an exercise in contemporary bush luxury.
Rates include chef-cooked meals and daily
guided wilderness safaris tailored to your
interests. Scenic flights and transfers also
available.

ℹ Information

Hawker Motors (☑ 08 8648 4014; www.
hawkermotors.com.au; cnr Wilpena & Cradock
Rds; ⊘7.30am-6pm) The town's petrol station
(fill up if you're heading north) doubles as the
visitor information centre.

Flinders Ranges National Park

One of SA's most treasured parks, Flinders
Ranges National Park (Ikara; ☑ 08 8648
0048; www.environment.sa.gov.au/parks; via
Wilpena; per vehicle $10; ⊘24hr) is laced
with craggy gorges, saw-toothed ranges,
abandoned homesteads, Aboriginal sites,
native wildlife and, after it rains, carpets
of wild flowers.

⊙ Sights

The park's big-ticket drawcard is the
80-sq-km natural basin Ikara (Wilpena
Pound) – a sunken elliptical valley ringed
by gnarled ridges (don't let anyone tell you
it's a meteorite crater!)

The only vehicular access to see Ikara
(Wilpena Pound) is via the Wilpena Pound
Resort's shuttle bus (☑ 1800 805 802, 08
8648 0004; www.wilpenapound.com.au; Wilpena
Pound Resort, Wilpena; return adult/child/family
$5/3/12), which drops you about 1km from
the old Hills Homestead, from where you
can walk to Wangarra Lookout (another
300m). The shuttle runs at 9am, 11am, 1pm
and 3pm. Otherwise, it's a three-hour, 8km
return walk between the resort and lookout
(guided walking tours available from the
resort for $45 per person).

The 20km Brachina Gorge Geologi-
cal Trail features an amazing layering of
exposed sedimentary rock, covering 120
million years of the earth's history. Grab a
brochure from the visitor centre.

The Bunyeroo–Brachina–Aroona
Scenic Drive is a 110km round trip, pass-
ing by Bunyeroo Valley, Brachina Gorge,
Aroona Valley and Stokes Hill Lookout.
The drive starts north of Wilpena off the
road to Blinman.

🏃 Activities

Bushwalking in the Flinders is unforgetta-
ble. Before you make happy trails, ensure
you've got enough water, sunscreen and a
massive hat, and tell someone where you're
going. Pick up the *Bushwalking in Flinders
Ranges National Park* brochure from the
visitor information centre. Many walks kick
off at Wilpena Pound Resort (p136).

For a really good look at Ikara, the walk
up to Tanderra Saddle (return 15km, six
hours) on the ridge of St Mary Peak is bril-
liant, though it's a thigh-pounding scram-
ble at times. The Adnyamathanha people
request that you restrict your climbing to
the ridge and don't climb St Mary Peak itself,
due to its traditional significance to them.

The quick, tough track up to Mt Ohlssen
Bagge (return 6.5km, four hours) rewards
the sweaty hiker with a stunning panorama.
Good short walks include the stroll to Hills
Homestead (return 6.5km, two hours), or
the dash up to the Wilpena Solar Power
Station (return 500m, 30 minutes).

Just beyond the park's southeast corner,
a one-hour, 1km return walk leads to the
Sacred Canyon Cultural Heritage Site,
with Aboriginal rock-art galleries featuring
animal tracks and designs.

ADNYAMATHANHA DREAMING

Land and nature are integral to the
culture of the traditional owners of the
Flinders Ranges. The people collectively
called Adnyamathanha (Hill People) are
actually a collection of the Wailpi, Kuy-
ani, Jadliaura, Piladappa and Pangkala
tribes, who exchanged and elaborated
on stories to explain their spectacular
local geography.

The walls of Ikara (Wilpena Pound),
for example, are the bodies of two
akurra (giant snakes), who coiled
around Ikara during an initiation cere-
mony, eating most of the participants.
The snakes were so full after their feast
they couldn't move and willed them-
selves to die, creating the landmark.

🛏 Sleeping

⭐ Rawnsley
Park Station   RESORT, CARAVAN PARK $$
(📞08 8648 0700; www.rawnsleypark.com.au;
Wilpena Rd, via Hawker; unpowered/powered sites
$26/36, hostel per adult/child $38/28, cabins/
units/villas/houses from $100/160/410/550;
※ 🤶 🏊) This rangy homestead 35km from
Hawker on the southern fringes of the
National Park offers everything from tent
sites to luxe eco-villas, a 1950s self-contained
house and a caravan park with cabins and
dorms. Activities include mountain-bike
hire ($15 per hour), bushwalks, 4WD tours
and scenic flights. The excellent **Woolshed
Restaurant** (mains $27-42; ⏱noon-2pm Wed-
Sun, 6-8.30pm daily) is also on-site.

Wilpena Pound Resort   RESORT $$
(📞1800 805 802, 08 8648 0004; www.wilpena
pound.com.au; Wilpena Rd, via Hawker; unpowered/
powered sites from $24/35, d/ste/safari tents from
$193/263/320; ※ 🤶 🏊) This far-flung resort
has lost some of its sheen, but remains an
interesting place to stay, with motel-style
rooms, self-contained suites, and a popular
camp site with plush safari tents (book way
in advance over winter). Don't miss a swim
in the pool, a drink at the bar and dinner at
the **bistro** (mains $26 to $40 – try the roo!)

ℹ Information

Wilpena Pound Visitor Information Centre
(📞08 8648 0048; www.wilpenapound.com.au/
do/visitors-centre; Wilpena Pound Resort,
Wilpena; ⏱8am-6pm) At the resort's info centre
you'll find a shop, petrol, park and bushwalking
info and bike hire (per half-/full day $35/65). Also
handles bookings for scenic flights and 4WD tours.

Blinman & Parachilna

About an hour north of Ikara on a sealed
road, ubercute Blinman (population 30)
owes its existence to the copper ore discovered here in 1859 and the smelter
built in 1903. But the boom went bust
and 1500 folks left town. Today Blinman's
main claim to fame is as SA's highest town
(610m above sea level). There are interesting tours of the old mines.

On the Hawker–Leigh Creek road, mid-
dle-of-nowhere Parachilna (population
somewhere between four and seven) is an
essential Flinders Ranges destination. The
drawcard here is the legendary Prairie
Hotel – a world-class stay.

⊙ Sights

Heritage Blinman Mine   HISTORIC SITE
(📞08 8648 4782; www.heritageblinmanmine.
com.au; Mine Rd, Blinman; tours adult/child/family
$28/11/65; ⏱9am-5pm, reduced hours Dec-Mar)
Much of Blinman's amazing, 150-year-old
copper mine has been redeveloped with
lookouts, audiovisual interpretation and
information boards. Excellent one-hour
tours run at 10am, noon and 2pm.

🛏 Sleeping

⭐ Prairie Hotel   HOTEL $$$
(📞1800 331 473, 08 8648 4844; www.prairiehotel.
com.au; cnr High St & West Tce, Parachilna; powered sites $35, budget cabins s/d/f $65/80/180,
hotel s/d/tr from $195/245/280; ※ 🤶) The
legendary Prairie Hotel has slick suites out
the back, plus camping and basic cabins
across the street. Don't miss a pub meal
(mains breakfast $8 to $28, lunch and dinner $18 to $42): try the feral mixed grill
(camel sausage, kangaroo fillet, emu and
bacon). 'Too early for a beer!? Whose rules
are those?', said the barman at 10.42am.

Leigh Creek & Copley

In the early 1980s, the previously nonexist-
ent town of Leigh Creek (population 500
and shrinking) emerged from the northern
Flinders desert. It was built by the state
government to house people working at the
huge open-cut coal mine here, with a school,
a pub, a shopping centre…the whole shebang. Population peaked at around 1000,
until in 2016 the mine shut down. What
happens next is anyone's guess: a new nat-
ural-gas project? The whole town up for
sale? A kooky resort? Swing by and check it
out: at least the pub is still open.

About 6km north of Leigh Creek is the
sweet meaninglessness of little Copley
(population 80). There's not a whole to see
or do here, other than try a slice of quandong pie at the cafe.

Further afield are the varied enticements
of the Aboriginal cultural centre Iga Warta,
Vulkathunha-Gammon Ranges National
Park and Arkaroola Wilderness Sanctuary.

⊙ Sights

**Arkaroola Wilderness
Sanctuary**   WILDLIFE RESERVE
(📞08 8648 4848; www.arkaroola.com.au; Copley-
Arkaroola Rd, via Copley) 🏍 129km east of

Copley on unsealed roads, Arkaroola Wilderness Sanctuary occupies a far-flung and utterly spectacular part of the Flinders Ranges. The visitor centre has natural-history displays, including a scientific explanation of the tremors that often shake things up hereabouts. The vertiginous 4WD Ridgetop Tour (www.arkaroola.com.au/ridgetop; adult/child $155/55; ⊙8am & 1pm daily) is a must! On site there's also motel and caravan park–style accommodation (www.arkaroola.com.au/accommodation.php; unpowered/powered sites $25/33, motel d $85-205, cottages f $149-230; ✳ ☎)

Vulkathunha-Gammon Ranges National Park   NATIONAL PARK
(☑08 8648 4829; www.environment.sa.gov.au/parks; Copley-Arkaroola Rd, via Copley; ⊙24hr) **FREE** Blanketing 1282 sq km of desert, this remote national park has deep gorges, rugged ranges, yellow-footed rock wallabies and gum-lined creeks. Most of the park is difficult to access (4WDs are near-compulsory) and has limited facilities. Bush camping is $12 per vehicle (BYO everything); pick up permits at the Balcanoona park HQ, 99km from Copley.

Iga Warta   CULTURAL CENTRE
(☑08 8648 3737; www.igawarta.com; Copley-Arkaroola Rd, via Copley; ⊙9am-5pm) Iga Warta, 57km east of Copley en route to Vulkathunha-Gammon Ranges National Park, is an Indigenous-run cultural centre and bush camp, offering authentic Adnyamathanha experiences ($25 to $84 – bush foods, campfire story telling, artefact making) plus 4WD and bush-walking tours ($138). There's accommodation here too (unpowered sites $22, tents per person $36, cabins and safari tents $104 to $150).

🛏 Sleeping

Copley Caravan Park   CARAVAN PARK $
(☑08 8675 2288; www.copleycaravan.com.au; Lot 100 Railway Tce W, Copley; unpowered/powered sites $30/40, cabins with/without bathroom from $110/80; ✳) Copley Caravan Park is a going concern: a small, immaculate park (not a whole lotta shade, but hey, this is the desert) and regular bonfire cook-ups for guests. The Quandong Cafe (items $5-12; ⊙8am-5pm) is here too.

THE OUTBACK

The area north of the Eyre Peninsula and the Flinders Ranges stretches into the vast, empty spaces of SA's outback – about 70% of the state! If you're prepared, travelling through this sparsely populated and harsh country is utterly rewarding.

Heading into the red heart of Australia, Woomera is the first pit stop, with its dark legacy of nuclear tests and shiny collection of left-over rockets. Further north on the Stuart Hwy and along the legendary Oodnadatta and Strzelecki Tracks, eccentric outback towns such as William Creek, Innamincka and Coober Pedy emerge from the heat haze. This is no country for the faint-hearted: it's waterless, fly-blown and dizzyingly hot. No wonder the opal miners in Coober Pedy live underground!

🧭 Tours

Sacred Earth Safaris   ADVENTURE
(☑08 8536 2234; www.sacredearthsafaris.com.au; tours per adult/child $4995/4795) Epic outback 4WD tours on the big three desert tracks – Oodnadatta, Strzelecki and Birdsville – plus Coober Pedy and the Flinders Ranges.

ℹ Getting There & Around

AIR
Regional Express (p268) flies most days between Adelaide and Coober Pedy (from $247, two hours).

BUS
Greyhound Australia (p266) runs a daily (overnight) bus from Adelaide to Pimba ($94, 6¾ hours) and Glendambo ($108, 8¼ hours), Coober Pedy ($167, 11¼ hours) and Marla ($228, 14¼ hours), continuing to Alice Springs.

CAR & MOTORCYCLE
The Stuart Hwy tracks from Port Augusta to Darwin. In SA, fuel and accommodation are available at Pimba (176km from Port Augusta), Glendambo (288km), Coober Pedy (542km), Cadney Homestead (693km) and Marla (775km). Pimba, Coober Pedy and Marla have 24-hour fuel sales.

The Oodnadatta, Birdsville and Strzelecki Tracks are subject to closure after heavy rains; check conditions with the **Royal Automobile Association** (p259) in Adelaide, online at www.dpti.sa.gov.au/outbackroads, or call the Outback Road Report on ☑1300 361 033.

TRAIN
Operated by Great Southern Rail (www.greatsouthernrail.com.au), the *Ghan* train runs through outback SA between Adelaide and Alice Springs, with a stop at Coober Pedy (or rather, near) a possibility; see the website for details.

Woomera & Around

A 6km detour off the Stuart Hwy from little truckstop Pimba (population 50; 481km north of Adelaide), Woomera (population 220) emerged as a settlement in 1947 as HQ for experimental British rocket and nuclear tests at notorious sites like Maralinga. Local Indigenous tribes suffered greatly from the resulting nuclear fallout. These days Woomera is an eerie artificial town that's still an active Department of Defence test site.

Beyond Woomera, drive-through Glendambo and quirky Roxby Downs offer different takes on the outback-town experience.

🛏 Sleeping

Glendambo Hotel-Motel & Caravan Park　　　　　MOTEL **$**
(✆08 8672 1030; www.turu.com.au/parks/sa/outback/glendambo-hotel-motel-and-caravan-park.aspx; Stuart Hwy, Glendambo; unpowered/powered sites $23/27, s/d/f from $94/99/140; ❄ ♨) If your eyelids are drooping out on the highway, bunk down at the oasis-like Glendambo Hotel-Motel, which has bars, a restaurant and a bunch of OK motel units. Outside are dusty camp sites; inside are meaty mains at the bistro ($18 to $32, serving noon to 2pm and 6pm to 8pm).

Eldo Hotel　　　　　　　　　　　MOTEL **$$**
(✆08 8673 7867; www.facebook.com/eldo-hotel; Kotara Pl, Woomera; d from $110; ❄) Built to house rocket scientists, the Eldo Hotel has comfortable budget and motel-style rooms, and serves à la carte meals in the urbane bistro (mains $20 to $35, serving 7am to 9am, noon to 2pm and 6pm to 8.30pm). Try the meaty game plate.

ℹ Information

Woomera Heritage & Visitor Information Centre (✆08 8673 7042; homepage.powerup.com.au/~woomera/herit1.htm; Dewrang Ave, Woomera; museum adult/child $6/3; ❄9am-5pm Mar-Nov, 10am-2pm Dec-Feb) Rocket into the info centre, with its displays on Woomera's past and present (plus a bowling alley!) Just across the car park is the **Lions Club Aircraft & Missile Park**, studded with jets and rocket remnants.

Coober Pedy

POP 3500

Coming into cosmopolitan Coober Pedy (yes, cosmopolitan – there are 44 nationalities represented in this little town!) the dry, barren desert suddenly becomes riddled with holes and adjunct piles of dirt – reputedly more than a million around the township. The reason for all this rabid digging is opals. Discovered here 100 years ago, these gemstones have made this small town a mining mecca. This isn't to say it's also a tourist mecca – with swarms of flies, no trees, 50°C summer days, cave-dwelling locals and rusty car wrecks, you might think you've arrived in a postapocalyptic wasteland – but it sure is interesting! The name derives from local Aboriginal words *kupa* (white man) and *piti* (hole).

The surrounding desert is jaw-droppingly desolate, a fact not overlooked by international film-makers who've come here to shoot end-of-the-world epics like *Mad Max III, Red Planet, Ground Zero, Pitch Black* and the slightly more believable *Priscilla, Queen of the Desert.*

◉ Sights

★**Old Timers Mine**　　　　　　　MUSEUM
(✆08 8672 5555; www.oldtimersmine.com; 1 Crowders Gully Rd; self-guided tours adult/child/family $12/5/40; ❄9am-5.30pm) This interesting warren of tunnels was mined in 1916, and then hidden by the miners. The mine was rediscovered when excavations for a dugout home punched through into the labyrinth of tunnels. As well as the great self-guided tunnel tours, there's a museum, a re-created 1920s underground home, and free mining-equipment demos daily (9.30am, 1.30pm and 3.30pm).

★**Spaceship**　　　　　　　　SCULPTURE
(Hutchinson St) Check out this amazing leftover prop from the film *Pitch Black,* which has crash-landed on Hutchinson St (...a minor *Millennium Falcon*?).

Umoona Opal Mine & Museum　　MUSEUM
(✆08 8672 5288; www.umoonaopalmine.com.au; 14 Hutchison St; museum free, tours adult/child $10/5; ❄8am-6pm) For a terrific introduction to Coober Pedy – including history, fossils, desert habitats, Aboriginal culture, ecology and mining – take a wander through this free museum, run by the Umoona shop. Book yourself on a guided tour (10am, 2pm and 4pm) if you want a deeper insight.

Catholic Church of St Peter & St Paul　　　　　CHURCH
(✆08 8672 5011; www.pp.catholic.org.au/about-our-parishes/coober-pedy-est-1965-; cnr Halliday Pl & Hutchison St; ❄10am-4pm, Mass 10am Sun) Coober Pedy's first underground church still

Coober Pedy

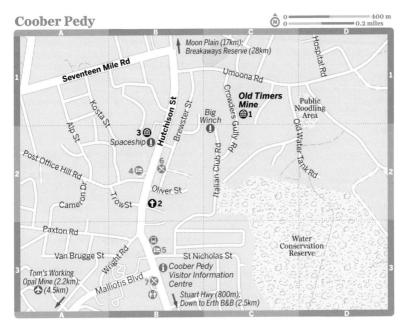

has a sweet appeal, with statue-filled nooks and hushed classical music.

Tours

Arid Areas Tours DRIVING

(☑ 0439 881 049, 08 8672 3008; www.aridareastours.com; 2/4/6hr tours per 2 people from $120/240/320) Offers 4WD tours around town, extending to the Breakaways. Full-day tours to Lake Eyre, the Painted Desert and the Oodnadatta Track also available.

Mail Run Tour DRIVING

(☑ 1800 069 911, 08 8672 5226; www.mailruntour.com; tours per person $195) Coober Pedy–based full-day mail-run tours, looping through the desert and along the Oodnadatta Track between Oodnadatta and William Creek.

Sleeping

Riba's CAMPGROUND $

(☑ 08 8672 5614; www.camp-underground.com.au; Lot 1811 William Creek Rd; underground sites $30, above-ground unpowered/powered sites $20/28, s & d $66; ☎) Around 5km from town, Riba's offers the unique option of underground camping! Extras include an underground TV lounge, cell-like underground budget rooms and a nightly opal-mine tour (adult/child $24/15; free for underground and unpowered-site campers, discounted for other guests).

Cadney Homestead CARAVAN PARK $

(☑ 08 7007 6591; www.turu.com.au/parks/sa/outback/cadney-homestead-caravan-park.aspx; Stuart Hwy, Cadney Park; unpowered/powered sites from $20/30, d cabin/motel from $52/110; ✴@☎) Cadney Homestead has caravan and tent sites, serviceable motel rooms and basic cabins (BYO towel), plus petrol, puncture repairs, takeaways, cold beer, an ATM, a swimming pool… On the Stuart Hwy, 151km north of Coober Pedy.

Marla Travellers Rest · CARAVAN PARK $

(☑ 08 8670 7001; www.marla.com.au; Stuart Hwy, Marla; unpowered/powered sites $20/30, cabins $40, d $110-140; ✳@≋) Marla Travellers Rest has fuel, motel rooms, camp sites, a kidney-shaped pool, a takeaway cafe, supermarket and a vast tiled bar area (easy to hose out?). On the Stuart Hwy at Marla, 234km north of Coober Pedy.

★ Down to Erth B&B · B&B $$

(☑ 08 8672 5762; www.downtoerth.com.au; Lot 1795 Wedgetail Cres; d incl breakfast $165; ≋≋) A real dugout gem about 3km from town: your own subterranean two-bedroom bunker (sleeps five – perfect for a family) with a kitchen/lounge area, a shady plunge pool for cooling off after a day exploring the earth, wood-fuelled BBQ and complimentary chocolates.

★ Mud Hut Motel · MOTEL $$

(☑ 08 8672 3003; www.mudhutmotel.com.au; cnr Hutchison & St Nicholas Sts; s/d/f/2-bedroom apt $130/150/180/218; ✳≋) The rustic-looking walls here are made from rammed earth, and despite the grubby name this is one of the cleanest (and newest) places in town – and by far the best motel option if you don't want to sleep underground. The two-bedroom apartments sleep six (extra person $20) and have kitchens. Central location.

Desert Cave Hotel · HOTEL $$$

(☑ 08 8672 5688; www.desertcave.com.au; Lot 1 Hutchison St; d above ground/underground $260/255; ✳≋≋) Top of the CP price tree, the Desert Cave brings a much-needed shot of luxury – plus a beaut pool, a daytime cafe, airport transfers and the excellent Umberto's (mains $28-43; ☺6-9pm) restaurant. Staff are supercourteous and can organise tours. Above-ground rooms cost a tad more (huge, but there are more soulful places to stay in town). Prices dive in summer.

✕ Eating

★ Outback Bar & Grill · FAST FOOD $$

(☑ 08 8672 3250; www.facebook.com/shellcoober pedy; 454 Hutchison St; mains $7-25; ☺7am-9pm Mon-Sat, to 8pm Sun; ≋) It may sound a bit odd, but this brightly lit, petrol-station diner is one of the best places to eat in Coober Pedy! Roasts, pastas, burgers, lasagne, schnitzels…and an awesome Greek-style lamb salad that's a bold departure from trucker norms and expectations. You can get a beer here too, if you're dry from the highway.

John's Pizza Bar & Restaurant · ITALIAN $$

(☑ 08 8672 5561; www.jpbr.com.au; Shop 24, 1 Hutchison St; mains $9-32; ☺10am-10pm) Serving up table-sized pizzas, hearty pastas and heat-beating gelato, you can't go past John's. Grills, salads, burgers, yiros, and fish and chips also available. Sit inside, order some takeaways, or pull up a seat with the bedraggled pot plants by the street.

ⓘ Information

Coober Pedy Visitor Information Centre
(☑ 08 8672 4600, 1800 637 076; www.coober pedy.sa.gov.au/tourism; Council Offices, lot 773 Hutchison St; ☺8.30am-5pm Mon-Fri, 10am-1pm Sat & Sun) Free 30-minute internet access (prebooked), history displays and comprehensive tour and accommodation info.

Oodnadatta Track

The legendary, lonesome Oodnadatta Track is an unsealed, 615km road between Marla on the Stuart Hwy and Marree in the northern Flinders Ranges. The track traces the route of the old Overland Telegraph Line and the defunct Great Northern Railway. Along the way are remote settlements, quirky desert sights and the enormous Lake Eyre (usually dry). Bring a 4WD – the track is often passable in a regular car, but it gets bumpy, muddy, dusty and potholed (how exciting!)

You can traverse the Oodnadatta Track in either direction. Rolling in from the north, around 209km from Marla, **Oodnadatta** (population 170) is where the main road and the old railway line diverged. Here you'll find the **Pink Roadhouse** (☑ 08 8670 7822, 1800 802 074; www.pinkroadhouse.com.au; Lot 42 Ikartuka Tce, Oodnadatta; unpowered/powered sites from $22/32, cabins with/without bathroom from $120/70), a solid source of track info and meals (try the stultifying 'Oodnaburger'). The roadhouse also has an attached caravan park; options run from basic camping through to self-contained cabins.

In another 201km you'll hit **William Creek** (population six!), best experienced in the weather-beaten **William Creek Hotel** (☑ 08 8670 7880; www.williamcreekhotel.com; Oodnadatta Track, William Creek; unpowered/powered sites $25/30, d cabin/hotel $90/150; ✳), an iconic 1887 pub festooned with photos, business cards, old licence plates and money stapled to the walls. There's a dusty camping ground, and modest cabins and motel rooms. Also on offer are fuel, cold beer, basic provisions, all-day meals (mains $16 to $32) and spare tyres.

William Creek is also a base for **Wrightsair** (08 8670 7962; www.wrightsair.com.au; 1 Bill Rivers Ave, William Creek; flights per person from $260), which runs scenic flights over Lake Eyre.

Some 130km shy of Marree, **Coward Springs Campground** (08 8675 8336; www.cowardsprings.com.au; Oodnadatta Track, Coward Springs; unpowered sites adult/child $12.50/6.25) is the first stop at the old Coward Springs railway siding. You can soak yourself silly in a natural hot-spring tub made from old railway sleepers (adult/child $2/1), or take a six-day camel trek to Lake Eyre from here (from $1760…or you can buy a camel!)

Next stop is the lookout over the southern section of **Lake Eyre** (Kati Thanda; 08 8648 5300; www.environment.sa.gov.au/parks; 24hr), the world's sixth-largest lake. It's usually dry but a couple of times in recent years has filled with flood waters running in from Queensland. When this happens (only once every decade or so) the explosion of bird life is astonishing! It's also the lowest point on the Australian continent, bottoming out at 15.2m below sea level.

Mutonia Sculpture Park – about 60km west of Marree – emerges from the desert unexpectedly. All sorts of wacky weldings stand mute in the heat, including several planes welded together with their tails buried in the ground to form *Planehenge.*

Marree (population 100) was once a vital hub for Afghan camel teams and the Great Northern Railway, and is the end (or start) of both the Oodnadatta and Birdsville Tracks. The big, stone 1883 **Marree Hotel** (08 8675 8344; www.marreehotel.com.au; Railway Tce S, Marree; unpowered sites free, hotel d without bathroom $120, cabins from $140;) has decent pub rooms (shared bathrooms), smart ensuite cabins and free camp sites!

The folks at the Marree Hotel can also hook you up with a scenic flight. From the air you'll get a good look at **Marree Man**, a 4.2km-long outline of a Pitjantjatjara Aboriginal warrior etched into the desert near Lake Eyre. It was only discovered in 1998, and no one seems to know who created it. Eroding away to nothingness for many years, in 2016 it was reploughed into the dirt…and still no-one knows who's responsible!

From Marree it's 80km south to Lyndhurst, where the bitumen kicks back in, then 33km down to Copley at the northern end of the Flinders Ranges.

Birdsville & Strzelecki Tracks

These two iconic outback stock routes tell stories of exploration and the opening up of the Australian continent… but also of landscape: this is ancient terrain, crossed by indigenous Australians for millenniums, from water source to water source. These days, if you pack plenty of H_2O in your 4WD, you won't need to rely on desert soaks and waterholes – but imagine doing it on foot!

Both of these tracks are hard-driving 4WD terrain – you'll need to keep your eyes on the dirt in front of you. But when you do stop to look around, the landscape here is dizzyingly bleak and beautiful, wildlife scurrying for shade and the desert air charged with ions. Completing either of these tracks is a real badge of honour – journeys into Australia's red heart that you won't hurriedly forget.

Birdsville Track

The Birdsville Track is an old droving trail running 517km from Marree in SA to Birdsville, just across the border in Queensland, passing between the Simpson Desert to the west and Sturt Stony Desert to the east. It's one of Australia's classic outback routes, made famous by stockmen in the late 1800s who drove cattle from Queensland's Channel Country to the railway at Marree, from where they were shunted to boats at Port Augusta – about 1000km shorter than the route to the coast near Brisbane. More recently, legendary outback mailman Tom Kruse (no, not that Tom Cruise) belted his mail truck along the track from 1936 until 1963.

Strzelecki Track

Meandering through the sand hills of the **Strzelecki Regional Reserve** (08 8648 5300; www.environment.sa.gov.au/parks; Strzelecki Track), the Strzelecki Track spans 460km from Lyndhurst, 80km south of Marree, to the tiny desert outpost of Innamincka. The discovery of oil and gas at Moomba (closed to travellers) saw the upgrading of the road from a camel track to a decent dirt road, though heavy transport travelling along it has created bone-rattling corrugations. The newer **Moomba–Strzelecki Track** is better kept, but longer and less interesting than the old track, which follows Strzelecki Creek.

Darwin & the Top End

Best Places to Eat

➜ Aboriginal Bush Traders Cafe (p153)

➜ Crustaceans (p154)

➜ Darwin Ski Club (p154)

➜ Crazy Acres Mango Farm & Cafe (p162)

➜ Border Store (p170)

Best Places to Sleep

➜ Wildman Wilderness Lodge (p161)

➜ Hawk Dreaming Wilderness Lodge (p169)

➜ Villa La Vue (p152)

➜ Adina Apartment Hotel (p152)

➜ Mt Bundy Station (p165)

Why Go?

The Top End is frontier country. It feels wild out here; time spent exploring the region's outer reaches will feel like exploring the Australia of childhood imaginings. This is the nation's most rewarding Indigenous homeland, a land of art centres, isolated communities and ancient rock art. It is also a world of iconic Aussie wildlife, from the jumping crocs of Mary River to the wildlife-rich flood plains and wetlands of Kakadu.

The wildness comes in many forms out here, from remote Arnhem Land to backpackers letting loose on Darwin's Mitchell St, from the mournful cries of Kakadu whistling kites and black cockatoos to the wild turtles laying their eggs within earshot of Darwin.

And Darwin itself is an intriguing place with a steamy, end-of-Australia feel, excellent markets, restaurants and galleries of Indigenous art, and a fine waterfront with terrific museums.

When to Go
Darwin

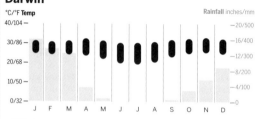

Apr–Sep Dry-season markets, fine weather and good festivals.

Oct & Nov The 'build-up' brings a chance of heavy rain and very humid conditions.

Dec–Mar The Wet brings monsoon rains and fewer visitors.

DARWIN

POP 135,000

Australia's only tropical capital city, Darwin gazes out confidently across the Timor Sea. It's closer to Bali than Bondi and can certainly feel removed from the rest of the country, which is just the way the locals like it.

Darwin has plenty to offer travellers. Chairs and tables spill out of streetside restaurants and bars, innovative museums celebrate the city's past, and galleries showcase the region's rich Indigenous art. Darwin's cosmopolitan mix – more than 50 nationalities are represented here – is typified by the wonderful markets held throughout the dry season.

⊙ Sights

◎ Central Darwin

★ **Crocosaurus Cove** ZOO
(☑ 08 8981 7522; www.crocosauruscove.com; 58 Mitchell St; adult/child $32/20; ◷ 9am-6pm, last admission 5pm) If the tourists won't go out to see the crocs, then bring the crocs to the tourists. Right in the middle of Mitchell St, Crocosaurus Cove is as close as you'll ever want to get to these amazing creatures. Six of the largest crocs in captivity can be seen in state-of-the-art aquariums and pools, while an eco boat cruise (adult/child $14/7) takes you out on the water with them.

You can be lowered right into a pool with the crocs in the transparent Cage of Death (1/2 people $165/250). If that's too scary, there's another pool where you can swim with a clear tank wall separating you from some mildly less menacing baby crocs. Other aquariums feature barramundi, turtles and stingrays, plus there's an enormous reptile house (allegedly displaying the greatest variety of reptiles in the country).

Aquascene AQUARIUM
(☑ 08 8981 7837; www.aquascene.com.au; Doctors Gully Rd; adult/child/family $15/10/43; ◷ high tide, check website) At Doctors Gully, an easy walk from the north end of the Esplanade, Aquascene runs a remarkable fish-feeding frenzy at high tide. Visitors, young and old, can hand-feed hordes of mullet, catfish, batfish and huge milkfish. Check the website and tourism publications for feeding times.

Bicentennial Park PARK
(◷ 24hr) Bicentennial Park (the Esplanade) runs the length of Darwin's waterfront and Lameroo Beach: a sheltered cove popular in the '20s when it housed the saltwater baths, and traditionally a Larrakia camp area. Shaded by tropical trees, the park is an excellent place to stroll.

Mason Gallery GALLERY
(☑ 08 8981 9622; www.masongallery.com.au; Shop 7, 21 Cavenagh St; ◷ 9am-5pm Mon-Fri, 10am-3pm Sat & Sun) FREE Features bold dot paintings from the Western and Central Desert regions, as well as works from Arnhem Land and Utopia.

George Brown Botanic Gardens GARDENS
(www.nt.gov.au/leisure/parks-reserves/george-brown-darwin-botanic-gardens; Geranium St; ◷ 7am-7pm, information centre 8am-4pm) FREE These 42-hectare gardens showcase plants from the Top End and around the world – monsoon vine forest, the mangroves and coastal plants habitat, baobabs, and a magnificent collection of native and exotic palms and cycads.

Myilly Point Heritage Precinct HISTORIC SITE
At the far northern end of Smith St is this small but important precinct of four houses built between 1930 and 1939 (which means they survived both the WWII bombings and Cyclone Tracy!) They're now managed by the National Trust. One of them, **Burnett House** (☑ 08 8981 0165; www.nationaltrust.org.au/places/burnett-house; $5; ◷ 10am-1pm Mon-Sat, 3-5pm Sun), operates as a museum.

◎ Darwin Waterfront Precinct

The bold redevelopment of the old Darwin Waterfront Precinct (www.waterfront.nt.gov.au) has transformed the city. The multi-million-dollar redevelopment features a cruise-ship terminal, luxury hotels, boutique restaurants and shopping, the Sky Bridge at the south end of Smith St, and a Wave Lagoon (☑ 08 8985 6588; www.waterfront.nt.gov.au; Wave Lagoon adult/child $9/6; ◷ Wave Lagoon 10am-6pm).

★ **Royal Flying Doctor Service** MUSEUM
(☑ 08 8983 5700; www.flyingdoctor.org.au; Stokes Hill Wharf; adult/child/family $26/16/70; ◷ 9.30am-6pm, last entry 5pm) This outstanding new museum on Stokes Hill Wharf is the way all museums should be. There's a 55-seat hologram cinema, virtual-reality glasses that enable you to relive in vivid detail the 1942 Japanese bombing raid on Darwin Harbour, a decommissioned Pilatus PC-12 aircraft from the Royal Flying Doctor

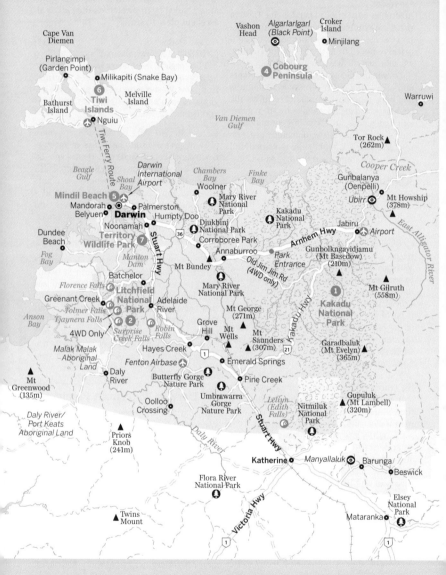

Darwin & the Top End Highlights

1 Kakadu National Park
(p166) Experiencing wildlife, rock art and Aboriginal culture in one of Australia's premier parks.

2 Litchfield National Park (p163) Plunging into a cascading, crystal-clear rock pool in this oasis-like national park.

3 Arnhem Land (p173) Touring this remote and hypnotically beautiful country and drawing near to Indigenous culture.

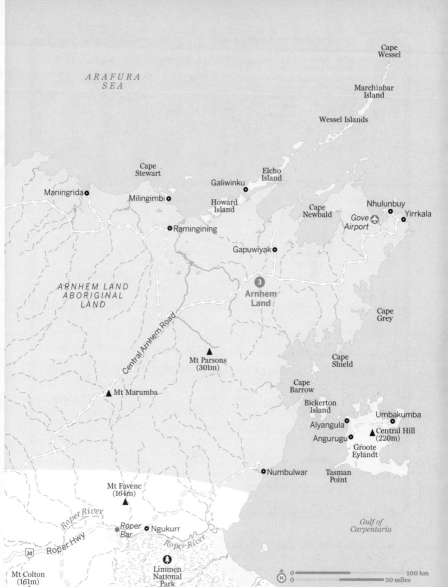

ARAFURA
SEA

Cape
Wessel

Marchinbar
Island

Wessel Islands

Cape
Stewart

Maningrida

Milingimbi

Galiwinku

Elcho
Island

Howard
Island

Cape
Newbald

Nhulunbuy

Gove
Airport

Yirrkala

Ramingining

Gapuwiyak

Arnhem
Land

ARNHEM LAND
ABORIGINAL
LAND

Central Arnhem Road

Cape
Grey

Mt Parsons
(301m)

Cape
Shield

Mt Marumba

Cape
Barrow

Bickerton
Island

Umbakumba

Alyangula

Central Hill
(220m)

Angurugu

Groote
Eylandt

Numbulwar

Tasman
Point

Gulf of
Carpentaria

Mt Favenc
(164m)

Roper River

Roper
Bar

Ngukurr

Roper River

Roper Hwy

20

Mt Colton
(161m)

Limmen
National
Park

N

0   100 km
0   50 miles

4 Cobourg Peninsula
(p175) Driving beyond the end
of the paved road into some
of Australia's most pristine
coastline.

**5 Mindil Beach Sunset
Market** (p154) Sampling a
satay and other exotic fare in
cosmopolitan Darwin.

6 Tiwi Islands (p157)
Drawing near to an ancient
culture on a day trip from
Darwin.

Darwin

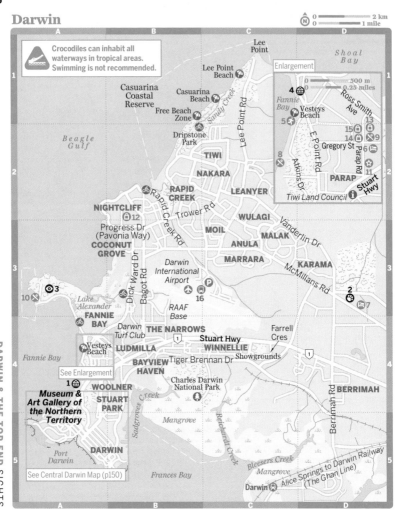

Crocodiles can inhabit all waterways in tropical areas. Swimming is not recommended.

See Central Darwin Map (p150)

Service (RFDS), a live map showing the current location of RFDS planes, and a series of touch screens that take you through the story of the RFDS and Darwin during WWII.

WWII Oil-Storage Tunnels TUNNEL
(☑08 8985 6322; www.darwintours.com.au/ ww2tunnels; self-guided tour per adult/child $8/5; ◷9am-4pm May-Oct, to 1pm Nov-Apr) You can escape from the heat of the day and relive your Hitchcockian fantasies by walking through the WWII oil-storage tunnels. They were built in 1942 to store the navy's oil

supplies (but never used); now they exhibit wartime photos.

Indo-Pacific Marine Exhibition AQUARIUM
(☑08 8981 1294; www.indopacificmarine.com.au; 29 Stokes Hill Rd; adult/child/family $24/10/58; ◷10am-4pm Apr-Oct, call for hours Nov-Mar) This excellent marine aquarium at the Waterfront Precinct (p143) gives you a close encounter with the denizens of Darwin Harbour. Each small tank is a complete ecosystem, with only the occasional extra fish introduced as food for some of the predators, such as stonefish or the bizarre angler fish.

Darwin

Also recommended is the **Coral Reef by Night** (adult/child $120/60; ◷ 6.30pm Wed, Fri & Sun), which consists of a tour of the aquarium, seafood dinner and an impressive show of fluorescing animals.

⊙ Fannie Bay & Parap

★ **Museum & Art Gallery of the Northern Territory**   MUSEUM
(MAGNT; ☏ 08 8999 8264; www.magnt.net.au; 19 Conacher St, Fannie Bay; ◷ 9am-5pm Mon-Fri, 10am-5pm Sat & Sun) **FREE** This superb museum and gallery boasts beautifully presented galleries of Top End–centric exhibits. The **Aboriginal art collection** is a highlight, with carvings from the Tiwi Islands, bark paintings from Arnhem Land and dot paintings from the desert. An entire room is devoted to **Cyclone Tracy**, in a display that graphically illustrates life before and after the disaster. You can stand in a darkened room and listen to the whirring sound of Tracy at full throttle – a sound you won't forget in a hurry.

East Point Reserve   GARDENS
(◷ mangrove boardwalk 8am-6pm) North of Fannie Bay, this spit of land is particularly attractive in the late afternoon when wallabies emerge to feed and you can watch the sun set over the bay.

    Lake Alexander, a small, recreational saltwater lake, was created so people could enjoy a swim year-round without having to worry about box jellyfish. There's a good children's playground here and picnic areas with BBQs. A 1.5km **mangrove boardwalk** leads off from the car park.

⊙ Outer East

Crocodylus Park   ZOO
(www.crocodyluspark.com.au; 815 McMillans Rd, Berrimah; adult/child $40/20; ◷ 9am-5pm) Crocodylus Park showcases hundreds of crocs and a minizoo comprising lions, tigers and other big cats, spider monkeys, marmosets, cassowaries and large birds. Allow about two hours to look around the whole park, and you should time your visit with a tour (10am, noon, 2pm and 3.30pm), which includes a feeding demonstration. Croc meat BBQ packs for sale!

🏃 Activities

Beaches & Swimming
Darwin is no beach paradise – naturally enough the harbour has no surf – but along the convoluted coastline north of the city centre is a string of sandy beaches. The most popular are **Mindil** and **Vesteys** on Fannie Bay. Further north, a stretch of the 7km **Casuarina Beach** is an official nude beach. Darwin's swimming beaches tend to be far enough away from mangrove creeks to make the threat of meeting a crocodile very remote. A bigger problem is the deadly box jellyfish, which makes swimming decidedly unhealthy between October and March (and often before October and until May).

You can swim year-round without fear of stingers in the western part of **Lake Alexander**, an easy cycle from the centre at East Point Reserve (p147), and at the very popular Wave & Recreation Lagoons (p143), the centrepiece of the Darwin Waterfront Precinct (p143). At the Recreation Lagoon, filtered seawater and nets provide a natural seawater swim.

Darwin Harbour Cruises CRUISE

(⏹ 08 8942 3131; www.darwinharbourcruises. com.au) Variety of cruises from Stokes Hill Wharf. The 20m schooner *Tumlaren* does a 'Tastes of the Territory' sunset cruise (adult/child $74/45), and there are day and evening cruise options aboard the *Charles Darwin,* a tri-level catamaran.

Spirit of Darwin CRUISE

(⏹ 0417 381 977; www.spiritofdarwin.com.au; tours per adult $65) This fully licensed, air-con motor-catamaran does a two-hour sightseeing cruise at 2pm and a sunset cruise at 5.30pm daily from Stokes Hill Wharf.

🧭 Tours

⭐ Turtle Tracks TOURS

(⏹ 1300 065 022; www.seadarwin.com; Stokes Hill Wharf; adult/child/family $250/175/790; ⏱ 4pm May-Sep) This late-afternoon tour goes out beyond Darwin Harbour and Charles Point Lighthouse to beautiful Bare Sand Island, where you'll arrive around sunset. Guides will take you around the island, explaining its history, then take you by torchlight to watch the wonderful sight of turtles laying their eggs; come late in the season and you may see the hatchlings emerge.

⭐ Ethical Adventures TOURS

(⏹ 0488 442 269; www.ethicaladventures.com) A cut above most of those offering day tours to Litchfield National Park from Darwin, Ethical Adventures runs sunrise-to-sunset tours that take in all of the main attractions, providing excellent food (including barbecued crocodile and buffalo) and good guides. Its focus on small groups, cultural engagement and ethical practices is a highlight.

⭐ NT Indigenous Tours CULTURAL TOUR

(⏹ 1300 921 188; www.ntitours.com.au; day tours adult/child from $249/124) Upmarket Indigenous tours to Litchfield and Kakadu.

AAT Kings TOURS

(⏹ 1300 228 546; www.aatkings.com; 52 Mitchell St) The big player in outback Australia, AAT Kings has loads of experience and plenty of tours to choose from, whether Darwin city tours or Kakadu and Litchfield. This is the antithesis of small-group travel, but it's still worth checking to see if it has a tour that suits.

Wallaroo Tours TOURS

(Darwin Tours; ⏹ 08 8981 6670; www.wallarootours. com; 50 Mitchell St; tours $95-170) A collection of half- and full-day tours that include Mary River National Park and its wetlands (good for birding and croc spotting), the jumping crocs of Mary River, scenic flights, Litchfield day trips and Darwin city tours.

Sacred Earth Safaris ADVENTURE

(⏹ 08 8536 2234; www.sacredearthsafaris.com. au; ⏱ May-Oct) Multiday, small-group 4WD camping tours around Kakadu, Katherine and the Kimberley. The two-day Kakadu tour starts at $850, while the five-day Top End National Parks Safari is $2600.

Sea Darwin OUTDOORS

(⏹ 1300 065 022; www.seadarwin.com; 1hr tour adult/child/family $35/20/100) Various eco tours around the city and Darwin Harbour, checking out mangroves, a crocodile trap, a shipwreck and (if you're lucky) dugongs and dolphins.

Darwin Walking Tours WALKING

(⏹ 08 8981 0227; www.darwinwalkingtours.com; 50 Mitchell St; adult/child $25/free) Two-hour guided history walks around the city, plus fishing, adventure and wildlife tours available from the Darwin Tours Shop.

Kakadu Dreams TOURS

(⏹ 1800 813 269; www.kakadudreams.com.au) Backpacker day tours to Litchfield ($149), and boisterous two-/three-day trips to Kakadu ($445/665).

✨ Festivals & Events

Darwin Festival ART

(www.darwinfestival.org.au; ⏱ Aug) This mainly outdoor arts and culture festival celebrates music, theatre, visual art, dance and cabaret and runs for 18 days in August. Festivities are centred in the large park next to Civic Sq, off Harry Chan Ave.

Darwin Aboriginal Art Fair ART

(www.darwinaboriginalartfair.com.au; ⏱ Aug) Held at the **Darwin Convention Centre** (www. darwinconvention.com.au), this three-day August festival showcases Indigenous art from communities throughout the NT.

Darwin Fringe Festival
CULTURAL

(www.facebook.com/darwinfringefestival; ◔ Jul) Showcases eclectic, local performing and visual arts at venues including **Brown's Mart** (☑ 08 8981 5522; www.brownsmart.com.au; 12 Smith St) theatre.

Beer Can Regatta
CULTURAL

(www.beercanregatta.org.au; ◔ Jul) An utterly insane and typically Territorian festival that features races for boats made out of beer cans. It takes place at Mindil Beach (p147) in July and is a good, fun day.

Darwin Cup Carnival
SPORTS

(www.darwinturfclub.org.au; ◔ Jul & Aug) The Darwin Cup racing carnival takes place in July and August at the Darwin Turf Club in Fannie Bay. The highlight of the eight-day program is the running of the Darwin Cup, along with the usual fashion and frivolities.

🛌 Sleeping

Darwin has a good range of accommodation, most of it handy to the CBD, but finding a bed in the peak May-to-September period can be difficult at short notice – book ahead, at least for the first night. Accommodation prices vary greatly with the season and demand; expect big discounts between November and March, especially for mid-range and top-end places.

City Centre & Waterfront

Melaleuca on Mitchell
HOSTEL $

(☑ 1300 723 437; www.momdarwin.com; 52 Mitchell St; dm $32, d with/without bathroom $130/116; ❄ @ 🛜 ☰) If you stay here take note: 24-hour check-in and it's plonked right in the action on Mitchell St. So, sleeping…maybe not. Partying? Oh yes! The highlight is the rooftop island bar and pool area – complete with waterfall spa and big-screen TV. Party heaven! This modern hostel is immaculate with great facilities and it's very secure. Third floor female only.

Chilli's
HOSTEL $

(☑ 1800 351 313, 08 8980 5800; www.chillis.com.au; 69a Mitchell St; dm $32, tw & d without bathroom $90; ❄ 🛜) Friendly Chilli's is a funky place with a small sun deck and spa (use the pool next door). There's also a pool table and a breezy kitchen/meals terrace overlooking Mitchell St. Rooms are compact but clean. There are nice touches to this place, such as pots with scented herbs hanging from the roof of the balcony.

WORTH A TRIP

CHARLES DARWIN NATIONAL PARK

With excellent birdwatching – watch for mangrove species such as the chestnut rail – is **Charles Darwin National Park** (☑ 08 8946 5126; www.nt.gov.au/leisure/parks-reserves; ◔ 8am-7pm) The park protects places of natural and cultural importance including part of Port Darwin wetland, one of the country's most significant wetland areas. It is available for day use only. There's a lookout, WWII displays and some pleasant short walks.

Darwin YHA
HOSTEL $

(☑ 08 8981 5385; www.yha.com.au; 97 Mitchell St; dm $27-38, d $125; ❄ @ 🛜 ☰) This place gets good reports from travellers (young and old). It's in a converted motel, so all 34 rooms have ensuites, and they're built around a decent pool. Some rooms can be noisy; try to get a room towards the back.

★ Vibe Hotel
HOTEL $$

(☑ 08 8982 9998; www.tfehotels.com/brands/vibe-hotels; 7 Kitchener Dr; r $207-240; P ❄ @ 🛜 ☰) You're in for an upmarket stay at this professional set-up with friendly staff and a great location at the Darwin Waterfront Precinct. Room prices creep upwards with more bed space and water views. The Wave Lagoon (p143) is right next door if the shady swimming pool is too placid for you.

Darwin Central Hotel
HOTEL $$

(☑ 1300 364 263, 08 8944 9000; www.darwincentral.com.au; 21 Knuckey St; d from $220; P ❄ @ 🛜 ☰ ☰) Right in the centre of town, this plush independent hotel oozes contemporary style and impeccable facilities. There is a range of stylish rooms with excellent accessibility for travellers with disabilities. Rack rates are steep, but internet, weekend, and three-night-stay discounts make it great value.

★ Argus
APARTMENT $$$

(☑ 08 8925 5000; www.argusaccommodation.com.au; 6 Cardona Ct; 1-/2-/3-bedroom apt from $330/421/509; P ❄ @ ☰) Apartments are *very* spacious at Argus, and the whole place rings with quality. There are lovely bathrooms, generous expanses of cool floor tiles, simple balcony living/dining spaces and snazzy kitchens with all the requisite appliances. The pool is shady and welcoming on a

Central Darwin

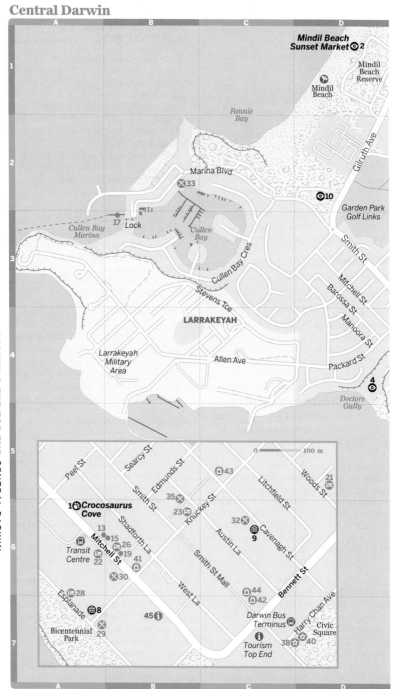

Mindil Beach
Sunset Market ⊚ 2

Mindil
Beach
Reserve

Mindil
Beach

Fannie
Bay

Gilruth Ave

Marina Blvd

⊗ 33

⊚ 10

Garden Park
Golf Links

17 Lock

Cullen Bay Marina

Cullen
Bay

Cullen Bay Cres

Smith St

Stevens Tce

Mitchell St

Barossa St

LARRAKEYAH

Manoora St

Larrakeyah
Military
Area

Allen Ave

Packard St

4 ⊚

Doctors
Gully

Peel St

Searcy St

Edmunds St

🔒 43

Woods St

0 —— 100 m

21

Smith St

Litchfield St

35 ⊗

1 🐊 **Crocosaurus
Cove**

23 🔒

Knuckey St

32 ⊗

🏛 9

Cavenagh St

13

Shadforth La

Austin La

15

Mitchell St

26

19

41 🔒

Transit
Centre

22

⊗ 30

Smith St Mall

West La

🔒 44

🔒 42

Bennett St

Esplanade

🖼 28

🏛 8

45 ℹ

Harry Chan Ave

Darwin Bus
Terminus

Civic
Square

Bicentennial
Park

⊗ 29

ℹ
Tourism
Top End

38 ✿

40

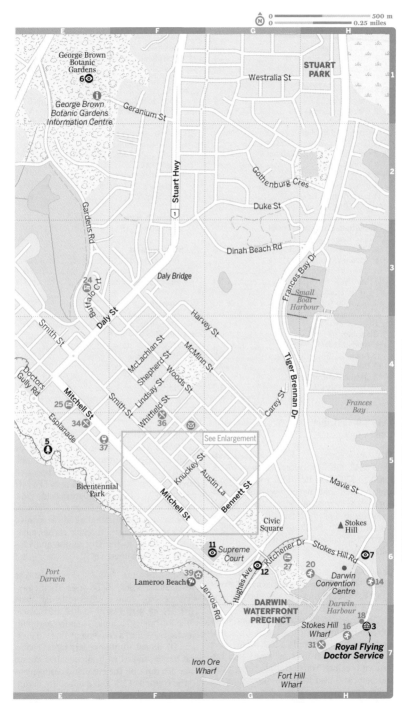

DARWIN & THE TOP END CENTRAL DARWIN

Central Darwin

sticky Top End afternoon. Wet-season prices drop by up to half.

★ **Villa La Vue**　　　　BOUTIQUE HOTEL $$$
(☑08 8942 3012; www.villalavue.com.au; 78 Esplanade; r $395-695) Beautiful rooms with a sophisticated but never overbearing old-world style, a gorgeous stone building as a backdrop, and professional service in a good central location. Put it all together and you have one of Darwin's classiest and more intimate places to stay.

★ **Adina Apartment Hotel**　　APARTMENT $$$
(☑08 8982 9999; www.tfehotels.com; 7 Kitchener Dr; apt $224-463) From the same people who brought the Vibe Hotel (p149) to Darwin, the Adina is a stylish place with contemporary apartments sporting clean lines and modern art on the walls. Most rooms have excellent views out over the water and waterfront precinct. You're close to restaurants and bars, and also within walking distance of downtown.

🛏 City Fringe & Suburbs

FreeSpirit Resort Darwin　　CARAVAN PARK $
(☑08 8935 0888; www.darwinfreespiritresort.com.au; 901 Stuart Hwy, Berrimah; unpowered/powered camp sites from $45/52, cabins & units $95-245; ❄@🖵❄) An impressive highway-side park about a 10-minute drive from the city, with loads of facilities (including three pools). With a jumping cushion, a kidz corner, a bar and live music in the Dry, adults and kids are easily entertained.

Darwin City Edge　　MOTEL $$
(Vitina Studio Motel; ☑08 8981 1544; www.vitinastudiomotel.com.au; 38 Gardens Rd; d/ste $199/229; 🅿❄@🖵❄) We like this place: value-for-money rooms, friendly and efficient service, and a convenient Darwin location. It's a deal. Contemporary motel rooms and larger studios with kitchenettes are on offer. It's right on the city fringe convenient to the Gardens Park golf course, the Botan-

ic Gardens (p143) and Mindil Beach (p147). Keep an eye on its website for discounts.

Grungle Downs B&B
B&B **$$**

(☑08 8947 4440; www.grungledowns.com.au; 945 McMillans Rd, Knuckey Lagoon; r incl breakfast $140-165, cottages $200-400; ✿ 🛜 🐾) Set on a 2-hectare property, this beautiful rural retreat seems worlds away from the city (but it's only 13km). When it's hot outside, hang out in the guest lounge or by the pool. There are four lodge rooms (one with ensuite) and a gorgeous two-bedroom cottage.

Casa on Gregory
MOTEL **$$**

(☑08 8941 3477; www.casaongregory.com.au; 52 Gregory St, Parap; r $83-220; ✿ 🛜 🐾) Describing itself as a 'boutique motel', this well-regarded Parap choice has motel-style rooms that are indeed a cut above your average motel with warm colour schemes and a hint of style in the decor.

✗ Eating

✗ City Centre & Waterfront

There are two large supermarkets in downtown Darwin: **Coles** (www.coles.com.au; Mitchell Centre, 55-59 Mitchell St; ⊙6am-10pm) and **Woolworths.** (www.woolworths.com.au; cnr Cavenagh & Whitfield Sts; ⊙6am-10pm)

★ **Aboriginal**
Bush Traders Cafe
CAFE, AUSTRALIAN **$**

(☑09-8942 4023; www.aboriginalbushtraders. com; cnr Esplanade & Knuckey St; mains & light meals $9.50-17; ⊙7.30am-2pm) In historic Lyons Cottage (p155) this fine little cafe has some really tasty dishes inspired by Aboriginal bush tucker from the desert. In addition to more conventional dishes such as gourmet toasted rolls, try the damper with jam (Kakadu plum or wild rosella jam), the kutjera (wild tomato) and aniseed myrtle feta damper, or the saltbush dukkah, avocado and feta smash.

Speaker's Corner Cafe
CAFE **$**

(☑08 8946 1439; www.karensheldoncatering.com. au/speakers; Parliament House, Mitchell St; breakfast $5-20, mains $12-18; ⊙7.30am-4pm Mon-Fri) In the grounds of Darwin's **Parliament House** (☑08 8946 1512; www.nt.gov.au/lant; Mitchell St; ⊙8am-4.30pm) FREE, and part of a project for training young Indigenous workers for the hospitality industry, Speaker's Corner is a great spot for lunch. In addition to the usual cafe fare, try the Speaker's Cor-

ner laksa and wash it down with a Kakadu plum spritzer. There are also toasties, creative salads and homemade waffles.

Hanuman
INDIAN, THAI **$$**

(☑08 8941 3500; www.hanuman.com.au; 93 Mitchell St; mains $13-36; ⊙noon-2.30pm, dinner from 6pm; 🖉) Ask locals about fine dining in Darwin and they'll usually mention Hanuman. It's sophisticated but not stuffy. Enticing aromas of innovative Indian and Thai Nonya dishes waft from the kitchen to the stylish open dining room and deck. The menu is broad, with exotic vegetarian choices and banquets also available. Respect the sign on the door: 'we appreciate neat attire'.

Little Miss Korea
KOREAN **$$**

(☑09-8981 7092; www.littlemisskorea.com; Austin Lane; lunch mains $14-19, dinner mains $19-32; ⊙11.30am-2.30pm & 5.30pm-late Tue-Fri, 5.30pm-late Sat & Sun) Darwin's first real Korean barbecue place is a good one, with a dining area that manages to be classy, casual and contemporary all at once. Dishes are fresh and tasty and could include chargrilled pork belly or local tiger prawns with lemongrass. The laneway location, Darwin's first, is very cool.

Darwin RSL
INTERNATIONAL **$$**

(☑08 8981 5437; www.darwinrsl.com.au; 27 Cavenagh St; mains $14-30; ⊙10am-9pm; 🖈) If you've spent any time travelling in provincial Australian towns, you'll know the RSL (Returned Services League) clubs are a good deal. There's nothing pretentious here – the atmosphere's very casual and good for families (save for the constant hum of pokies). The food is similarly no-frills excellent, covering great burger choices, pasta, steak and seafood.

> ## PARAP VILLAGE
>
> Parap Village is a foodie's heaven with several good restaurants, bars and cafes as well as the highly recommended deli **Parap Fine Foods** (p154). However, it's the Saturday morning **market** (p154) that attracts locals like bees to honey. It's got a relaxed vibe as breakfast merges into brunch and then lunch. Between visits to the takeaway food stalls (most serving spicy Southeast Asian snacks) shoppers stock up on tropical fruit and vegetables – all you need to make your own laksa or rendang. The produce is local so you know it's fresh.

★**Crustaceans** SEAFOOD $$$
(☑ 08 8981 8658; www.crustaceans.net.au; Stokes Hill Wharf; mains $26-65; ⊙ 5.30-11pm; 🖪) This casual, licensed restaurant features fresh fish, Moreton Bay bugs, lobster, oysters, even crocodile, as well as succulent steaks. It's all about the location, perched right at the end of Stokes Hill Wharf with sunset views over Frances Bay. The cold beer and a first-rate wine list seal the deal.

Char Restaurant STEAK $$$
(☑ 08 8981 4544; www.chardarwin.com.au; cnr Esplanade & Knuckey St; mains $29-69; ⊙ noon-11pm Wed-Fri, 6-11pm Sat-Tue) Housed in the grounds of historic Admiralty House is Char, a carnivore's paradise. The speciality here is chargrilled steaks – aged, grain-fed and cooked to perfection – but there's also a range of clever seafood creations. It's an upmarket atmosphere so dress nicely.

DARWIN'S MAGICAL MARKETS

Mindil Beach Sunset Market (www.mindil.com.au; off Gilruth Ave; ⊙ 5-10pm Thu, 4-9pm Sun May-Oct) Food is the main attraction here – from Thai, Sri Lankan, Indian, Chinese and Malaysian to Brazilian, Greek, Portuguese and more – all at around $6 to $12 a serve. But that's only half the fun – arts and crafts stalls bulge with handmade jewellery, fabulous rainbow tie-dyed clothes, Aboriginal artefacts, and wares from Indonesia and Thailand. Mindil beach (p147) is about 2km from Darwin's city centre; it's an easy walk or hop on buses 4 or 6, which go past the market.

Parap Village Market (www.parapvillage.com.au; Parap Shopping Village, Parap Rd, Parap; ⊙ 8am-2pm Sat) This compact, crowded food-focused market is a local favourite. There's the full gamut of Southeast Asian cuisine, as well as plenty of ingredients to cook up your own tropical storm. It's open year-round.

Nightcliff Market (www.nightcliffmarkets.com.au; Pavonia Way, Nightcliff; ⊙ 6am-2pm Sun) A popular community market north of the city in the Nightcliff Shopping Centre. You'll find lots of secondhand goods and designer clothing.

✗ **City Fringe & Suburbs**

Parap Fine Foods MARKET $
(☑ 08 8981 8597; www.parapfinefoods.com; 40 Parap Rd, Parap; ⊙ 8am-6.30pm Mon-Fri, 8am-6pm Sat, 9am-1pm Sun) A gourmet food hall in Parap shopping centre, stocking organic and health foods, deli items and fine wine – perfect for a picnic.

Laneway Specialty Coffee CAFE $
(☑ 08 8941 4511; www.facebook.com/lanewayspecialtycoffee; 4/1 Vickers St, Parap; mains $12-18; ⊙ 8am-3pm Mon-Sat) The pared-back, industrial interior, corner location and powerhouse coffee here have locals wondering if they could be in Melbourne. Getting rave reviews, this place is fast becoming popular. Its well-prepared dishes use local and organic ingredients; the almost artistic bacon-and-egg roll is worth the trip here alone. For lunch the wagyu beef burger beckons.

★**Darwin Ski Club** MODERN AUSTRALIAN $$
(☑ 08 8981 6630; www.darwinskiclub.com.au; Conacher St, Fannie Bay; mains $18-28; ⊙ noon-10pm) This place just keeps getting better. Already Darwin's finest location for a sunset beer (p155), it now does seriously good tucker too. The dishes are well prepared, and the menu is thoughtful and enticing. We had the red curry and were impressed. Highly recommended by locals.

★**Exotic North Indian Cuisine** INDIAN $$
(☑ 08 8941 3396; www.exoticnorthindiancuisine.com.au; Cullen Bay Marina; mains $14-23; ⊙ 5-10pm; 🖪) Offering outstanding value for quality Indian cuisine, this place has taken over the mantle of Darwin's best Indian restaurant. It's positioned right on the waterfront at Cullen Bay, making for extremely pleasant waterside dining in the evening. The service is attentive, there are high chairs for young 'uns and, unusually for Darwin, you can BYO wine.

Pee Wee's at the Point MODERN AUSTRALIAN $$$
(☑ 08 8981 6868; www.peewees.com.au; Alec Fong Lim Dr, East Point Reserve; mains $41-68; ⊙ from 6.30pm) With Hahndorf venison striploin kicking in at $68 a serve, this is indeed a place for a treat. One of Darwin's finest restaurants, it is well worth shelling out for the experience. Enjoy your double-roasted duckling among tropical palms at East Point Reserve (p147), right on the waterfront.

🍷 Drinking & Nightlife

★**Darwin Ski Club** PUB
(📞08 8981 6630; www.darwinskiclub.com.au; Conacher St, Fannie Bay; ☺noon-late) Leave Mitchell St behind and head for a sublime sunset at this laid-back waterski club on Vesteys Beach (p147). The view through the palm trees from the beer garden is a winner, and there are often live bands. Hands down the best venue for a sunset beer in Darwin.

Discovery & Lost Arc CLUB
(📞08 8942 3300; www.discoverydarwin.com.au; 89 Mitchell St; ☺noon-late) Discovery is Darwin's biggest nightclub and dance venue, with three levels featuring hip hop, techno and house, bars, private booths, karaoke, an elevated dance floor and plenty of partygoers. The Lost Arc is the classy chill-out bar opening on to Mitchell St, which starts to thaw after about 10pm.

Bogarts BAR
(📞08 8981 3561; 52 Gregory St, Parap; ☺4pm-late Tue-Sat) Bogarts is one of Darwin's best bars and well worth the trek out into the suburbs. The decor is old movie posters, cane furniture and animal-print lounges in a mishmash that, strangely enough, works beautifully. It has a low-key ambience and is a local favourite for the over-30s crowd.

Darwin Sailing Club SPORTS BAR
(📞08 8981 1700; www.dwnsail.com.au; Atkins Dr, Fannie Bay; ☺noon-2pm & 5.30-9pm) More upmarket than the ski club (p155), the sailing club is always filled with yachties enjoying a sunset beer overlooking the Timor Sea. Tunes on the sound system are surprisingly un-yacht club (no Christopher Cross or Rod Stewart). Sign in as a visitor at the door.

☆ Entertainment

Off the Leash (www.offtheleash.net.au) magazine lists events happening around town.

★**Deckchair Cinema** CINEMA
(📞08 8981 0700; www.deckchaircinema.com; Jervois Rd, Waterfront Precinct; adult/child $16/8; ☺box office from 6.30pm Apr-Nov) During the Dry, the Darwin Film Society runs this fabulous outdoor cinema below the southern end of the Esplanade. Watch a movie under the stars while reclining in a deckchair. There's a licensed bar serving food or you can bring a picnic (no BYO alcohol). There are usually double features on Friday and Saturday nights (adult/child $24/12).

Happy Yess LIVE MUSIC
(www.happyyess.tumblr.com; Brown's Mart, 12 Smith St; ☺6pm-midnight Thu-Sat) This venue is Darwin's leading place for live music. A not-for-profit venue for musicians run by musicians, you won't hear cover bands in here. Original, sometimes weird, always fun.

Darwin Railway Club LIVE MUSIC
(📞08 8981 4171; 17 Somerville Gardens, Parap; ☺4-11.30pm Mon-Fri, noon-2am Sat, noon-10pm Sun) Big supporters of Darwin's live music scene, this place pulls in some class acts.

🛍 Shopping

★**Outstation Gallery** ART
(📞08 8981 4822; www.outstation.com.au; 8 Parap Pl; ☺10am-1pm Tue, 5pm Wed-Fri, 2pm Sat) One of Darwin's best galleries of Indigenous art, Outstation presents the works of nine different Aboriginal art centres from across the NT, from Arnhem Land to the Western Desert.

Nomad Art Gallery ART
(📞08 8981 6382; www.nomadart.com.au; 1/3 Vickers St, Parap; ☺10am-5pm Mon-Fri, 9am-2pm Sat) Around since 2005, this high-end gallery sells contemporary Indigenous art, including limited-edition paintings, textiles, carpets, bronze and jewellery.

Mbantua Fine Art Gallery ART
(📞08 8941 6611; www.mbantua.com.au; 2/30 Smith St Mall; ☺9am-5pm Mon-Sat) Vivid Utopian designs painted on everything from canvases to ceramics.

Aboriginal Bush Traders ARTS & CRAFTS
(📞0487 007 070; www.aboriginalbushtraders. com; 74 Esplanade; ☺9am-2pm) Inhabiting the fine old heritage building of **Lyons Cottage** (📞0488 329 933; cnr Esplanade & Knuckey St) 🆓, this is a collection of artworks, carvings, weaving, jewellery and a small number of books and CDs. There's also a cafe (p153).

The Bookshop BOOKS
(📞08 8941 3489; www.bookshopdarwin.com.au; 1/30 Smith St Mall; ☺9am-5pm Mon-Fri, 9am-3pm Sat, 10am-2pm Sun) Probably Darwin's best bookshop with a good general selection.

Darwin Art Trail ART
(www.darwinarttrail.com.au; ☺10am-4pm 3rd Sun of month May-Sep) This online resource is a good way to get to know the lesser-known art galleries and artists around Darwin with around seven studios involved. Aside from the studios' normal opening hours, they all have monthly open days.

NT General Store
SPORTS & OUTDOORS

(☑08 8981 8242; www.thentgeneralstore.com.
au; 42 Cavenagh St; ⊙8.30am-5.30pm Mon-Wed,
6pm Thu & Fri, 1pm Sat) This casual, corrugated-iron warehouse has shelves piled high
with camping and bushwalking gear, as well
as a range of maps.

Aboriginal Fine Arts Gallery
ART

(☑08 8981 1315; www.aaia.com.au; 1st fl, cnr Mitch-
ell & Knuckey Sts; ⊙9am-5pm Mon-Fri, 9am-3pm
Sat, 10am-3pm Sun) Displays and sells art from
Arnhem Land and the Central Desert region.

Tiwi Art Network
ART

(☑08 8941 3593; www.ankaaa.org.au/art-centre/
tiwi-art-network-tiwi-islands; 3/3 Vickers St, Parap;
⊙10am-5pm Wed-Fri, to 2pm Sat) 🖋 The office
and showroom for three arts communities
on the Tiwi Islands.

ℹ Information

DANGERS & ANNOYANCES

➡ Darwin is a generally safe city to visit but the
usual rules apply: petty crime can be a problem, particularly late at night, so avoid walking
alone in unlit areas and don't leave valuables
in your car.

➡ In response to several reports of drugged
drinks, authorities are advising women to refuse drinks offered by strangers in bars and to
drink bottled alcohol rather than from a glass.

➡ Always assume that there are crocodiles in
waterholes and rivers in the Darwin area.

➡ Cyclones can happen from November to
April, while heavy monsoon rains can curtail
outdoor activities from December to March.

➡ **Fire** (☑000; www.pfes.nt.gov.au) For local
fire services.

INTERNET ACCESS

Most accommodation in Darwin provides some
form of internet access, and there's free wi-fi
available in the Smith Street Mall.

NT Library (☑1800 019 155; www.dtc.nt.gov.
au/arts-and-museums/northern-territory-
library; Parliament House, Mitchell St; ⊙10am-
5pm Mon-Fri, 1-5pm Sat & Sun; 🛜)

MEDICAL SERVICES

Ark Aid (☑0409 090 840; www.wildlifedarwin.
org.au) The people to call if you come across
injured wildlife.

Royal Darwin Hospital (☑08 8920 6011;
www.health.nt.gov.au; 105 Rocklands Dr, Tiwi;
⊙24hr)

MONEY

There are 24-hour ATMs dotted around the city
centre, and exchange bureaux on Mitchell St.

POST

General Post Office (☑13 13 18; www.
auspost.com.au; 48 Cavenagh St; ⊙9am-5pm
Mon-Fri, to 12.30pm Sat)

TOURIST INFORMATION

**George Brown Botanic Gardens Information
Centre** (⊙8am-4pm)

Northern Land Council (☑08 8920 5100;
www.nlc.org.au; 45 Mitchell St) Permits for Arnhem Land and other northern mainland areas.

Tiwi Land Council (p270) Permits for the Tiwi
Islands.

Tourism Top End (☑1300 138 886, 08 8980
6000; www.tourismtopend.com.au; cnr Smith
& Bennett Sts; ⊙8.30am-5pm Mon-Fri, 9am-
3pm Sat & Sun) Helpful office with hundreds of
brochures; books tours and accommodation.

ℹ Getting There & Away

AIR

Darwin International Airport (☑08 8920
1811; www.darwinairport.com.au; Henry
Wrigley Dr, Marrara) is 12km north of the
city centre, and handles both international
and domestic flights. **Darwin City Airport
Shuttle Service** (☑08 8947 3979; www.
darwincityairportshuttleservice.com.au; per
person $15) is one of a number of private
airport shuttle companies who will pick up or
drop off almost anywhere in the centre. When
leaving Darwin book a day before departure. A
taxi fare into the centre is about $40.

The following airlines operate from the airport:
Airnorth (www.airnorth.com.au), **Jetstar** (www.
jetstar.com), **Qantas** (www.qantas.com.au) and
Virgin Australia (www.virginaustralia.com).

BUS

Greyhound Australia (☑1300 473 946; www.
greyhound.com.au) operates long-distance
bus services from the **Transit Centre** (p269).
There's at least one service per day up and
down the Stuart Hwy, stopping at Pine Creek
(from $62, three hours), Katherine ($75,
four hours), Mataranka ($102, seven hours),
Tennant Creek ($206, 14½ hours) and Alice
Springs ($265, 22 hours).

For Kakadu, there's a daily return service from
Darwin to Jabiru ($75, 3½ hours).

Backpacker buses and tours can also get you
to out-of-the-way places.

CAR & CAMPERVAN

For driving around Darwin, conventional vehicles
are cheap enough, but most companies offer
only 100km per day free, which won't get you
very far out of town. Rates start at around $40
per day for a small car with 100km per day.

There are also plenty of 4WD vehicles available
in Darwin, through companies like **Britz** (☑1800

331 454; www.britz.com.au; 17 Bombing Rd, Winnellie), but you usually have to book ahead and fees/deposits are higher than for 2WD vehicles. Larger companies offer one-way rentals plus better mileage deals for more-expensive vehicles. Campervans are a great option for touring around the NT and you generally get unlimited kilometres even for short rentals. Prices start at around $60 a day for a basic camper or $100 to $120 for a three-berth hi-top camper, to $250-plus for the bigger mobile homes or 4WD bushcampers. Additional insurance cover or excess reduction costs extra.

Most rental companies are open every day and have agencies in the city centre. **Avis** (☑ 08 8936 0600; www.avis.com.au; 89 Smith St), **Budget** (☑ 08 8981 9800; www.budget.com. au; McLachlan St), **Hertz** (☑ 08 8941 0944; www.hertz.com.au; Shop 41, Mitchell Centre, 55-59 Mitchell St; ☺ 8am-5pm Mon-Fri, to noon Sat & Sun) and **Thrifty** (☑ 08 8924 2454; www. rentacar.com.au; 50 Mitchell St) all have offices at the airport.

There's also:

Europcar (☑ 08 8941 0300; www.europcar. com.au; 77 Cavenagh St; ☺ 8am-5pm Mon-Fri, to noon Sat & Sun)

JJ's Car Hire (☑ 0427 214 229; www.jjscarhire. com.au; 7 Goyder Rd, Parap) A good local operator.

Mighty Cars & Campervans (www.mighty campers.com.au; 17 Bombing Rd, Winnellie)

Travellers Autobarn (☑ 1800 674 374; www. travellers-autobarn.com.au; 19 Bishop St)

For assistance or information try one of the following:

AANT Roadside Assistance (☑ 13 11 11; www. aant.com.au)

Automobile Association of the Northern Territory (p269)

TRAIN

The legendary *Ghan* train, operated by Great Southern Rail (www.greatsouthernrail.com.au), runs weekly (twice weekly May to July) between Adelaide and Darwin via Alice Springs. The Darwin terminus is on Berrimah Rd, 15km/20 minutes from the city centre. A taxi fare into the centre is about $35, though there is a shuttle service to/from the **Transit Centre** (p269).

ℹ Getting Around

BUS

Darwinbus (☑ 08 8944 2444; www.nt.gov. au/driving/public-transport-cycling) runs a comprehensive bus network that departs from the **Darwin Bus Terminus** (Harry Chan Ave), opposite Brown's Mart.

A $3 adult ticket gives unlimited travel on the bus network for three hours (validate your ticket

when you first get on). Daily ($7) and weekly ($20) travel cards are also available from bus interchanges, newsagents and the **visitor centre** (p156). Bus 4 (to Fannie Bay, Nightcliff, Rapid Creek and Casuarina) and bus 6 (Fannie Bay, Parap and Stuart Park) are useful for getting to **Aquascene** (p143), the **Botanic Gardens** (p143), **Mindil Beach** (p147), the **Museum & Art Gallery** (p147), **East Point Reserve** (p147) and the markets.

TAXI

Taxis wait along Knuckey St, diagonally opposite the north end of Smith St Mall, and are usually easy to flag down. Call **Darwin Radio Taxis** (☑ 13 10 08; www.131008.com).

AROUND DARWIN

In Darwin's hinterland you'll come across some real gems, particularly Litchfield National Park, the Mary River region, Pine Creek and the Tiwi Islands. You're never more than a couple of hours from the capital but, with the exception of the Tiwi Islands, we recommend doing more than just a day visit from Darwin – every one of these places is worth lingering over.

Tiwi Islands

The Tiwi Islands – Bathurst Island and Melville Island – lie about 80km north of Darwin, and are home to the Tiwi Aboriginal people. A visit here is one of the cultural highlights of the Top End. The Tiwis (We People) have a distinct culture and today are well known for producing vibrant art and the odd champion Aussie Rules football player. Tourism is restricted on the islands and for most travellers the only way to visit is on one of the daily organised tours from Darwin.

The main settlement on the islands is Wurrumiyanga in the southeast of Bathurst Island, which was founded in 1911 as a Catholic mission. On Melville Island the settlements are Pirlangimpi and Milikapiti.

☞ Tours

There's no public transport, so the best way to see the islands is on a tour. You can catch the Sealink (p159) ferry over to Wurrumiyanga on Bathurst Island and have a very quick ook around the town without taking a tour or buying a permit, but if you want to explore further you'll need a permit from the Tiwi Land Council (p270).

DARWIN & THE TOP END TIWI ISLANDS

Around Darwin

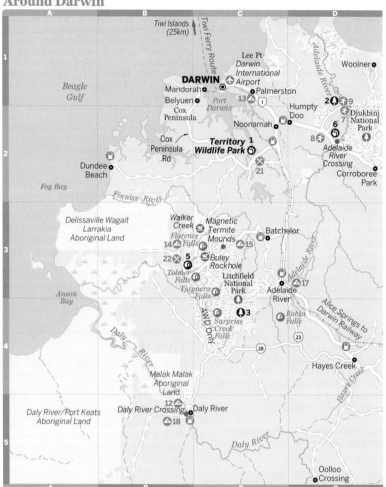

Tiwi Tours Aboriginal
Cultural Experience   CULTURAL
(☑1300 228 546; www.aatkings.com/tours/
tiwi-tours-aboriginal-cultural-experience-by-ferry;
adult/child $285/143) Runs fascinating day
trips to the Tiwis, although interaction with
the local community tends to be limited to
your guides and the local workshops and
showrooms. The tour is available by ferry
(2½ hours each way Thursday and Friday).

Tiwi by Design   CULTURAL
(☑1300 130 679; www.sealinknt.com.au; adult/
child $345/289; ⊙8am-5.45pm Thu & Fri Apr–mid-
Dec, 8am-5.45pm Mon mid-Jun–Aug) Leaving

from Cullen Bay ferry terminal, this tour
to the Tiwi Islands includes permits, lunch
and a welcome ceremony, as well as visits to
a local museum, church and art workshop,
where you get to create your own design. It's
run by Sealink (p159), the ferry operator.

✿ Festivals & Events

Tiwi Grand Final   SPORTS
(⊙Mar) Held at the end of March on Bathurst
Island, this sporting spectacular displays the
Tiwis' sparkling skills and passion for Aussie
Rules football. Thousands come from Dar-
win for the day, which coincides with the

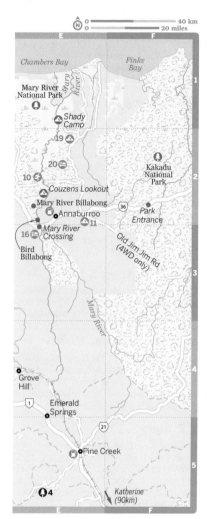

operate from Darwin's Cullen Bay to the Tiwi Islands daily at noon (less often during the Wet); the journey takes 2½ hours and departs Wurrumiyanga on the islands at 3.15pm. If you visit the islands on the public ferry, you'll only have 45 minutes to have a quick look around Wurrumiyanga.

Tiwi Art Sale (www.tiwidesigns.com). Book your tour or ferry trip well in advance.

🛏 Sleeping & Eating

Visitors are not allowed to stay on the island without permission and there are no hotels. Visit instead on a day trip from Darwin.

Some of the tour operators provide lunch, but otherwise there are no restaurants or supermarkets so you'll need to bring your own food.

ⓘ Getting There & Away

Sealink (www.sealinknt.com.au; adult/child one-way $52.50/27.50, return $105/55) ferries

Arnhem Highway

The Arnhem Highway (Rte 36) connects Darwin to Kakadu National Park – it branches off towards Kakadu 34km southeast of Darwin – and while many travellers stop for little more than petrol along the way, there are a number of worthwhile sights and activities if you have the time. These include river cruises and wetland birdwatching, as well as the small agricultural hub (and gloriously named) Humpty Doo where you can see The Big Boxing Crocodile.

◎ Sights

Djukbinj National Park
NATIONAL PARK

(☑08 8988 8009; www.nt.gov.au/leisure/parks-reserves) Flood plains and billabongs make for good birdwatching at this pretty park 80km southeast of Darwin off the Arnhem Hwy. This was once the hunting grounds for the Limilngan people who now comanage the park, and the waterbirds here can be epic in numbers, especially the magpie geese. There are lookouts at Scotts Creek, Little Sister Billabong and Twin Billabong, and a picnic area at Calf Billabong. The park is often closed or otherwise inaccessible from December to March due to heavy rains.

Window on the
Wetlands Visitor Centre
WILDLIFE RESERVE

(www.nt.gov.au/leisure/parks-reserves; Arnhem Hwy; ⊙8am-5.30pm) FREE Three kilometres past the Fogg Dam (p160) turn-off east along the Arnhem Hwy is this dashing-looking structure full of displays explaining the wetland ecosystem, as well as the history of the local Limilngan-Wulna Aboriginal people. There are great views over the Adelaide River flood plain from the observation deck.

Fogg Dam
Conservation Reserve
NATURE RESERVE

(www.foggdamfriends.org) There are ludicrous numbers of waterbirds living at the fecund green Fogg Dam Conservation Reserve. The dam walls are closed to walkers (crocs), but there are a couple of nature walks (2.2km and 3.6km) through the forest and woodlands. Bird numbers are highest between December and July. The turn-off for the reserve is about 15km southeast along the Arnhem Hwy from Humpty Doo.

⚡ Activities

Adelaide River Cruises
WILDLIFE WATCHING

(☑08 8983 3224; www.adelaiderivercruises.com.au; tours adult/child/family $45/20/110; ⊙9am, 11am, 1pm & 3pm May-Oct) See the jumping crocodiles on a private stretch of river past the Fogg Dam turn-off. Also runs small-group full-day wildlife cruises.

Spectacular Jumping
Crocodile Cruise
WILDLIFE WATCHING

(☑08 8978 9077; www.jumpingcrocodile.com.au; tours adult/child $40/25; ⊙9am, 11am, 1pm & 3pm) Along the Window on the Wetlands (p160) access road, this outfit runs one-hour tours. Ask about trips ex-Darwin.

Adelaide River Queen
WILDLIFE WATCHING

(☑08 8988 8144; www.jumpingcrocodilecruises.com.au; tours adult/child $45/30; ⊙9am, 10am, 11am, 1pm, 2pm & 3pm Mar-Oct) Well-established jumping-crocodile operator on the highway just before Adelaide River Crossing.

🛏 Sleeping & Eating

Humpty Doo Hotel
PUB FOOD $$

(☑08 8988 1372; www.humptydoohotel.net; Arnhem Hwy; mains $19-32; ⊙10am-9pm; ❀) Some people stop here because, well, it's the sort of name you'd like to tell your friends about when you're back home, but there's more to this place than novelty. The self-proclaimed 'world famous' Humpty Doo Hotel is a popular local serving up big meals, big Sunday sessions and Friday night bands. There are unremarkable motel rooms and cabins out the back (rooms $130 to $160).

ℹ Getting There & Away

There's not much public transport along the Arnhem Hwy, but most visitors either drive or visit on a tour. There's a petrol station at Humpty Doo.

Mary River Region

Often overlooked in the rush to Kakadu, Mary River is worth dedicating some time to, with the wetlands and wildlife of the Mary River National Park (p161), north of the Arnhem Hwy, the centrepiece.

🐾 Tours

Pudakul Aboriginal Cultural Tours
TOURS

(☑08 8984 9282; www.pudakul.com.au; adult/child/family $99/55/250; ⊙May-Oct) This fine small operator runs two-hour Indigenous cultural tours in the Adelaide River and Mary River regions, with Aboriginal guides taking you through everything from painting, spear-throwing and didgeridoo lessons to bush-tucker and bush-medicine guided walks.

Wetland Cruises –
Corroboree Billabong
TOURS

(☑08 8985 5855; www.wetlandcruises.com.au; ⊙Mar-Oct) These excellent boat excursions show the Mary River Wetlands in all their glory. You're almost guaranteed to see saltwater crocs, as well as plenty of bird life. There are one-hour morning cruises (adult/child $40/30) and lunch or sunset cruises along with full-day excursions from Darwin (adult/child $130/100).

DARWIN & THE TOP END ARNHEM HIGHWAY

MARY RIVER NATIONAL PARK

With an interesting mix of barramundi fishing, pretty landscapes and history, Mary River National Park (08 8978 8986; www.nt.gov.au/leisure/parks-reserves) has good bird life, saltwater crocodiles and paperbark-fringed swamps. Bird Billabong, just off the Arnhem Hwy a few kilometres before Mary River Crossing if you're coming from the west, is a back-flow billabong, filled by creeks flowing off the nearby Mt Bundy Hill during the Wet. It's 4km off the highway and accessible by 2WD year-round. The scenic loop walk (4.5km, two hours) passes through tropical woodlands, with a backdrop of Mt Bundy granite rocks. About another 2km along the same road is the emerald-green Mary River Billabong, with a BBQ area (no camping). From here the 4WD-only Hardies Track leads deeper into the national park to Corroboree Billabong (25km) and Couzens Lookout (37km); the sunsets are especially pretty from Couzens Lookout, where there's a camp site.

Further east and north of the Arnhem Hwy, the partly sealed Point Stuart Rd leads to a number of riverside viewing platforms and to Shady Camp. The causeway barrage here, which stops fresh water flowing into saltwater, creates the ideal feeding environment for barramundi, and the ideal fishing environment.

In the park's northern reaches, devotees of explorer history will not want to miss the 6km-return walk in Point Stuart Coastal Reserve out to Stuart's Memorial Cairn – it marks the northernmost point reached by John McDouall Stuart in 1862.

🛏 Sleeping

Annaburroo Billabong CAMPGROUND $
(🖰08 8978 8971; Arnhem Hwy; unpowered sites per adult/family $10/22, cabins $75-160) With a private billabong, bush camp sites, a wandering menagerie and friendly owners, this place seems a world away from the highway only 2km down the road, and is a great alternative to the roadhouses. The elevated African-style safari cabins with fridge and ensuite are cosy, and there are cabins, lodge rooms and immaculate tin-and-bamboo amenity blocks.

★ **Mary River**
Wilderness Retreat RESORT $$
(🖰08 8978 8877; www.maryriverpark.com.au; Mary River Crossing, Arnhem Hwy; unpowered/powered sites $30/43, cabins & safari tents $145-220; ❄🛜🏊) Boasting 3km of Mary River frontage, this bush retreat has excellent poolside and bush cabins with decks surrounded by trees, as well as some fine safari tents. Pool cabins are the pick of the bunch with high ceilings, walk-in showers and more space to knock around in; both sleep up to three people. Camping on the grassy slopes here is delightful.

Point Stuart
Wilderness Lodge CAMPGROUND $$
(🖰08 8978 8914; www.pointstuart.com.au; Point Stuart Rd; camping per adult/child $17.50/6, safari tents s/d $35/50, d $130-195; ❄🏊) Accessible by 2WD and only 36km from the Arnhem Hwy, this remote-feeling lodge is part of an old cattle station and ideal for exploring the Mary River region. Accommodation ranges from camp sites and simple safari tents to budget rooms and decent lodge rooms. Two-hour wetland cruises on croc-rich Rockhole Billabong cost $65/25 per adult/child, and boat hire is available.

★ **Wildman Wilderness Lodge** RESORT $$$
(🖰08 8978 8955; www.wildmanwildernesslodge. com.au; Point Stuart Rd; safari tent/cabin half-board $615/769; ❄🏊) One of the best places to stay in the Top End, Wildman Wilderness Lodge is an upmarket safari lodge with an exceptional program of optional tours and activities, not to mention some gorgeous, supremely comfortable accommodation in a beautiful and remote setting. There are just 10 air-conditioned, stylish, architect-designed cabins and 15 fan-cooled, clean-lined luxury tents.

❶ Getting There & Away

You'll need a 4WD to explore anywhere in the national park beyond the Arnhem Hwy, although a few park trails may be passable in a 2WD during the dry season. Petrol is available along the Arnhem Highway. Some accommodation places offer transfers from Darwin and elsewhere.

Berry Springs

The only two reasons to come to Berry Springs – and they're good ones – are to visit one of the NT's best zoos, home to a brilliant collection of Australia's native wildlife, and a fine waterhole. It's a perfect day trip from Darwin.

◉ Sights

★ **Territory Wildlife Park** ZOO
(📞08 8988 7200; www.territorywildlifepark.com.au; 960 Cox Peninsula Rd; adult/child/family $32/16/54.50; ⊙9am-5pm) This excellent park, 60km from Darwin, showcases the best of Aussie wildlife. Pride of place must go to the aquarium, where a clear walk-through tunnel puts you among giant barramundi, stingrays, sawfish and saratogas, while a separate tank holds a 3.8m saltwater crocodile. To see everything you can either walk around the 4km perimeter road, or hop on and off the shuttle trains that run every 15 to 30 minutes and stop at all the exhibits.

Berry Springs Nature Park NATURE RESERVE
(www.nt.gov.au/leisure/parks-reserves; ⊙8am-6.30pm) This wonderful waterhole is the closest to Darwin and very popular with locals. It's a beautiful series of spring-fed swimming holes shaded by paperbarks and pandanus palms and serenaded by abundant birds; native flowers bloom here in March and April. Facilities include a kiosk, a picnic area with BBQs, toilets, changing sheds and showers. And there are large grassed areas to lounge around on in between swims.

✗ Eating

★ **Crazy Acres**
Mango Farm & Cafe CAFE $
(📞08 8988 6227; www.crazyacres.com.au; Reedbeds Rd; light meals $10-16; ⊙9am-5.30pm May-Sep) Homemade ice cream, mango smoothies, local honey, Devonshire teas and a range of light meals from mango chicken (of course) to a gorgeous Farmer's Platter – what's not to like about this lovely little place just off Cox Peninsula Rd?

❶ Getting There & Away

The turn-off to Berry Springs is 48km down the Stuart Hwy from Darwin; it's 10km from the turn-off to the nature park, and a further 2km to the wildlife park.

Batchelor

POP 336

The little town of Batchelor was once so sleepy the government gave blocks of land away for a time to encourage settlement. That was before uranium was discovered and the nearby Rum Jungle mine developed (it closed in 1971 after operating for almost 20 years). These days, Batchelor is an important gateway and service centre for neighbouring Litchfield National Park.

◉ Sights

From the Visitor Information Centre, pick up a copy of the photocopied *Batchelor Heritage Walk* to guide your steps. It provides a potted history of the town and a self-guided route for a leisurely amble with a focus on local history.

⌁ Sleeping & Eating

Litchfield Tourist Park CARAVAN PARK $
(📞08 8976 0070; www.litchfieldtouristpark.com.au; 2916 Litchfield Park Rd; camp sites $38, bunkhouse $79, ensuite cabins from $148; ❄@🛜🏊) Just 4km from Litchfield National Park (p163), there's a great range of accommodation here and it's the closest option to the park. There's also a breezy, open-sided bar-restaurant (all-day food $11 to $21, open breakfast and dinner) where you can get a beer, a burger or a real coffee.

★ **Rum Jungle Bungalows** BUNGALOW $$
(📞08 8976 0555; 10 Meneling Rd; r $170; ❄🏊) With more personality than most Batchelor places and rooms with warm and eclectic decor, Rum Jungle is an excellent choice. It's set in soothing and beautiful gardens and is open year-round.

Batchelor Butterfly Farm RESORT $$
(📞08 8976 0110; www.butterflyfarm.net.au; 8 Meneling Rd; d Apr-Sep $160, Oct-Mar $80-150; ❄@🛜🏊) This compact, slightly eclectic retreat divides itself between a low-key tourist attraction and friendly tropical-style resort. There's a butterfly farm (adult/child $10/5), mini zoo (free for staying guests), ensuite cabins, a large homestay, and a busy all-day cafe-restaurant (mains $18 to $32) featuring Asian-inspired dishes. It's all a bit Zen with Buddha statues, chill music and wicker chairs on the shaded deck.

Litchfield Motel RESORT $$
(☑08 8976 0123; www.litchfieldmotel.com.au; 37-49 Rum Jungle Rd; d Apr-Oct $195-215, Nov-Mar $150-170; ❀ 🖶 ⛆) On the edge of town, this sprawling orange-brick complex has decent motel rooms and energetic new managers. It's good for families, with bird feeding, two pools and two restaurants. There's also a bar and a grocery shop.

Batchelor General Store MARKET $
(cnr Takarri Rd & Nurndina St; ⊘6am-6pm) Combines a well-stocked supermarket, takeaway, newsagent and post office.

🛍 Shopping

Coomalie Cultural Centre ARTS & CRAFTS
(☑08 8939 7404; www.facebook.com/coomalie artcentre; cnr Awilla Rd & Nurndina St; ⊘10am-5pm Tue-Sat Apr-Sep, 10am-4pm Tue-Fri Oct-Mar) The community-based Coomalie Cultural Centre displays and sells a range of Indigenous art and crafts from throughout the NT, and runs an artist-in-residence program, so you'll often see artists at work.

ℹ Information

Visitor Information Centre (☑08 8976 0444; Takarri Rd; ⊘8.30am-5pm)

ℹ Getting There & Away

Batchelor is 98km south of Darwin and 14km west of the Stuart Highway along a sealed road. There's a **petrol station** in the town centre.

Litchfield National Park

It may not be as well known as Kakadu, but many NT locals rate Litchfield (☑08 8976 0282; www.nt.gov.au/leisure/parks-reserves) even higher. Our response? Why not visit both? The rock formations and the rock pools in cliff shadow here are simply stunning and Litchfield is smaller and more manageable than Kakadu. The 1500-sq-km national park encloses much of the spectacular Tabletop Range, a wide sandstone plateau mostly surrounded by cliffs. The waterfalls that pour off the edge of this plateau are a highlight of the park, feeding crystal-clear cascades and croc-free plunge pools.

The only downside is that, given its proximity to and ease of access from Darwin, it's often busy, and the road can be full of tour buses. Even so, it remains a beautiful place and certainly one of the best spots in the Top End for bushwalking and swimming.

👁 Sights & Activities

About 17km after entering the park from Batchelor you come to what look like tombstones. But only the very tip of these magnetic termite mounds is used to bury the dead; at the bottom are the king and queen, with workers in between. They're perfectly aligned to regulate temperature, catching the morning sun, then allowing the residents to dodge the midday heat. Nearby are some giant mounds made by the aptly named cathedral termites.

Another 6km further along is the turn-off to Buley Rockhole (2km), where water cascades through a series of rock pools big enough to lodge your bod in. This turn-off also takes you to Florence Falls (5km), one of Litchfield's more agreeable waterholes and accessed by a 15-minute, 135-step descent to a deep, beautiful pool surrounded by monsoon forest. Alternatively, you can see the falls from a lookout, 120m from the car park. There's a walking track (1.7km, 45 minutes) between the two places that follows Florence Creek.

About 18km beyond the turn-off to Florence Falls is the turn-off to the spectacular Tolmer Falls, which are for looking at only. A 1.6km loop track (45 minutes) offers beautiful views of the valley. Tolmer Falls doesn't quite get the crowds because of the absence of swimming and we like it all the more for that.

It's a further 7km along the main road to the turn-off for Litchfield's big-ticket attraction, Wangi Falls (wong-guy), 1.6km up a side road. The falls flow year-round, spilling either side of a huge orange-rock outcrop and filling an enormous swimming hole bordered by rainforest. Bring swimming goggles to spot local fish. It's immensely popular during the Dry (when there's a portable refreshment kiosk here, and free public wi-fi), but water levels in the Wet can make it unsafe; look for signposted warnings.

The park offers plenty of bushwalking, including the Tabletop Track (39km), a circuit of the park that takes three to five days to complete depending on how many side tracks you follow. You can access the track at Florence Falls, Wangi Falls and Walker Creek. You must carry a topographic map of the area, available from tourist and retail outlets in Batchelor. The track is closed late September to March.

🛏 Sleeping

There is excellent public camping (adult/child $6.60/3.30) with toilets and fireplaces at Florence Falls (p163), Florence Creek, Buley Rockhole (p163), Wangi Falls (p163) (better for vans than tents) and Tjaynera Falls (Sandy Creek; 4WD required). There are more-basic camp sites at Surprise Creek Falls (4WD required) and Walker Creek. Otherwise, most people who stay overnight do so in one of the motels or caravan parks in Batchelor or on the road into Litchfield.

Litchfield Safari Camp CAMPGROUND $
(☑ 08 8978 2185; www.litchfieldsafaricamp.com.au; Litchfield Park Rd; unpowered/powered sites $25/35, dm $30, d safari tents $150; ☀) Shady grassed sites make this a good alternative to Litchfield's bush camping sites, especially if you want power and to stay inside the park. The safari tents are great value as they comfortably sleep up to four folks. There's also a camp kitchen, a kiosk and a pint-sized pool.

🍴 Eating

Wangi Falls Centre CAFE $
(www.wangifallscentre.com.au; mains from $10; ☾ 10am-4pm Jun-Oct; 🐾) This busy cafe at Wangi Falls (p163) is arguably the best place in the park for a light meal. There are hot rolls and other bites to eat as well as a small souvenir shop. Try the smoothies made from local mangoes or the homemade iced coffee.

Litchfield Cafe CAFE $$
(Litchfield Park Rd; mains $14-36; ☾ noon-3pm & 6-8pm Apr-Sep, noon-3pm Oct-Mar) Filo parcels make for a super lunch at this excellent licensed cafe, or you could go for a meal of grilled local barramundi or roo fillet, topped off with a good coffee and some wicked mango cheesecake.

ℹ Getting There & Away

The two routes to Litchfield (115km south of Darwin) from the Stuart Hwy join up and loop through the park. The southern access road via Batchelor is all sealed, while the northern access route, off the Cox Peninsula Rd, is partly unsealed, corrugated and often closed in the Wet. Many travellers visit on a day tour from Darwin.

Daly River

POP 171

The Daly River is considered some of the best barramundi-fishing country in the NT and the hub is this small community.

There's a shop and fuel here and visitors are welcome without a permit, but note that this is a dry community (no alcohol). Other than fishing, there's a fine art centre and a fine arts festival. And don't be fooled by the river's enticing waters on a hot afternoon – crocs live here.

👁 Sights

Merrepen Arts GALLERY
(☑ 08 8978 2533; www.merrepenarts.com.au; ☾ 8am-5pm Mon-Fri) FREE Around 20 artists work in a variety of traditional and contemporary media at this centre. Displays may include etchings, screen prints, acrylic paintings, carvings, weaving and textiles.

Daly River Crossing LANDMARK
Popular barramundi-fishing haunt and the crocs know it – ask about local conditions and advice before casting.

🎉 Festivals & Events

Merrepen Arts Festival CULTURAL
(www.merrepenfestival.com.au; adult/child $20/10) The excellent, three-day Merrepen Arts Festival celebrates arts and music from communities around the district, including Nauiyu, Wadeye and Peppimenarti, with displays, art auctions, workshops and dancing. The festival is held in Nauiyu, about 5km northwest of Daly River. It's usually held in May but it has moved around a little in recent years.

🛏 Sleeping & Eating

You can find basic supplies and takeaway food at the petrol station and general store.

Perry's CAMPGROUND $
(☑ 08 8978 2452; www.dalyriver.com; Mayo Park; unpowered/powered sites $28/38, fisherman's hut $110; ☀) A very peaceful place with 2km of river frontage and gardens where orphaned wallabies bound around. Dick Perry, a well-

---

LOCAL KNOWLEDGE

FLORENCE FALLS ALTERNATIVE ROUTE

An alternative to climbing the steep staircase up to the Florence Falls car park is Shady Creek Walk (950m), which begins by the waterhole and climbs gently through riverine monsoon forest then into the more open savannah woodland country. En route, watch for the shy short-eared rock wallaby.

known fishing expert, operates guided trips, and boat hire is available. The fisherman's hut has no air-con and is pretty basic with queen bed and bunks.

Daly River Mango Farm   CAMPGROUND **$**
(🖉 08 8978 2464; www.mangofarm.com.au; unpowered/powered sites $32/37, d $130-210; ❄ ❋) The camping ground here, on the Daly River 9km from the crossing (p164), is shaded by a magnificent grove of near-century-old mango trees. Other accommodation includes simple budget and self-contained cabins. Guided fishing trips and boat hire available.

ⓘ Getting There & Away

Daly River is 117km southwest of Hayes Creek, reached by a narrow sealed road off the Dorat Rd (Old Stuart Hwy; Rte 23), and 221km from Darwin.

Pine Creek

POP 380

A short detour off the Stuart Highway, Pine Creek is a small settlement that was once the scene of a frantic gold rush. The recent closing of the nearby iron-ore mine has dealt another blow to this boom-bust place, which somehow always seems to survive. It's a quietly pretty little town with a nice park in the centre and it's a good place to break up the journey, thanks to its good places to sleep and eat, and its proximity to the Kakadu Hwy turn-off.

◉ Sights

Umbrawarra Gorge
Nature Park   NATURE RESERVE
(🖉 08 8976 0282; www.nt.gov.au/leisure/parks-reserves) About 3km south of Pine Creek on the Stuart Highway is the turn-off to pretty Umbrawarra Gorge, with a safe swimming hole, a little beach and a basic camping ground (adult/child $3.30/1.65). It's 22km southwest on a rugged dirt road (just OK for 2WDs in the Dry; often impassable for everyone in the Wet). The walk along the water's edge is easy but will have you clambering over boulders every now and then. Bring plenty of water and mosquito repellent.

🛏 Sleeping & Eating

Lazy Lizard
Caravan Park & Tavern   CAMPGROUND **$**
(🖉 08 8976 1019; www.lazylizardpinecreek.com.au; 299 Millar Tce; unpowered/powered sites $16/30, d cabins $120; ❋) The small, well-grassed

WORTH A TRIP

MT BUNDY STATION

If you're into horse riding, fishing and country-style hospitality, **Mt Bundy Station** (🖉 08 8976 7009; www.mtbundy.com.au; Haynes Rd; unpowered/powered sites $22/30, s/d $70/100, cottage d from $140; ❋ ❋) is the perfect detour, 3km off the highway after Adelaide River. The original station buildings have become spotless guest accommodation, plus there are simple safari tents. There are 4WD tours and plenty of animals on the property.

camping area at the Lazy Lizard seems like an afterthought to the pulsing pub next door, but the sites are fine. The open-sided bar supported by carved ironwood pillars is a busy local watering hole with a pool table and old saddles slung across the rafters.

Pine Creek Railway Resort   BOUTIQUE HOTEL **$$**
(🖉 08 8976 1001; www.pinecreekrailwayresort.com.au; s/d $90/130, cabins $150-170; ❄ 🛜 ❋) This charming hotel uses raw iron, steel and wood in its modern rooms, which are easily the best for quite a distance in any direction. The dining area has been designed with romantic rail journeys of yore in mind; it's a scene-stealer with pressed-tin ceilings and elaborate chandeliers.

The menu (mains $21 to $30) is, however, modern, with steaks, pasta, ribs and risotto on offer.

Mayse's Cafe   CAFE **$**
(🖉 08 8976 1241; Moule St; breakfast $8-19, mains $9-13; ⊙8am-3pm) Offering Pine Creek's best lunches, Mayse's does sandwiches, homemade pies, fish burgers, steak sandwiches and a mean lamb souvlaki in a cavernous dining area that feels vaguely like an American diner.

ⓘ Getting There & Away

The Kakadu Hwy (Rte 21) branches off the Stuart Hwy here, connecting Pine Creek to Cooinda and Jabiru. There's a **petrol station** in the centre of town.

Greyhound buses (www.greyhound.com.au) connect Pine Creek with Darwin (from $62, three hours) and Katherine ($75, four hours) twice daily.

DARWIN & THE TOP END PINE CREEK

KAKADU NATIONAL PARK

Kakadu (☑ 08 8938 1120; parksaustralia.gov.au/kakadu/; adult/child/family Apr-Oct $40/20/100, Nov-Mar $25/12.50/65) is more than a national park. It's also a vibrant, living acknowledgement of the elemental link between the Aboriginal custodians and the country they have nurtured, endured and respected for thousands of generations. Encompassing almost 20,000 sq km (about 200km north–south and 100km east–west), it holds within its boundaries a spectacular ecosystem, periodically scorched and flooded, and mind-blowing ancient rock art.

In just a few days you can cruise on billabongs bursting with wildlife, examine 25,000-year-old rock paintings with the help of an Indigenous guide, swim in pools at the foot of tumbling waterfalls and hike through ancient sandstone escarpment country.

If Kakadu has a downside it's that it's very popular – in the Dry at least. Resorts, camping grounds and rock-art sites can be very crowded. But this is a vast park and with a little adventurous spirit you can easily leave the crowds behind.

Geography

The circuitous Arnhem Land escarpment, a dramatic 30m- to 200m-high sandstone cliff line, forms the natural boundary between Kakadu and Arnhem Land and winds 500km through eastern and southeastern Kakadu.

Creeks cut across the rocky plateau and, in the wet season, tumble off it as thundering waterfalls. They then flow across the lowlands to swamp Kakadu's vast northern flood plains. From west to east, the rivers are the Wildman, West Alligator, South Alligator and East Alligator (the latter forming the eastern boundary of the park). The coastal zone has long stretches of mangrove swamp, important for halting erosion and as a breeding ground for bird and marine life. The southern part of the park is dry lowlands with open grassland and eucalyptuses. Pockets of monsoon rainforest crop up throughout the park.

More than 80% of Kakadu is savannah woodland. It has more than 1000 plant species, many still used by Aboriginal people for food and medicinal purposes.

Wildlife

Kakadu has more than 60 mammal species, more than 280 bird species, 120 recorded species of reptile, 25 species of frog, 55 freshwater fish species and at least 10,000 different kinds of insect. Most visitors see only a fraction of these creatures (except the insects), since many of them are shy, nocturnal or scarce.

Rock Art

Kakadu is one of Australia's richest, most accessible repositories of rock art. There are more than 5000 sites, which date from 20,000 years to 10 years ago. The vast majority of these sites are off limits or inaccessible, but two of the finest collections are the easily visited galleries at Ubirr and Nourlangie.

Rock paintings have been classified into three roughly defined periods: Pre-estuarine, which is from the earliest paintings up to around 6000 years ago; Estuarine, which covers the period from 6000 to around 2000 years ago, when rising sea levels brought the coast to its present level; and Freshwater, from 2000 years ago until the present day.

For local Aboriginal people, these rock-art sites are a major source of traditional knowledge and represent their archives. Aboriginal people rarely paint on rocks anymore, as they no longer live in rock shelters and there are fewer people with the requisite knowledge. Some older paintings are believed by many Aboriginal people to have been painted by mimi spirits, connecting people with Creation legends and the development of Aboriginal lore.

As the paintings are all rendered with natural, water-soluble ochres, they are very susceptible to water damage. Drip lines of clear silicon rubber have been laid on the rocks above the paintings to divert rain. As the most accessible sites receive up to 4000 visitors a week, boardwalks have been erected to keep the dust down and to keep people at a suitable distance from the paintings.

☞ Tours

★ **Guluyambi Cultural Cruise**   CULTURAL
(☑ 1800 525 238; www.kakaduculturaltours.com; adult/child $76/49; ⊙ 9am, 11am, 1pm & 3pm May-Nov) 🌿 Launch into an Aboriginal-led river cruise from the upstream boat ramp on the East Alligator River near Cahill's Crossing. Highly recommended by Darwin locals and a wonderful way to see crocodiles, see a little

of Arnhem Land from the riverbank and listen to Indigenous stories as you go.

★ **Yellow Water Cruises**   CRUISE
(☑1800 500 401; www.kakadutourism.com; per person $72-99) Cruise the South Alligator River and Yellow Water Billabong spotting wildlife. Purchase tickets from Gagudju Lodge, Cooinda; a shuttle bus will take you from here to the tour's departure point. Two-hour cruises depart at 6.45am, 9am and 4.30pm; 1½-hour cruises leave at 11.30am, 1.15pm and 2.45pm.

★ **Kakadu Air**   SCENIC FLIGHTS
(☑08 8941 9611, 1800 089 113; www.kakaduair.com.au; 30min flight adult/child $150/120, 60min flight $250/200, 45/60min helicopter flight adult $485/650) Offers both fixed-wing and helicopter scenic flights and both are a wonderful way to get a sense of the sheer scale and beauty of Kakadu and Arnhem Land. Note that flights are only available over Jim Jim Falls in the wet season – traditional owners request that the 'skies are rested' in the Dry.

★ **Arnhemlander**
Cultural & Heritage Tour   CULTURAL
(☑08 8979 2548; www.kakaduculturaltours.com.au; adult/child $269/215) ✔ Aboriginal-owned and operated tour into northern Kakadu and Arnhem Land. See ancient rock art, learn bush skills and meet local artists at Injalak Arts Centre (p176) in Oenpelli.

Ayal Aboriginal Tours   CULTURAL
(☑0429 470 384; www.ayalkakadu.com.au; adult/child $220/99) ✔ Full-day Indigenous-run tours around Kakadu, with former ranger and local, Victor Cooper, shining a light on art, culture and wildlife.

Kakadu Animal Tracks   CULTURAL
(☑0409 350 842; www.animaltracks.com.au; adult/child $220/110; ⊙1pm) ✔ Based at Cooinda, this outfit runs seven-hour tours with an Indigenous guide combining a wildlife safari and Aboriginal cultural tour. You'll see thousands of birds, get to hunt, gather, prepare and consume bush tucker and crunch on some green ants.

ⓘ Information

Bowali Visitor Information Centre (☑08 8938 1121; parksaustralia.gov.au/kakadu/plan-your-trip/visitor-centres.html; Kakadu Hwy, Jabiru; ⊙8am-5pm) This excellent information centre has walk-through displays that sweep you across the land, explaining Kakadu's

ecology from Aboriginal and non-Aboriginal perspectives. The helpful, staffed info window has 'Park Notes' flyers on all walks, with superb information about plants, animals and salient features you might encounter on each walk plus explanations of their uses and significance.

ⓘ Getting There & Away

The Arnhem Hwy and Kakadu Hwy traverse the park; both are sealed and accessible year-round. The 4WD-only Old Jim Jim Rd is an alternative access from the Arnhem Hwy, joining the Kakadu Hwy 7km south of Cooinda. Fuel is available at Kakadu Resort, Cooinda and Jabiru.

Many people choose to access Kakadu on a tour, which shuffles them around the major sights with a minimum of hassle, but it's just as easy with your own wheels if you know what kinds of road conditions your trusty steed can handle (Jim Jim and Twin Falls, for example, are 4WD-access only).

Greyhound Australia (p156) runs a return service from Darwin to Jabiru ($75, 3½ hours).

Ubirr & Around

Magnificent Ubirr is one of the jewels in Kakadu's rather well-studded crown. Even if you know what to expect, coming here feels like wandering into a lost and beautiful world that is at once playful art gallery of the ancients and soulful history book of Kakadu's extraordinary human and natural history. There are real treasures here – the

> **ⓘ KAKADU PARK ADMISSION**
>
> Admission to the park is via a seven-day Park Pass (adult/child/family Apr-Oct $40/20/100, Nov-Mar $25/12.50/65). Passes can be bought online (parksaustralia.gov.au/kakadu/plan-your-trip/passes-and-permits.html) or at various places around the park, including Bowali Visitor Information Centre where you can pick up a pass, along with the excellent *Visitor Guide* booklet. Carry your pass with you at all times as rangers conduct spot checks – penalties apply for nonpayment.
>
> Other places to purchase the pass are:
>
> ➜ Tourism Top End (p156)
>
> ➜ Cooinda Lodge & Campground (p172)
>
> ➜ Katherine Visitor Information Centre (p184)

DARWIN & THE TOP END UBIRR & AROUND

Kakadu National Park

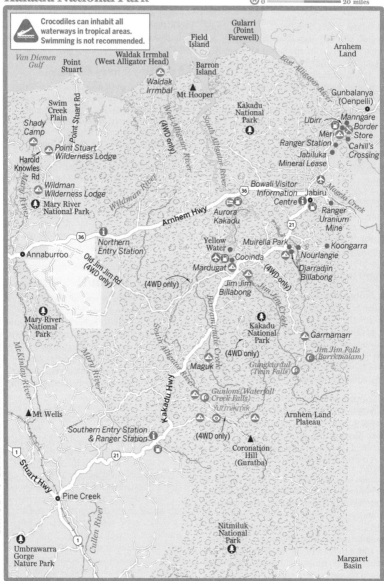

Crocodiles can inhabit all waterways in tropical areas. Swimming is not recommended.

NT's best sunset, a rare and accessible depiction of the Rainbow Serpent, the intriguing and improbable representation of the thylacine (Tasmanian tiger) and mesmerising Ubirr rock art. It's a spiritual place, and very, very beautiful.

⦿ Sights

★ **Ubirr** ROCK ART
(⊙ 8.30am-sunset Apr-Nov, from 2pm Dec-Mar)
Ubirr is 39km north of the Arnhem Hwy via a sealed road. It'll take a lot more than the busloads of visitors to disturb Ubirr's

inherent majesty and grace. Layers of rock-art paintings, in various styles and from various centuries, command a mesmerising stillness.

Part of the main gallery reads like a menu, with images of kangaroos, tortoises and fish painted in X-ray, which became the dominant style about 8000 years ago. Predating these are the paintings of mimi spirits: cheeky, dynamic figures who, it's believed, were the first of the Creation Ancestors to paint on rock. (Given the lack of cherry-pickers in 6000 BC, you have to wonder who else but a spirit could have painted at that height and angle.) Look out for the yam-head figures, where the head is depicted as a yam on the body of a human or animal; these date back around 15,000 years.

The magnificent **Nardab Lookout** is a 250m scramble accessed from the main gallery. Surveying the exotic flood plain, watching the sun set in the west and the moon rise in the east like they're on an invisible set of scales gradually exchanging weight is humbling to say the least.

★**Cahill's Crossing**   RIVER
It may be small, but there can be few more dramatic frontiers in Australia. This shallow causeway, which is impassable when the tide's in, crosses the East Alligator River from Kakadu National Park on the west bank to Arnhem Land to the east. And watching you as you cross is the river's healthy and rather prolific population of saltwater crocs. Ask at Border Store (p170) for tide timings.

Activities

Manngarre Monsoon Forest Walk   WALKING
Mainly sticking to a boardwalk, this walk (1.5km return, 30 minutes, easy) starts by the boat ramp near the Border Store and winds through heavily shaded vegetation, palms and vines.

Bardedjilidji Sandstone Walk   WALKING
Starting from the upstream picnic-area car park, this walk (2.5km, 90 minutes, easy) takes in wetland areas of the East Alligator River and some interesting eroded sandstone outliers of the Arnhem Land escarpment. Informative track notes point out features on this walk; watch for both rock wallabies and the much-prized-among-birders chestnut-quilled rock pigeon. These are sacred rocks – no climbing.

Sleeping & Eating

Merl Camping Ground   CAMPGROUND $
(adult/child/family $15/7.50/38) The turn-off to this camping ground is about 1km before the Border Store. It is divided into a quiet zone and a generator use zone, each with a block of showers and toilets. It can get mighty busy at peak times and, be warned, the mosquitoes are diabolical. The site is closed in the Wet.

★**Hawk Dreaming**
Wilderness Lodge   LODGE $$$
(☑1800 525 238; www.kakaduculturaltours.com.au/hawk-dreaming-wilderness-lodge; s/d half-board $415/578) In a restricted area of the park (ie only guests and local Indigenous residents are allowed in), this deliciously remote lodge sits in the shadow of the stunning Hawk Dreaming sandstone escarpment and is as close to sweeping flood plains and billabongs as it is far from the clamouring crowds of Kakadu. The safari tents are simple but nicely spread through shady grounds inhabited by wallabies,

---

WATCHING WILDLIFE IN KAKADU

Species to watch out for include:

Saltwater crocodiles Cahill's Crossing over the East Alligator River – you can't miss them.

Dingoes At once elusive and possible everywhere; you may seem them at the flood plains stretching out from Ubirr, but they're also seen around Jabiru and along the Kakadu Hwy.

Black wallaroo This shy species is unique to Kakadu and Arnhem Land – look for them at Nourlangie Rock, where individuals rest under rocky overhangs.

Short-eared rock wallabies Can be spotted in the early morning around Ubirr.

Northern quoll Possible at night out the back of the Border Store and the surrounding area.

Northern brown bandicoot Find this and you've hit the jackpot; watch for it if you're driving at night.

Buffalo and wild horses Non-native species you might spot from the Yellow Water cruise.

whistling kites and blue-winged kookaburras. There's a small hot tub and rates include dinner and breakfast, transfers from the Border Store (p170) in Ubirr, sundowners and excursions to see local rock art that will be yours and yours alone to enjoy.

★ **Border Store** CAFE **$$**
(☑ 08 8979 2474; www.facebook.com/ubirrborder store; mains $28; ☉ 8.30am-8pm Jun-Oct) Run by Michael and Amm, charming little Border Store is full of surprises, including real coffee, sweet cakes and delicious Thai-cooked Thai food – a real treat. You can book a Guluyambi Cultural Cruise (p166) on the East Alligator River or a tour to Arnhem Land or browse the small selection of books and artwork.

ⓘ Getting There & Away

Ubirr is 39km north of the Arnhem Hwy via a sealed road.

Jabiru

POP 1200

It may seem surprising to find a town of Jabiru's size and structure in the midst of a wilderness national park, but it exists solely because of the nearby Ranger uranium mine. It's Kakadu's major service centre, with a bank, newsagent, medical centre, supermarket, bakery and service station. You can even play a round of golf here. It also has some good accommodation and simple restaurants, making it an agreeable if relatively unexciting base.

🎉 Festivals & Events

Mahbilil Festival CULTURAL
(www.mahbililfestival.com; ☉ Sep) A one-day celebration in early September of Indigenous culture in Jabiru. There are exhibitions showcasing local art as well as craft demonstrations, such as weaving and painting. Also on offer are competitions in spear throwing, didgeridoo blowing and magpie goose cooking. In the evening the focus is on Indigenous music and dance.

🛏 Sleeping

★ **Anbinik Kakadu Resort** CABIN **$$**
(☑ 08 8979 3144; www.kakadu.net.au; 27 Lakeside Dr; ensuite powered sites $42, bungalows/d/cabins $135/150/250; ❄ ☀) This Aboriginal-owned park is one of Kakadu's best, with a range of tropical-design bungalows set in lush gardens. The doubles share a communal kitchen, bathroom and lounge and also come equipped with their own TV and fridge. The 'bush bungalows' are stylish, elevated safari designs (no air-con) with private, open-air bathroom out the back and a nice verandah out front.

Aurora Kakadu
Lodge & Caravan Park RESORT **$$**
(☑ 08 8979 2422, 1800 811 154; www.auroraresorts.com.au; Jabiru Dr; powered/unpowered sites $42/30, cabins from $275; ❄ 🐾 ☀) One of the best places to camp in town with lots of grass, trees and natural barriers between camping areas, creating a sense of privacy. This sprawling, impeccable resort/caravan park also has a lagoon-style swimming pool. Self-contained cabins sleep up to five people. The restaurant is a lovely outdoor place for meals overlooking the pool.

Mercure Kakadu
(Crocodile Hotel) HOTEL **$$$**
(☑ 08 8979 9000; www.accorhotels.com; 1 Flinders St; d from $275; ❄ 🐾 ☀) Known locally as 'the Croc', this hotel is designed in the shape of a crocodile, which, of course, is only obvious when viewed from the air. The rooms are clean and comfortable if a little pedestrian for the price (check their website for great deals). Try for one on the ground floor opening out to the central pool.

🍴 Eating

Kakadu Bakery BAKERY **$**
(Gregory Pl; meals $4-19; ☉ 6am-4pm Mon-Fri, 6.30am-3pm Sat, 8am-3pm Sun) Grab a made-to-order sandwich on home-baked bread to walk out the door. There are also mean burgers, slices, breakfast fry-ups, pizzas, cakes and basic salads. There are a few outdoor tables but it's mostly takeaway and we can think of plenty of places where we'd rather enjoy our burger out in the park.

Escarpment Restaurant INTERNATIONAL **$$**
(mains $22-38; ☉ 7am-9pm) This restaurant inside the Mercure Kakadu gets very mixed reviews – some love it, others hate it and we lie somewhere in between. While probably Jabiru's best restaurant, it's pretty uninspiring but you won't leave hungry. Dishes on the regularly changing menu cover the usual meat and seafood staples (steaks, burgers, barra) with the occasional nod to local bush tucker tastes.

Jabiru Sports & Social Club   PUB FOOD **$$**
(☑ 08 8979 2326; www.jabirusportsandsocialclub.
com.au; Lakeside Dr; mains $16-35; ⊘ 6-8.30pm
Mon-Sat, noon-2pm & 6-8.30pm Sun) Along with
the golf club, this low-slung hangar is the
place to meet locals over a beer or glass of
wine. The bistro meals, such as steak, chick-
en parma or fish and chips, are honest and
there's an outdoor deck overlooking the
lake, a kids playground and sport on TV.

❶ Information

Northern Land Council (☑ 1800 645 299, 08
8938 3000; www.nlc.org.au; 3 Government
Bldg, Flinders St, Jabiru; ⊘ 8am-4.30pm Mon-
Fri) Issues permits for Arnhem Land, including
Gunbalanya (Oenpelli).

❶ Getting There & Away

Jabiru lies 257km from Darwin along the Stuart
and then Arnhem Hwys. There's no public trans-
port out here, but nor is there any shortage of
tours that can get you here.

Nourlangie

The sight of this looming outlier of the Arn-
hem Land escarpment makes it easy to un-
derstand its ancient importance to Aboriginal
people. Its long red-sandstone bulk, striped
in places with orange, white and black, slopes
up from surrounding woodland to fall away
at one end in stepped cliffs. Below is Kakadu's
best-known collection of rock art.

◎ Sights

The name Nourlangie is a corruption of
nawulandja, an Aboriginal word that re-
fers to an area bigger than the rock itself.
The 2km looped walking track (open 8am to
sunset) takes you first to the Anbangbang
Shelter, used for 20,000 years as a refuge
and canvas. Next is the Anbangbang Gal-
lery, featuring vivid Dreaming characters
repainted in the 1960s. Look for the virile
Nabulwinjbulwinj, a dangerous spirit who
likes to eat females after banging them on
the head with a yam. From here it's a short
walk to Gunwarddehwarde Lookout, with
views of the Arnhem Land escarpment.

⚡ Activities

Nawurlandja Lookout   WALKING
This is a short walk (600m return, 30 min-
utes, medium) up a gradual slope, but it
gives excellent views of the Nourlangie rock
area and is a good place to catch the sunset.

Barrk Walk   WALKING
This long day walk (12km loop, five to six
hours, difficult) will take you away from
the crowds on a circuit of the Nourlangie
area. Barrk is a male black wallaroo and
you might see this elusive marsupial if you
set out early. Pick up a brochure from the
Bowali Visitor Information Centre.

Nanguluwur Gallery   WALKING
This outstanding rock-art gallery sees far
fewer visitors than Nourlangie simply be-
cause it's further to walk (3.5km return, 1½
hours, easy) and has a gravel access road.
Here the paintings cover most of the styles
found in the park, including very early dy-
namic style work, X-ray work and a good
example of 'contact art', a painting of a
two-masted sailing ship towing a dinghy.

Anbangbang Billabong Walk   WALKING
This picturesque, lily-filled billabong lies
close to Nourlangie and the picnic tables
dotted around its edge make it a popular
lunch spot. The track (2.5km loop, 45 min-
utes, easy) circles the billabong and passes
through paperbark swamp. It's a lovely ad-
junct to the rock art.

🛏 Sleeping

Muirella Park   CAMPGROUND **$**
(Djarradjin;   adult/child/family $15/7.50/38)
Basic camping ground at Djarradjin Bil-
labong, with BBQs, excellent amenities
and the 5km-return Bubba Wetland Walk.
Look for the turn-off from the Kakadu
Hwy, about 7km south from the turn-off to
Nourlangie.

❶ Getting There & Away

Nourlangie is well signposted at the end of a
12km sealed road that turns east off Kakadu Hwy.

Jim Jim Falls & Twin Falls

Remote and spectacular, these two falls
epitomise the rugged Top End. Jim Jim
Falls, a sheer 215m drop, is awesome after
rain (when it can only be seen from the
air), but its waters shrink to a trickle by
about June. Twin Falls flows year-round
(no swimming), but half the fun is getting
here, involving a little boat trip (adult/child
$15/free, 7.30am-5pm, last boat 4pm) and
an over-the-water boardwalk.

🛏 Sleeping

Garrnamarr Camping Ground CAMPGROUND $
(www.parksaustralia.gov.au/kakadu/plan-your-trip/
camping-and-caravans.html; adult/child/family
$15/7.50/38) Basic camping ground in a won-
derful place and there's plenty of shade.

ℹ Getting There & Away

These two iconic waterfalls are reached via a
4WD track that turns south off the Kakadu Hwy
between the Nourlangie and Cooinda turn-offs.
Jim Jim Falls is about 56km from the turn-off
(the last 1km on foot) and it's a further five
corrugated kilometres to Twin Falls. The track is
open in the Dry only and can still be closed into
late May; it's off limits to most rental vehicles
(check the fine print). A couple of tour companies make trips here in the Dry.

Cooinda & Yellow Water

Cooinda is one of the main tourism hubs in
Kakadu. A slick resort has grown up around
the wetlands, which are known as Yellow
Water, or to give it's rather challenging Indigenous name, *Ngurrungurrundjba*. The
cruises, perferably around sunrise or sunset, are undoubted highlights of any visit to
Kakadu.

◉ Sights

**Warradjan Aboriginal
Cultural Centre** MUSEUM
(www.kakadutourism.com/tours-activities/warra
djan-cultural-centre/; Yellow Water Area; ⊙9am-
5pm) FREE About 1km from the Cooinda
resort (an easy 15 minutes' walk), the Warradjan Aboriginal Cultural Centre depicts Creation stories and has an excellent permanent
exhibition that includes clap sticks, sugarbag holders and rock-art samples. You'll be
introduced to the moiety system (the law
of interpersonal relationships), languages
and skin names, and there's a minitheatre
with a huge selection of films from which
to choose. A mesmeric soundtrack of chants
and didgeridoos plays in the background.

🛏 Sleeping

Mardugal Park Campground CAMPGROUND $
(www.parksaustralia.gov.au/kakadu/plan-your-
trip/camping-and-caravans.html; camping per
adult/child/family $15/7.50/38) Just south of
the Kakadu Hwy, 2km south of the Cooinda turn-off, is the National Parks Mardugal
Park campground – an excellent spot with
shower and toilets.

Cooinda Lodge & Campground RESORT $$
(☑1800 500 401; www.kakadutourism.com/
accommodation/cooinda-lodge/; Cooinda; pow-
ered/unpowered sites $50/38; budget/lodge
r from $159/189; ✳🖨❄) This sprawling
place has a good variety of accommodation
options and is Kakadu's most popular re-
sort – even with 380 camp sites, facilities
can get very stretched. The budget air-con
units share camping ground facilities and
are compact and comfy enough. The lodge
rooms are spacious and more comfortable,
sleeping up to four people.

There's a grocery shop, tour desk, fuel
pump and the excellent open-air **Barra Bar
& Bistro** (☑1800 500 401; www.kakadutourism.
com/accommodation/cooinda-lodge/; Cooinda;
mains $25-35; ⊙6.30am-9pm) here too.

Ask about the 'Flash Camp @ Kakadu', a
semimobile camp of tents set up out in the
bush with all the comforts of a tented camp.

ℹ Getting There & Away

The turn-off to the Cooinda accommodation
complex and Yellow Water wetlands is 47km down
the Kakadu Hwy from the Arnhem Hwy intersec-
tion. It's then 4.5km to the Warradjan Aboriginal
Cultural Centre, a further 1km to the Yellow Water
turn-off and another 1km to Cooinda.

Southwestern Kakadu

Kakadu's southwestern reaches shelter two
of Kakadu's most underrated attractions –
the gorgeous waterhole at Maguk and the
dramatic Gunlom. Both require a 4WD or
high-clearance 2WD to get there and may
be impassable in the Wet – all of which is
precisely why you won't see any tour buses
down here.

◉ Sights

★**Maguk** WATERFALL
(Barramundi Gorge) This southern section of
Kakadu National Park sees far fewer tour
buses. Though it's unlikely you'll have dreamy
Maguk to yourself, you might time it right to
have the glorious natural pool and falls be-
tween just a few of you. The walk in from the
car park passes through monsoon forest rich
in endemic anbinik trees and then opens out
into a nicely bouldered river section.

The waterhole is 2km return walk from
the car park (count on about an hour plus
swimming time). Where the trail emerges
from the forest into a broader valley and
where the marked trail crosses the river to

the right, stay on the left bank (or return here later) to climb up high above the falls for great views and a series of small rock pools to plunge into. Wildlife here includes freshwater crocs (swimming is generally safe but check the signs) as well as birds such as rainbow pittas and emerald doves.

★**Gunlom**   WATERFALL
(Waterfall Creek) Gunlom is an utterly superb escarpment waterfall and plunge pool 40-odd kilometres south of Maguk and 37km along an unsealed, though easily doable, gravel road. The reward is a gloriously large waterhole and drama-filled scenery, and that's just 200m through the paperbark forest from the car park. There's also a lovely picnic area here. If you're keen to explore more, take the steep **Lookout Walk** (one hour, 1km), which affords incredible views.

❶ Getting There & Away

Both Maguk and Gunlom are clearly signposted off the Kakadu Hwy along unsealed tracks – Gunlom is easier to access in a 2WD. There's no public transport to either site and few tour operators come this way.

ARNHEM LAND

Arnhem Land is a vast, overwhelming and mysterious corner of the NT. About the size of the state of Victoria and with a population of only around 17,000, mostly Yolngu people, this Aboriginal reserve is one of Australia's last great untouched wilderness areas. Most people live on outstations, combining traditional practices with modern Western ones, so they might go out for a hunt and be back in time to watch the 6pm news. Travelling out here requires careful planning, but it's a small price to pay for visiting one of Australia's most ruggedly beautiful and culturally intriguing corners.

☞ Tours

★**Kakadu Cultural Tours**   CULTURAL
(☑1800 525 238; www.kakaduculturaltours. au; adult/child $269/215; ⊙May-Nov) This eight-hour Arnhemlander 4WD Cultural Tour is outstanding. It takes you to ancient rock-art sites (hopefully it will include the Mountford site, but access depends on the age and mobility of the group), Inkiyu Billabong and Injalak art centre at Gunbalanya (Oenpelli). The tour leaves from Border Store (p170) at Ubirr in Kakadu National Park.

Outback Spirit   TOURS
(☑1800 688 222; www.outbackspirittours.com.au) This experienced operator has an epic 12-day traverse of Arnhem Land's north, from the Cobourg Peninsula to Yirrkala. Prices start at $10,995 per person.

Venture North Australia   TOURS
(☑08 8927 5500; venturenorth.com.au; 4-/5-day tours $2890/3290; ⊙May-Oct) Four-wheel drive tours to remote areas and featuring expert guidance on rock art. The four-day Arnhem Land and Cobourg Peninsula Tour (per person $2890) is the pick of numerous Arnhem Land options. Also runs Cobourg Coastal Camp with safari-style tents overlooking the water near Smith Point on the Cobourg Peninsula for the exclusive use of Venture tour guests.

Davidson's Arnhemland Safaris   CULTURAL
(☑08 8979 0413; www.arnhemland-safaris.com) Experienced operator taking tours to Mt Borradaile, north of Oenpelli. Meals, guided tours, fishing and safari-camp accommodation at its Safari Lodge (p173) are included in the daily price (from $750 per person); transfers from Darwin can be arranged.

🛏 Sleeping

★**Davidson's**
Arnhemland Safari Lodge   LODGE $$$
(www.arnhemland-safaris.com; s/d cabins all-inclusive from $1025/1500; ❄) An oasis of good taste with high levels of comfort out in the wilds of western Arnhem Land, Davidson's has appealing cabins on stilts, good food and a lovely setting. It's generally worth paying a little extra for the deluxe cabins. Excursions include billabong boat trips, hikes into the nearby escarpments and birdwatching.

Barramundi Lodge   LODGE $$$
(☑08 8983 1544; www.barralodge.com.au; d from $550; ☎) Out in the wilds of Arnhem Land, close to Maningrida, this lovely lodge is a haven for sport-fishers and birdwatchers from March to November. The safari-style tents are beautifully appointed in the finest African safari style with just canvas between you and the great outdoors but with high levels of comfort.

❶ Getting There & Away

Most visitors to Arnhem Land come as part of an organised tour.

Indigenous Art & Culture

The intricate and mesmerising art, stories and dances of Australia's Aboriginal peoples resonate with a deep association with the land itself. The Top End and the outback are the best places to engage with Aboriginal culture: take a cultural tour, hear spoken stories of the Dreaming, see galleries of ancient rock art or check out some contemporary canvasses in modern acrylics.

Cultural Tours

There's a proliferation of Indigenous-owned and -operated cultural tours across outback Australia – a chance to learn about the outback from the people who know it best. Sign up for a cultural tour in Darwin, Kakadu National Park and Arnhem Land in the tropical north; and Alice Springs and Uluru-Kata Tjuta National Park in the Red Centre.

Rock Art

Evidence of Australia's ancient Indigenous culture can be found at the outdoor rock-art sites scattered across the outback. Highlights include the 5000-plus sites in Kakadu National Park that document a timeline of spirits from the Dreaming, extinct fauna, and remarkable 'contact art', portraying the interaction between Indigenous Australians, Macassan fishermen and early European settlers. Standout Kakadu sites include Ubirr and Nourlangie. More rock art can easily be seen at Nitmiluk (Katherine

1. Aboriginal dancers at Barunga Festival (p25).

2. Mbantua Fine Art Gallery (p155).

3. Contemporary dot painting on a souvenir didgeridoo.

Gorge) and Keep River National Parks, the MacDonnell Ranges near Alice, and Uluru (Ayers Rock).

Contemporary Indigenous Art

Contemporary Australian Indigenous art – the lion's share of which is produced in outback communities – has soared to global heights of late. Traditional methods and spiritual significance are fastidiously maintained, but often find a counterpart in Western materials – the results can be wildly original interpretations of traditional stories and ceremonial designs. Dot paintings (acrylic on canvas) are the most recognisable form, but you may also see synthetic polymer paintings, weavings, bark paintings, weapons, boomerangs and sculptures.

Indigenous Festivals

For an unforgettable Aboriginal cultural experience, time your outback visit to coincide with a traditional Indigenous festival. These celebrations offer visitors a look at Aboriginal culture in action. Witnessing a timeless dance and feeling the primal beats is a journey beyond time and place. The Northern Territory plays host to several Indigenous festivals and events, including the popular Walking With Spirits in Beswick, Barunga Festival near Katherine, Merrepen Arts Festival at Daly River, and Arnhem Land's Stone Country Festival.

Gunbalanya (Oenpelli)

POP 1200

Gunbalanya is a small Aboriginal community 17km into Arnhem Land across the East Alligator River from the Border Store in Kakadu. Home to one of the NT's best Indigenous art centres, Gunbalanya makes an excellent add-on to a visit to Kakadu.

The drive in itself is worth the trip, with brilliant green wetlands and spectacular escarpments lining the road. Road access is only possible between May and October: check the tides at Cahill's Crossing on the East Alligator River before setting out so you don't get stuck on the other side.

◉ Sights

★ Injalak Arts & Crafts Centre   GALLERY
(☐08 8979 0190; www.injalak.com; ⊙8.30am-5pm Mon-Fri, 9am-2pm Sat) FREE At this centre, artists and craftspeople display traditional paintings on bark and paper, plus didgeridoos, pandanus weavings and baskets, and screen-printed fabrics; the shop is excellent and half of the sale price goes directly to the artists.

Take the time to wander around and watch the artists at work (morning only): the women usually make baskets out in the shade of the trees on the centre's west side, while the men paint on the verandah to the east. Some of the works come from remote outstations throughout Arnhem Land.

---

❶ ARNHEM LAND PERMITS

Visits to Arnhem Land are strictly regulated through a permit system, designed to protect the environment, rock art and ceremonial grounds, as *balanda* (white people) are unaware of the locations of burial grounds and ceremonial lands. Basically, you need a specific purpose for entering, usually to visit an arts centre, in order to be granted a permit. It's also worth remembering that some of the permits issued are transit permits (others are called recreational permits) that allow you to travel along certain roads but not either side of them – check when picking up your permit.

If you're travelling far enough to warrant an overnight stay, you'll need to organise accommodation (which is in short supply) in advance. It's easy to visit Gunbalanya (Oenpelli) and its arts centre on a day trip from Kakadu National Park, just over the border, either on a tour or independently. Elsewhere, it's best to travel with a tour, which will include the necessary permit(s) to enter Aboriginal lands.

If you're travelling independently, you'll need to arrange the following permits:

PLACE	ISSUED BY	COST	DURATION	PROCESSING TIME
Central Arnhem Highway	Northern Land Council (p176)	free	transit	10 days to issue
East Arnhem Land	Dhimurru Aboriginal Corporation (www.dhimurru.com.au)	$15/35/45	1 day/7 days/2 months	varies
Gunbalanya (Oenpili)	Northern Land Council (p176)	$16.50	1 day	issued on the spot
West Arnhem Land (incl Cobourg Peninsula & Garig Gunak Barlu National Park)	Northern Land Council (p176; transit permit); Parks & Wildlife Commission (dtc.nt.gov.au; camping permit)	$88 (plus $232.10 per vehicle for camping permit)	5 days	10 days to issue

There are good views from the centre's grounds south towards the wetlands to the escarpment and Injalak Hill (Long Tom Dreaming).

Kakadu Cultural Tours (p173) and **Lord's Kakadu & Arnhemland Safaris** (☑ 0438 808 548; www.lords-safaris.com; adult/child $225/180) both offer excellent day tours that include a visit here.

Tours

★ **Rock Art Tours**   TOURS
(☑ 08 8979 0190; www.injalak.com/rock-art-tours/; adult/child $110/33; ⊘ 9am Mon-Sat Jun-Sep) Five kilometres south of the Injalak Arts & Crafts Centre (p176), Injalak Hill (Long Tom Dreaming) is one of Western Arnhem Land's best collections of rock art. To see it you'll need to join one of the three-hour tours run out of the arts centre.

Festivals & Events

Stone Country Festival   CULTURAL
(⊘ Aug) This open day and cultural festival is held in August in Gunbalanya (Oenpelli). It has traditional music, dancing and arts and crafts demonstrations and is the only day you can visit Gunbalanya without a permit. Camping allowed; no alcohol.

Getting There & Away

There is no public transport to Gunbalanya and most travellers visit as part of an organised tour. The road here from Cahill's Crossing is only partly sealed and is impassable in the Wet (usually from October or November to March).

Cobourg Peninsula

Sights

★ **Garig Gunak Barlu**
National Park   NATIONAL PARK
(nt.gov.au/leisure/parks-reserves; ⊘ May-Oct) The entire wilderness of remote Cobourg Peninsula forms the Garig Gunak Barlu National Park which includes the surrounding sea. It's a stunning, isolated place and one of the loveliest spots on Australia's northern coast. You'll likely see dolphins and turtles and – what most people come for – a threadfin salmon thrashing on the end of your line.

Port Essington   RUINS
(Victoria) On the shores of Port Essington are the stone ruins and headstones of Victoria settlement – Britain's 1838 attempt to es-

tablish a military outpost here. It's an eerie place with stone ruins and echoes a doomed dream to build a city in such remote country.

Activities

The Cobourg Peninsula is well-known among fisherfolk for its fabulous barramundi fishing in March, April, October and November, while wildlife-watching is excellent during the Dry (the Peninsula is difficult to access at other times).

Wildlife Watching

The waters of Garig Gunak Barlu National Park are home to six species of marine turtle: green, loggerhead, olive ridley, hawksbill, flatback and leatherback; some of these nest on remote beaches in the later months of the year. Watch for the northern snake-necked turtle in the park's inland billabongs. Whales, dolphins, various shark species and saltwater crocodiles are all found in the waters off the coast – swimming here would be extremely dangerous.

Mammal species, though elusive, are always possible, especially around dawn, dusk and overnight. Species include dingoes, echidnas and northern brown bandicoots. The park is also home to more than 200 bird species.

Tours

Cobourg Fishing Safaris   FISHING
(☑ 08 8927 5500; www.cobourgfishingsafaris.com.au) These fishing safaris run by Venture North Australia (p173) are outstanding, with the fishing camps and food on offer a cut above others, not to mention excellent fishing guides.

Sleeping & Eating

There are two camping grounds in the park with showers, toilets, BBQs and limited bore water; generators are allowed in one area. Camping fees (per person per day $16.50) are covered by your vehicle permit. Other accommodation is available in pricey fishing resorts, while Cobourg Fishing Safaris (p177) has a tented safari camp for those on its tours at Smith Point.

You'll need to bring your own supplies, although **Garig Store** (☑ 08 8979 0455; Algarlarlgarl (Black Point); ⊘ 4-6pm Mon-Sat) sells basic provisions, ice and camping gas.

Wiligi Outstation   TENTED CAMP, CAMPING $$$
(☑ 08 8979 0069; www.wiligiarnhemland.com.au; camping per person $47, eco tents $275) On a remote outstation on the cusp of the Cobourg

Peninsula's Garig Gunak Barlu National Park, Wiligi has some rather lovely eco tents, each with a private verandah looking out over Morris Bay, as well as some shady waterfront campsites. The eco tents in particular are a fine alternative to wild camping.

ℹ️ Getting There & Away

The quickest route here is by private charter flight, which can be arranged by accommodation providers. If you're driving, the track to Cobourg starts at Gunbalanya (Oenpelli) and is accessible by 4WD vehicles only from May to October. The 270km drive to Black Point from the East Alligator River takes about five hours.

Eastern Arnhem Land

The wildly beautiful coast and country of Eastern Arnhem Land (www.eastarnhemland.com.au) is really off the beaten track. About 4000 people live in the region's main settlement, Nhulunbuy, built to service the bauxite mine here. The 1963 plans to establish a manganese mine were hotly protested by the traditional owners, the Yolngu people; though mining proceeded, the case became an important step in establishing land rights. Some of the country's most respected art comes out of this region, too, including bark paintings, carved mimi figures, *yidaki* (didgeridoos), woven baskets and mats, and jewellery.

⊙ Sights

★ Buku Larrnggay Mulka
Art Centre & Museum   GALLERY
(☑ 08 8987 1701; www.yirrkala.com; Yirrkala; by donation; ⊙ 8am-4.30pm Mon-Fri, 9am-noon Sat) This museum, 20km southeast of Nhulunbuy in Yirrkala, is one of Arnhem Land's best. No permit is required to visit from Nhulunbuy or Gove airport.

★☆ Festivals & Events

★ Garma Festival   CULTURAL
(www.yyf.com.au; ⊙ Aug) A four-day festival in northeastern Arnhem Land. Garma is one of the most significant regional festivals, a celebration of Yolngu culture that includes ceremonial performances, bushcraft lessons, a *yidaki* masterclass and an academic forum. Serious planning is required to attend, so start early.

🛏️ Sleeping & Eating

Walkabout Lodge   MOTEL $$
(☑ 08 8939 2000; www.walkaboutlodge.com.au; 12 Westal St, Nhulunbuy; s/d Aug & Sep $250/290, Oct-Jul $218/245) Air-conditioned, motel-style rooms in a leafy Nhulunbuy setting. They'd be overpriced elsewhere, but they're not bad value for here.

BanuBanu Wilderness Retreat   LODGE $$$
(☑ 08 8987 8085; www.banubanu.com; Bremer Island; d $720-1220) These eco tents on Bremer Island off the Gove Peninsula couldn't be closer to the beach – and it's the location (and the fishing) that is most memorable here. The tents themselves are fairly simple and the surrounding area a little bare and shadeless, but as you'll spend most of your day out fishing, this latter point may prove less significant.

🛍️ Shopping

Nambara Arts &
Crafts Aboriginal Gallery   ART
(Melville Bay Rd, Nhulunbuy; ⊙ 10am-4pm Mon-Fri, 10am-2pm Sat) Sells art and crafts from northeast Arnhem Land and often has artists-in-residence.

ℹ️ Getting There & Away

AIR
Airnorth (☑ 1800 627 474; www.airnorth.com.au) and **Qantas** (p156) fly from Darwin to Gove Airport (for Nhulunbuy) daily.

4WD
Overland, it's a 10-hour 4WD trip and only possible in the Dry. The Central Arnhem Hwy to Gove leaves the Stuart Hwy (Rte 87) 52km south of Katherine.

Uluru & Outback Northern Territory

Best Places to Eat

➡ Marksies Camp Tucker (p183)

➡ Sounds of Silence (p218)

➡ Black Russian Caravan Bar (p183)

➡ Montes (p204)

Best Places to Sleep

➡ Desert Gardens Hotel (p219)

➡ Lorella Springs Wilderness Park (p195)

➡ Seven Emu Station (p197)

Why Go?

The remote and largely untamed chunk of the Northern Territory from Katherine to Uluru is where dreams end and adventure begins. If you enjoy off-road driving, meeting real characters of the Australian outback, and contortions of an ancient land sliced into escarpments, canyons, gorges and pockets of verdant bush, then you've come to the right place.

The Stuart Hwy from Katherine to Alice Springs is still referred to as 'the Track' – it has been since WWII, when it was literally a dirt track connecting the NT's two main towns. It's dead straight most of the way. The Red Centre is Australia's heartland, boasting the iconic attractions of Uluru (Ayers Rock) and Kata Tjuta (The Olgas), plus an enigmatic Central Desert culture that continues to produce extraordinary abstract art. And delighting travellers with its eccentric offerings, pioneering spirit and weathered mountain setting, Alice Springs is the city at the centre of a continent.

When to Go
Alice Springs

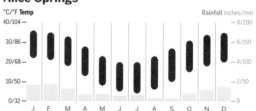

Apr–Aug Peak season with cooler temperatures in the Red Centre.

Jun & Jul Festival season: Beanie Festival and Camel Cup in Alice Springs.

Sep–Mar It's hot, hot, hot around Alice Springs; storms bring relief in Katherine.

Map labels:

Joseph Bonaparte Gulf

Katherine

❸ Nitmiluk National Park

Roper River

Giwining/Flora River Nature Park

Beswick Elsey National Park

Roper Bar

Ngukurr

Gulf of Carpentaria

Cutta Cutta Caves National Park

Keep River National Park

Victoria River

Timber Creek

Matarajka

Limmen National Park

Sir Edward Pellew Group

Kununurra

Judbarra/ Gregory National Park

Victoria River Crossing

Judbarra/ Gregory National Park

Larrimah

Alawa Aboriginal Land

Daly Waters

Top Springs

Dunmarra

Borroloola

Kalkarinji

Newcastle Waters

Elliott

Cape Crawford

❺ Pungalina – Seven Emu Wildlife Sanctuary

Lajamanu

Lake Woods

Renner Springs

Barkly Tablelands

Tarrabool Lake

Tablelands Hwy

Waanyi/ Garawa Aboriginal Land

Karlantijpa North Aboriginal Land

Tanami Desert

Karlantijpa South Aboriginal Land

Stuart Hwy

Ranken Road

Central Desert Aboriginal Land

Three Ways

Tennant Creek

Camooweal

Tanami Rd

Wakaya Aboriginal Land

Wauchope

Devil's Marbles

Anurrete Aboriginal Land

Alpururulam

NORTHERN TERRITORY

Wycliffe Well Roadhouse & Holiday Park

Barrow Creek

Lake Mackay Aboriginal Land

Ampilatwatja

Urandangi

Yuendumu

Red Centre Farm

Ti Tree

Sandover Hwy

Aileron

Plenty Hwy

West MacDonnell National Park

Harts Range

Atnetye Aboriginal Land

QUEENSLAND

WESTERN AUSTRALIA

Mt Zeil (1531m) ❼

Kintore

Haasts Bluff Aboriginal Land

MacDonnell Ranges

East MacDonnell Range

❻ Alice Springs

Hermannsburg

Ewaninga Rock Carvings Conservation Reserve

Santa Teresa

Watarrka National Park ❹

Finke Gorge National Park

Rainbow Valley Conservation Reserve

Pmere Nyente Aboriginal Land

Petermann Aboriginal Land

Kings Canyon

Lake Amadeus

Erldunda

Central Australia Railway

Kata Tjuta ❷ Yulara

❶ Uluru

Uluru-Kata Tjuta National Park

Mt Conner (350m)

Finke (Aputula)

Pmer Ulperre Ingwemirne Aboriginal Land

Simpson Desert

Kulgera

0 — 200 km
0 — 100 miles

Uluru & Outback Northern Territory Highlights

❶ **Uluru** (p222) Watching the sunrise and sunset alter the earth's colour palette on this strangely spiritual rock.

❷ **Kata Tjuta** (p224) Hiking through the hidden valleys and deep-red monoliths of the Olgas.

❸ **Nitmiluk National Park** (p181) Swimming in croc-free waters and hiking through splendid gorge country.

❹ **Kings Canyon** (p216) Admiring one of the outback's icons, looking for wildlife.

❺ **Pungalina – Seven Emu Wildlife Sanctuary** (p197) Journeying to remote Gulf Country in search of wildlife.

❻ **Alice Springs** (p198) Shopping for Indigenous art in one of Australia's most remote cities.

❼ **West MacDonnell Ranges** (p209) Exploring the dramatic escarpment country, with its wildlife and waterholes west of Alice.

KATHERINE

POP 10,766

Katherine is probably best known for the **Nitmiluk (Katherine Gorge) National Park** (☑08 8972 1886, 08 8972 1253; nt.gov.au/leisure/parks-reserves/) to the east; the town makes an obvious base, with plenty of accommodation. It also has a handful of interesting outback attractions to tempt you into staying an extra day or two.

Katherine is considered a big town in this part of the world, and you'll certainly feel like you've arrived somewhere if you've just made the long trip up the highway from Alice Springs (its namesake river is the first permanent running water on the road north of Alice Springs) or down from Darwin.

◉ Sights

★ Top Didj Cultural Experience & Art Gallery GALLERY

(☑08 8971 2751; www.topdidj.com; cnr Gorge & Jaensch Rds; cultural experience adult/child $70/45; ⊙cultural experience 9.30am & 2.30pm Sun-Fri, 9.30am & 1.30pm Sat) Run by the owners of the now-onsite Katherine Art Gallery, Top Didj is a good place to see Aboriginal artists at work. The cultural experience is hands on with fire sticks, spear throwing, painting and basket weaving, and is a somewhat more dynamic take on the Indigenous cultural experience.

Godinymayin Yijard Rivers Arts & Culture Centre GALLERY

(☑08 8972 3751; www.gyracc.org.au; Stuart Hwy, Katherine East; ⊙10am-5pm Tue-Fri, to 3pm Sat) This stunning arts and culture centre in Katherine is housed in a beautiful, contemporary building that is a real landmark for the town. The centre is designed to be a meeting place for Indigenous and non-Indigenous people, and a chance to share cultures. Don't miss this place when you're in town.

Djilpin Arts GALLERY

(☑08 8971 1770; www.djilpinarts.org.au; 27 Katherine Tce; ⊙9am-4pm Mon-Fri) This Katherine gallery is Aboriginal owned and represents art from the Ghunmarn Culture Centre (p191) in the remote community of Beswick (Wugularr). Exhibits include paintings, weavings and termite-bored didgeridoos.

Katherine School of the Air CULTURAL CENTRE

(☑08 8972 1833; www.ksa.nt.edu.au; Giles St; adult/child $12/free, VIP tour $20; ⊙9am, 10am & 11am mid-Apr–Oct) At the School of the Air,

1.5km from the town centre, you can listen into a class and see how 170 kids from preschool to Year 9 are educated in areas where there is no physical school – it is sometimes called the world's biggest classroom. The standard tour doesn't get much beyond the front room but is interesting nonetheless, while the 10am VIP tour takes you into the classrooms for a closer look at what goes on.

⛯ Tours

★ Nitmiluk Tours TOURS

(☑1300 146 743, 08 8972 1253; www.nitmiluktours.com.au; 4/52 Katherine Terrace (Stuart Hwy)) This excellent operator runs scenic flights, canoeing and boat cruises in Nitmiluk National Park and is a good place to begin as plan your time in the area.

Gecko Canoeing & Trekking OUTDOORS

(☑1800 634 319, 0427 067 154; www.geckocanoeing.com.au) ✎ Exhilarating guided canoe trips on the more remote stretches of the Katherine River. Trips include three days ($1090) on the Katherine River and six days ($1895) on the Daly and Katherine Rivers. A five-day hike along the Jatbula Trail in Nitmiluk National Park costs $1895.

✵ Festivals & Events

Katherine Country Music Muster MUSIC

(adult/child $35/free; ⊙May or Jun) 'We like both kinds of music: country *and* western.' Plenty of live music in the pubs and entertainment at the Tick Market Lindsay St Complex on a weekend in May or June.

⌷ Sleeping

BIG4 Katherine Holiday Park CARAVAN PARK $

(☑08 8972 3962; www.big4.com.au/caravan-parks/nt/katherine-surrounds/katherine-holiday-park; Shadforth Rd; powered/unpowered sites $48/45, cabin/safari tent $198/115; ❉�🛜🏊) A well-manicured park with plenty of shady sites, a great swimming pool adjoining a bar and an excellent bistro (mains $21 to $29) that is sheltered by a magnificent fig tree. The amenities are first rate, making it the pick of the town's several caravan parks.

Coco's Backpackers HOSTEL $

(☑08 8971 2889; coco@21firstst.com.au; 21 First St; camping per person $22, dm $40) Travellers love this place, with Indigenous art on the walls and didgeridoos in the tin shed next door helping to provide an authentic

Katherine

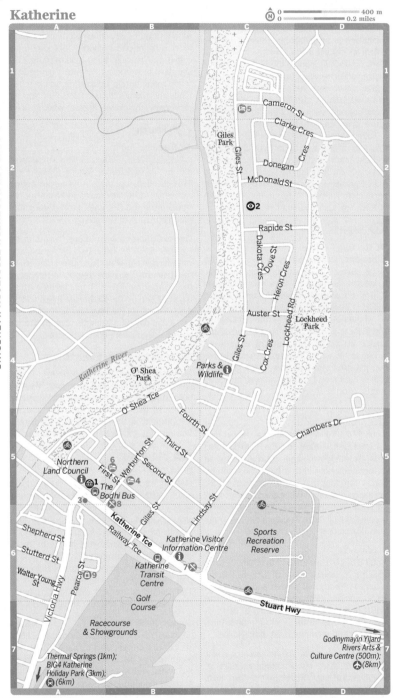

N
0 — 400 m
0 — 0.2 miles

Katherine

Katherine experience. Coco's is a converted home where the owner chats with the guests and has great knowledge about the town and local area. Aboriginal artists are often here painting didgeridoos.

Knott's Crossing Resort   MOTEL **$$**
(✐08 8972 2511; www.knottscrossing.com.au; cnr Cameron & Giles Sts; powered/unpowered sites $46/28, cabin/motel d from $110/160; ❄@✆➳✉☰) Probably the pick of Katherine's accommodation options. There is variety to suit most budgets, a fantastic restaurant and the whole place is very professionally run. Everything is packed pretty tightly into the tropical gardens at Knott's, but it's easy to find your own little nook.

St Andrews Apartments   APARTMENT **$$$**
(✐1800 686 106, 08 8971 2288; www.standrews apts.com.au; 27 First St; apt $240-290; ❄➳✉) In the heart of town, these serviced apartments are great for families and those pining for a few home comforts and a little more space. The two-bedroom apartments sleep four (six if you use the sofa bed) and come with fully equipped kitchen and lounge/dining area. Nifty little BBQ decks are attached to the ground-floor units.

✕ Eating

★ **Black Russian**
Caravan Bar   INTERNATIONAL **$**
(✐0409 475 115; www.facebook.com/theblack russiancaravanbar/; Stuart Hwy; mains $7.80-12.50; ☺7am-1pm) Street food has arrived in Katherine! This cutesy little caravan sits

just across the car park from the visitor centre (although it may have moved by the time you get there; check it out on Facebook) and it serves Katherine's best coffee, which you can enjoy on the lawn.

Coffee Club   CAFE **$$**
(www.coffeeclub.com.au; cnr Katherine Tce & Warburton St; meals $13-19; ☺6.30am-3pm Mon-Fri, 7am-3pm Sat & Sun) This is the best place in town for breakfast, as well as a good bet at lunchtime. Dining is in a light-filled contemporary space. On offer is decent coffee, healthy all-day breakfast options including fruit and muesli, plus burgers, sandwiches, wraps and salads all day.

Savannah Bar &
Restaurant   MODERN AUSTRALIAN **$$**
(✐08 8972 2511; knottscrossing.com.au/ facilities/#dining; Knott's Crossing Resort, cnr Giles & Cameron Sts; mains $25-35; ☺6.30-9am & 6-9pm) Undoubtedly one of the best dining choices in Katherine. It's predominantly an outdoors garden restaurant, with a cool breeze wafting through the tropical vegetation. The menu includes steak, barramundi, croc croquettes and Venus Bay prawn dishes. There's even a suckling pig you can tuck into. Service is fast and friendly and the whole place is very well run.

★ **Marksies Camp Tucker**   AUSTRALIAN **$$$**
(✐0427 112 806; www.marksiescamptucker.com. au; 363 Gorge Rd; adult/child $75/35; ☺7pm Apr-Sep) Now here's something special. Head to this re-created stockman's camp 7km from town for a night of fabulous food and fun storytelling by Geoff Mark (Marksie), a warm and wily raconteur and one of Katherine's great characters. The meal consists of a three-course set menu that might include crocodile, wild-caught barramundi, camel, buffalo and/or kangaroo, all leavened with bush spices and hilarious bush yarns. Bookings essential. Marksies shares an entrance with Top Didj (p181).

☆ Entertainment

Katherine
Outback Experience   LIVE PERFORMANCE
(✐0428 301 580; www.katherineoutbackexperi ence.com.au; 115 Collins Rd, Uralla; adult/student/ senior $50/25/45; ☺4.30pm Mon, Thu & Fri, 5pm Wed, closed Nov-Mar) You get a little bit of everything for your money out here – the 90-minute show is about horse training and working station dogs, but don't be surprised

if presenter Tom Curtain bursts into song at some stage during proceedings. Sometimes it falls a bit flat, but it's great when it works, which is often.

🛍 Shopping

★ **Mimi Aboriginal**
Art & Craft   ARTS & CRAFTS
(☑ 08 8971 0036; www.mimiarts.com; 6 Pearce St; ⊙ 8.30am-4.30pm Mon-Fri) Aboriginal owned and not-for-profit, Mimi is arguably Katherine's best Indigenous art centre. It's a small but carefully chosen collection of works from the Katherine region, as well as the Tanami Desert and all the way up to the Kimberleys. They also sell postcards and a small selection of books, music and didgeridoos.

ℹ Information

Katherine Wildlife Rescue Service (☑ 0407 934 252; www.fauna.org.au) The place to call if you come across injured wildlife.

Katherine Visitor Information Centre (☑ 1800 653 142; www.visitkatherine.com.au; cnr Lindsay St & Stuart Hwy; ⊙ 8.30am-5pm daily in the Dry (mid-Apr–Sep), 8.30am-5pm Mon-Fri, 10am-2pm Sat & Sun in the Wet (Oct–mid-Apr)) Modern, air-con information centre stocking information on all areas of the NT. Pick up the handy *Katherine Region Visitor Guide*.

Northern Land Council (☑ 08 8971 9899; www.nlc.org.au; 5/29 Katherine Tce) Permits for the Central Arnhem Hwy towards Gove.

Parks & Wildlife (☑ 08 8973 8888; nt.gov.au/leisure/parks-reserves; 32 Giles St; ⊙ 8am-4.20pm) National park information and notes.

Katherine Hospital (☑ 08 8973 9211; www. health.nt.gov.au; Giles St) About 3km north of town, with an emergency department.

ℹ Getting There & Away

Katherine is a major road junction: from here the Stuart Hwy tracks north and south and the Victoria Hwy heads west to Kununurra in WA.

AIR

Airnorth (p265) connects Katherine with Darwin, Alice Springs and Tennant Creek a few times a week.

BUS

Greyhound Australia (p266) has regular services between Darwin and Alice Springs, Queensland or Western Australia. Buses stop at **Katherine Transit Centre** (☑ 08 8971 9999; 6 Katherine Tce). One-way fares from Katherine include: Darwin ($75, four hours), Alice Springs (from $175, 16 hours), Tennant Creek ($139, 8½ hours) and Kununurra ($108, six hours).

An alternative is the **Bodhi Bus** (p269), which travels to remote communities (including Borroloola and Timber Creek). It also services the Katherine–Darwin route ($70 one way, Monday, Thursday and Saturday) via Adelaide River ($50, 2½ hours) and Pine Creek ($50, one hour), dropping off passengers at the Palmerston bus exchange or Darwin airport.

TRAIN

The *Ghan* train, operated by **Great Southern Rail** (www.gsr.com.au), travels between Adelaide and Darwin twice a week, stopping at Katherine for four hours – enough for a whistle-stop tour to Katherine Gorge! **Nitmiluk Tours** (☑ 1300 146 743; www.nitmiluktours.com.au; Katherine Tce; ⊙ 9am-5pm Mon-Sat) runs shuttles between the station and town.

AROUND KATHERINE

The area around Katherine has plenty to keep you occupied, none more so than Nitmiluk National Park. The Indigenous community of Beswick (Wugularr) is a wonderful place to draw near to Aboriginal people and their culture.

Nitmiluk (Katherine Gorge) National Park

◉ Sights & Activities

Leliyn (Edith Falls)   NATURE RESERVE
Reached off the Stuart Hwy 40km north of Katherine and a further 20km along a sealed road, Leliyn is an idyllic, safe haven for swimming and hiking. The moderate **Leliyn Trail** (2.6km loop, 1½ hours; medium) climbs into escarpment country through grevillea and spinifex and past scenic lookouts (Bemang is best in the afternoon) to the Upper Pool, where the moderate **Sweetwater Pool Trail** (8.6km return, three to five hours) branches off.

The peaceful Sweetwater Pool has a small camping ground; overnight permits are available at the kiosk. The main Lower Pool – a gorgeous, mirror-flat swimming lagoon – is a quick 150m dash from the car park. The Parks & Wildlife **camping ground** (☑ 08 8975 4869; adult/child $12/6) next to the car park has grassy sites, lots of shade, toilets, showers, a laundry and facilities for travellers with disabilities. Fees are paid at the **kiosk** (⊙ 8am-6pm May-Oct, 9.30am-3pm Nov-Apr), which sells snacks and basic supplies. Nearby is a picnic area with BBQs and tables.

★ **Nitmiluk Tours** CRUISE
(✆ 08 8972 1253, 1300 146 743; www.nitmiluktours.
com.au; 2hr cruise per adult/child $89/44.50, 4hr
cruise adult/child $129/63.50) An easy way to
see far into the gorge is on a cruise. Bookings on some cruises can be tight in the peak
season; make your reservation at least a day
in advance. The two-hour cruise goes to the
second gorge and visits a rock-art gallery
(including an 800m walk). The four-hour
cruise goes to the third gorge and includes
a chance to swim. There's also a more leisurely two-hour breakfast cruise (adult/child
$94/48), and a sunset cruise with a candlelit
buffet dinner and champagne (adult/child
$164.50/119). There's wheelchair access to
the top of the first gorge only.

Jatbula Trail WALKING
This renowned walk (66km one way, five
days, difficult) to Leliyn (Edith Falls) climbs
the Arnhem Land escarpment, passing the
swamp-fed Biddlecombe Cascades, Crystal
Falls, the Amphitheatre and Sweetwater Pool.
This walk can only be done one way (ie you
can't walk from Leliyn to Katherine Gorge),
is closed from October to April and requires
a minimum of two walkers. A ferry service
takes you across the gorge to kick things off.

Nitmiluk Tours SCENIC FLIGHTS
(✆ 1300 146 743; www.nitmiluktours.com.au)
Nitmiluk Tours offers a variety of flights
ranging from an eight-minute buzz over the
first gorge (per person $104) to a 20-minute
flight over all 13 gorges ($226). There are
broader tours that take in Aboriginal rock-
art sites and Kakadu National Park. Book at
the Nitmiluk Visitor Centre (p185).

Nitmiluk Tours CANOEING
(✆ 1300 146 743, 08 8972 1253; www.nitmiluktours.
com.au) From April to November, Nitmiluk
Tours hires out single/double canoes for a
half-day ($57/91 plus $50 deposit), including
the use of a splash-proof drum for cameras
and other gear, a map and a life jacket.

Butterfly Gorge WALKING
A challenging, shady walk (12km return, 4½
hours, difficult) through a pocket of monsoon rainforest, often with butterflies, leads
to midway along the second gorge and a
deep-water swimming spot.

Jawoyn Valley WALKING
A difficult (40km loop, overnight) wilderness trail leading off the Eighth Gorge walk
into a valley with rock outcrops and rock-art
galleries.

Barrawei (Lookout) Loop WALKING
Starting with a short, steep climb, this walk
(3.7km loop, two hours, moderate difficulty)
provides good views over the Katherine River.

🛏 Sleeping

**Nitmiluk National Park
Campground** CAMPGROUND $
(✆ 1300 146 743, 08 8972 1253; www.nitmiluktours.
com.au; powered/unpowered sites $49.50/37, safa-
ri tents $160; 🌀 🛜 🏊) Plenty of grass and shade,
hot showers, toilets, BBQs, a laundry and a
kiosk by the good-lookin' swimming pool.
Wallabies, goannas and night curlews are
frequent visitors. There's a 'tent village' here
with permanent safari tents sleeping two
people. Book at the Nitmiluk Visitor Centre
(p185).

★ **Cicada Lodge** BOUTIQUE HOTEL $$$
(✆ 1800 242 232, 08 8974 3100; www.cicadalodge.
com.au; Nitmiluk National Park; d incl breakfast
$750; 🌀 @ 🛜 🏊) This luxury lodge has been
architecturally designed to meld modern so-
phistication and traditional Jawoyn themes.
It has just 18 luxury rooms overlooking the
Katherine River. Decor is tasteful and styl-
ish and features include full-length louvred
doors that open onto private balconies.
Indigenous artworks decorate the walls.
Breakfast included.

Nitmiluk Chalets CABIN $$$
(✆ 1300 146 743, 08 8972 1253; www.nitmiluktours.
com.au; 1-/2-bedroom cabins $218/275; 🌀 🛜 🏊)
Next door to the caravan park, these cabins
are a serviceable choice if you'd rather have
a solid roof over your head (and a flat-screen
TV). Has access to all the caravan park facilities (pool, BBQs, kiosk etc).

🍴 Eating

Sugarbag Café CAFE $$
(Nitmiluk Visitor Centre; salads $12-20, mains $17-
22, breakfast buffet adult/child $26/11, lunch buf-
fet $26/21; ☉ 7am-3pm) The food here at the
visitor centre is excellent, with highlights
including the Nitmiluk burger or the lem-
on-myrtle barra bites. It also does breakfast
and lunch buffets from April to October. The
elevated deck looking out over the river and
filled with blue-faced honeyeaters is a fine
place to rest after a walk or cruise.

ℹ Information

The **Nitmiluk Visitor Centre** (✆ 1300 146 743,
08 8972 1253; www.nitmiluktours.com.au;
☉ 6.30am-5.30pm) has excellent displays and

information on the park's geology, wildlife, the traditional owners (the Jawoyn) and European history. There's also **Sugarbag Cafe** (p185) here and a desk for Parks & Wildlife, which has information sheets on a wide range of marked walking tracks that start here and traverse the picturesque country south of the gorge. Registration for overnight walks and camping permits ($3.30 per night) is from 8am to 1pm; canoeing permits are also issued.

ℹ️ Getting There & Away

Car & 4WD It's 30km by sealed road from Katherine to the Nitmiluk Centre, and a few hundred metres further to the car park, where the gorge begins and the cruises start.

Bus Daily transfers between Katherine and the gorge are run by **Nitmiluk Tours** (p184), departing the Nitmiluk Town Booking Office and also picking up at local accommodation places on request. Buses leave Katherine three times daily.

Katherine to Western Australia

The sealed Victoria Hwy – part of the Savannah Way – stretches 513km from Katherine to Kununurra in WA. A 4WD will get you into a few out-of-the-way national parks accessed off the Victoria Hwy or you can meander through semiarid desert and sandstone outcrops until bloated baobab trees herald your imminent arrival in WA. All fruits, vegetables, nuts and honey must be left at the quarantine inspection post on the border.

Victoria River Crossing

The red sandstone cliffs surrounding the spot where the highway crosses the Victoria River (194km west of Katherine) create a dramatic setting. Much of this area forms the eastern section of Judbarra/Gregory National Park.

⊙ Sights & Activities

Park up at the roadhouse and wander down to Victoria River Crossing and the old bridge for lovely river views and good birding; watch the tall grass for the prized purple-crowned fairy wren, as well as other bird species such as the star finch, chestnut-breasted mannikin and the blue-winged kookaburra.As you continue west of Victoria River in the direction of Timber Creek, you'll pass through some lovely escarpment country where the river cuts its way through. A number of signposted walks head off up into the hills around here, while the old river crossing (signposted) is a gorgeous spot.

🛏️ Sleeping

Victoria River Roadhouse Caravan Park   CAMPGROUND $
(☑08 8975 0744; Victoria Hwy; powered/unpowered sites $25/20, r $50-150; @) Well-run camping ground behind the roadhouse with very good facilities and a range of cabins from the budget variety with shared bathrooms to more expansive options. It also has a shop, a bar and can provide meals ($10 to $37). It's on a rise on the west side of the bridge over the river.

ℹ️ Getting There & Away

The **Bodhi Bus** (p269) that runs between Katherine ($60, 2½ hours) and Wyndham ($50, 3½ hours) passes through the Victoria River Crossing – make sure that the driver knows that this is as far as you're going.

Timber Creek

POP 232

Tiny Timber Creek is the only town between Katherine and Kununurra. It has a pretty big history for such a small place, with an early European exploration aboard the *Tom Tough* requiring repairs to be carried out with local timber (hence the town's name). The expedition's leader, AC Gregory, inscribed his arrival date into a baobab; it is still discernable (and is explained in detail through interpretive panels) at Gregory's Tree; 15km northwest of town. The tree is off the Victoria Hwy down a 3km unsealed road, which can become corrugated.

Other worthwhile detours just out of town include tracks to achingly pretty Policeman's Point (2km) and Escarpment Lookout (5km), the latter has fine views over town and the surrounding country.

👉 Tours

A highlight of Timber Creek is the Victoria River Cruise (☑0427 750 731; www.victoriarivercruise.com.au; sunset cruises adult/child $95/50; ⊙4pm daily Apr-Sep), which takes you 40km downriver spotting wildlife and returning in time for a fiery sunset.

🛏 Sleeping

There are a couple of caravan parks along the main road through town. Basic meals and takeaway food are possible along the main road – that's about as good as it gets.

**Timber Creek Hotel
& Circle F Caravan Park**   CARAVAN PARK $
(☑ 08 8975 0722; www.timbercreekhotel.com.au; Victoria Hwy; powered/unpowered sites $33/29, s/d $80/110; ✳ ❄) The town is dominated by this roadside hotel and caravan park. Enormous trees shade parts of the camping area, which is next to a small creek where there's croc feeding every evening (5pm). The complex includes the Timber Creek Hotel (pub) and a small supermarket.

ℹ Getting There & Away

The Bodhi Bus has a daily service to/from Katherine ($60, 3¼ hours) on its way through to Kununurra and Wyndham.

Judbarra / Gregory National Park

The remote and rugged wilderness of the little-visited Judbarra / Gregory National Park (☑ 08 8975 0888; nt.gov.au/leisure/parks-reserves) will swallow you up – this is right off the beaten track and ripe for 4WD exploration. Covering 12,860 sq km, it sits at the transitional zone between the tropical and semiarid regions. The park consists of old cattle country and is made up of two separate sections: the eastern (Victoria River) section and the much larger Bullita section in the west. This is croc country; swimming isn't safe.

🛏 Sleeping & Eating

You'll need to bring your own food. There are basic supplies in the small grocery stores in Timber Creek.

Big Horse Creek   CAMPGROUND $
(adult/child $3.30/1.75) There's accessible bush camping at Big Horse Creek, 10km west of Timber Creek.

ℹ Information

Parks & Wildlife (☑ 08 8975 0888; nt.gov.au/leisure/parks-reserves; Timber Creek; ☉ 7am-4.30pm) in Timber Creek has park and 4WD notes. It can also provide a map featuring the various walks, camping spots, tracks and the historic homestead and ruggedly romantic original stockyards – a must before heading in.

ℹ Getting Around

You'll need a 4WD vehicle to explore the park.

Keep River National Park

The remote Keep River National Park (☑ 08 9167 8827; nt.gov.au/leisure/parks-reserves) is noted for its stunning sandstone formations, beautiful desolation and rock art.

Pamphlets detailing walks are available at the start of the excellent trails. Don't miss the rock art walk (5.5km return, two hours) near Jarnem and the gorge walk (3km return, two hours) at Jinumum.

🛏 Sleeping

There are basic, sandstone-surrounded camping grounds (adult/child $3.30/1.65) at Gurrandalng (18km into the park) and Jarnem (32km). Tank water is available at Jarnem.

ℹ Getting There & Away

The park entrance is just 3km from the WA border. You can reach the park's main points by conventional 2WD vehicle during the Dry.

DON'T MISS

LARRIMAH

Tiny roadside Larrimah, 185km south of Katherine, offers a couple of reasons to pull over.

Pink Panther (Larrimah) Hotel (☑ 08 8975 9931; larrimahwaysideinn. wordpress.com; powered/unpowered sites $25/18, r $65-100; ✳ ❄) Originally a WWII officers' mess, now a cheerfully rustic and quirky pub offering basic rooms, meals (mains $12 to $34) and a small menagerie of animals. Its specialities are the homemade pies (which often sell out by midafternoon) and excellent burgers. The atmosphere is a cross between a cheerfully dishevelled forgotten outpost of the outback and an ageing art installation.

Fran's Devonshire Teahouse (Stuart Hwy; meals $6-20; ☉ 8am-4pm) Fran's Devonshire Teahouse is in Fran's house, where she cooks up legendary pies and pastries. This is the place to stop for a filling camel or buffalo pie, roast lamb with damper or just a Devonshire tea (no, you couldn't be further from Exeter) or fresh coffee.

ALAN COPSON/GETTY IMAGES ©

1. Uluru (Ayers Rock) **2.** Kata Tjuta (The Olgas)
3. Kings Canyon

3

Ultimate Outback

'Outback' means different things to different people and in different parts of Australia – deserts, tropical savannah, wetlands... But what's consistent is the idea that it's far from the comforts of home. The outback is 'beyond the black stump' and holds many surprises.

Uluru (Ayers Rock)

Uluru-Kata Tjuta National Park is the undisputed highlight of central Australia. There's not much that hasn't been said about Uluru, and not many parts of it that haven't been explored, photographed and documented. Still, nothing can prepare you for its almighty bulk, spiritual stories, remarkable textures and camera-worthy colours.

Kata Tjuta (The Olgas)

The tallest dome of Kata Tjuta is taller than Uluru (546m versus 348m), and some say exploring these 36 mounded monoliths is a more intimate, moving experience. Trails weave in amongst the red rocks, leading to pockets of silent beauty and spiritual gravitas.

Watarrka National Park

In Watarrka National Park, about 300km north of Uluru by road, Kings Canyon is the inverse of Uluru – as if someone had grabbed the big rock and pushed it into the desert sand. Here, 270m-high cliffs drop away to a palm-lined valley floor, home to 600 plant species and delighted-to-be-here native animals. The 6km canyon rim walk is four hours well spent.

MacDonnell Ranges

The 'Macs' stretch east and west of Alice Springs. In their ancient folds are hidden worlds where rock wallabies and colourful birds can find water even on the hottest days.

WORTH A TRIP

CUTTA CUTTA CAVES NATURE PARK

About 30km south of Katherine, turn your back on the searing sun and dip down 15m below terra firma into this mazelike limestone cave system. The 1499-hectare **Cutta Cutta Caves Nature Park** (☑ 1300 146 743, 08 8972 1940; nt.gov.au/parks-reserves; tours adult/child $20/10; ◷ 8.30am-4.30pm guided tours 9am, 10am, 11am, 1pm, 2pm and 3pm) has a unique ecology and you'll be sharing the space with brown tree snakes and pythons, plus the endangered ghost bats and orange horseshoe bats that they feed on. Cutta Cutta is a Jawoyn name meaning 'many stars'; it was taboo for Aboriginal people to enter the cave, which they believed was where the stars were kept during the day. Admission is by guided tour only.

Mataranka

POP 244

With soothing, warm thermal springs set in pockets of palms and tropical vegetation, you'd be mad not to pull into Mataranka for at least a few hours to soak off the road dust. The small settlement regularly swells with towel-toting visitors shuffling to the thermal pool. But Mataranka has more calling cards than most roadside outback towns: nearby spring-fed **Elsey National Park** (☑ 08 8975 4560; www.nt.gov.au/leisure/parks-reserves) and a history linked to one of Australia's most enjoyable outback tales, not to mention the welcoming tree-lined road through town, add considerable appeal to a stop here.

◉ Sights

★**Elsey Cemetery** CEMETERY
This lonely cemetery under the eucalypts is a poignant footnote to *We of the Never Never*, with so many of the larger-than-life characters from the book buried here, among them Aeneas Gunn (alongside a memorial to his wife), Henry Peckham, John MacLennan and Tom Pearce. The last remains of the homestead (destroyed during roadworks in the 1940s) lie 300m to the southeast at the end of the gravel track. The cemetery is

around 20km south of Mataranka and signposted off the Stuart Hwy.

Elsey Station Homestead HISTORIC BUILDING
(admission by donation; ◷ daylight hours) Outside the entrance to the Mataranka Homestead Resort (p190) is a replica of the Elsey Station Homestead, constructed for the filming of *We of the Never Never*, which is screened daily at noon in the resort bar. The low-lying and overgrown ruins of the actual site are a few hundred metres past the Elsey Cemetery (p190).

🏃 Activities

Mataranka Thermal Pools THERMAL BATHS
Mataranka's crystal-clear thermal pool, shrouded in rainforest, is 10km from town beside the Mataranka Homestead Resort. The warm, clear water, dappled by light filtered through overhanging palms, rejuvenates a lot of bodies on any given day; it's reached via a boardwalk from the resort and can get mighty crowded.

🛏 Sleeping & Eating

Territory Manor Motel & Caravan Park MOTEL $
(☑ 08 8975 4516; www.matarankamotel.com; Martin Rd; powered/unpowered sites $30/26, s/d $110/120; ❋ @ 🞷) Mataranka's best caravan park is well positioned and a class act – no surprise it's also popular. Smallish motel rooms are well decked out and have good-sized bathrooms, and the grounds are well shaded for camping. In the licensed bistro (mains $22 to $35) they serve barramundi, along with steaks, salad, lamb chops with a honey mint glaze and other surprises.

Mataranka Homestead Resort CAMPGROUND $
(☑ 08 8975 4544; www.matarankahomestead.com.au; Homestead Rd; powered/unpowered sites $30/26, d/cabins $89/115; ❋ 🞷) Only metres from the main thermal pool and with a range of accommodation, this is a *very* popular option. The large camping ground is dusty but has a few shady areas and decent amenities. The rudimentary air-con motel rooms have fridge, TV and bathroom, while the cabins have a kitchenette and sleep up to six people. Book ahead.

Bitter Springs Cabins CABIN $$
(☑ 08 8975 4838; www.bitterspringscabins.com.au; 4705 Martin Rd, Bitter Springs; powered/unpowered sites $35/30, cabins $130; ❋ @ 🞷 🞷)

On the banks of the Little Roper River, only a few hundred metres from Bitter Springs thermal pool, this quiet bush setting has some amazing termite mounds adorning the front paddock. The TV-equipped, open-plan cabins have a balcony with bush views.

★ **Stockyard Gallery** CAFE $
(☑ 08 8975 4530; Stuart Hwy; snacks & light meals $6-13; ☺ hours vary) This casual cafe is a little gem and the lovely shaded garden area is a great respite from the heat and dust. There's a delicious range of homemade snacks (sandwiches and kebabs) plus fresh espresso coffee and divine mango smoothies. The art gallery here sells Aboriginal art, books and souvenirs. The only problem is that the opening hours change regularly.

❶ Getting There & Away

Mataranka lies 108km south of Katherine and 568km north of Tennant Creek along the Stuart Hwy. Daily **Greyhound buses** (p266) connect Mataranka with Katherine ($37, 1¼ hours) and Tennant Creek ($126, 7½ hours).

Beswick (Wugularr)

If you're interested in seeing genuine Aboriginal art produced by local communities, it's worth detouring off the Stuart Hwy to the remote cultural centre and small community of Beswick (Wugularr). It's an opportunity to draw near to the great artistic traditions of Arnhem Land, without straying down detours along long and lonely dirt tracks.

⊙ Sights

★ **Ghunmarn Culture Centre** GALLERY
(Djilpin Arts; ☑ 08 8977 4250; www.djilpinarts. org.au; Beswick; ☺ 9.30am-4pm Mon-Fri Apr-Nov) The Ghunmarn Culture Centre, opened in 2007, displays local artworks, prints, carvings, weavings and didgeridoos from western Arnhem Land. The centre also features the Blanasi Collection, a permanent exhibition of works by elders from the western Arnhem Land region. Visitors are welcome to visit the centre without a permit; call ahead to check that it's open.

★✲ Festivals & Events

Walking With Spirits CULTURAL
(www.djilpinarts.org.au; ☺ Jul) A two-day Indigenous cultural festival in July at Beswick Falls, 130km from Katherine. In a magical setting, traditional dance and music is combined with theatre, films and a light show. Camping is allowed at the site (only during the festival). A 4WD is recommended for the last 20km to the falls; alternatively, a shuttle bus runs from Beswick.

🛏 Sleeping & Eating

Beswick has a general store with limited supplies.

★ **Djakanimba Pavilions** GUESTHOUSE $$
(☑ 08 8977 4250; www.djilpinarts.org.au/djaka nimba-pavillions-beswick/; Cameron Rd, Beswick; d $140-180, 2-night all-inclusive package $880; ❄) These four attractive guestrooms attached to the impressive Djilpin Arts complex in Beswick are a wonderful chance to sleep overnight in a predominantly Aboriginal community. The accommodation, on stilts and with a contemporary Outback aesthetic with louvred windows to catch the prevailing breezes, is simple but stylish and smart casual – an excellent choice.

❶ Getting There & Away

Beswick, reached via the sealed Central Arnhem Hwy, is 56km east of the Stuart Hwy on the southern fringes of Arnhem Land.

BARKLY TABLELAND & GULF COUNTRY

East of the Stuart Hwy lies some of the NT's most remote cattle country, but parts are accessible by sealed road and the rivers and inshore waters of the Gulf coast are regarded as some of the best fishing locales in the country. Other than the fishing, the reason to venture out here is to immerse yourself in the silence of this remote and empty land – the last time we passed this way, we encountered two cars and one road train in the entire 390km from Daly Waters to Borroloola. Just the way we like it.

Roper Highway

Not far south of Mataranka on the Stuart Hwy, the mostly sealed single-lane Roper Hwy strikes 175km eastwards to Roper Bar, crossing the paperbark- and pandanus-lined Roper River, where freshwater meets saltwater. It's passable only in the Dry.

◉ Sights

★**Limmen National Park**   NATIONAL PARK
(☎08 8975 9940; nt.gov.au/leisure/parks-reserves) A vast and rugged landscape, this 9608 sq-km national park is in the heart of tropical savannah country and appeals particularly to fisherfolk and 4WD enthusiasts. This is home to some of the most striking sandstone-escarpment country in southern Arnhem Land and the 'lost cities', upthrusts of rocky pinnacles that are simply spectacular and worth exploring on foot. For an aerial view, contact Heartbreak Hotel (p193) along the Carpentaria Highway.

There are two 'lost cities'. The first if you're coming from the north is Southern Lost City, 35km south of the Nathan River Ranger Station; a 2.5km walking track loops among the rocks. More difficult to access (you'll need a high-clearance 4WD), the Western Lost City lies at the end of a rough 28km track that begins just northwest of the Ranger Station (where you'll need to get the access code to unlock the gate; it's posted on the whiteboard).

★**Ngukurr Arts Centre**   GALLERY
(☎08 8975 4260; www.ngukurrarts.net; ⊘10am-4pm Mon-Fri) This community-owned-and-run Indigenous arts centre is well worth the long trip out here, showcasing as it does works by artists from local Alawa, Mara, Ngalakan, Ngandi, Nunggubuyu, Rittarrngu and Wandarang clans; 60% of sales go back to the artist.

🍽 Sleeping & Eating

Roper Bar Store has some takeaway meals and sells basic groceries, but you'll otherwise need to bring all of your food with you.

Roper Bar Store   CARAVAN PARK $
(☎08 8975 4636; www.roperbar.com.au; unpowered sites per adult/child $15/10, s/d $115/135; ☞) You can't be choosy out here; rooms are simple and would be overpriced anywhere else. The nearby campground has plenty of shade and sits next to the river. Takeaway food is available at the general store.

❶ Getting There & Away

4WD Roper Bar is a 4WD-only access point to Borroloola, a more beautiful but more rugged alternative to the route via the sealed Stuart and Carpentaria Hwys. Not deterred? Head south along the rough-going Nathan River Rd through Limmen National Park – high-clearance with two spares required – and across southeastern Arnhem Land. They sell petrol at the Roper Bar Store.

Bus The **Bodhi Bus** (p269) runs a dry-season service from Katherine to Numbulwar ($130, eight hours, Monday and Thursday) that only

---

WE OF THE NEVER NEVER

Few outback stories have captured the national imagination quite like *We of the Never Never*, Jeannie Gunn's account of life on Elsey Station at Mataranka.

Originally from Melbourne, where she ran a girls' school, Gunn arrived in the NT in 1902 with her husband, Aeneas, who had already spent some years there and was returning to take up the manager's position at Elsey Station at Mataranka, south of Katherine. At that time there were very few white women living in the NT, especially on isolated cattle stations. Station life was tough, but Jeannie adapted and interacted with the local Najig and Guyanggan Nganawirdbird Aboriginal people, a number of whom worked on the station. Only a year after their arrival at Elsey, Aeneas contracted malarial dysentery and died. Jeannie returned to Melbourne and recorded her Top End experiences in the novel, which was published in 1908. She was a keen observer of the minutiae of station life and managed to spark the interest of people down south who led such a different existence. These days, however, her depiction of Aboriginal people seems naive and patronising.

Jeannie was awarded an OBE in 1939 for her contribution to Australian literature and died in Melbourne at the age of 91. *We of the Never Never* was made into a film in 1981. Interestingly, in 2012 native title to Mataranka was granted to the Najig and Guyanggan Nganawirdbird Aboriginal groups, represented in court by Jessie Roberts, who played Nellie in the film.

A number of sites around Mataranka pay tribute to this history, most notably Elsey Cemetery (p190), the replica of Elsey Station Homestead (p190) and the Never Never Museum (120 Roper Tce; adult/child $4/2; ⊘9am-4.30pm Mon-Fri). In the park along the Stuart Hwy in the centre of town, there are life-sized figures meant to represent the story's main characters.

goes as far as Ngukurr ($90, 4½ hours, Tuesday and Friday) in the Wet. It stops at Roper Bar on request.

Carpentaria & Tablelands Highways

The Carpentaria Hwy connects the deserts of the outback with the subtropical hinterland of the Gulf of Carpentaria and it's one of the NT's most remote stretches of tarmac. Part of the Savannah Way (a loose network of highways from Broome to Cairns), it runs for 390km from Daly Waters on the Stuart Hwy to Borroloola. The only 'town' en route is Cape Crawford, which is little more than a roadhouse and petrol station.

🏃 Activities

★ **Scenic Flights**   SCENIC FLIGHTS
(Heartbreak Hotel, Cape Crawford; 15/20/30min flights $155/210/315) You just expect to find helicopter scenic flights out here, but we're very glad that you do. Flights zip out over Limmen National Park and its dramatic rock formations known as 'lost cities' – you'll need to take the longer flights to get that far, while the shorter trips take in smaller versions of same.

🛏 Sleeping

Heartbreak Hotel   HOTEL $
(☑08 8975 9928; www.heartbreakhotel.com.au; cnr Carpentaria & Tablelands Hwys, Cape Crawford; powered/unpowered sites $28/20, s/d $75/90, deluxe cabins $165; ❋) The Heartbreak Hotel, a fairly standard Outback roadhouse and fuel stop, is 267km west of Daly River, 123km short of Borroloola and 374km from the Barkly Homestead Roadhouse...yes, you're in the middle of nowhere. Pitch the tent on the shaded grassy lawn and then nurse a cold beer on the wide verandah.

★ **Barkly Homestead**
Roadhouse   CARAVAN PARK $$
(☑08 8964 4549; www.barklyhomestead.com.au; powered/unpowered sites $36/28, cabins & motel d $150; ❋❋) You're a *long* way from anywhere out here; from Cape Crawford it's a desolate 374km south across the Barkly Tableland along the Tablelands Hwy (Rte 11), 210km west to Tennant Creek and 252km east to the Queensland border. And yet it's here you'll find one of the NT's best roadhouses.

ℹ Getting There & Away

The only public transport along the Carpentaria Hwy is the daily Bodhi Bus (www.thebodhibus.com.au) from Katherine to Borroloola.

Borroloola

POP 926

On the McArthur River out near the Gulf of Carpentaria, Borroloola has a wonderful end-of-the-road feel to it – it's a sleepy, slightly neglected place that revels in its remoteness. There's a good Indigenous art centre, some fine wildlife and conservation reserves in neighbouring country and fabulous barramundi fishing.

The town isn't actually on the Gulf of Carpentaria – it's a further 59km to the Bing Bong port loading facility, from which you'll have obscured views of the Gulf of Carpentaria. The nearby Macarthur River zinc mine is the town's lifeblood.

◉ Sights

★ **Waralungku Arts Centre**   ARTS CENTRE
(☑08 8975 8677; www.waralungku.com; Robinson Rd, opposite Macarthur River Caravan Park; ☺8.30am-4pm Mon-Fri, 10am-1pm Sat May-Oct) This relaxed art centre on the main road through town showcases work by artists from the four different Indigenous-language groups in the area; the Yanyuwa, Garrwa, Marra and Gudanji people. Unlike the dot-painting styles of the Western Desert or the bark paintings of Arnhem Land, the paintings here have a style all their own, with a more figurative style.

There are also locally made screen prints and baskets. Ask about the 'Craft & Culture Experiences', a fine program that offers immersion into local culture and which may include painting, weaving, making didgeridoos, lessons in bush tucker and bush medicine and traditional dance and singing. Advance reservations essential.

Borroloola Museum   MUSEUM
(www.nationaltrust.org.au/places/old-police-station-borroloola/; Robinson Rd; $5; ☺8am-5pm Mon-Fri May-Sep) About three-quarters of the population of Borroloola is Indigenous and the town's colourful history is displayed at the Borroloola Museum, alongside mining memorabilia, within the 1887 police station. If you find it closed, ask any of the businesses around town and someone should be able to track down the key.

🏃 Activities

Borroloola is big news for fishing fans and bagging a barramundi in these parts is the stuff of fishing legend. The barramundi season peaks from February to April, but October and November can also be good. Whereas the big fishing charter companies dominate up in Arnhem Land, things can be a little more low-key here. The following companies can arrange for boat and equipment hire:

J & A Charters & Tours (☑ 0448 804 855)

KAB Fishing Club (☑ 0448 804 855)

✨ Festivals & Events

Malandarri Festival   CULTURAL
(☑ 08 8941 1444, 08 8975 8677; www.artbacknt. com.au/index.php/itdp/dancesite/; per day $5; ☉ Oct) This two-day event in October is Borroloola's biggest celebration, with traditional dance the focal point alongside artworks, markets, workshops and other activities.

🛏 Sleeping

Borroloola Hotel Motel   MOTEL $
(☑ 08 8975 8766; www.borroloolahotelmotel.com. au; Robinson Rd; r $75-110; ⊠) Simple rooms at the pub are nothing to write home about, but we do like the large saltwater swimming pool.

McArthur River Caravan Park   CARAVAN PARK $
(☑ 08 89758734; www.mcarthurcaravanpark. com.au; Robinson Rd; powered/unpowered site $30/25, budget unit s/d $100/110, self-contained unit s/d $130/140) This fairly simple camp site and caravan park on the main road into town is a little dusty during the Dry, but the owners are keen fishers and it's a good place to stay if that's why you're here. Ask for one of the newer cabins that are much better than their older counterparts.

Savannah Way Motel   MOTEL $
(☑ 08 8975 8883; www.savannahwaymotel.com. au; Robinson Rd; r & cabins $80-130; ❄ 🛜 ⊠) This motel, close to the airstrip on the main road through town, is clean and comfortable, with cabins and guesthouse rooms set in tropical gardens. It's often full so book ahead.

🍴 Eating

Carpentaria Grill   AUSTRALIAN $$
(☑ 08 8975 8883; Savannah Way Motel, Robinson Rd; mains $17-37; ☉ 5.30-10pm) Easily the best place to eat in town, the Carpentaria Grill

does Aussie pub staples, but the best choice is always the barra – served with garlic prawns or on its own cooked just the way you like it. There are special nights: Monday is steak night, Fridays is all about barra, while Sunday is roasts.

Borroloola Hotel   AUSTRALIAN $$
(166 Robinson Rd; meals $12-32; ☉ noon-2pm & 5.30-10pm) Borroloola Hotel serves the usual pub fare of burgers, chops and mixed grills within a lounge bar that's heavily reinforced with steel mesh.

ℹ Getting There & Away

AIR

Airnorth (www.airnorth.com.au) has up to two daily flights between Darwin and the Macarthur River Mine Airport (70km from Borroloola) for $579, but it's mainly for miners. Tour companies sometimes use Borroloola's in-town air strip.

BUS

Bodhi Bus (☑ in Katherine 08 8971 0774) has a daily bus service between Borroloola and Katherine ($120, 8½ hours), which runs via Mataranka, Larrimah, Daly Waters and Cape Crawford. Borroloola's stop is outside the Malandari General Store.

CAR & MOTORCYCLE

Under normal conditions, it's a 5½-hour drive (390km) from Daly Waters to Borroloola. In the other direction, it's 479km along a mostly unsealed road to Burketown in Queensland; parts of this latter route are impassable in the Wet.

CENTRAL NORTHERN TERRITORY

Central NT (basically the Stuart Hwy from Katherine to Alice Springs) is still referred to as 'the Track' – as it has been since WWII when it was literally a dirt track connecting the NT's two main towns, roughly following the Overland Telegraph Line. It's dead straight most of the way and gets progressively drier and flatter as you head south, but there are quite a few notable diversions.

Daly Waters

POP 50

The tiny community of Daly Waters is home to one of the NT's great outback pubs. It was an important staging post in the early days of aviation – Amy Johnson landed here on her epic flight from England to

Australia in 1930. High on novelty value, it's worth the detour off the highway.

Sleeping

Daly Waters Pub CARAVAN PARK $
(☑08 8975 9927; www.dalywaterspub.com; powered/unpowered sites $28/16, d $70-110, cabins $135-175; ❄⚡) Decorated with business cards, bras, banknotes and memorabilia from passing travellers, this pub claims to be the oldest in the NT (its liquor licence has been valid since 1893). Beside the pub is a dustbowl camping ground with a bit of shade; book ahead or arrive early to secure a powered site.

Accommodation ranges from basic dongas (small, transportable buildings) to spacious self-contained cabins.

The pub has become a bit of a legend along the Track. Every evening from April to September there's the popular beef 'n' barra barbecue, along with entertainment some nights from a visiting country muso. Otherwise, hearty meals (mains $11 to $30), including the filling barra burger, roast beef rolls, kangaroo loin and home-made damper bread are served.

ⓘ Getting There & Away

Daly Waters is 3km off the highway; the turn-off is 160km south of Mataranka or 407km north of Tennant Creek. The petrol station here is expensive – fill up instead at the one out on the main highway at the junction of the Stuart and Carpentaria Hwys.

Tennant Creek

POP 3062

Tennant Creek is the only town of any size between Katherine, 680km to the north, and Alice Springs, 511km to the south, and is the NT's fifth-largest town (which says more about the NT's small population than it does about Tennant Creek). It's a good place to break up a long drive and check out the town's few attractions. Tennant Creek is known as Jurnkurakurr to the local Warumungu people and almost half of the population is of Aboriginal descent.

◉ Sights

★**Nyinkka Nyunyu** GALLERY
(☑08 8962 2699; www.nyinkkanyunyu.com.au; Paterson St; guided tour $15; ☺9am-5pm Mon-Fri, 10am-2pm Sat & Sun Oct-Apr, 8am-6pm Mon-Sat, 10am-2pm Sun May-Sep) This innovative museum and gallery highlights the dynamic art

WORTH A TRIP

LORELLA SPRINGS

One of our favourite places to stay in the entire Gulf region, **Lorella Springs Wilderness Park** (☑08 8975 9917; www.lorellasprings.com.au/accommodation; camping per adult/child $20/5, s $130-230, d $130-250; ☺Apr-Sep) has a marvellously isolated setting, a thermal spring and river frontage, a restaurant and self-contained air-con cabins, rooms with ceiling fans and good camp sites. Activities include fishing, swimming, birdwatching, bushwalking, 4WD expeditions and even helicopter scenic flights.

Lorella Springs is 130km from Cape Crawford, 180km from Borroloola and 275km from Roper Bar close to the Gulf of Carpentaria coast. You'll need a 4WD to get here, unless you have your own plane.

and culture of the local Warumungu people. The absorbing displays focus on contemporary art, traditional objects, bush medicine and regional history. The diorama series, or bush TVs as they became known within the community, are particularly special.

Battery Hill Mining Centre MINE
(☑08 8962 1281; www.barklytourism.com.au; Peko Rd; adult/child $30/20; ☺9am-5pm) Relive life in Tennant Creek's 1930s gold rush at this mining centre, which doubles as the Visitor Information Centre, 2km east of town. There are **underground mine tours** and audio tours of the 10-head **battery**. In addition there is a superb **Minerals Museum** and you can try your hand at gold panning.

🏃 Activities

Kelly's Ranch HORSE RIDING
(☑08 8962 2045; www.kellysranch.com.au; 5 Fazaldeen Rd; trail rides/lesson per person $150/50) Experience the Barkly from the back of a horse with local Warumungu man Jerry Kelly. His two-hour trail rides start with a lesson and then a ride through some superb outback scenery with bush-tucker stops along the way. Jerry entertains with stories about Aboriginal culture and life on the cattle stations.

Sleeping

Outback Caravan Park CAMPGROUND $
(☑08 8962 2459; 71 Peko Rd; powered/unpowered sites $36/30, cabins $70-150; ❄⚡) In a town that often feels parched, it's nice to be in the

WORTH A TRIP

CARANBIRINI CONSERVATION RESERVE

Just off the Carpentaria Hwy, 46km south of Borroloola, the Caranbirini Conservation Reserve (☑ 08 8975 8792; www.nt.gov.au/leisure/parks-reserves) is good for wildlife – including euros (wallaroos), agile wallabies and water goannas – and birdwatching (prize species include the Gouldian finch, Carpentaria grasswren and sandstone rockthrush) and plays an important role in many Aboriginal Dreaming stories. But Caranbirini is also remarkable for the drama of its sandstone spires and pinnacles – this is the most accessible of all of the 'lost-city' rock formations for which the area is renowned.

A number of walks take you into the heart of the pinnacles and surrounding country. From the car park, a 150m trail goes to the waterhole where a bird hide overlooks the billabong. The Barrawulla Loop (2km, one to two hours, easy) gets you into the heart of the rocky outcrops, while the Jagududgu Loop (5km, three hours, easy to medium) ranges further afield with some good views before joining the Barrawulla Loop.

shade of this grassy caravan park about 1km east of the centre. There's a well-stocked kiosk, camp kitchen and fuel. You may even be treated to some bush poetry and bush tucker, courtesy of yarn spinner Jimmy Hooker, at 7.30pm ($10). Decent outdoor bar area, but be quick, it closes early.

Bluestone Motor Inn MOTEL **$**
(☑ 08 8962 2617; www.bluestonemotorinn.com.au; 1 Paterson St; standard/deluxe d $100/123;) At the southern end of town, this 3½-star motel has comfortable standard rooms in leafy surrounds. In addition there are spacious hexagonal deluxe rooms with queen-size beds and a sofa. There are also wheelchair-accessible units and a restaurant.

Safari Lodge Motel MOTEL **$$**
(☑ 08 8962 2207; www.arrahotels.com.au/safari-lodge-motel; Davidson St; s/d $110/130; ✱ @ 🛜) You should book ahead to stay at this family-run motel. Safari Lodge is centrally located next to the best restaurant in town and has clean, fairly standard rooms with phone, fridge and TV.

✕ Eating

Top of the Town Cafe CAFE **$**
(☑ 08 8962 1311; www.facebook.com/TopOfTownCafe/; 163 Paterson St; breakfast $7-15; ⊙ 7am-3pm Mon-Fri, 7am-2pm Sat) Home of pinkmolly cupcakes, this little gem is slightly twee. It's cute, quirky and a little cramped inside, but there are tables and chairs on the footpath, too. There are a range of toasties and bacon-and-egg options for brekky, making it the best place in town for breakfast.

Tennant Creek Memorial Club AUSTRALIAN **$$**
(www.tennantcreekmemorialclub.com/dining; 48 Schmidt St; mains $16-32; ⊙ noon-2pm & 6-9pm)

In a town where eating rarely rises above the mediocre, the Memorial Club is a reliable if generally unexciting option. It has standard rural club fare, with oysters, burgers, steaks, pasta, curry, Asian noodle dishes… It's also a friendly place with a courtesy bus back to your hotel.

ℹ Information

MEDICAL SERVICES
Tennant Creek Hospital (☑ 08 8962 4399; Schmidt St)

POLICE
Police Station (☑ 08 8962 4444; Paterson St)

TOURIST INFORMATION
Central Land Council (☑ 08 8962 2343; www.clc.org.au; 63 Paterson St, Tennant Creek)
Visitor Information Centre (☑ 1800 500 879; www.barklytourism.com.au; Peko Rd; ⊙ 9am-5pm Mon-Fri, 9am-1pm Sat)

ℹ Getting There & Around

All long-distance buses stop at the **Transit Centre** (☑ 08 8962 2727; 151 Paterson St; 9am-5pm Mon-Fri, 8.30-11.30am Sat), where you can purchase tickets. **Greyhound Australia** (☑ 1300 473 946; www.greyhound.com.au) has daily buses from Tennant Creek to Alice Springs ($115, six hours), Katherine ($145, 8½ hours), Darwin (from $135, 14 hours) and Mount Isa ($163, eight hours). As few of the buses originate in Tennant Creek, departure times are sometimes 3.15am.

The weekly *Ghan* rail link between Alice Springs and Darwin can drop off passengers in Tennant Creek, although cars can't be loaded or offloaded. The train station is about 6km south of town so you will need a **taxi** (☑ 08 8962 3626).

Car hire is available from **Thrifty** (☑ 08 8962 2207, 1800 891 125; www.thrifty.com.au;

Davidson St, Safari Lodge Motel) and there's a **petrol station** (☑ 08 8962 2626; 218 Paterson St) in the town centre.

Devil's Marbles & Around

The Stuart Hwy between Tennant Creek and Alice Springs is a long and lonely stretch of tarmac. The standout attractions are the Devils Marbles; otherwise, roadside roadhouses, no matter how basic, can seem like oases amid the great emptiness.

◉ Sights

★ **Devil's Marbles** RELIGIOUS SITE
(www.nt.gov.au/leisure/parks-reserves) The gigantic granite boulders piled in precarious piles beside the Stuart Hwy, 105km south of Tennant Creek, are known as the Devil's Marbles (or Karlu Karlu in the local Warumungu language) and they're one of the more beautiful sights along this road. The Marbles are a sacred site to the traditional Aboriginal owners of the land, who believe the rocks are the eggs of the Rainbow Serpent.

🛏 Sleeping & Eating

Camping Ground CAMPGROUND $
(☑ 08 8962 4599; nt.gov.au/leisure/parks-reserves; adult/child $3.30/1.65) Basic camping available.

Barrow Creek Hotel PUB $
(☑ 08 8956 9753; Stuart Hwy; powered camp sites $24, s/d $65/80) The Barrow Creek Hotel is one of the highway's oddball outback pubs. In the tradition of shearers who'd write their name on a banknote and pin it to the wall to ensure they could afford a drink when next they passed through, travellers have left notes, photos, bumper stickers and knick-knacks. Dinner, basic motel-style rooms and campsites are available.

**Wycliffe Well
Roadhouse & Holiday Park** CARAVAN PARK $
(☑ 1800 222 195, 08 8964 1966; powered/unpowered sites $38/35, budget s/d from $65/75, s/d cabins with bathroom $130/150; ☺ 6.30am-9pm; ✷ @ ☒) At Wycliffe Well Roadhouse & Holiday Park, 17km south of Wauchope, you can fill up with fuel and food (mains $14 to $29; open 7am to 9pm) or stay and spot UFOs that apparently fly over with astonishing regularity. The park has a pleasant lawn camping ground, a kids' playground,

WORTH A TRIP

PUNGALINA-SEVEN EMU WILDLIFE SANCTUARY

A groundbreaking collaboration between the Australian Wildlife Conservancy and local traditional owners, Pungalina-Seven Emu Wildlife Sanctuary (www.australianwildlife.org/sanctuaries/pungalina-seven-emu-sanctuary.aspx) merges wildlife conservation with a working cattle station in an area rich in coastal rainforest, mangroves, eucalypt woodlands, wetlands and thermal springs.

The sanctuary is home to a recorded 292 bird species and 48 mammals, among them little-known species such as the Carpentarian Pseudantechinus (small carnivorous marsupial),along with northern brown bandicoots, dingoes and a host of wallaby and rock wallaby species. Birds to watch out for include the Gouldian finch, red goshawk and purple-crowned fairy wren.

The sanctuary covers 3060 sq km and includes 55km of Gulf shoreline and 100km of the Calvert River. Seven Emu Station (p197) makes a good base.

Seven Emu Station (☑ 08 8975 8307, 08 8975 9904; www.sevenemustation.com.au; camping per vehicle $50) Deep in the heart of Gulf country and on the doorstep of Pungalina – Seven Emu Wildlife Sanctuary (p197), Seven Emu Station is a remote, working cattle station which offers a unique package of fishing, remote camping and wildlife watching. The campsites are in the stockman tradition, with shelter sheds, fire pits and long-drop loos-with-a-view.

an indoor pool, a cafe and a range of international beer.

The place is decorated with alien figures and newspaper clippings ('That UFO Was Chasing Us!').

Aileron Hotel Roadhouse MOTEL, CAMPGROUND $
(☑ 08 8956 9703; www.aileronroadhouse.com.au; Stuart Hwy; powered/unpowered sites $18/15, dm $40, s/d $120/130; ☺ 5am-9pm; ✷ ☒) Aileron Hotel Roadhouse has camp sites (power available until 10pm), a 10-bed dorm and decent motel units. There's an ATM, a bar, shop and licensed restaurant. The owner's collection of Namatjira watercolours (at

least 10 by Albert) is displayed around the roadhouse's bar and dining area – quite the find in this otherwise standard roadside roadhouse.

Devils Marbles Hotel   HOTEL **$**
(☑08 8964 1963; www.wauchopehotel.com.au; Stuart Hwy; powered/unpowered sites $30/10, budget s/d $70/130; ❄❉) At Wauchope (*war-kup*), 8km south of the Devil's Marbles, are the well-kept rooms of the Wauchope Hotel. The budget rooms are dongas (small, transportable buildings); the more expensive rooms are more spacious, with ensuite. Meals from the restaurant (☑08 8964 1963; www.wauchopehotel.com.au; Stuart Hwy; breakfast $10-32, mains $18-33) are more than satisfactory.

ℹ Getting There & Away

Greyhound buses run up and down the Stuart Hwy, stopping off in the major towns along the way. The road is tarmac and, at the time of writing, there were no speed limits between Tennant Creek and Alice Springs, part of an experiment by the local authorities – do check whether this remains the case before you put your foot to the floor.

Tanami Track

Welcome to one of the longest short cuts on the planet. Synonymous with isolated outback driving, the 1055km Tanami Rd connects Alice Springs with Halls Creek, the Red Centre with the Kimberley. The Tanami Desert and surrounding country are the homeland of the Warlpiri, Arrente, Luritja and Pintubi peoples and much of the land has reverted to their traditional ownership. The only real attractions along the way are the important Indigenous settlement of Yuendemu and Wolfe Creek Crater (on the Western Australian side of the border). It's a long haul and only occasionally beautiful; watch for the termite mounds, up to 800 per hectare in places. Crossing the Tanami does have huge cachet and is a journey to remember.

⦿ Sights

The NT section is wide and usually well graded and starts 20km north of Alice Springs. The road is sealed to Tilmouth Well (☑08 8956 8777; www.tilmouthwell.com; powered/unpowered sites $40/30, cabins without bathroom $80; ❄@❉) on the edge of Napperby Station, which bills itself as an oasis in the desert with a sparkling pool and lush, sprawling lawns.

ROADSIDE STOPS

Threeways Roadhouse (☑08 8962 2744, 1800 448 163; www. threewaysroadhouse.com.au; Stuart Hwy; powered/unpowered sites $32/24, d $115; ❄@❉), 537km north of Alice Springs at the junction of the Stuart and Barkly Hwys, is a potential stopover with a bar and restaurant. Rooms are simple but better than most roadhouse stops.

Banka Banka (☑08 8964 4511; adult/child $12/6) is a historic cattle station 100km north of Tennant Creek, with a grassy camping area (no power), marked walking tracks (one leading to a tranquil waterhole), a mudbrick bar and a small kiosk selling basic refreshments.

The next fuel stop is at Yuendumu, the largest remote community in the region and home to the Warlpiri people who were made famous in the 2001 *Bush Mechanics* documentary. It's worth popping in to the Warlukurlangu Art Centre (☑08 8956 4133; www.warlu.com) a locally owned venture specialising in acrylic paintings.

From here there is no fuel for another 600km until you cross the WA border and hit the community of Billiluna (08 9168 8076). Note, Rabbit Flat Roadhouse has closed permanently. Another 170km will have you resting your weary bones in Halls Creek.

ℹ Getting There & Away

In dry conditions it's possible to make it through the unsealed dust and corrugations in a well-prepared 2WD. Stay alert, as rollovers are common, and stock up with fuel, tyres, food and water.

ALICE SPRINGS

POP 28,667

Alice Springs wouldn't win a beauty contest, but there's a lot more going on here than first meets the eye. For a start it has a lot to offer travellers, from the inspirational (excellent museums, a fine wildlife park and outstanding galleries of Indigenous art) to the practical (a wide range of accommodation, some good dining options and travel connections).

It serves as the gateway to some of central Australia's most stirring landscapes: Uluru-Kata Tjuta National Park is a relatively short four-hour drive away, while closer still, the ruggedly beautiful MacDonnell Ranges stretch east and west from the town centre; you don't have to venture far to find yourself among ochre-red gorges, pastel-hued hills and ghostly white gum trees.

Alice is also a key touchstone for understanding Aboriginal Australia in all its complexity (where else can you hear six uniquely Australian languages in the main street?) and present-day challenges.

◎ Sights

★ Alice Springs
Desert Park   WILDLIFE RESERVE
(☑08 8951 8788; www.alicespringsdesertpark.com.au; Larapinta Dr; adult/child $32/16, nocturnal tour adult/child $44/28; ⊙7.30am-6pm, last entry 4.30pm, nocturnal tour 7.30pm Mon-Fri) If you haven't glimpsed a spangled grunter or marbled velvet gecko on your travels, head to Desert Park where the creatures of central Australia are all on display in one place. The predominantly open-air exhibits faithfully re-create the animals' natural environments in a series of habitats: inland river, sand country and woodland. It's an easy 2.5km cycle to the park. Pick up a free audioguide (available in various languages) or join one of the free ranger-led talks throughout the day.

Araluen Arts Centre   GALLERY
(☑08 8951 1122; www.araluenartscentre.nt.gov.au; cnr Larapinta Dr & Memorial Ave; ⊙10am-4pm) For a small town, Alice Springs has a thriving arts scene and the Araluen Arts Centre is at its heart. There is a 500-seat theatre, and four galleries with a focus on art from the Central Desert region. The Albert Namatjira Gallery features works by the artist, who began painting watercolours in the 1930s at Hermannsburg. The exhibition draws comparisons between Namatjira and his initial mentor, Rex Battarbee, and other Hermannsburg School artists.

Olive Pink Botanic Garden   NATURE RESERVE
(☑08 8952 2154; www.opbg.com.au; Tuncks Rd; by donation; ⊙8am-6pm) A network of meandering trails leads through this lovely arid zone botanic garden, which was founded by the prominent anthropologist Olive Pink. The garden has more than 500 central Australian plant species and grows bush foods and medicinal plants like native lemon grass, quandong and bush passionfruit.

Royal Flying Doctor Service Base   MUSEUM
(RFDS; ☑08 8958 8411; www.rfdsalicesprings.com.au; Stuart Tce; adult/child $16/9; ⊙9am-5pm Mon-Sat, 1-5pm Sun, cafe 8.30am-4.30pm Mon-Sat) A $3 million facelift, which includes interactive information portals, has given this excellent museum a new lease of life. It is the home of the Royal Flying Doctor Service, whose dedicated health workers provide 24-hour emergency retrievals across an area of around 1.25 million sq km. State-of-the-art facilities includes a hologram of John Flynn (the RFDS founder) and a look at the operational control room, as well as some ancient medical gear and a flight simulator. Guided tours leave every half-hour, with the last at 4pm.

Araluen Cultural Precinct   CULTURAL CENTRE
(☑0889511122; dtc.nt.gov.au/arts-and-museums/araluen-cultural-precinct; cnr Larapinta Dr & Memorial Ave; precinct pass adult/child $15/10) The Araluen Cultural Precinct is Alice Springs' cultural hub; leave at least an afternoon aside for exploration of its excellent sights. You can wander around freely outside, accessing the cemetery and grounds, but the 'precinct pass' provides entry to the exhibitions and displays for two days (with 14 days to use the pass).

Grave of John Flynn   CEMETERY
On the western edge of Alice on the road to the West MacDonnell Ranges, the grave of John Flynn is topped by a boulder donated by the Arrernte people (the original was a since-returned Devil's Marble). Opposite the car park is the start of the sealed cycling track to Simpsons Gap, a recommended three- to four-hour return ride.

Alice Springs Reptile Centre   ZOO
(☑08 8952 2900; www.reptilecentre.com.au; 9 Stuart Tce; adult/child $17/9; ⊙9.30am-5pm) It may be small, but this reptile centre packs a poisonous punch with its impressive collection of venomous snakes, thorny devils and bearded dragons. Inside the cave room are 11 species of NT geckos and outside there's Terry, a 3.3m saltwater croc, plus Bub, a magnificent perentie, Australia's largest lizard. The enthusiastic guides will happily plonk a python around your neck during the handling demonstrations (11am, 1pm and 3.30pm) or let you pet a blue-tongued lizard.

Anzac Hill   LANDMARK
For a tremendous view, particularly at sunrise and sunset, take a hike (use Lions Walk from Wills Tce) or a drive up to the top of

Alice Springs

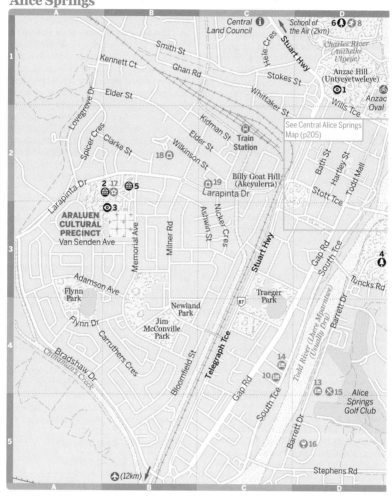

Anzac Hill, known as Untyeyetweleye in Arrernte. From the war memorial there is a 365-degree view over the town down to Heavitree Gap and the MacDonnell Ranges.

Telegraph Station Historical Reserve PARK
(☑ 08 8952 1013; nt.gov.au/leisure/parks-reserves; adult/child $9/4.50; ⊗ reserve 8am-9pm, building 9am-5pm) The old Telegraph Station, which used to relay messages between Darwin and Adelaide, offers a fascinating glimpse of the town's European beginnings. It's an easy 4km walk or cycle north from Todd Mall; follow the path on the riverbed's western

side. Nearby is the original 'Alice' spring (Thereyurre to the Arrernte Aboriginal people), a semipermanent waterhole in the Todd River after which the town is named.

Museum of Central Australia MUSEUM
(☑ 08 8951 1121; www.magnt.net.au/museum-of-central-australia; cnr Larapinta Dr & Memorial Ave; ⊗ 10am-5pm Mon-Fri) The natural history collection at this compact museum recalls the days of megafauna – when hippo-sized wombats and 3m-tall flightless birds roamed the land. Among the geological displays are meteorite fragments and fossils. There's a

Alice Springs

◎ Sights
1 Anzac Hill D1
2 Araluen Arts Centre............................... B2
3 Araluen Cultural Precinct B3
   Museum of Central Australia ...... (see 5)
4 Olive Pink Botanic Garden.................. D3
5 Strehlow Research Centre B2
6 Telegraph Station Historical
   Reserve D1

⦿ Activities, Courses & Tours
7 Dreamtime Tours................................... F5
8 Outback Cycling.................................... D1

⌾ Sleeping
9 Alice Lodge Backpackers E2
10 Alice on Todd....................................... C4
11 Alice's Secret Traveller's Inn.............. E2
12 Chifley Alice Springs E3
13 Doubletree by Hilton D4
14 Quest Alice Springs C4

⊗ Eating
   Bean Tree Cafe............................. (see 4)
15 Hanuman Restaurant.......................... D4

⦿ Drinking & Nightlife
16 Juicy Rump D5

✪ Entertainment
17 Araluen Arts Centre.............................. B2

⌂ Shopping
18 Ngurratjuta Iltja Ntjarra B2
19 Tjanpi Desert Weavers.........................C2

broadcasting lessons to children over an area of 1.3 million sq km. While transmissions were originally all done over high-frequency radio, satellite broadband internet and web-cams now mean students can study in a virtual classroom. The guided tour of the centre includes a video. The school is about 3km north of the town centre.

free audio tour, narrated by a palaeontologist, which helps bring the exhibition to life.

Upstairs is the **Strehlow Research Centre** (www.magnt.net.au/strehlow-research-centre) with a display on the work of Professor TGH Strehlow, a linguist, anthropologist and avid collector of Indigenous artefacts.

School of the Air   MUSEUM
(☑ 08 8951 6834; www.assoa.nt.edu.au; 80 Head St; adult/child $9/7; ☺ 8.30am-4.30pm Mon-Sat, 1.30-4.30pm Sun) Started in 1951, this was the first school of its type in Australia,

🏃 Activities

Bushwalking

Experience the bush around Alice with several easy walks radiating from the Olive Pink Botanic Garden (p199) and the Telegraph Station (p200), which marks the start of the first stage of the Larapinta Trail.

Central Australian Bushwalkers WALKING
(centralaustralianbushwalkers.com; walks $5) A group of local bushwalkers that schedules a wide variety of walks in the area,

particularly the West MacDonnell Ranges, from March to November.

Lone Dingo Adventure
HIKING

(☑ 08 8953 3866; www.lonedingo.com.au; cnr Todd Mall & Gregory Tce; ⊘ 9am-5.30pm Mon-Fri, 9am-4pm Sat, 10am-3pm Sun) If you're keen to tackle part of the Larapinta Trail but don't have your own equipment, Lone Dingo Adventure can put together packs of camping and hiking gear for hire, as well as GPS and EPIRB (Emergency Positioning Indicating Radio Beacon) equipment.

Camel Riding

Pyndan Camel Tracks
CAMEL TOURS

(☑ 0416 170 164; www.cameltracks.com; Jane Rd; 1hr rides adult/child $70/40; ⊘ noon, 2.30pm & sunset) Local cameleer Marcus Williams offers one-hour rides at his base 17km southwest of Alice.

Cycling & Mountain Biking

Bikes are the perfect way to get around Alice Springs. There are cycle paths along the Todd River to the Telegraph Station, west to the Alice Springs Desert Park and further out to Simpsons Gap. For a map of cycling and walking paths go to the visitor information centre (p208).

Mountain-bike trails are easily accessed from town or meet up for a social sunset ride with the **Central Australian Rough Riders' Club** (☑ 08 8952 5800; www.centralaustralianroughriders.asn.au; rides $5).

Outback Cycling
CYCLING

(☑ 08 8952 3993; www.outbackcycling.com/alice-springs/; Alice Springs Telegraph Station; hire per day/week from $40/160) Bike hire with urban and mountain bikes available, as well as baskets, kids' bikes and baby seats. Also offer cycling tours of Alice and at Uluru.

☞ Tours

★ Earth Sanctuary
TOURS

(☑ 08 8953 6161; www.earth-sanctuary.com.au; astronomy tour adult/child $36/25) See the stars of central Australia in the desert outside Alice with Earth Sanctuary's terrific nightly Astronomy Tours. Tours last for an hour and the informative guides have high-powered telescopes to get you up close and personal with the stars. You'll need to ring ahead – they'll know by 4pm if clear skies are forecast.

They also run food-themed events and tours like outback dinners and bush-tucker tours.

★ Wayoutback Desert Safaris
DRIVING

(☑ 08 8952 4324, 1300 551 510; www.wayoutback.com) Numerous small group, 4WD safari tours including the chance for remote desert camping near Uluru. There are also three-day safaris that traverse 4WD tracks to Uluru and Kings Canyon for $795 and five-day safaris that top it up with the West MacDonnell Ramges for $1195.

★ Trek Larapinta
HIKING

(☑ 1300 133 278; www.treklarapinta.com.au; 3/6 days from $1295/2695) 🏃 Guided multiday walks along sections of the Larapinta Trail. Also runs volunteer projects involving trail maintenance, and bush regeneration on Aboriginal outstations.

Rainbow Valley Cultural Tours
TOURS

(☑ 08 8956 0661; www.rainbowvalleyculturaltours.com; afternoon walking tours adult/child $90/50; ⊘ 2pm-sunset Mon, Wed & Fri) Tour beautiful Rainbow Valley with a traditional owner and visit rock art sites not open to the general public. Tours can include overnight camping and dinner for an extra $20 per person. They also run birdwatching tours at the site upon request. You'll need your own transport to get there.

Dreamtime Tours
CULTURAL

(☑ 08 8955 5095; 72 Hillside Garden; adult/child $85/42, self-drive $66/33; ⊘ 8.30-11.30am) Runs the three-hour Dreamtime & Bushtucker Tour, where you meet Warlpiri Aboriginal people and learn a little about their traditions. As it caters for large bus groups it can be impersonal, but you can tag along with your own vehicle.

Emu Run Experience
TOURS

(☑ 08 8953 7057, 1800 687 220; www.emurun.com.au; 72 Todd St) Operates day tours to Uluru ($226) and two-day tours to Uluru and Kings Canyon ($536). Prices include park entry fees, meals and accommodation. There are also recommended, small-group day tours through the West MacDonnell Ranges (from $119).

RT Tours
TOURS

(☑ 08 8952 0327; www.rttoursaustralia.com; tours $160) Chef and Arrernte guide Bob Taylor runs a popular lunch and dinner tour at Simpsons Gap or the Telegraph Station Historical Reserve, where he whips up a bush-inspired meal. Other tours available.

✦ Festivals & Events

Alice Springs Cup Carnival SPORTS
(www.alicespringsturfclub.org.au; ⊘ May) On the first Monday in May, don a hat and gallop down to the Pioneer Park Racecourse for the main event of this five-day carnival.

Uluru Camel Cup SPORTS
(www.uluruoutbackfest.com.au; ⊘ May) Over two days in May, Yulara hosts camel racing against a desert backdrop.

Finke Desert Race SPORTS
(www.finkedesertrace.com.au; ⊘ Jun) Motorcyclists and buggy drivers vie to take out the title of this crazy race 240km from Alice along the Old South Rd to Finke; the following day they race back again. Spectators camp along the road to cheer them on.

Alice Springs Beanie Festival ART
(www.beaniefest.org; ⊘ Jun/Jul) This four-day festival in June/July, held at the Araluen Art Centre, celebrates the humble beanie (knitted woollen hat), handmade by women throughout the Central Desert.

★ Camel Cup SPORTS
(www.camelcup.com.au; ⊘ mid-Jul) A carnival atmosphere prevails during the running of the Camel Cup at Blatherskite Park in mid-July.

★ Henley-on-Todd Regatta SPORTS
(www.henleyontodd.com.au; ⊘ 3rd Sat in Aug) These boat races in September on the dry bed of the Todd River are a typically Australian, light-hearted denial of reality. The boats are bottomless; the crews' legs stick through and they run down the course.

Alice Desert Festival ART
(www.alicedesertfestival.com.au; ⊘ late Aug) A cracker of a festival, including a circus program, music, film and comedy. A colourful parade down Todd Mall marks the beginning of the festival. It's held in September. The festival didn't run in 2016 but was expected to return in 2017.

Desert Song Festival MUSIC
(☏ 0409 003 004; www.desertsong.com.au; ⊘ Sep) Held over ten days in September with choirs from across central Australia and occasional international acts performing in venues across Alice.

🛏 Sleeping

Alice's Secret Traveller's Inn HOSTEL $
(☏ 08 8952 8686; www.asecret.com.au; 6 Khalick St; dm $25-27, d from $65; ❄ @ ☂) Get the best accommodation deals here by booking your tour to Uluru through the inn. One of our favourite hostels in Alice, just across the Todd River from town, this place gets a big thumbs up for cleanliness and the helpful, friendly owner. Relax around the pool, blow on a didgeridoo or lie in a hammock in the garden.

Alice Lodge Backpackers HOSTEL $
(☏ 08 8953 1975, 1800 351 925; www.alicelodge. com.au; 4 Mueller St; dm $27-30, d $74-105; ❄ @ ☂ ☂) Alice Lodge gets great feedback from travellers, particularly for the friendly and helpful management. An easy 10-minute walk from town, this is a small, highly recommended, low-key hostel.

MacDonnell Range Holiday Park CARAVAN PARK $
(☏ 1800 808 373, 08 8952 6111; www.macrange. com.au; Palm Pl; powered/unpowered sites $48/42, cabins d $100-250; ❄ @ ☂) Probably Alice's biggest and best kept, this caravan park has grassy sites and spotless amenities. Accommodation ranges from simple cabins with shared bathroom to self-contained, two-bedroom villas. Kids can cavort in the adventure playground, on the BMX track and on the basketball court.

Quest Alice Springs APARTMENT $$
(☏ 08 8959 0000; www.questapartments.com. au; 10 South Tce; d studio/1-bedroom apt from $135/196; P ❄ ☂ ☂) These stylish modern apartments just across the road from the Todd River are an excellent choice. The Quest chain is reliably comfortable and well run and the quality of the rooms is well above most Alice choices.

Doubletree by Hilton HOTEL $$
(☏ 1300 666 545, 08 8950 8000; www.double tree3.hilton.com; Barrett Dr; d from $150, ste $175-350; ❄ @ ☂ ☂) With its spacious resort-style facilities, this is widely considered one of Alice's top hotels. Choose from the garden-view rooms or the better mountain range–view rooms – they're decked out with floor-to-ceiling windows, cane furniture and pastel colours. There's a lovely pool and spa, well-equipped gym and sauna, tennis courts and a house peacock.

WORTH A TRIP

LARAPINTA TRAIL

The 230km Larapinta Trail extends along the backbone of the West MacDonnell Ranges and is one of Australia's great long-distance walks. The track is split into 12 stages of varying difficulty, stretching from the Telegraph Station in Alice Springs to the craggy 1380m summit of Mt Sonder. Each section takes one to two days to navigate and the trail passes many of the attractions in the West MacDonnell Ranges.

Trail notes and maps are available from Parks & Wildlife. Walking groups of eight or more should contact Parks & Wildlife (p207) with a trip plan.

There's no public transport out to this area, but transfers can be arranged through the Alice Wanderer (☑1800 722 111, 08 8952 2111; www.alicewanderer.com.au); see the website for the various costs. For guided walks, including transport from Alice Springs, go through Trek Larapinta (p202).

Alice on Todd   APARTMENT $$
(☑08 8953 8033; www.aliceontodd.com; cnr Strehlow St & South Tce; studio/1-bed apt $135/158; ✳@☎☲) This place has a great set-up, with friendly and helpful staff. It's an attractive and secure apartment complex on the banks of the Todd River offering one- and two-bedroom self-contained units with kitchen and lounge. There are also studios. The balconied units sleep up to six so they're a great option for families.

Chifley Alice Springs   HOTEL $$
(☑08 8951 4545; www.silverneedlehotels.com/chifley; 34 Stott Tce; standard/superior/deluxe d $139/155/179; ✳@☎☲) With a circle of double-storey buildings arranged around a swath of lawns and gum trees, the Chifley has a relaxed country club vibe. Avoid the standard rooms and go for the recently refurbished superior and deluxe accommodation overlooking the Todd River. There's an attractive pool area with a swim-up bar, plus a seafood restaurant.

Bond Springs Outback Retreat   B&B $$
(☑08 8952 9888; www.outbackretreat.com.au; cottage d $231; ✳☲) Experience a taste of outback station life at this retreat, about 25km north of town. The private self-contained cottage is a refurbished stockman's quarters. A full breakfast is included but other meals are self-catering. Have a game of tennis or mooch around the enormous property including the original station school, which operated through the School of the Air.

✗ Eating

★ Piccolo's   CAFE $
(☑08 8953 1936; Shop 1, Cinema Complex 11, Todd Mall; breakfast from $12; ☺7am-3pm Mon-Fri, 7am-2pm Sat, 8am-noon Sun) This modern cafe is popular with locals for its excellent food and probably Alice's best coffee. Try the toasties or one of the breakfast rolls.

★ Montes   MODERN AUSTRALIAN $$
(☑08 8952 4336; www.montes.net.au; cnr Stott Tce & Todd St; mains $13-26; ☺11am-late; ☻) Travelling circus meets outback homestead. It's family friendly with a play area for kids, and the food ranges from gourmet burgers, pizzas and tapas to curries and seafood. Sit in the leafy beer garden (with a range of beers) or intimate booth seating. Patio heaters keep patrons warm on cool desert nights.

★ Hanuman Restaurant   THAI $$
(☑08 8953 7188; www.hanuman.com.au/alice-springs; Doubletree by Hilton, 82 Barrett Dr; mains $25-36; ☺noon-10pm Mon-Fri, 6pm-midnight Sat, 6-10pm Sun; ☻) You won't believe you're in the outback when you try the incredible Thai- and Indian-influenced cuisine at this stylish restaurant. The delicate Thai entrees are a real triumph as are the seafood dishes, particularly the Hanuman prawns. Although the menu is ostensibly Thai, there are enough Indian dishes to satisfy a curry craving.

Epilogue Lounge   TAPAS $$
(☑08 8953 4206; www.facebook.com/epiloguelounge/; 58 Todd Mall; mains $16-25; ☺8am-11.30pm Wed-Sat, 8am-3pm Sun & Mon) This urban, retro delight is definitely the coolest place to hang in town. With a decent wine list, food served all day and service with a smile, it is a real Alice Springs standout. Expect dishes like halloumi burgers or steak sandwiches and a cooling breeze under the shade cover. They also have live music some nights.

Central Alice Springs

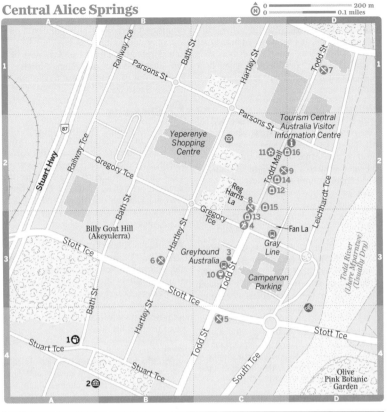

Central Alice Springs

⦿ Sights
1 Alice Springs Reptile Centre A4
2 Royal Flying Doctor Service Base......... A4

⦿ Activities, Courses & Tours
3 Emu Run Experience C3
4 Lone Dingo Adventure C3

⦿ Eating
Epilogue Lounge ....(see 8)
5 Montes C4
6 Overlanders Steakhouse B3
7 Piccolo's D1
8 Red Dog Cafe..................................... C2
9 Red Ochre Grill C2

⦿ Drinking & Nightlife
10 Rock C3

⦿ Entertainment
11 Sounds of Starlight Theatre..................C2

⦿ Shopping
12 Jila Arts...C2
13 Mbantua Gallery C3
14 Papunya Tula Artists...............................C2
15 Red Kangaroo Books C2
16 Talapi...C2

Red Dog Cafe   CAFE **$$**
(☑08 8953 1353; 64 Todd Mall; breakfast $5-17, mains $15-18.50; ☺7am-5pm) With tables and chairs strewn out over Todd Mall, this place is good for people watching, hearty breakfasts and fresh, well-brewed coffee. Lunch is

all about burgers, with a few veggie options thrown in. We enjoyed the kangaroo salad.

Bean Tree Cafe   CAFE **$$**
(☑08 8952 0190; www.opbg.com.au/beantree-cafe; Olive Pink Botanic Garden, Tuncks Rd;

breakfast $7-18, mains $15-19; ⊘8am-4pm)
Breakfast with the birds at this superb outdoor cafe tucked away in the Olive Pink Botanic Garden. It's a relaxing place to sit and the wholesome, homestyle dishes, such as the roo burger or kangaroo salad in a smoked native pepperberry sauce, are well worth the wait.

Overlanders Steakhouse   STEAK $$$
(⊘08 8952 2159; 72 Hartley St; mains $32-55; ⊘6pm-late) The place for steaks, big succulent cuts of beef – and crocodile, camel, kangaroo or emu. Amid the cattle station decor you can try Stuart's Tucker Bag: a combo of croc, kangaroo, emu and camel.

The 'Drovers Blowout' set menu will satisfy your need to eat as many local animalsas possible in one go, it features all of the meats and you'll never want to eat meat again.

Red Ochre Grill   MODERN AUSTRALIAN $$$
(⊘08 8952 9614; www.alicespringsaurora.com.au/red-ochre-grill; Todd Mall; mains $18.50-39; ⊘10am-9pm) Offering innovative fusion dishes with a focus on outback cuisine, the menu here usually features traditional meats plus locally bred proteins, such as kangaroo and emu, matched with native herbs such as lemon myrtle, pepperberries and bush tomatoes. Keep an eye out for special deals such as tapas with a bottle of wine or discounts for an early-bird dinner.

🍷 Drinking & Nightlife

Rock   BAR
(⊘08 8953 8280; 78 Todd St; ⊘noon-2am) There is an excellent beer selection at this Alice classic. It's blessed with a beer garden and is ideal for a cold drink by the windows that open onto the street. The Rock pulls in a good mix of locals and tourists, although it can get seedy in the evenings.

Juicy Rump   BAR
(93 Barrett Dr; ⊘10am-late) Not as bad as the name suggests but still an acquired taste, this is the late-night favourite if you want to have a dance to cheesy R&B or watch a big sporting event on the town's largest plasma screen. Also has a deck with a view to the ranges, lovely for sunset drinks.

☆ Entertainment

★ Sounds of Starlight Theatre   LIVE MUSIC
(⊘08 8953 0826; www.soundsofstarlight.com; 40 Todd Mall; adult/concession/family $30/25/90; ⊘8pm Tue, Fri & Sat) This atmospheric 1½-hour musical performance evoking the spirit of the outback with didgeridoos, drums and keyboards, plus wonderful photography and lighting, is an Alice institution. Musician Andrew Langford also runs free didgeridoo lessons (11am Monday to Friday). You can add dinner to the mix or just see the show.

🛍 Shopping

Alice is the centre for Aboriginal arts from all over central Australia. The places owned and run by community art centres ensure that a better slice of the proceeds goes to the artist and artist's community. Look for the black-over-red Indigenous Art Code (www.indigenousartcode.org) displayed by dealers dedicated to fair and transparent dealings with artists.

★ Papunya Tula Artists   ART
(⊘08 8952 4731; www.papunyatula.com.au; Todd Mall; ⊘9am-5pm Mon-Fri, 10am-2pm Sat) This stunning gallery showcases artworks from the Western Desert communities of Papunya, Kintore and Kiwikurra – even if you're not buying, it's worth stopping by to see the magnificent collection.

Talapi   ART
(⊘08 8953 6389; www.talapi.com.au; 45 Todd Mall; ⊘9am-6pm Mon-Fri, 10am-5pm Sat) One of Alice Spring's newest galleries, Talapi is a beautiful space in the heart of Alice Springs, exhibiting and promoting Central Desert indigenous art. It sources its artworks directly from Aboriginal-owned art centres and is a member of the Indigenous Art Code. Drop in to ask about upcoming exhibitions.

Mbantua Gallery   ART
(⊘08 8952 5571; www.mbantua.com.au; 64 Todd Mall; ⊘9am-6pm Mon-Fri, 9am-3pm Sat, 10am-2pm Sun) This privately owned gallery includes extensive exhibits of works from the renowned Utopia region, as well as watercolour landscapes from the Namatjira school. Collectors should ask to see their collection of bark paintings, old boomerangs and high-end works out the back.

Tjanpi Desert Weavers   ART
(⊘08 8958 2377; www.tjanpi.com.au; 3 Wilkinson St; ⊘10am-4pm Mon-Fri) This small enterprise employs and supports Central Desert weavers from 18 remote communities. The shop is well worth a visit to see the magnificent woven baskets and quirky sculptures created from grasses collected locally.

Ngurratjuta Iltja Ntjarra ART
(☑ 08 8951 1953; www.ngurart.com.au; 29 Wilkinson St; ☺9am-3.30pm Mon-Fri) The 'many hands' art centre is a small gallery and studio for visiting artists from all over central Australia. Watercolour and dot paintings are reasonably priced and you buy directly from the artists. You can see artists at work from 10am to 3pm Monday to Thursday.

Red Kangaroo Books BOOKS
(☑ 08 8953 2137; www.redkangaroobooks.com; 79 Todd Mall; ☺9am-5pm Mon-Fri, 9am-3pm Sat & Sun) Excellent bookshop specialising in central Australian titles: history, art, travel, novels, guidebooks and more. It also has small but excellent wildlife section.

Jila Arts ART
(☑ 08 8953 3005; www.jilaarts.com.au; 63 Todd Mall; ☺9am-5pm Mon-Fri, 9am-3pm Sat, 10am-2pm Sun) One of the better galleries selling original works, with a focus on contemporary paintings from the Western Desert.

❶ Information

DANGERS & ANNOYANCES
Avoid walking alone at night anywhere in town. Catch a taxi back to your accommodation if you're out late.

MEDICAL SERVICES
Alice Springs Hospital (☑ 08 8951 7777; Gap Rd)
Alice Springs Pharmacy (☑ 08 8952 1554; shop 19, Yeperenye Shopping Centre, 36 Hartley St; ☺8.30am-7.30pm)
Ambulance (☑ 000)

MONEY
Major banks with ATMs, such as ANZ, Commonwealth, National Australia and Westpac, are located in and around Todd Mall in the town centre.

POST
Main Post Office (☑ 13 13 18; auspost.com.au; 31-33 Hartley St; ☺8.15am-5pm Mon-Fri)

TOURIST INFORMATION
Central Land Council (☑ 08 8951 6211; www.clc.org.au; PO Box 3321, 27 Stuart Hwy, Alice Springs; ☺8.30am-noon & 2-4pm) For Aboriginal land permits and transit permits.
Parks & Wildlife (☑ 08 8951 8250, 08 8999 4555; www.nt.gov.au/leisure/parks-reserves; Arid Zone Research Institute, off Stuart Hwy) Information on national parks and for the Larapinta Trail.
Tourism Central Australia Visitor Information Centre (p208) This helpful centre can load you up with stacks of brochures and the free visitors guide. Weather forecasts and road conditions are posted on the wall. National parks information is also available. Ask about the unlimited kilometre deals if you are thinking of renting a car.
Wildcare Inc Alice Springs (☑ 0419 221 128; www.fauna.org.au) The people to call if you find injured wildlife

❶ Getting There & Away

AIR
Alice Springs is well connected, with **Qantas** (☑ 13 13 13, 08 8950 5211; www.qantas.com.au) and **Virgin Australia** (☑ 13 67 89; www.virginaustralia.com) operating regular flights to/from capital cities. Airline representatives are based at Alice Springs airport.

BUS
Greyhound Australia (☑ 1300 473 946; www.greyhound.com.au; Shop 3, 113 Todd St) has regular services from Alice Springs (check the website for timetables and discounted fares). Buses arrive at, and depart from, the Greyhound office in Todd St. The following are Flexi Fares:

DESTINATION	ONE-WAY FARE ($)	DURATION (HR)
Adelaide	155	20
Coober Pedy	145	8
Darwin	185	22
Katherine	175	16½
Tennant Creek	115	6

Emu Run (p202) runs cheap daily connections between Alice Springs and Yulara (one way $120). **Gray Line** (☑ 1300 858 687; www.grayline.com; Capricornia Centre 9, Gregory Tce) also runs between Alice Springs and Yulara (one way $120).

Backpacker buses roam to and from Alice providing a party atmosphere and a chance to see some of the sights along the way. **Groovy Grape Getaways Australia** (☑ 1800 661 177; www.groovygrape.com.au) plies the route from Alice to Adelaide on a seven-day, backpacker camping jaunt for $975.

CAR & MOTORCYCLE
Alice Springs is a long way from everywhere. It's 1180km to Mt Isa in Queensland, 1490km to Darwin and 441km (4½ hours) to Yulara (for Uluru). Although the roads to the north and south are sealed and in good condition, these are still outback roads and it's wise to have your vehicle well prepared, particularly as you won't get a mobile phone signal outside Alice or Yulara. Carry plenty of drinking water and emergency food at all times.

All the major car-hire companies have offices in Alice Springs and many have counters at the airport. Prices drop by about 20% between November and April, but rentals don't come cheap, as most firms offer only 100km free per day, which won't get you far. Talk to the **Tourism Central Australia Visitor Information Centre** (☑ 1800 645 199, 08 8952 5800; www.discovercentralaustralia.com; cnr Todd Mall & Parsons St; ⏰ 8.30am-5pm Mon-Fri, 9.30am-4pm Sat & Sun; ☎) about its unlimited kilometres deal before you book. A conventional (2WD) vehicle will get you to most sights in the MacDonnell Ranges and out to Uluru and Kings Canyon via sealed roads. If you want to go further afield, say to Chambers Pillar, Finke Gorge or even the Mereenie Loop Rd, a 4WD is essential.

TRAIN

A classic way to enter or leave the NT is by the *Ghan,* which can be booked through **Great Southern Rail** (☑ 13 21 47; www.greatsouthernrail.com.au). Discounted fares are sometimes offered, especially in the low season (February to June). Bookings are essential.

The train station is at the end of George Cres off Larapinta Dr.

ⓘ Getting Around

BUS

The public bus service, **Asbus** (☑ 08 8944 2444), departs from outside the Yeperenye Shopping Centre. Buses run about every 1½ hours Monday to Friday and Saturday morning. There are three routes of interest to travellers: 400/401 has a detour to the cultural precinct, 100/101 passes the School of the Air, and 300/301 passes many southern hotels and caravan parks along Gap Rd and Palm Circuit. The **visitor information centre** (p208) has timetables.

TAXI

Taxis congregate near the **visitor information centre** (p208). To book one, call 13 10 08 or 08 8952 1877.

MACDONNELL RANGES

The beautiful, weather-beaten MacDonnell Ranges, stretching 400km across the desert, are a hidden world of spectacular gorges, rare wildlife and poignant Aboriginal heritage all within a day from Alice.

East MacDonnell Ranges

Although overshadowed by the more popular West Macs, the East MacDonnell Ranges are extremely picturesque and, with fewer visitors, can be a more enjoyable outback experience. With gorges, some stunning scenery (especially around sunset or sunrise) and the old gold-mining ruins of Arltunga, there's enough to fill a day trip from Alice.

⊙ Sights

★ Arltunga
Historical Reserve   HISTORIC SITE

At the eastern end of the MacDonnell Ranges, 110km east of Alice Springs, the old gold-mining ghost town of Arltunga (33km on an unsealed road from the Ross Hwy) has lonely ruins and a wonderful end-of-the-road feel. Old buildings, a couple of cemeteries and the many deserted mine sites in this parched landscape give visitors an idea of what life was like for the miners.

★ Trephina Gorge
Nature Park   NATURE RESERVE

If you only have time for a couple of stops in the East MacDonnell Ranges, make Trephina Gorge Nature Park (75km from Alice) one of them. The play between the pale sandy river beds, the red and purple gorge walls, the white tree trunks, the eucalyptus-green foliage and the blue sky is spectacular. Depending on the time of year, you'll also find deep swimming holes and abundant wildlife. There's a **rangers station** (☑ 08 8956 9765) and **camping grounds** (Trephina Gorge Nature Park; adult/child $3.30/1.65) with barbecues, water and toilets.

N'dhala Gorge Nature Park   NATURE RESERVE

Just southwest of the Ross River Resort, a strictly 4WD-only track leads 11km south to N'Dhala Gorge. More than 5900 ancient Aboriginal rock carvings (some date back 10,000 years) and some rare endemic plants decorate a deep, narrow gorge, although the art isn't easy to spot. There's a small, exposed **camping ground** (N'Dhala Gorge; adult/child $3.30/1.65) without reliable water. From the car park, there's a 1.5km (one hour) return walk to the gorge with some signposts to rock art walls.

Ruby Gap Nature Park   NATURE RESERVE

This remote park rewards visitors with wild and beautiful scenery. The sandy bed of the Hale River sparkles with thousands of tiny garnets. It's an evocative place and is well worth the considerable effort required to reach it – by high-clearance 4WD. **Camping** (Ruby Gap Nature Park; adult/child $3.30/1.65) is permitted anywhere along the river; make sure to BYO drinking water and a camp cooker. Allow two hours each way for the 44km trip from Arltunga.

Emily & Jessie Gaps
Nature Park
NATURE RESERVE

Both of these gaps in the rock wall of the East MacDonnells are associated with the Eastern Arrernte Caterpillar Dreaming trail. Emily Gap, 16km out of Alice, has stylised rock paintings and a fairly deep waterhole in the narrow gorge. The gap is a sacred site with some well-preserved paintings on the eastern wall, although some of the paintings have been vandalised. Jessie Gap, 8km further on, is usually much quieter. Both sites have toilets, but camping is not permitted.

Corroboree Rock
Conservation Reserve
HISTORIC SITE

Corroboree Rock, 51km from Alice Springs, is one of many strangely shaped dolomite outcrops scattered over the valley floor. Despite the name, it's doubtful the rock was ever used as a corroboree area, but it is associated with the Perentie Dreaming trail. The perentie lizard, Australia's largest, grows in excess of 2.5m and takes refuge within the area's rock falls. There's a short walking track (15 minutes) around the rock.

🛏 Sleeping

Most people visit on a day trip from Alice, but there are basic campsites at Arltunga, Trephina Gorge, John Hayes Rockhole, Arltunga, Ruby Gap Nature Park and N'Dhala Gorge, as well as two fine options, one at Ross River, the other along the Arltunga Tourist Drive.

Arltunga Bush Hotel
CAMPGROUND $

(🖉08 8956 9797; sites per person $5, dm $10, family cottage $50; ☺Mar-Nov) Arltunga Bush Hotel, close to the entrance of the Arltunga Historical Reserve, has a camping ground with showers, toilets, barbecue pits and picnic tables. Fees are collected in the late afternoon. It's a lovely spot with plenty of shade and nicely spaced sites.

⭐Hale River Homestead
at Old Ambalindum
FARMSTAY $$

(🖉08 8956 9993; www.haleriverhomestead.com. au; powered/unpowered sites from $35/30, dm $60-80, d cottage/homestead $190/240; ❄🌊) This remote spot run by NT veterans Sean and Lynne offers a great range of accommodation including a nicely renovated

homestead, a cottage sleeping five people, simple bunkhouses and lovely campsites, all on a working cattle station. Bookings are essential and ring ahead to ask whether you need to bring your own food.

It's on the Arltunga Tourist Dr, which runs from Arltunga to the Stuart Hwy, about 50km north of Alice Springs.

Ross River Resort
CARAVAN PARK $$

(🖉08 8956 9711; www.rossriverresort.com.au; Ross Highway; powered/unpowered sites $33/25, bunkhouse with/without linen $35/30, d/f cabin $135/160; ❄🌊🐾) Nine kilometres along the continuation of the Ross Hwy past the Arltunga turn-off (coming from Alice Springs) is the secluded Ross River Resort. Built around a historic stone homestead, timber cabins encircle a swimming pool.

There's a store with fuel and it's worth stopping to check out the old homestead and maybe grab lunch (mains $17 to $25) or a beer in the Stockman's Bar. Ring first to check that the restaurant is open.

ℹ Getting There & Away

The sealed Ross Hwy runs 100km along the Ranges. Arltunga is 33km off the Ross Hwy along an unsealed road that is usually OK for 2WD vehicles; the first 13km off the Ross Hwy require careful driving as the road bucks and weaves through the hills, but the final 20km into Arltunga cross more open floodplains.

You'll need a 4WD to access John Hayes Rockhole (in Trephina Gorge Nature Park), N'Dhala Gorge and Ruby Gap.

From Arltunga it's possible to loop back to Alice along the Arltunga Tourist Dr, which pops out at the Stuart Hwy about 50km north of town.

West MacDonnell Ranges

With their stunning beauty and rich diversity of plants and animals, the West MacDonnell Ranges are not to be missed. Their easy access by conventional vehicle makes them especially popular with day-trippers. Although it is possible to visit all of the sights in the West MacDonnells in one very long day, we recommend spreading it out over two, allowing you time to linger at special places like Simpsons Gap, Ormiston Gorge, Hermannsburg and Palm Valley. Most sites in the West MacDonnell Ranges lie within the Tjoritja/West MacDonnell National Park, except for Standley Chasm, which is privately owned.

South of Alice Springs

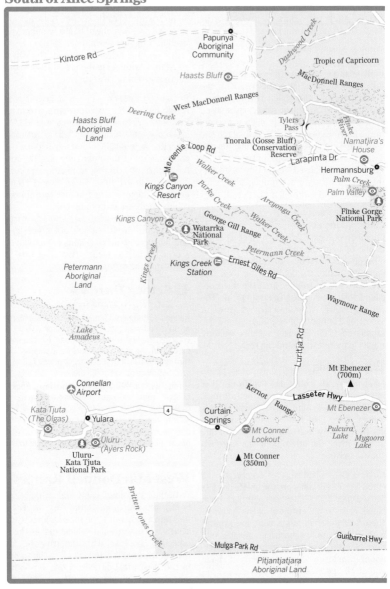

⊙ Sights

If you choose Namatjira Dr, one of your first stops might be **Ellery Creek Big Hole**, 91km from Alice Springs and with a large permanent waterhole – a popular place for a swim on a hot day (the water is usually freezing).

It's good for wildlife and birdwatching, too. About 11km further west along Namatjira Dr, a rough gravel track leads to narrow, ochre-red **Serpentine Gorge**, which has a lovely waterhole blocking the entrance and a lookout at the end of a short, steep track

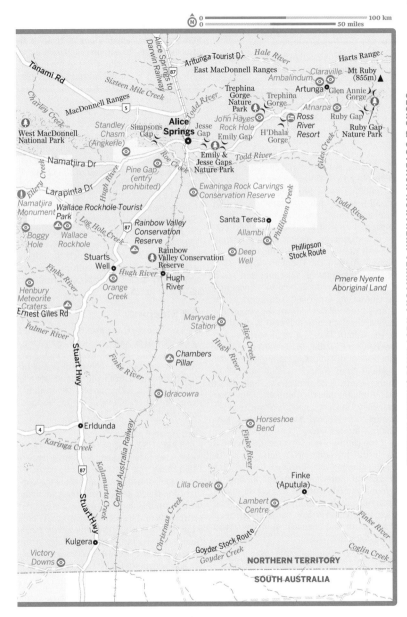

(30 minutes return), where you can view ancient cycads.

The **Ochre Pits** line a dry creek bed 11km west of Serpentine and were a source of pigment for Aboriginal people. The various coloured ochres – mainly yellow, white and red-brown – are weathered limestone, with iron-oxide creating the colours.

The car park for the majestic **Ormiston Gorge** is 25km beyond the Ochre Pits. It's the most impressive chasm in the West Mac-Donnells. There's a waterhole shaded with

CATERPILLAR DREAMING

Known to the Arrernte as Anthwerrke, Emily Gap in the East MacDonnell Ranges is one of the most important Aboriginal sites in the Alice Springs area; it was from here that the caterpillar ancestral beings of Mparntwe originated before crawling across the landscape to create the topographical features that exist today.

ghost gums, and the gorge curls around to the enclosed Ormiston Pound. It's a haven for wildlife (dingo, red kangaroo and euro are all possible, and look for the fat-tailed false antechinus near sunrise) and birds (western bowerbird, rufous-crowned emu-wren and spinifex pigeon among others). The only drawback? It's also the busiest site along Namatjira Dr. There are some excellent walking tracks – take one and you'll soon leave the crowds behind – including the Ghost Gum Lookout (20 minutes), which affords brilliant views down the gorge, and the excellent, circuitous Pound Walk (three hours, 7.5km). There's a small visitor centre (☑ 08 8956 7799; ⊙ 10am-4pm), a kiosk (open 10am to 4pm) and camping ground.

About 2km further is the turn-off to Glen Helen Gorge, where the Finke River cuts through the MacDonnells. Only 1km past Glen Helen is a good lookout over Mt Sonder; sunrise and sunset here are particularly impressive.

If you continue northwest for 25km you'll reach the turn-off (4WD only) to multi-hued, cathedral-like Redbank Gorge. This permanent waterhole runs for kilometres through the labyrinthine gorge and makes for an incredible swimming and scrambling adventure on a hot day. Namatjira Dr then heads south and is sealed as far as Tylers Pass Lookout.

Tylers Pass Lookout   VIEWPOINT
Tylers Pass Lookout provides a dramatic view of Tnorala (Grosse Bluff), the legacy of an earth-shattering comet impact. It's a 30- to 40-minute drive beyond Glen Helen Gorge.

Standley Chasm   GORGE
(☑ 08 8956 7440; www.standleychasm.com.au; adult/concession/family $12/10/30; ⊙ 8am-5pm, last chasm entry 4:30pm) Standley Chasm is owned and run by the local Iwupata-ka community. The narrowest of the West

Macdonnell defiles, Standley Chasm is a stunning spot with sheer rock walls rising 80m from the canyon floor. A rocky path into the gorge (20 minutes, 1.2km) follows a creek bed lined with ghost gums and cycads. There's a kiosk, camping (☑ 08 8956 7440; per person $18.50; 🐾), picnic facilities and toilets near the car park.

Although it may not look like there's a lot of water, this is one of eight permanent water sources in the ranges; note the many different rock types along the chasm floor, all carried here by water. Hikes radiate out from here, but the far end of the chasm is closed off as an Aboriginal sacred site lies beyond.

From 9am to 1pm on Thursdays (and at other times by appointment), you can take the Angkerle Cultural Experience (☑ 08 8956 7440; www.standleychasm.com.au; per person $85; ⊙ 9am-1pm Thu), which includes a presentation about local cultural and natural history, an art workshop, morning tea and buffet lunch.

🛏 Sleeping

Ormiston Gorge Campground   CAMPGROUND $
(☑ 08 8954 6198; Ormiston Gorge; adult/child/family $10/5/25) Has showers, toilets, gas barbecues and picnic tables and is just far enough removed from the day visitor car park to offer a little privacy; we wouldn't leave anything of value lying around, however.

Glen Helen Resort   HOTEL $
(☑ 08 8956 7489; www.glenhelen.com.au; Namatjira Dr; powered/unpowered sites $30/24, dm $35, r $160-175; 🅿🐾❄) At the western edge of the West MacDonnell National Park is the popular Glen Helen Resort, which has an idyllic back verandah slammed up against the red ochre cliffs of the spectacular gorge. There's a busy restaurant-pub serving hearty meals (mains $29 to $42) and live music on the weekend. There are also 4WD tours available and helicopter flights (from $175).

Ellery Creek Campground   CAMPGROUND $
(per adult/child $5/1.50) These simple camp sites in the Ellery Creek car park are not as good as those at Ormiston Gorge, but are otherwise fine.

❶ Getting There & Away

Heading west from Alice, Namatjira Dr turns northwest off Larapinta Dr 6km beyond Standley Chasm and is sealed all the way to Tylers

Pass. Beyond Tylers Pass, there is a 43km stretch of unsealed road – reports of this section being sealed (and hence closing the loop between Larapinta and Namatjira Drs) often circulate but funding was frozen at the time of our visit.

Hermannsburg

POP 624

The Aboriginal community of Hermannsburg (Ntaria), about 125km from Alice Springs, is famous as the one-time home of artist Albert Namatjira and as the site of the Hermannsburg Mission. It's an appealingly rundown and sleepy place which belies its significance as one of the most important Aboriginal communities in the area.

Just west of Hermannsburg is Namatjira's House.

◉ Sights

Hermannsburg Mission   HISTORIC SITE
(☑08 8956 7402; www.hermannsburg.com.au; adult/child $10/5; ⊙9am-5pm Mon-Sat, 10.30am-5pm Sun) The whitewashed walls of the old mission are shaded by tall river gums and date palms. This fascinating monument to the NT's early Lutheran missionaries includes a school building, a church and various outbuildings. The 'Manse' houses an art gallery and a history of the life and times of Albert Namatjira (a one-time resident) as well as work of 39 Hermannsburg artists.

✖ Eating

Kata-Anga Tea Rooms   CAFE $
(mains $8-15; ⊙9am-4pm) Within Hermannsburg Mission, Kata-Anga Tea Rooms, in the old missionary house, serves Devonshire teas, sandwiches and strudel, and displays historic photographs, plus a good range of traditional and watercolour paintings. There are distinctive ceramic works by the Hermannsburg potters on display and available for sale.

❶ Getting There & Away

There's no public transport to/from Hermannsburg.

Finke Gorge National Park

With its primordial landscape, the Finke Gorge National Park, south of Hermannsburg, is one of central Australia's premier wilderness reserves. It's hard going getting

here and even harder getting around, but that also tends to keep the numbers of visitors down, which only adds to the park's already considerable appeal.

◉ Sights

★Palm Valley   GORGE
Top attraction Palm Valley is famous for its red cabbage palms (up to 12,000 of them!) which exist nowhere else in the world. These relics from prehistoric times give the valley a picture-book oasis feel. In Palm Valley, walking tracks include Arankaia walk (2km loop, one hour), which traverses the valley, returning via the sandstone plateau; the Mpulungkinya track (5km loop, two hours), heading down the gorge before joining the Arankaia walk; and the Mpaara track (5km loop, two hours).

🛏 Sleeping

There's a camping ground (Finke Gorge National Park; adult/child $6.60/3.30) with basic facilities inside the national park.

❶ Getting There & Away

Access to the park follows the sandy bed of the Finke River and rocky tracks, so a high-clearance 4WD is essential. If you don't have one, several tour operators go to Palm Valley from Alice Springs. The turn-off to Palm Valley starts about 1km west of the Hermannsburg turn-off on Larapinta Dr.

WEST MACDONNELL WILDLIFE

The West MacDonnell Ranges offer some fine possibilities when it comes to native Australian wildlife. The main species to watch out for include:

Black-footed rock wallaby Most easily seen at Simpsons Gap.

Common brushtail possum Any riverine woodland across the range.

Dingo Possible at Ormiston Gorge or Ellery Creek Big Hole.

Euro or common wallaroo Simpsons Gap or Ormiston Gorge.

Fat-tailed false Antechinus Small, rodent-like marsupial sometimes seen early morning around Ormiston Gorge.

Red kangaroo Around Simpsons Gap, along Larapinta Dr around sunset and Ormiston Gorge.

NORTHERN TERRITORY'S FAR SOUTH

Most travellers clocking long desert kilometres along the Stuart and Lasseter Hwys often do so oblivious to the fact that some fascinating and dramatic sites lie off in the hinterland. You'd need a few days to see all of them, but possibilities for those with limited time include Rainbow Valley Conservation Reserve, Henbury Meteorite Craters, the views of Mt Connor and Australia's geographic centre.

Old South Road

The Old South Road, which runs close to the old *Ghan* railway line, is a pretty rough 4WD track that takes you about as far off the beaten track as you go this close to Alice Springs. Attractions, beyond that sense of being somewhere deliciously remote, are few, but you may end up at Australia's geographical centre if you go far enough.

⊙ Sights

It's only 39km from Alice Springs to Ewaninga, where prehistoric Aboriginal petroglyphs are carved into sandstone. The rock carvings found here and at N'Dhala

RED CENTRE WAY & MEREENIE LOOP

The Red Centre Way is the 'back road' from Alice Springs to Uluru. It incorporates part of the West MacDonnell Ranges, an 'inner loop' comprising Namatjira and Larapinta Drs, plus the rugged Mereenie Loop Rd, the short cut to Kings Canyon. This dusty, heavily corrugated road is not to be taken lightly and hire-car companies won't permit their 2WDs to be driven on it.

To travel along this route, which passes through Aboriginal land, you need a Mereenie Tour Pass ($5), which is valid for one day and includes a booklet with details about the local Aboriginal culture and a route map. The pass is issued on the spot (usually only on the day of travel) at the visitor information centre in Alice Springs, Glen Helen Resort, Kings Canyon Resort and Hermannsburg service station.

Gorge are thought to have been made by Aboriginal people who lived here before those currently in the region, between 1000 and 5000 years ago.

The eerie, sandstone **Chambers Pillar**, southwest of Maryvale Station, towers 50m above the surrounding plain and is carved with the names and visit dates of early explorers – and, unfortunately, some much less worthy modern-day graffiti. To the Aboriginal people of the area, Chambers Pillar is the remains of Itirkawara, a powerful gecko ancestor. Most photogenic at sunset and sunrise, it's best to stay overnight at the **camping ground** (Chambers Pillar; adult/child $3.30/1.65). It's 160km from Alice Springs and a 4WD is required for the last 44km from the turn-off at Maryvale Station.

Back on the main track south, you eventually arrive at **Finke** (Aputula), a small Aboriginal community 230km from Alice Springs. When the old *Ghan* was running, Finke was a thriving town; these days it seems to have drifted into a permanent torpor, except when the Finke Desert Race (p203) is staged. Fuel and basic supplies are available here at Aputula Store.

Just 21km west of Finke, and 12km north of the road along a signposted track, is the **Lambert Centre**. The point marks Australia's geographical centre and features a 5m-high version of the flagpole found on top of Parliament House in Canberra.

✗ Eating

Basic supplies are available at the **Aputula Store** (☑08 8956 0968; ⊙9am-noon & 2-4pm Mon-Fri, 9am-noon Sat) in Finke, but we strongly recommend that you carry with you everything you think you're likely to need as supplies sometimes run low and prices are high.

ⓘ Getting There & Away

You'll need a fully equipped, high-clearance 4WD to travel this route. The road begins south of Alice Springs, close to where the road branches to the airport and the newer Stuart Hwy. At the southern end, from Finke, you can turn west along the Goyder Stock Rte to join the Stuart Hwy at Kulgera (150km) or east to Old Andado station on the edge of the Simpson Desert (120km). (Expensive) fuel is sold at the Aputula Store.

WORTH A TRIP

WALLACE ROCKHOLE

You'll be virtually guaranteed seclusion at the **Wallace Rockhole Tourist Park** (☑ 08 8956 7993; www.wallace rockholetours.com.au; powered/unpowered sites $28/22, cabins $120; ❄), situated at the end of an 18km dirt road branching off Larapinta Dr. The park has a camping area with good facilities. Tours here include a 1½-hour rock art and bush medicine tour (adult/child $10/8) with billy tea and damper (advance booking essential).

Rainbow Valley Conservation Reserve

Visit this series of free-standing sandstone bluffs and cliffs, in shades ranging from cream to red, at sunset or sunrise and you'll encounter one of central Australia's more underrated sights. Visit in the middle of the day and you're likely to wonder what all the fuss is about, save for one thing – deep-desert silence will overwhelm you whatever time of day you are here. A marked walking trail takes you past claypans and in between the multihued outcrops to the aptly named Mushroom Rock.

🛏 Sleeping

Rainbow Valley Camping Ground CAMPGROUND $
(Rainbow Valley Conservation Reserve; adult/child/family $3.30/1.65/7.70) We love staying here, but there's barely a scrap of shade (apart from the picnic shelters), so set up late afternoon and pack up by midmorning – if you do this, you'll leave with fond memories of the silence and the wonderful sunrise and sunset views.

❶ Getting There & Away

The park lies 22km off the Stuart Hwy along a 4WD track; the turn-off is 77km south of Alice Springs. If it hasn't rained for a while, the track should be passable in a 2WD vehicle.

Ernest Giles Road

The Ernest Giles Rd heads off to the west of the Stuart Hwy, about 140km south of Alice, and is a shorter but much rougher route to Kings Canyon only recommended for 4WD vehicles. The main attraction, apart from the sense of adventure that comes from travelling such a remote and challenging route, is the chance to visit Henbury Meteorite Craters.

◉ Sights

Henbury Meteorite Craters LANDMARK
Eleven kilometres west of the Stuart Hwy, a corrugated track leads 5km off Ernest Giles Rd to this cluster of 12 small craters, formed after a meteor fell to earth 4700 years ago. The largest of the craters is 180m wide and 15m deep. It's well worth the detour: the road is fine for 2WDs if you proceed carefully and the craters are surrounded by some beautiful country.

There are no longer any fragments of the meteorites at the site, but the Museum of Central Australia (p200) in Alice Springs has a small chunk that weighs 46.5kg.

There are some pretty exposed camp sites (adult/child/family $3.30/1.65/7.70) available.

❶ Getting There & Away

The turn-off to the Ernest Giles Rd is 132km south of Alice Springs and 68km north of Erldunda. Even if you have a 4WD, remember that many car-rental companies won't allow you to travel this road and doing so without permission may mean that your insurance is invalid.

Lasseter Highway

The Lasseter Hwy connects the Stuart Hwy with Uluru-Kata Tjuta National Park, 244km to the west from the turn-off at Erldunda. For much of the way, it's fairly standard central Australian scenery with red sand, scrub and spinifex to the horizon, but there are two main attractions: the first sighting of Uluru as you approach Yulara and free-standing Mt Conner.

◉ Sights

Mt Connor MOUNTAIN
Mt Conner, the large mesa (tabletop mountain) that looms 350m out of the desert, is the outback's most photographed red herring – on first sighting many mistake it for Uluru. It has great significance to local Aboriginal people, who know it as Atila. There's a well-signposted **lookout** around 20km east of Curtin Springs; from the lookout's summit, there are also views to the

north over the salt pan, which often has standing water.

According to local Indigenous beliefs, Mt Connor is the home of the Ice Men, who venture out on winter nights and leave frost upon the ground as a sign that they have passed.

🛏 Sleeping

Desert Oaks Resort   MOTEL $$
(☎08 8956 0984; www.desertoaksresort.com; Stuart Hwy, Erldunda; powered/unpowered sites $32/22, motel s/d from $115/149; ❄🌐🏊) Motel rooms here are a good standard and look out onto a lovely red-dirt native garden. Rooms 23 to 27 enjoy the best views. There's a roadhouse restaurant (mains $10 to $16), a bar and fuel.

Curtin Springs Wayside Inn   MOTEL $$
(☎08 8956 2906; www.curtinsprings.com; Lasseter Hwy; powered/unpowered sites $40/free, s/d with shared bathroom $90/130, r with private bathroom $180; ❄) There's a jolly air at this inn where they pride themselves on their friendliness. Pitch a tent for free or bed down in a well-maintained cabin. There's (expensive) fuel, a store with limited supplies and takeaway and bistro meals (mains $18 to $34), plus an eccentric outback bar full of history and tall tales.

❶ Getting There & Away

Lasseter Hwy is sealed all the way from Erldunda to Yulara (and beyond as far as Kata Tjuta inside the national park).

WATARRKA NATIONAL PARK & KINGS CANYON

The yawning chasm of Kings Canyon in Watarrka National Park is one of the most spectacular sights in central Australia. While there is a certain soulfulness and mystique to those two other outback icons, Uluru and Kata Tjuta, Kings Canyon impresses with its scale and raw beauty, with its sheer red cliffs and by the opportunity it presents to climb high on the precipitous walls for fabulous aerial views.

Plan to explore the canyon on foot, and therefore to spend at least two nights here, so that you can go walking on a number of occasions in the cool of the morning or late afternoon.

Wildlife is another highlight out here, from native mammals (dingoes and red

kangaroos) to feral camels and brumbies (wild horses) and around 100 bird species (watch for the handsome spinifex pigeon).

🏃 Activities

Walkers are rewarded with awesome views on the **Kings Canyon Rim Walk** (6km loop, four hours; you must begin before 9am on hot days), which many travellers rate as a highlight of their trip to the Centre. After a short but steep climb (the only 'difficult' part of the trail), the walk skirts the canyon's rim before descending down wooden stairs to the Garden of Eden: a lush pocket of ferns and prehistoric cycads around a tranquil pool. The next section of the trail winds through a swarm of giant beehive domes: weathered sandstone outcrops, which to the Luritja represent the men of the Kuniya Dreaming.

The **Kings Creek Walk** (2km return) is a short stroll along the rocky creek bed to a raised platform with views of the towering canyon rim.

About 10km east of the car park, the **Kathleen Springs Walk** (one hour, 2.6km return) is a pleasant, wheelchair-accessible track leading to a waterhole at the head of a gorge.

The **Giles Track** (22km one way, overnight) is a marked track that meanders along the George Gill Range between Kathleen Springs and the canyon; fill out the logbook at Reedy Creek rangers office so that in the event of an emergency, rangers can more easily locate you.

🍳 Tours

Kings Creek Helicopters   SCENIC FLIGHTS
(☎08 8956 7474; www.kingscreekstation.com.au; flights per person $60-460) Flies from Kings Creek Station, including a breathtaking 30-minute canyon flight (from $275).

Professional Helicopter Services   SCENIC FLIGHTS
(PHS; ☎08 8956 2003; www.phs.com.au; flights per person 8/15/30mins $95/150/285) Picking up from Kings Canyon Resort, PHS buzzes the canyon on demand.

🛏 Sleeping & Eating

Kings Creek Station   CAMPGROUND $$
(☎08 8956 7474; www.kingscreekstation.com.au; Luritja Rd; powered/unpowered sites for 2 people $51/45, safari cabins s/d incl breakfast $117/189, luxury safari tents all inclusive $950;

(@ 🏊) Located 35km before the canyon, this family-run station offers a bush camping experience among the desert oaks. Cosy safari-style cabins (small canvas tents on solid floors) share amenities and a kitchen-BBQ area, while the luxury glamping experience is very cool. You can also tear around the desert on a quad bike (one-hour ride $105).

Kings Canyon Resort RESORT **$$$**
(📞 08 8956 7442, 1300 863 248; www.kingscanyonresort.com.au; Luritja Rd; powered/unpowered sites $50/42, dm $40, d $285-500; ✳ @ 🛜 🏊)
Only 10km from the canyon, this well-designed resort boasts a wide range of accommodation, from a grassy camping area with its own pool and bar to deluxe rooms looking out onto native bushland. Eating and drinking options are as varied, with a bistro, the Thirsty Dingo bar and an outback BBQ for big steaks and live entertainment.

Under the Desert Moon AUSTRALIAN **$$$**
(www.kingscanyonresort.com.au/Under-A-Desert-Moon.aspx; per person $149; ⏱ 6pm Apr-Oct)
Dine out under the stars and around a campfire in great comfort and with fine food at the Kings Canyon Resort. There's a five-course set menu and the whole experience lasts from three to four hours.

🛈 Getting There & Away

There are three routes to Kings Canyon from Alice Springs, but no public transport.

The only sealed route leaves the Stuart Highway at Erldunda, 199km south of Alice Springs, then take the sealed Lasseter Hwy for 108km and then 169km along the Luritja Rd. The other options are the 4WD-only Mereenie Loop or Red Centre Way from Hermannsburg and the unsealed Ernest Giles Rd.

ULURU-KATA TJUTA NATIONAL PARK

There are some world-famous sights touted as unmissable that end up being a let-down when you actually see them. And then there's Uluru: nothing can really prepare you for the immensity, grandeur, changing colour and stillness of 'the Rock'. It really is a sight that will sear itself onto your mind.

The World Heritage–listed icon has attained the status of a pilgrimage. Uluru, the equally impressive Kata Tjuta (the Olgas) and the surrounding area are of deep cultural significance to the traditional owners, the Pitjantjatjara and Yankuntjatjara Aboriginal peoples (who refer to themselves as Anangu). The Anangu officially own the

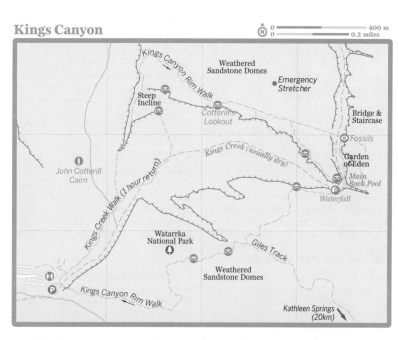

Kings Canyon

national park, which is leased to Parks Australia and jointly administered.

There's plenty to see and do: meandering walks, bike rides, guided tours, desert culture and simply contemplating the many changing colours and moods of the great monolith itself.

👉 Tours

★ Sounds of Silence   TOURS
(☑ 08 8957 7448; www.ayersrockresort.com.au/sounds-of-silence; adult/child $195/96) Waiters serve champagne and canapés on a desert dune with stunning sunset views of Uluru and Kata Tjuta. Then it's a buffet dinner (with emu, croc and roo) beneath the southern sky, which, after dinner, is dissected and explained with the help of a telescope. If you're more of a morning person, try the similarly styled Desert Awakenings 4WD Tour (☑ 1300 134 044; www.ayersrockresort.com.au/experiences/detail/desert-awakenings-tour; adult/child $185/145). Neither tour is suitable for children under 10 years.

Uluru Aboriginal Tours   CULTURAL TOUR
(☑ 0447 878 851; www.facebook.com/Uluru-Aboriginal-Tours-248457278623328/; guided tours from $99) Owned and operated by Anangu from the Mutitjulu community, this company offers a range of trips to give you an insight into the significance of Uluru through the eyes of the traditional owners. Tours operate and depart from the cultural centre (p223), as well as from Yulara Ayers Rock Resort (through AAT Kings) and from Alice Springs.

Professional Helicopter Services   SCENIC FLIGHTS
(PHS; ☑ 08 8956 2003; www.phs.com.au; per person 15/30/120min scenic flight $150/285/950) Fabulous aerial views. The 120-minute option is part of a 4½-hour package that takes in Uluru, Kata Tjuta and Kings Canyon, including two hours' flying time.

Ayers Rock Helicopters   SCENIC FLIGHTS
(☑ 08 8956 2077; www.new.helicoptergroup.com/arh-index; 20/40/60min scenic flight per person $115/230/360) One of the most memorable ways to see Uluru; you'll need the 40-minute flight to also take in Kata Tjuta.

Seit Outback Australia   BUS
(☑ 08 8956 3156; www.seitoutbackaustralia.com.au) This small-group tour operator has dozens of Uluru and Kata Tjuta tours, including sunset tours around Uluru and sunrise tours at Kata Tjuta. Food is increasingly a part of what they offer as well.

AAT Kings   BUS
(☑ 08 8956 2171; www.aatkings.com) Operating the largest range of coach tours to Uluru, AAT offers a range of half- and full-day tours from Yulara. Check the website or enquire at the Tour & Information Centre (p222) in Yulara.

Uluru Camel Tours   OUTDOORS
(☑ 08 8956 3333; www.ulurucameltours.com.au) View Uluru and Kata Tjuta from a distance atop a camel ($80, 1½ hours) or take the popular Camel to Sunrise and Sunset tours ($129, 2½ hours).

Uluru Motorcycle Tours   TOURS
(☑ 08 8956 2019; www.ulurucycles.com; rides $119-429) Approach Uluru on a Harley – now that's the way to arrive! Check the website for the many possible tours on offer.

ℹ Information

The park is open from half an hour before sunrise to sunset daily (varying slightly between months; check the website for exact times). Entry permits are valid for three days and are available at the drive-through entry station on the road from Yulara.

Yulara

POP 888

Yulara is the service village for the Uluru-Kata Tjuta National Park and has effectively turned one of the world's least hospitable regions into a comfortable place to stay. Lying just outside the national park, 20km from Uluru and 53km from Kata Tjuta, the complex is the closest base for exploring the park.

◉ Sights

Wintjiri Arts & Museum   GALLERY
(Yulara Dr; ⊘ 8.30am-5pm) A fascinating overview of local natural and cultural history, with plenty of artworks, an artist-in-residence and an excellent small shop. It's just north of reception for the Desert Gardens Hotel.

Mulgara Gallery   GALLERY
(Sails in the Desert Hotel; ⊘ 8.30am-5pm) Wide range of quality, handmade Australian arts and crafts are displayed here, such as textiles, paintings and crafty Indigenous knick-knacks.

⚘ Activities

Uluru Outback Sky Journey   STARGAZING
(☎ 08 8956 2563; Town Sq, Yulara; adult/child $45/free) Takes an informative one-hour look at the startlingly clear outback night sky with a telescope and an astronomer. Tours start at the Yulara Town Sq, 30 minutes after sunset.

✵ Festivals & Events

★ Tjungu Festival   CULTURAL
(www.ayersrockresort.com.au/tjungu; ☺ late Apr) A new festival that runs over four days in late April, hosted at Ayers Rock Resort and celebrating Indigenous culture. Food, art, film and music, plus plenty to keep the kids entertained.

Australian Outback Marathon   SPORTS
(www.australianoutbackmarathon.com; ☺ Jul) Yulara is abuzz in late July when runners converge on Ayers Rock Resort. The route of the outback marathon cuts an impressive path through the heart of Australia's Red Centre, taking in views of Uluru and Kata Tjuta.

⯾ Sleeping

All of the accommodation in Yulara, including the camping ground and hostel, is owned by the Ayers Rock Resort. Even though there are almost 5000 beds, it's wise to make a reservation, especially during school holidays. Substantial discounts are usually offered if you book for more than two or three nights.

**Ayers Rock Resort
Campground**   CAMPGROUND $
(☎ 08 8957 7001; www.ayersrockresort.com.au/arrcamp; off Yulara Dr; powered/unpowered sites $49/40, cabins $174; ✳ @ ⊠) A saviour for the budget conscious, this sprawling camp ground is set among native gardens. There are good facilities including a kiosk, free BBQs, a camp kitchen and a pool. During the peak season it's very busy and the inevitable predawn convoy heading for Uluru can provide an unwanted wake-up call.

Outback Pioneer Hotel & Lodge   HOSTEL $$
(☎ 1300 134 044; www.ayersrockresort.com.au/accommodation/outback-pioneer-hotel; Yulara Dr; dm/d from $42/198; ✳ @ 🖧 ⊠) With a lively bar, barbecue restaurant and musical entertainment, this is the budget choice for noncampers. The cheapest options are the 20-bed YHA unisex dorms and squashy four-bed budget cabins with fridge, TV and shared bathroom. There are also more spacious motel-style rooms that sleep up to four people.

★ Desert Gardens Hotel   HOTEL $$$
(☎ 1300 134 044; Yulara Dr; r $192-480; ✳ 🖧 ⊠) One of Yulara's original hotels, the four-and-a-half-star Desert Gardens is undergoing gradual renovations – the updated rooms have a lovely Scandinavian minimalist look and are supremely comfortable. Some rooms have partial or distant Uluru views. Prices drop considerably, depending on the number of nights you stay.

Sails in the Desert   HOTEL $$$
(☎ 1300 134 044; www.ayersrockresort.com.au/sails; Yulara Dr; superior d from $404; ✳ @ 🖧 ⊠) The rooms seem overpriced at the resort's flagship hotel, but they're still the most upmarket choice in Yulara. There's a lovely pool and surrounding lawn shaded by sails and trees. There are also tennis courts, several restaurants, a health spa and piano bar. The best rooms have balcony views of Uluru – request one when you make a booking.

ULURU WILDLIFE

Birds

Before you go anywhere, download the *Uluru Birds* app to your smartphone or tablet. A fantastic resource, it covers where best to see the flagship species and plays recordings of their call to aid in identification. The park is home to an estimated 178 species.

Mammals

If you come here expecting to see plains filled with kangaroos you'll be disappointed. Perhaps not surprisingly given the numbers of people who visit here, wildlife tends to be fairly shy. Even so, there's a reasonable chance that you'll see red kangaroos on or around the roads through the park, especially close to sunset. Dingoes have proved elusive in recent years, but they occasionally turn up near the sunset-viewing car park close to when the last cars are leaving. For the euro (wallaroo), the Walpa Gorge walk is said to be good early in the morning or late afternoon.

Emu Walk Apartments   APARTMENT $$$

(☎ 1300 134 044; www.ayersrockresort.com.au/emu; Yulara Dr; apt from $258; ❄ 🛜 🗲) The pick of the bunch for families looking for self-contained accommodation, Emu Walk has comfortable, modern apartments, each with a lounge room (with TV) and a well-equipped kitchen with washer and dryer. The one-bedroom apartments accommodate four people, while the two-bedroom version sleeps six.

✗ Eating

Kulata Academy Cafe   CAFE $

(Town Sq, Yulara; light meals $6.50-10; ⊙ 8am-5pm) Run by trainees of Uluru's Indigenous training academy, Kulata is a good place to pick up a coffee in the morning and a light lunch (including pies) later in the day.

Yulara IGA Supermarket   SUPERMARKET $

(Town Sq, Yulara; ⊙ 8am-9pm) This well-stocked supermarket has a delicatessen and sells picnic portions, fresh fruit and vegetables, meat, groceries, ice and camping supplies.

Outback Pioneer Barbecue   BARBECUE $$

(Outback Pioneer Hotel & Lodge; burgers $20, meat $32, salad bar $18; ⊙ 6-9pm) For a fun, casual night out, this lively tavern is the popular choice for everyone from backpackers to grey nomads. Choose between kangaroo skewers, prawns, veggie burgers, steaks and emu sausages, and grill them yourself at the communal BBQs. The deal includes a salad bar.

Geckos Cafe   MEDITERRANEAN $$

(Town Sq, Yulara; mains $19-25; ⊙ noon-2.30pm & 6.30-9pm; 🗲) For great value, a warm atmosphere and tasty food, head to this buzzing licensed cafe. The wood-fired pizzas, pulled pork sliders and kangaroo burgers go well with a carafe of sangria, and the courtyard tables are a great place to enjoy the desert night air. There are several veggie and gluten-free options, plus meals can be made to takeaway.

Ayers Wok Noodle Bar   ASIAN $$

(Town Square, Yulara; stir-fried noodles $16; ⊙ 6-8.30pm) This takeaway-only joint does a reasonable job with stir-fries and is a good change of pace from the hotel restaurants.

Tali Wiru   AUSTRALIAN $$$

(☎ 02-8296 8010; www.ayersrockresort.com.au; per person $325; ⊙ Apr–mid-Oct) One way to combine creature comfort with the ruggedness of the central Australian landscape is the Tali Wiru outdoor dining experience. Organised by the Ayers Rock Resort between April and October, it involves walking to a dune-top 'restaurant' to eat and drink as the sun sets over timeless Uluru.

★ Bough House   AUSTRALIAN $$$

(Outback Pioneer Hotel & Lodge; mains $35-45; ⊙ 6.30-10am & 6.30-9.30pm; 🗲) This family-friendly, country-style place overlooks the pool at the Outback Pioneer. Intimate candlelit dining is strangely set in a barn-like dining room. Bough House specialises in native ingredients such as lemon myrtle, kakadu plums and bush tomatoes. The entree or buffet dessert is free with your main course or you can opt for the whole three courses.

Walpa Lobby Bar   MODERN AUSTRALIAN $$$

(Sails in the Desert; mains $35; ⊙ 11am-10pm) if you want to treat yourself, this is the place to try. With a recent makeover, and the feel of a Hilton Hotel bar, the excellent food and friendly service make up for the slight sterility. Hot and cold seafood platters are a treat and most dishes feature Australian bush ingredients. Salads and antipasto are also available.

🔒 Shopping

Newsagency   BOOKS

(⊙ 8.30am-8pm) Excellent newsagents with magazines, a wide range of books with outback Australian themes and good maps.

ℹ Information

Visitor Information Centre (☎ 08 8957 7377; Town Square, Yulara; ⊙ 8.30am-4.30pm)

SUNRISE & SUNSET VIEWING AREAS

About halfway between Yulara and Uluru, the sunset viewing area has plenty of car and coach parking for that familiar postcard view. The Talinguru Nyakunytjaku sunrise viewing area is perched on a sand dune and captures both Uluru and Kata Tjuta in all their glory. It also has two great interpretive walks (1.5km) about women's and men's business. There's a shaded viewing area, toilets and a place to picnic. There also the sand-dune viewpoint for a panoramic view of Kata Tjuta.

Yulara (Ayers Rock Resort)

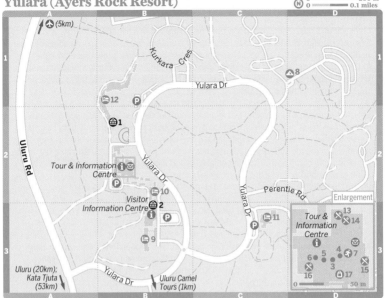

Yulara (Ayers Rock Resort)

◎ Sights
1 Mulgara Gallery B2
2 Wintjiri Arts & Museum B3

⊕ Activities, Courses & Tours
3 AAT Kings D3
4 Ayers Rock Helicopters D3
5 Professional Helicopter Services D3
6 Seit Outback Australia D3
7 Uluru Outback Sky Journey D3

⊜ Sleeping
8 Ayers Rock Resort Campground D1
9 Desert Gardens Hotel B3
10 Emu Walk Apartments B2

11 Outback Pioneer Hotel &
   Lodge C3
12 Sails in the Desert B1

⊗ Eating
13 Ayers Wok Noodle Bar D3
   Bough House .... (see 11)
14 Geckos Cafe D3
15 Kulata Academy Cafe D3
   Outback Pioneer Barbecue .... (see 11)
   Walpa Lobby Bar .... (see 12)
16 Yulara IGA Supermarket D3

⊜ Shopping
17 Newsagency D3

Contains displays on the geography, wildlife and history of the region. There's a short audio tour ($2) if you want to learn more. It also sells books and regional maps.

Post Office (☑ 08 8956 2288; Resort Shopping Centre; ☺ 9am-5pm Mon-Fri, 9am-noon Sat) An agent for the Commonwealth and NAB banks. Pay phones are outside.

Royal Flying Doctor Service Medical Centre (☑ 08 8956 2286; Yulara Dr; ☺ 9am-noon & 2-5pm Mon-Fri, 10-11am Sat & Sun) The resort's medical centre and ambulance service.

ANZ bank (☑ 08 8956 2070; ☺ 10am-noon & 12.30-3pm Mon-Thu, 10am-noon & 12.30-4pm Fri) Currency exchange and 24-hour ATMs.

❶ Getting There & Away

Yulara is the gateway to the park and has an airport with flights from major Australian cities. There are also buses and tours from Alice Springs. If you're driving, the sealed route from Alice Springs (447km) is via the Stuart and then Lasseter Hwys.

AIR

Yulara's **Connellan Airport** (☑ 08 8956 2266), serviced by a number of **Qantas** (☑ 13 13 13; www.qantas.com.au), **Virgin Australia** (☑ 13 67 89; www.virginaustralia.com) and **Jetstar** (www.jetstar.com) flights, is about 4km north from Yulara.

CLIMBING ULURU

Many visitors consider climbing Uluru to be a highlight of a trip to the Centre, and even a rite of passage. But for the traditional owners, the Anangu, Uluru is a sacred place. The path up the side of Uluru is part of the route taken by the Mala ancestors on their arrival at Uluru and has great spiritual significance – and is not to be trampled by human feet. When you arrive at Uluru you'll see a sign from the Anangu saying 'We don't climb', and a request that you don't climb either.

The Anangu are the custodians of Uluru and take responsibility for the safety of visitors. Any injuries or deaths that occur are a source of distress and sadness to them. For similar reasons of public safety, Parks Australia would prefer that people didn't climb. It's a very steep ascent, not to be taken lightly, and each year there are several air rescues, mostly from people suffering heart attacks. Furthermore, Parks Australia must constantly monitor the climb and close it on days where the temperature is forecast to reach 36°C or over, and when strong winds are expected.

So if the Anangu and Parks Australia don't want people to climb Uluru, why does the climb remain open? The answer is tourism. The tourism industry believes visitor numbers would drop significantly – at least initially – if the climb was closed, particularly among those who think there is nothing else to do at Uluru.

A commitment has been made to close the climb for good, but only when there are adequate new visitor experiences in place or when the proportion of visitors climbing falls below 20%. Until then, it remains a personal decision and a question of respect. Before deciding, visit the Uluru-Kata Tjuta Cultural Centre and perhaps take an Anangu guided tour (p218).

BUS
Emu Run (p202) runs cheap daily connections between Alice Springs and Yulara (one way adult/child $135/80).

CAR & MOTORCYCLE
One route from Alice to Yulara is sealed all the way, with regular food and petrol stops. It's 200km from Alice to Erldunda on the Stuart Hwy, where you turn west for the 245km journey along the Lasseter Hwy. The journey takes four to five hours.

There's also a much longer route that requires a 4WD and goes via Hermannsburg and Kings Canyon.

Renting a car in Alice Springs to go to Uluru and back is an excellent way to see a little of the country en route if you have the time.

ⓘ Getting Around
A free shuttle bus meets all flights (pick-up is 90 minutes before your flight) and drops off at all accommodation points around the resort. Another free shuttle bus loops through the resort – stopping at all accommodation points and the shopping centre – every 15 minutes from 10.30am to 6pm and from 6.30pm to 12.30am daily.
Uluru Express (☑ 08 8956 2152; www. uluruexpress.com.au; adult/child $45/15) falls somewhere between a shuttle-bus service and an organised tour. It provides return transport

from the resort to Uluru and Kata Tjuta – see website for details.

Hiring a car will give you the flexibility to visit Uluru and Kata Tjuta whenever you want. Car-rental offices are at the **Tour & Information Centre** (☑ 08 8957 7324; Resort Shopping Centre; ⊘ 8am-7pm) and **Connellan Airport** (p221).

Uluru (Ayers Rock)

The first sight of Uluru on the horizon will astound even the most jaded traveller. Uluru is 3.6km long and rises a towering 348m from the surrounding sandy scrubland (867m above sea level). If that's not impressive enough, it's believed that two-thirds of the rock lies beneath the sand. Closer inspection reveals a wondrous contoured surface concealing numerous sacred sites of particular significance to the Anangu. If your first sight of Uluru is during the afternoon, it appears as an ochre-brown colour, scored and pitted by dark shadows. As the sun sets, it illuminates the rock in burnished orange, then a series of deeper reds before it fades into charcoal. A performance in reverse, with marginally fewer spectators, is given at dawn.

⊙ Sights

Uluru-Kata Tjuta Cultural Centre (☑ 08 8956 1128; www.parksaustralia.gov.au/uluru/do/cultural-centre.html; ⊙ 7am-6pm) is 1km before Uluru on the road from Yulara and should be your first stop. Displays and exhibits focus on *tjukurpa* (Aboriginal law, religion and custom) and the history and management of the national park. The information desk in the Nintiringkupai building is staffed by park rangers who supply the informative *Visitor Guide,* leaflets and walking notes.

Walkatjara Art Centre (☑ 08 8956 2537; ⊙ 9am-5.30pm) is a working art centre owned by the local Mutitjulu community. It focuses on paintings and ceramics created by women from Mutitjulu.

🏃 Activities

Walking

There are walking tracks around Uluru, and ranger-led walks explain the area's plants, wildlife, geology and cultural significance. All the trails are flat and suitable for wheelchairs. Several areas of spiritual significance are off limits to visitors; these are marked with fences and signs. The Anangu ask you not to photograph these sites.

The excellent *Visitor Guide & Maps* brochure, which can be picked up at the Cultural Centre, gives details on a few self-guided walks.

Base Walk   WALKING
This track (10.6km, three to four hours) circumnavigates the rock, passing caves, paintings, sandstone folds and geological abrasions along the way.

Kuniya Walk   WALKING
A short walk (1km return, 45 minutes) from the car park on the southern side leads to the most permanent waterhole, Mutitjulu, home of the ancestral water snake. Great birdwatching and some excellent rock art are highlights of this walk.

Liru Walk   WALKING
Links the Cultural Centre with the start of the Mala walk and climb, and winds through strands of mulga before opening up near Uluru (4km return, 1½ hours).

Mala Walk   WALKING
From the base of the climbing point (2km return, one hour), interpretive signs explain the *tjukurpa* (Aboriginal law, religion and custom) of the Mala (hare-wallaby people), which is significant to the Anangu. There are also fine examples of rock art. A ranger-guided walk (free) along this route

ULURU & OUTBACK NORTHERN TERRITORY ULURU (AYERS ROCK)

Uluru (Ayers Rock)

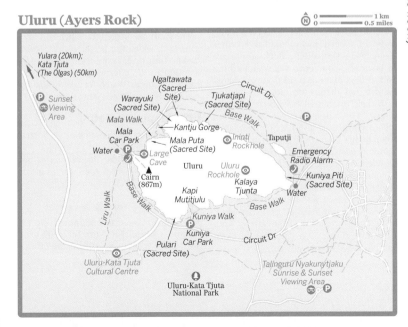

departs at 10am (8am from October to April) from the car park.

Cycling

Bike Hire at Uluru   CYCLING

(☎ 0437 917 018; outbackcycling.com/uluru; 3hr hire adult/child $45/30; ☺ Feb-Nov) Adult and kids' bikes as well as toddler seats and tag-alongs for hire to ride around the base of Uluru. It's a terrific way to experience Uluru, especially if you want to do so a bit quicker than on foot.

🛏 Sleeping & Eating

The only places to stay close to Uluru are at Yulara, around 20km away, with all accommodation run by Ayers Rock Resort.

The only places to eat inside the park are the kiosk/cafe at the Uluru-Kata Tjuta Cultural Centre or the numerous wonderful places for a picnic (bring your own food). Otherwise, there are plenty of restaurants and a good supermarket at Yulara.

ℹ Getting There & Away

It's around 20km from Uluru to Yulara and 51km to Kata Tjuta. Unless you're here on a tour, or take the Uluru Express, you'll need your own wheels.

Kata Tjuta (The Olgas)

No journey to Uluru is complete without a visit to Kata Tjuta (the Olgas), a striking group of domed rocks huddled together about 35km west of the Rock. There are 36 boulders shoulder to shoulder forming deep valleys and steep-sided gorges. Many visitors find them even more captivating than their prominent neighbour, but why choose? The tallest rock, Mt Olga (546m, 1066m above sea level) is approximately 200m higher than Uluru. Kata Tjuta means 'many heads' and is of great *tjukurpa* significance (relating to Aboriginal law, religion and custom), particularly for Indigenous men, so stick to the tracks.

There's a picnic and sunset-viewing area with toilet facilities just off the access road, a few kilometres west of the base of Kata Tjuta. Like Uluru, Kata Tjuta is at its glorious, blood-red best at sunset.

Kata Tjuta (The Olgas)

🏃 Activities

The 7.4km **Valley of the Winds** loop (two to four hours) is one of the most challenging and rewarding bushwalks in the park. It winds through the gorges giving excellent views of the surreal domes and traversing varied terrain. It's not particularly arduous, but wear sturdy shoes and take plenty of water. Starting this walk at first light often rewards you with solitude, enabling you to appreciate the sounds of the wind and bird calls carried up the valley. When the weather gets too hot, trail access is often closed by late morning.

The short signposted track beneath towering rock walls into pretty **Walpa Gorge** (2.6km return, 45 minutes) is especially beautiful in the afternoon, when sunlight floods the gorge. Watch for rock wallabies in the early morning or late afternoon.

🛏 Sleeping & Eating

The nearest accommodation is at Yulara, 53km away.

There are, of course, no restaurants out here. Bring your own food for a picnic lunch or head to Yulara.

ℹ Getting There & Away

Unless you're here on a tour, you'll need your own wheels to reach Kata Tjuta. The road is paved all the way from Uluru (51km) and Yulara (53km).

Understand South Australia & Northern Territory

South Australia & Northern Territory Today

If Australia is agonising over its relationship between Indigenous Australians and the rest of the country, they're old hands at it in outback Australia where questions of self-determination and land rights are anything but abstract issues. The not-unrelated issue of the treatment of prisoners in youth detention centres brought down a government and ushered in a new political landscape, while natural resources and the question of a treaty sit front and centre in South Australia.

Best on Film

Samson & Delilah (2009) A devastating portrait of life in a remote outback Indigenous community.

Storm Boy (1976) A young boy, his dad and a pelican living in the Coorong.

Crocodile Dundee I & II (1986/88) Outback Australia hits the cinematic jackpot.

Utopia (2013) John Pilger documentary tracing life in the remote central Australian community of Utopia.

Another Country (2015) Renowned actor David Gulpilil takes you on an arresting visit to his remote Arnhem Land community.

Best in Print

Adelaide (Kerryn Goldsworthy; 2011) Eccentric, personal biography of Adelaide that brings the city alive.

The Dog Fence (James Woodford; 2004) A modern-day crossing of the outback from SA's north.

An Intruder's Guide to East Arnhem Land (Andrew McMillan; 2001) Arguably the NT's best history book.

The Red Highway (Nicolas Rothwell; 2009) A lyrical exploration of Australia's interior.

King Brown Country (Russell Skelton; 2010) Searing exposé of the mismanagement of a remote Aboriginal community.

Dark Emu (Bruce Pascoe; 2014) A rewriting of the history of Aboriginal Australia.

The Northern Territory's Shame

In July 2016 Australia's national broadcaster, the ABC, aired an investigative report into the treatment of youth detainees in the Northern Territory's prisons on its *Four Corners* program. The appalling footage prompted outrage across the country and shone an uncomfortably bright spotlight upon issues – including that of Indigenous people making up a disproportionate number of prisoners in the NT's jails – that never seem to be resolved. In the fallout from the program, Australia's federal government launched a royal commission of inquiry into youth detention practices in the NT. The revelations also led to a stunning electoral turnaround a month after the program was aired, a turnaround that saw the ruling conservative Country Liberal Party reduced to a rump of just two seats in the 25-seat NT parliament. The Labor Party was swept to power with 18 seats (five seats were won by independents) and its leader Michael Gunner became chief minister.

Questions of Governance

Nowhere in Australia does policy towards Aboriginal Australians mean quite so much as it does here. Indigenous communities are now recognised as the owners of roughly half of the NT, and some communities have negotiated lucrative royalty deals with mining companies working on their traditional lands. But many Aboriginal communities remain in crisis – poorly governed and beset with problems of alcohol and substance abuse, high crime levels and the concomitant high levels of incarceration.

This is by no means universal – many Aboriginal communities are winning the struggle to balance the demands of the modern and traditional world views. Governments trying to 'solve the problem' have not helped, from the patronising paternalism of the 1960s to the free-wheeling self-determination policies ushered in by the Whitlam government in the 1970s. The pendulum of government policy may have swung back with the 2007 Northern Territory National Emergency Response (aka 'The Intervention'), but as a country, it seems, Australia is no closer to moving towards reconciliation with Aboriginal Australians in the 21st century.

Treaty?

With Australia's federal government dragging its feet on the question of a treaty with Indigenous Australians, some of the states have taken up the mantle. South Australia has long been known as one of the most progressive corners of Australia – it was here that Australian women were first allowed to vote – so it should scarcely be surprising that they are leading the way. In 2016 the South Australian government began formal negotiations with the state's Indigenous leaders, declaring them to be open-ended; compensation, one of the more controversial issues, is part of a process that the government has implemented, with the Stolen Generations Reparations Scheme closing its first funding round in March 2017. Other issues expected to form part of the conversation include giving Aboriginal people a voice in policy on issues relating to Indigenous Australians and the form of wording used in the treaty to recognise past wrongs.

Murray River Flows

The mighty Murray River, Australia's version of the Mississippi, is flowing freely again after years of salination and habitat degradation, but it continues to play an important role in Australian political debates on the country's environmental future. River-land irrigators, lower-lakes farmers and environmentalists – each with their own agendas – remain locked in ongoing battles with the Murray-Darling Basin Authority, state and federal governments over water allocations within SA and upstream. In the aftermath of the 2016 federal election, senators from SA used the question of the Murray-Darling waters as a bargaining chip in their negotiations over whether or not to allow government legislation to pass. In the meantime, the South Australian state government remained sufficiently unsure of reliable water flows from Australia's longest river that it finally opened the $1.83-billion Adelaide Desalination Plant south of the city, commissioned at the height of the drought in 2007. Just in case.

POPULATION: **1.92 MILLION**

AREA: **2,332,611 SQ KM**

GDP: **$120.9 BILLION**

GDP GROWTH: **3.13%**

UNEMPLOYMENT:
NT 4%, SA 6.4%

POPULATION GROWTH:
NT 0.22%, SA 0.55%

if Central Australia were 100 people

94 would be non-Indigenous
6 would be Indigenous

where people live
(% of population)

65	7	2
Adelaide	Darwin	Alice Springs
1	1	24
Mt Gambier	Whyalla	other

population per sq km

NT   SA   AUSTRALIA

⬤ ≈ 1 person

History

In many ways, the history of central Australia, from civilised Adelaide to frontier Darwin, is a distillation of a broader Australian history. Far-reaching Indigenous heritage collides with European ambitions, settlements rise and fall, resources and politics intertwine... Presiding over it all, the harsh environment has proved an indomitable force.

Aboriginal Settlement

For a timely account of central Australian Indigenous history, check out the ABC TV series *First Footprints* (2013; www.abc.net.au/tv/firstfootprints) and the accompanying book by Scott Cane. Alternatively, try the SBS TV series *First Australians* (2008; www.sbs.com.au/firstaustralians) and the companion book, edited by Rachel Perkins and Marcia Langton.

Human contact with Australia began around 60,000 years ago, when Aboriginal people journeyed across the straits from what is now Indonesia and Papua New Guinea – the beginning of the world's longest continuous cultural history.

Within a few thousand years, Aboriginal people populated much of Australia. In South Australia, the earliest known Aboriginal relics are rock carvings near Olary, dated at 43,000 years – around the same era as the paintings in the Cave of El Castillo in northern Spain. In Kakadu National Park in the Northern Territory, the oldest rock-art sites date back 20,000 years; further east in Arnhem Land, evidence suggests that rock art was being produced as far back as 60,000 years ago. Central Australia was occupied about 24,000 years ago.

Aboriginal peoples traded goods, items of spiritual significance, songs and dances, using routes that followed the paths of ancestors from the Dreaming, the complex system of country, culture and beliefs that defines Indigenous spirituality. An intimate understanding of plant ecology and animal behaviour ensured that food shortages were rare. Even central Australia's hostile deserts were occupied year-round, thanks to scattered permanent wells. Fire-stick farming was practised in forested areas to the south and north of the deserts, involving the burning of undergrowth and dead grass to encourage new growth, to attract game and reduce the threat of bushfires.

Early Contact

The Chinese eunuch Admiral Cheng Ho (Zheng He) may have been the first non-Aboriginal visitor to northern Australia. He reached Timor in

TIMELINE	60,000 BC	AD 1627	1836
	Experts believe Aboriginal people settled in Australia around this time. Evidence suggests the oldest rock-art sites in the NT are 60,000 years old; those in SA date from 43,000 years.	Dutch captain Francois Thijssen, aboard the *Gulden Zeepaard*, is the first European to spy the coast of SA. The French follow in the 1700s, the British in the 1800s.	The Province of South Australia is proclaimed. The first official colonial settlement at Kingscote on Kangaroo Island is soon replaced by Adelaide, on the advice of Colonel William Light.

the 15th century, and some suggest he also made it to Australia. In 1879 a small, carved figure of the Chinese god Shao Lao was found lodged in the roots of a banyan tree in Darwin. That's the clincher, the pro-Zheng camp says: the carving apparently dates from the Ming dynasty (1368–1644).

There's evidence to suggest that the Portuguese were the first Europeans to sight Australia's northern coast, sometime during the 16th century, followed promptly by the Dutch. Famed Dutch navigator Abel Tasman charted the north coast, from Cape York to the Kimberley in Western Australia, in 1664.

Other 17th-century visitors to the north were Macassan traders from the island of Celebes (today's Sulawesi in Indonesia), who set up seasonal camps to gather trepang (sea cucumber). Interracial relationships were common, with some local Aboriginal people journeying to Celebes to live.

Down south, the Dutch ship *Gulden Zeepaard* made the first European sighting of the South Australian coast in 1627. The French ships *Recherche* and *L'Esperance* followed in 1792, while the first British explorer on the scene was Lieutenant James Grant in 1800. In 1802 Englishman Matthew Flinders charted Fowlers Bay, Spencer and St Vincent Gulfs and Kangaroo Island on his ship the *Investigator*.

The Explorers (1998), by Tim Flannery, brings together excerpts from the writings of explorers across Australia, including numerous journeys through outback Australia.

HISTORY EUROPEAN COLONISATION

European Colonisation

In 1829 Captain Charles Sturt headed inland from Sydney and fell into the Murray River, floating downstream to Lake Alexandrina. His glowing reports inspired the National Colonisation Society to propose a utopian, self-supporting South Australian colony founded on planned immigration with land sales, rather than convict-based grants. The British Parliament then passed the *South Australian Colonisation Act* in 1834, making SA the only Australian colony established entirely by free colonists (a distinction most South Australians happily highlight).

The first official settlement was established in 1836 at Kingscote on Kangaroo Island, before colonial Surveyor-General Colonel William Light chose Adelaide as the site for the capital. The first Governor,

DINNER ON KANGAROO ISLAND

British explorer Matthew Flinders bumped into Kangaroo Island on 2 March 1802. His crew of hungry sailors stormed ashore in search of sustenance – their eyes boggled at the thousands of kangaroos bouncing around on the beach. Flinders described the inevitable feeding frenzy in his journal: 'The whole ship's company was employed this afternoon in the skinning and cleaning of kangaroos. After four months' privation they stewed half a hundredweight of heads, forequarters and tails down into soup for dinner … In gratitude for so seasonable a supply, I named this south land 'Kangaroo Island'.'

1862	1869	1894	1901
John McDouall Stuart makes the first south–north crossing of the continent from SA into the NT, the highlight of his many epic explorations.	After three other NT colonies all fail to take hold, Palmerston (renamed Darwin in 1911) is established by George Goyder, SA's Surveyor-General.	South Australian women are the first in Australia permitted to vote, and the first in the world eligible to stand for parliament.	With the federation of the disparate Australian colonies, SA becomes a state of the Commonwealth of Australia.

Captain John Hindmarsh, landed at present-day Glenelg on 28 December 1836, and proclaimed the Province of South Australia.

In the NT, early European attempts at settlement – on Melville Island in 1824, Raffles Bay in 1829 and the Cobourg Peninsula in 1838 – all failed in the face of Indigenous resistance, disease and climate, until the settlement of Palmerston (renamed Darwin in 1911) was established in 1869.

Conflict marked the arrival of European cattle farmers across central Australia. The Arrernte (*uh*-rahn-da) people defended their lands and spiritual heritage, spearing cattle for food as farmers had destroyed many of their hunting grounds. In return, those waterholes not already ruined by cattle were poisoned, and reprisal raids saw many massacres.

Dark Emu (2014), by Bruce Pascoe, draws on the accounts of early explorers to argue for a reassessment of precolonial Aboriginal society, arguing that it was much more sophisticated than has hitherto been recognised.

Immigration & Second-Wave Explorations

The first immigrants to SA were poor, young English, Scots and Irish. About 12,000 landed in the first four years of settlement, followed by 800 German farmers and artisans between 1838 and 1841 – mainly Lutherans fleeing religious persecution. Around 5400 more Germans arrived by 1850; many more followed during the next decade. They settled mainly in the Adelaide Hills and the Barossa Valley, their vineyards forming the beginning of the SA wine industry. Thousands of Cornish people also arrived following the discovery of copper in the 1840s, many of them jumping ship to Victoria in the 1850s when gold was discovered there.

In the NT, the discovery of gold and copper south of Darwin (then Palmerston) attracted miners, and settlers with cattle moved into the area from SA and northern Queensland. In 1877 the first Lutheran mission was established at Hermannsburg; Catholic and Methodist missions followed elsewhere.

Successive waves of immigration fuelled the search for new arable land. Between 1839 and 1841, Edward John Eyre made the first traverse of the Flinders Ranges in SA. In 1839, Charles Bonney drove the first herd of cattle from Melbourne to Adelaide via Mt Gambier.

THE LONG WALK TO BALLARAT

On South Australia's Limestone Coast, Robe set up shop as a fishing port in 1846 – one of SA's earliest settlements. During the 1850s gold rush in Victoria, Robe came into its own when the Victorian government whacked a $10-per-head tax on Chinese gold miners arriving to work the goldfields. Thousands of Chinese miners dodged the tax by landing at Robe in SA, then walking the 400-odd kilometres to Bendigo and Ballarat; 10,000 arrived in 1857 alone. But the flood stalled as quickly as it started when the SA government instituted its own tax on the Chinese. The Chinamen's Wells along their route (including one in the Coorong) can still be seen today.

1942	1974	1978	1980
Darwin is bombed by the Japanese during WWII – 243 people lose their lives in 64 raids. A mass exodus cripples the Top End economy.	Cyclone Tracy tears through Darwin on Christmas Eve, demolishing 70% of the city's buildings and killing 71 people. Much of the city was rebuilt (more strongly) within four years.	The NT is granted legislative self-government, but remains under the constitutional auspices of the federal government (and does to this day).	The rickety, wash-out-prone old *Ghan* railway line through the Flinders Ranges and Oodnadatta is replaced by new, more reliable standardgauge line 160km further west.

Five years later, Charles Sturt set off from Adelaide towing a whale-boat to find the mythical central Australian inland sea, but after 18 months of hardship he abandoned it in a waterless red expanse of stones and sandhills. If nothing else, he had discovered the Simpson Desert.

In 1844 Prussian scientist Ludwig Leichhardt set off from Queensland to blaze an overland route into the NT. The party reached the Gulf of Carpentaria and headed northwest. Leichhardt was afforded hero status for his efforts, but his route was too difficult for regular use and no promising grazing areas were discovered.

The hard-drinking John McDouall Stuart made several epic forays into central Australia between 1858 and 1862. His successful south-north crossing of the continent led to SA wresting governmental control of the NT from New South Wales in 1863. The Stuart Hwy, from Port Augusta in SA to Darwin, is named in his honour.

Wheat, Sheep, Copper & Gold

By 1865 SA was growing half of Australia's wheat. Overcropping in the Adelaide Hills and Fleurieu Peninsula led to more land being opened up in the Mid-North and Flinders Ranges. A 'wheat boom' ensued. Enthusiastic trumpeting of 'a rich golden harvest' extending into the NT continued until drought struck in the mid-1880s.

Sheep farmers also helped to open up SA, but a tendency to overestimate carrying capacity led to overstocking, and with no pasture kept in reserve, the 1880s drought ruined many. The SA breeders survived by developing a strain of merino sheep suited to semiarid conditions.

By the 1870s, SA had replaced Cornwall as the British Empire's leading copper producer, making many South Australians wealthy and leaving a legacy of fine public buildings in mining towns such as Burra.

The NT was opened up with the discovery of gold at Yam Creek, 160km south of Darwin. The find fired up local prospectors, and it wasn't long before other discoveries at Pine Creek, south of Darwin, sparked a minor rush. The South Australian government built a railway line in 1883 from Darwin to Pine Creek, but the gold rush was soon over. Subsequent government-backed NT projects such as sugar, tobacco and coffee plantations, peanut farming, pearling and crocodile- and snake-skin trading either failed completely or provided only minimal returns.

Finding Federation

When parliament sprang up in 1856, SA began with the most democratic constitution of any colony. Before that it was governed by representatives from the SA Board of Commissioners and the British government.

Fighting off recession, SA's transport and communications systems grew rigorously. By 1890 railways connected Adelaide with

The History Trust of South Australia website (www.history. sa.gov.au) is a rich resource, with links to the Migration Museum, the National Motor Museum and SA's Maritime Museum.

Adelaide's King William St is 40m wide – the broadest Australian capital-city thoroughfare. It was once famed for its mud; picking up a stray hat would likely reveal someone underneath (and possibly a horse below them!).

1982	1986	1998	1998
Lindy Chamberlain is jailed for the murder of her baby daughter Azaria, who was taken by a dingo at Uluru in 1980. She is finally exonerated in 2012.	Paul Hogan stars as Mick 'Crocodile' Dundee and launches Kakadu National Park (in the NT's Top End) onto the world cinematic stage.	The NT narrowly returns a negative result in a referendum on whether it should become a state rather than federally administered territory. The result surprises many.	Ross Fargher stubs his toe on the world's oldest vertebrate fossil on his Flinders Ranges property in SA. At 560 million years old, it beats the previous oldest find by 30 million years.

Melbourne, Oodnadatta in the outback, and Cockburn on SA's border with NSW. There were also 3200km of sealed roads and 100-plus steamboats trading on the Murray River. The South Australian parliament established Australia's first juvenile court in 1890, and granted free education in 1891. In 1894 SA became the first Australian colony to recognise women's right to vote in parliamentary elections, and the first place in the world to allow women to stand for parliament.

With federation in 1901 – the amalgamation of disparate colonies into the states of the Commonwealth of Australia – SA experienced slow but steady growth, but South Australian speculators and investors in the NT were getting cold feet. Soon after federation the South Australian government threw in the towel, offering control of the ugly NT duckling back to the federal government.

Twentieth-Century Trials

After federation, manufacturing and heavy engineering became important in SA. The Port Pirie smelter was enlarged during WWI, and was soon producing 10% of the world's lead, as well as silver and zinc.

WWI was a time of division in SA. Before 1914 the state had many German place names, but in a fit of anti-German zeal many of these were replaced. Most were reinstated during the 1936 centennial celebrations, when the German settlers' huge contribution to SA's development was officially recognised.

The early 1920s brought prosperity across Australia, before a four-year drought led into the Great Depression. All states suffered during this period, but SA fared worst of all: in 1931 more than 70,000 people out of a population of 575,000 were dependent on welfare.

Industrial development in SA quickened during WWII – water-pipeline construction, ship building and coal mining all took off – but people in the NT had more pressing issues to contend with. At 9.57am on 19 February 1942, nearly 200 Japanese aircraft bombed Darwin's harbour and the RAAF base at Larrakeyah. Darwin was attacked 64 times during the war and 243 people lost their lives; it was the only place in Australia to suffer prolonged attacks. In March 1942 the entire NT north of Alice Springs was placed under military control and by December there were 32,000 troops stationed in the Top End.

After WWII, the Australian government launched an ambitious scheme to attract immigrants. Thousands of people from Britain, Greece, Italy, Serbia, Croatia, the Netherlands, Poland, Turkey, Malta and Lebanon took up the offer of government-assisted passage. The immigration boom fuelled growth in SA, which shifted from a rural economy to a predominantly industrial one. In the NT, the urban areas of Darwin and Alice Springs also grew.

The Australian Museum's Indigenous Australia website (australianmuseum.net.au/indigenous-australia) is chock-full of historical and cultural information, plus Dreaming stories, an Indigenous glossary and insights into Aboriginal spiritual values.

I Saw a Strange Land (1950), by Arthur Groom, is a classic memoir of Groom's mid-20th-century camel expedition through the heart of Australia in the company of Indigenous guides.

2000	2001	2004	2007
Mandatory-sentencing laws and zero-tolerance policing in the NT increase the jailing of Aboriginal people for trivial offences, causing national outrage. The laws are repealed in 2001.	The federal government incarcerates asylum seekers at the Baxter Detention Centre in SA's outback. Some Adelaidians display signs 'Asylum seekers welcome here' in their windows; others go to jail for protesting.	After a 70-year wait, the *Ghan* passenger train runs from Adelaide to Darwin, finally linking the Top End with the southern states.	Causing general public outrage, the NT government introduces speed limits of 130km/h on the Stuart, Victoria, Arnhem and Barkly Hwys.

LAND RIGHTS IN THE NORTHERN TERRITORY

Britain colonised Australia on the legal principle of 'terra nullius', meaning the country was unoccupied. While patently not true, this legal fiction ensured that early colonists could take land from Aboriginal peoples without signing treaties or providing compensation. This principle remained legally potent until the landmark Mabo High Court decision in 1992, which voided the presumption of terra nullius and officially recognised native title as a traditional connection to or occupation of Australian lands.

Preceding the Mabo decision, in 1966 the South Australian government made the first move of any Australian state to give Aboriginal peoples title to their land. The Aboriginal Lands Trust was created, vesting title to the missions and reserves still operating in SA. These lands are leased back to their Aboriginal occupants, who have repeated rights of renewal. The South Australian parliament then passed two pieces of legislation, the *Prohibition of Discrimination Act* and the *Aboriginal Affairs Act*, giving South Australian Aboriginal peoples the right to run their own communities.

In 1981 the *Pitjantjatjara Land Rights Act* came into effect, granting freehold title over a vast area of northwest SA to the Anangu-Pitjantjatjara. A further 76,000 sq km, occupied by the federal government as part of the Maralinga project, was returned to its traditional owners in 1984. Land held under Aboriginal freehold title cannot be sold or taken back into public ownership, and no development of any kind can take place without the permission of traditional owners.

A more convoluted land-rights path has been navigated in the NT. In 1962 a bark petition was presented to the federal government by the Yolngu peoples of Yirrakala, in northeast Arnhem Land, demanding the government recognise Aboriginal peoples' occupation and ownership of Australia since time immemorial. The petition was ignored, so the Yolngu peoples took the matter to court – and lost.

But the wheels had begun to turn, and under increasing pressure the federal government passed the *Aboriginal Land Rights (Northern Territory) Act* in 1976, establishing three Aboriginal land councils empowered to claim land on behalf of traditional owners.

Under the act, the only claimable land is crown land outside town boundaries that no one else owns or leases – usually semidesert or desert. So when the Anangu, Uluru's traditional owners, claimed ownership of Uluru and Kata Tjuta, their claim was overruled because the land was within a national park. It was only by amending two acts of parliament that Uluru-Kata Tjuta National Park was handed back to its traditional owners, providing it was leased back to the federal government as a national park.

Around half of the NT has been claimed, or is under claim. The native-title process is tedious and can take years to complete, often without success. Many claims are opposed by state and territory governments, and claimants are required to prove they have continuous connection to the land and are responsible for sacred sites under Aboriginal law. If a claim is successful, Aboriginal peoples have the right to negotiate with mining interests and ultimately accept or reject exploration and mining proposals. This right is often opposed by Australia's mining lobby, despite traditional Aboriginal owners in the NT rejecting only about a third of such proposals outright.

2007 The federal government's 'Intervention' policy in NT Indigenous communities causes controversy in both black and white communities.

2011 Cyclone Yasi and monumental rainfalls across Qld and NSW bring relief to the drought-stricken Murray River in SA.

2012 Coroner deems that a dingo did in fact kill baby Azaria Chamberlain at Uluru in 1980. Lindy Chamberlain states, 'We live in a beautiful country but it is dangerous.'

2012 The NT elects a new conservative Country Liberal Party (CLP) government. Incoming Chief Minister Terry Mills is thirsty: 'It's waiting in the fridge...so I'm going to finish [his victory speech] shortly.'

The 1960s and '70s were difficult times in SA: economic and population growth were stagnating, and overseas competition heightened a deepening industrial recession. Socially, however, South Australian premier Don Dunstan's progressive Labor government was kicking goals, passing an act prohibiting racial discrimination (the first in Australia), and creating the South Australian Film Corporation (1972).

The NT was also ailing economically, and the good citizens of Darwin were soon brought to their knees once more. On Christmas Eve 1974, Cyclone Tracy ripped through the city, killing 65 people and destroying more than 70% of Darwin's buildings.

From the late '70s into the 1990s, mining dug a tunnel to economic recovery. In SA, huge deposits of uranium, copper, silver and gold were found at Roxby Downs, plus oil and gas in the Cooper Basin. In the NT, copper and gold were unearthed at Tennant Creek, and oil and gas in the Amadeus basin. Bauxite was found at Gove, manganese at Groote Eylandt, and uranium at Batchelor and (more controversially) Kakadu.

In the aftermath of Cyclone Tracy in 1974, an exodus saw Darwin's population fall from 45,000 to just 11,000. These days it's bounced back to around 135,000.

In 1996 the NT government became the first in the world to legalise voluntary euthanasia. Although the legislation was soon overturned by the federal government, by then three people had voluntarily died.

These Days

Today, mining continues to drive the economies of SA and the NT (and Australia as a nation), but tourism is the big success story in central Australia. SA has an extremely well-oiled governing tourist body extolling the virtues of the state's diverse regions. In the NT, the tourist magnets of Uluru and Kakadu each receive more than half a million visitors per year. At the end of WWII the population of Alice Springs (Uluru's main access point) was around 1000; today it's approaching 30,000 – a direct result of selling the central Australian outback as 'the real-deal Aussie experience'. The rise in environmental awareness and ecotourism has also boosted Kakadu's popularity.

2014	2016	2016	2016
After 12 years in power, Labor narrowly wins a fourth term in office in elections in SA. Independents hold the balance of power.	The ABC's *Four Corners* program broadcasts an explosive report on conditions inside the NT's youth detention system, causing outrage across the country. The federal government announces a royal commission.	Elections called after the *Four Corners* report result in the worst outcome for a sitting government in NT history – Labor wins power with 18 seats, while the conservative CLP (who governed for four years) wins just two seats.	Unseasonal heavy rains in the Red Centre cause the temporary closure of Uluru-Kata Tjuta National Park, while outback communities such as a Kintore and Kiwikurra are cut off by floods.

Aboriginal Australia

Aboriginal and Torres Strait Islander culture has evolved over thousands of years with strong links between the spiritual, economic and social lives of the people. This heritage has been kept alive from one generation to the next by the passing of knowledge and skills through rituals, art, cultural material and language. From the cities to the bush, there are opportunities to get up close with Australia's Indigenous peoples and learn from a way of life that has existed for over 50,000 years.

Aboriginal Culture

Aboriginal and Torres Strait Islander society is a diverse group of several hundred sovereign nations. Torres Strait Islanders are a Melanesian people with a separate culture from that of Aboriginal Australians, though they have a shared history. Together, these two groups form Australia's Indigenous peoples.

Aboriginal and Torres Strait Islander peoples have an oral tradition and languages that have played an important role in preserving Indigenous cultures. Today there is a national movement to revive Aboriginal languages and a strong Aboriginal art sector. Traditional knowledge is being used in science, natural resource management and government programs. Aboriginal culture has never been static, and continues to evolve with the changing times and environment. New technologies and media are now used to tell Aboriginal stories, and cultural tourism ventures, through which visitors can experience an Aboriginal perspective, have been established. You can learn about ancestral beings at particular natural landmarks, look at rock art that is thousands of years old, taste traditional foods or attend an Aboriginal festival or performance.

Government support for cultural programs is sporadic and depends on the political climate at the time. However, Aboriginal people are determined to maintain their links with the past and to also use their cultural knowledge to shape a better future.

Land

Aboriginal cultures view humans as part of the ecology, not separate from it. Everything is connected, a whole environment that sustains the spiritual,

KEY EVENTS

1928
Anthony Martin Fernando, the first Aboriginal activist to campaign internationally against racial discrimination in Australia, is arrested for protesting outside Australia House in London.

26 January 1938
To mark the 150th anniversary of the arrival of the British, the Aborigines Progressive Association holds a meeting at Australia Hall in Sydney. The conference, called 'A Day of Mourning and Protest', is the first national Aboriginal civil rights gathering and is a milestone in the campaign for policy reform.

15 August 1963
A bark petition is presented to the House of Representatives from the people of Yirrikala in the Northern Territory. Written in their own language on a length of stringy bark, the petition objected to mining on their land, which the federal government had approved without consultation.

27 May 1967
A federal referendum allows the Commonwealth to make laws on Aboriginal issues and include them in the national census. They will now have the same citizen rights as other Australians.

12 July 1971
The Aboriginal flag first flies on National Aborigines Day in Adelaide. Designed by central Australian man Harold Thomas, the flag has become a unifying symbol of identity for Aboriginal people.

The *Macquarie PEN Anthology of Aboriginal Literature* (www.macquariepenanthology.com.au) offers over 200 years of Aboriginal culture, history and life. It starts with Bennelong's letter in 1796 and includes works from some of Aboriginal Australia's best writers.

economic and cultural lives of the people. In turn, Aboriginal people have sustained the land over thousands of years, through knowledge passed on in ceremonies, rituals, songs and stories. For Aboriginal people land is intrinsically connected to identity and spirituality. All land in Australia is reflected in Aboriginal lore but particular places may be significant for religious and cultural beliefs.

Sacred sites can be parts of rocks, hills, trees or water and are associated with an ancestral being or an event that occurred. Often these sites are part of a Dreaming story and link people across areas. The ranges around Alice Springs are part of the Caterpillar Dreaming (p212) with many sites including Akeyulerre (Billy Goat Hill), Atnelkentyarliweke (Anzac Hill) and rock paintings at Emily Gap. The most well known are Uluru and Kata Tjuta, which is the home of the snake Wanambi. His breath is the wind that blows through the gorge. Pirla Warna Warna, a significant site in the Tanami Desert for Warlpiri people, is 435km northwest of Alice and is where several Walpiri Dreaming stories meet.

Cultural tours to Aboriginal sites provide opportunities to learn about plants and animals, hunting and fishing, bush food or dance.

Please note that many Aboriginal sites are protected by law and are not to be disturbed in any way.

The Arts

When Europeans first saw a corroborree they described it as a 'bush opera'. These festive social events combined music, dance and drama with body art. One of the first recorded corroborees was in 1791 at Bennelong Point, now the site of the Sydney Opera House.

Aboriginal art has impacted the Australian cultural landscape and is now showcased at national and international events and is celebrated as a significant part of Australian culture. It still retains the role of passing on knowledge but today it is also important for economic, educational and political reasons. Art has been used to raise awareness of issues such as health and has been a primary tool for the reconciliation process in Australia. In many communities art has become a major source of employment and income.

Performing Arts

Dance and theatre are a vital part of Aboriginal culture. Traditional styles varied from one nation to the next; imitation of animals, birds and the elements was common across all nations, but arm, leg and body movements differed greatly. Ceremonial or ritual dances, often telling stories to pass on knowledge, were highly structured and were distinct from the social dancing at corroborees (festive events). Like other art forms, dance

THE IMPORTANCE OF STORYTELLING

Aboriginal people had an oral culture so storytelling was an important way to learn. Stories gave meaning to life and were used to teach the messages of the spirit ancestors. Although beliefs and cultural practices vary according to region and language groups, there is a common world view that these ancestors created the land, the sea and all living things. This is often referred to as the Dreaming. Through stories, the knowledge and beliefs are passed on from one generation to another and set out the social mores. They also recall events from the past. Today artists have continued this tradition but are using new media such as film and writing. The first Aboriginal writer to be published was David Unaipon, a Ngarrindjeri man from SA who was a writer, scientist and advocate for his people. Born in 1872, he published *Aboriginal Legends* (1927) and *Native Legends* (1929).

Other early published writers were Oodgeroo Noonuccal, Kevin Gilbert and Jack Davis. Contemporary writers of note include Alexis Wright, Kim Scott, Anita Heiss and Ali Cobby Eckerman. Award-winning novels to read are Kim Scott's *Deadman Dancing* (2010) and *Benang* (1999), Alexis Wright's *Carpentaria* (2006) and Ali Cobby Eckerman's *Little Bit Long Time* (2009) and *Ruby Moonlight* (2012).

has adapted to the modern world, with contemporary dance groups bringing a modern interpretation to traditional forms. The most well-known dance company is the internationally acclaimed Bangarra Dance Theatre.

Theatre also draws on the storytelling tradition, where drama and dance came together in ceremonies or corroborees, and this still occurs in many contemporary productions. Today, Australia has a thriving Aboriginal theatre industry and many Aboriginal actors and writers work in or collaborate with mainstream productions. There are two major Aboriginal theatre companies, Ilbijerri (www.ilbijerri.com.au) in Melbourne and Yirra Yakin (www.yirrayaakin.com.au) in Perth, as well as several mainstream companies specialising in Aboriginal stories who have had successful productions in Australia and overseas.

TV, Film & Media

Aboriginal people have developed an extensive media network of radio, print and television services. There are over 120 Aboriginal radio stations and programs operating across Australia – in cities, rural areas and remote communities. Program formats differ from location to location. Some broadcast only in Aboriginal languages or cater to specific music tastes.

After many years of lobbying to have Aboriginal languages and culture reflected in the media, NITV (www.nitv.org.au) hit the airwaves in 2007. It broadcasts via the free-to-air TV channel SBS, with news, views and current affairs, and also produces programs for children, documentaries and sports programs.

There is a thriving Aboriginal film industry and in recent years feature films such as *The Sapphires*, *Bran Nue Day*, *Samson and Delilah* and *Putuparri – And the Rainmakers* have had mainstream success. Since the first Aboriginal television channel, NITV, was launched in 2007, there has been a growth in the number of filmmakers wanting to tell their stories.

From its base in Brisbane, the National Indigenous Radio Service (NIRS; www.nirs.org.au) broadcasts four radio channels of Aboriginal content via satellite and over the internet.

The Aboriginal-owned national newspaper, the *Koori Mail* (www.koorimail.com) was set up by several Aboriginal communities in 1991 to give a voice to Aboriginal people. It provides news and information on politics, sport and social and cultural life from communities across Australia. It is published fortnightly and can be purchased at some newsagents.

Visual Arts

It is difficult to define Aboriginal art (p240) as one style because form and practice vary from one area to another. From the traditional forms of rock art, carving and body decoration, a dynamic contemporary art industry has grown into one of the success stories of Aboriginal Australia.

26 January 1972

The Aboriginal Tent Embassy is set up on the lawns of Parliament House in Canberra to oppose the treatment of Aboriginal people and the government's recent rejection of a proposal for Aboriginal Land Rights.

10 August 1987

The *Royal Commission into Aboriginal Deaths in Custody* investigates the high number of Aboriginal deaths in jails. Aboriginal people are still over-represented in the criminal system today.

3 June 1992

The previous legal concept of terra nullius is overturned by the Australian High Court in its landmark decision in the Mabo case, declaring Australia was occupied before the British settlement.

26 January 1988

As Australia celebrates its bicentenary, over 40,000 Aboriginal people and their supporters march in Sydney to mark the 200-year anniversary of invasion.

28 May 2000

Over 300,000 people walk together across Sydney Harbour Bridge to highlight the need for reconciliation between Aboriginal people and other Australians.

21 June 2007

The federal government suspends the *Racial Discrimination Act* to implement a large-scale intervention – the Northern Territory Emergency Response – to address child abuse in NT Aboriginal communities.

Music

Described by *Rolling Stone* magazine as 'Australia's Most Important Voice', blind singer Geoffrey Gurrumul Yunupingu sings in the Yolngu language from Arnhem Land. His angelic voice tells of identity, connecting with land and ancestral beings. Gurrumul has entranced Australian and overseas audiences and reached platinum with his two albums, *Gurrumul* (2008) and *Rralaka* (2011). His latest is *The Gospel Album* (2015).

Music has always been a vital part of Aboriginal culture. Songs were important for teaching and passing on knowledge and musical instruments were often used in healing, ceremonies and rituals. The most well-known instrument is the *yidaki* (didgeridoo), which was traditionally only played by men in northern Australia. Other instruments included clap-sticks, rattles and boomerangs; in southern Australia animal skins were stretched across the lap to make a drum.

This rich musical heritage continues today with a strong contemporary-music industry. Like other art forms, Aboriginal music has developed into a fusion of new ideas and styles mixed with strong cultural identity. Contemporary artists such as Dan Sultan and Jessica Mauboy have crossed over successfully into the mainstream and have won major music awards and can be seen regularly on popular programs and at major music festivals. Aboriginal radio is the best and most accessible way to hear Aboriginal music.

History of Aboriginal Australia

First Australians

Many academics believe Aboriginal people came here from somewhere else, with scientific evidence placing Aboriginal people on the continent at least 40,000 to 60,000 years ago. However, Aboriginal people believe they have always inhabited the land.

At the time of European contact the Aboriginal population was grouped into 300 or more different nations with distinct languages and land boundaries. Most Aboriginal people did not have permanent shelters but moved within their territory and followed seasonal patterns

THE STOLEN GENERATIONS

When Australia became a Federation in 1901, a government policy known as the 'White Australia policy' was put in place. It was implemented to restrict nonwhite immigration to Australia but the policy also impacted on Aboriginal Australia. Assimilation into the broader society was 'encouraged' by all sectors of government with the intent to eventually fade out the Aboriginal race. A policy of forcibly removing Aboriginal and Torres Strait Islander children from their families was official from 1909 to 1969, although the practice was happening before and after those years. Although accurate numbers will never be known, it is estimated that around 100,000 Aboriginal children were taken from their families (or one in three children).

A government agency, the Aborigines Protection Board, was set up to manage the policy and had the power to remove children without consent from families or without a court order. Many children never saw their families again and those that did manage to find their way home often found it difficult to maintain relationships. The generations of children who were taken from their families became known as the Stolen Generations.

In the 1990s the Australian Human Rights Commission held an inquiry into the practice of removing Aboriginal children. The 'Bring Them Home' report was tabled in parliament in May 1997 and told of the devastating impact that these polices had on the children and their families. Governments, churches and welfare bodies all took part in the forced removal. Sexual and physical abuse and cruelty were common in many of the institutions where children were placed. Today many of the Stolen Generations still suffer trauma associated with their early lives.

On 13 February 2008 Kevin Rudd, the then prime minister of Australia, offered a national apology to the Stolen Generations. For many Aboriginal people it was the start of a national healing process and today there are many organisations working with the Stolen Generations.

of animal migration and plant availability. The diversity of landscapes in Australia meant that each nation varied in their lifestyles. Although these nations were distinct cultural groups, there were also many common elements. Each nation had several clans or family groups who were responsible for looking after specific areas. For thousands of years Aboriginal people lived within a complex kinship system that tied them to the natural environment. From the desert to the sea Aboriginal people shaped their lives according to their environments and developed different skills and a wide body of knowledge on their territory.

Colonised

The effects of colonisation started immediately after the Europeans arrived. It began with the appropriation of land and water resources and an epidemic of diseases. Smallpox killed around half of the Sydney Harbour natives. A period of resistance occurred as Aboriginal people fought back to retain their land and way of life. As violence and massacres swept the country, many Aboriginal people were pushed away from their traditional lands. Over a century, the Aboriginal population was decimated by 90%.

By the late 1800s most of the fertile land had been taken and most Aboriginal people were living in poverty on the fringes of settlements or on land unsuitable for settlement. Aboriginal people had to adapt to the new culture but had few to no rights. Employment opportunities were scarce and most worked as labourers or domestic staff. This disadvantage has continued and even though successive government policies and programs have been implemented to assist Aboriginal people, most have had little effect on improving lives.

Rights & Reconciliation

The relationship between Aboriginal people and other Australians hasn't always been an easy one. Over the years several systematic policies have been put in place, but these have often had an underlying purpose, including control over the land, decimating the population, protection, assimilation, self-determination and self-management.

The history of forced resettlement, removal of children, and the loss of land and culture can't be erased even with governments addressing some of the issues. Current policies focus on 'closing the gap' and centre on better delivery of essential services to improve lives, but there is still great disparity between Aboriginal people and other Australians, including lower standards of education, employment, health and living conditions, high incarceration and suicide rates, and a lower life expectancy.

Throughout all of this, Aboriginal people have managed to maintain their identity and link to country and culture. Although there is a growing recognition and acceptance of Aboriginal people's place in this country, there is still a long way to go. Aboriginal people have no real political or economic wealth, but their struggle for legal and cultural rights continues today and are always at the forefront of politics. Any gains for Aboriginal people have been hard won and initiated by Aboriginal people themselves.

13 February 2008

Prime minister Kevin Rudd makes a national apology to Aboriginal people for the forced removal of their children and the injustices that occurred.

10 July 2010

Aboriginal leader Yagan is put to rest in a Perth park bearing his name. He was murdered in 1833 and his head sent to England. Aboriginal people have campaigned for decades to repatriate their people's remains.

22 January 2015

A Barngarla native-title claim over a vast section of SA's Eyre Peninsula is upheld in the Federal Court.

Local Histories of Aboriginal Australia

First Footprints (2013), Scott Cane

An Intruder's Guide to East Arnhem Land (2001), Andrew McMillan

A Handful of Sand (2016), Charlie Ward

Craft for a Dry Lake (2000), Kim Mahood

King Brown Country (2010), Russell Skelton

ABORIGINAL AUSTRALIA HISTORY OF ABORIGINAL AUSTRALIA

Indigenous Visual Art

Visual imagery is a fundamental part of Aboriginal and Torres Strait Islander culture and life: a connection between the past, present and future, and between Indigenous peoples and their traditional homelands. The earliest forms of Indigenous visual cultural expression were rock carvings (petroglyphs) and paintings on rock galleries, body painting and ground designs, with the earliest engraved designs known to exist dating back up to 60,000 years.

Visual Art

Visual art, including painting, sculpture and *tjanpi* (weaving) in central Australia has flourished to such a degree that it is now a substantial source of income for many communities. It has also been an important educational tool for children, through which they can learn different aspects of spiritual and ceremonial knowledge. In the past decade or so women have played a huge role in the visual-arts movement, with some of the most innovative work being created by women artists, working equally alongside their male counterparts. More recently, significant efforts have been made to involve youth in cultural maintenance and revival projects, as well as contemporary art production to ensure continuity of art centres and local culture.

Indigenous art, with some notable exceptions, was either largely disregarded by non-Indigenous people or viewed in an ethnographic context, with most examples of Indigenous material culture placed in natural-history museums, as opposed to fine-art museums. The first exception to this was the acquisition of a work of Aboriginal art by a fine-art museum in 1939, when the Art Gallery of South Australia bought a watercolour by Western Arrernte artist Albert Namatjira (1902–59). Other state galleries followed suit, developing similarly themed collections.

Papunya Tula Art

In the 1980s acclaimed Papunya Tula artists were invited to submit work for the new Parliament House in Canberra. Michael Nelson Jagamarra's *Possum and Wallaby Dreaming* is embedded in the mosaic forecourt: www. papunyatula. com.au

In 1971 an event took place that would challenge non-Indigenous perceptions about Indigenous art. At the remote government-established community of Papunya, 240km northwest of Alice Springs, a group of elders were encouraged to paint a mural on one of the school's external walls by art teacher Geoffrey Bardon (1940–2003). The group was led by Kaapa Mbitjana Tjampitjinpa (Anmatyerre/Arrernte people; 1925–89), along with Long Jack Phillipus Tjakamarra (Pintupi/ Luritja/Warlpiri people; born 1932) and Billy Stockman Tjapaltjarri (Anmatyerre people; 1927–2015). This was the genesis of the Papunya Tula Artists movement. Shortly after painting commenced, other members of the community became enthused by the project and joined in creating the mural *Honey Ant Dreaming*. Government regulations later saw the mural destroyed, but its effect on the community was profound. Images of spiritual significance had taken on a very public form. Notwithstanding the debate the mural caused at Papunya, other members of the community expressed a desire to paint.

Initially many of the paintings were executed on smallish boards, but within a short time larger canvases were used.

Although Indigenous artists were working in other regions throughout the country, this fraught beginning in a remote Aboriginal community arguably instigated the contemporary Indigenous art movement in Australia. That it developed in Papunya is not without irony, since the community was established in 1960 under the auspices of the Australian government's cultural assimilation policy.

In the four decades since the genesis of the Papunya Tula movement, a huge diversity of contemporary visual art and culture has blossomed across the Northern Territory and South Australia, with myriad art centres being established to represent the breadth of this creativity, supported by advocacy organisations, state and territory public art museums, and commercial galleries.

With the growing importance of art as both an economic and a cultural activity, an association was formed to help the artists from Papunya community sell their work. Papunya Tula Artists (p206) in Alice Springs is the longest-running Aboriginal-owned and -directed gallery in the country, and operates from a stylish contemporary gallery space in Todd Mall.

Rock Art of Arnhem Land & Kakadu

Arnhem Land, in the Top End of the NT, is an area of abundant, diverse artistic and cultural heritage. Recent scientific discoveries have confirmed that rock paintings were being produced as long as 28,000 years ago, possibly up to 60,000 years, and some of the rock-art galleries in the huge sandstone Arnhem Land plateau are at least 18,000 years old.

The rock art (pictographs, petroglyphs, stencils, prints, beeswax, and geoglyphs) of Arnhem Land depicts ancestral stories for the many language groups and clans of the region, with stylised designs, often hatched and *rarrk* (cross-hatched), of ancestral beings, spirits,

ALBERT NAMATJIRA

No discussion of Indigenous visual arts would be complete without mention of Albert Namatjira (1902–59), the pioneer of Australia's Aboriginal artists and whose work predated by decades the 1970s flowering of Indigenous art. A member of the Western Arrernte–speaking people of the West MacDonnell Ranges, Namatjira was born and grew up in the **Hermannsburg Mission** (p213).

Namatjira's style was very different from the more abstract forms that we would come to associate with Indigenous art later in the 20th century: his watercolour paintings of the outback drew more on Western artistic traditions. This may, of course, account for his popularity among white Australians at a time when Aboriginal culture was little understood and artistic expressions rarely encouraged. However, Namatjira drew on a more recognisably Aboriginal colour palette, especially in his use of ochres, and he rendered the outback with an expert eye, as seen in his rugged mountains and ghostly gums.

Namatjira held his first exhibition in Melbourne in 1938 to popular and critical acclaim, with more exhibitions following in cities around the country. He won the Queen's Coronation medal in 1953 and, in 1957, he became the first Aboriginal Australian to be granted Australian citizenship, nearly a decade before a referendum would extend this right to all Indigenous Australians. He would also later become such a household name that he pops up in songs by everyone from Midnight Oil to Slim Dusty. By the time of his death in 1959, he had painted more than 2000 paintings, many of which now appear in major art galleries around the country.

A lonely monument to the great man stands 2km outside Hermannsburg (p213).

Rock Art Sites in the Northern Territory

....

Ubirr

....

Nourlangie – Nanguluwur Gallery

....

Arnhem Land/ Gunbalanya (Oenpelli) – Injalak Hill

totems, and cultural exchanges with Macassans – Indonesian mariners from Sulawesi who regularly visited the north coast for at least three centuries until their visits were banned by South Australian government regulations in 1906 (a time when the region was known as the Northern Territory of South Australia).

The paintings contained in the Arnhem Land rock-art sites constitute one of the world's most significant and fascinating rock-art collections. They provide a record of changing environments and lifestyles over millenniums.

In some places they are concentrated in large galleries, with paintings from more recent eras sometimes superimposed over older paintings. Some sites are kept secret – not only to protect them from damage, but also because they are private or sacred to the Aboriginal owners. Some are believed to be inhabited by malevolent spirit beings sometimes known as Namorrodo, who must not be approached by those who are ignorant of the Indigenous customs of the region. However, two of the finest sites have been opened up to visitors, with access roads, walkways and explanatory signs. These are Ubirr and Nourlangie in Kakadu National Park, although a terrible irony is that the original custodians no longer paint at these sites, though descendants ensure cultural maintenance and management of the sites as part of their ongoing cultural obligations through work at the park.

The rock paintings show how the main styles succeeded each other over time. The earliest hand-prints were followed by a 'naturalistic/figurative' style, with outlines of people or animals filled in with colour. Some of the animals depicted at Ubirr and elsewhere, such as the thylacine (Tasmanian tiger), have long been extinct on mainland Australia.

After the naturalistic style came the 'dynamic', in which motion was often depicted (a dotted line, for example, to show a spear's path through the air). In this era the first ancestral beings appeared, with human bodies and animal heads.

The next style mainly showed simple human silhouettes, and was followed by the curious 'yam figures', in which people and animals were drawn in the shape of yams. Other painting styles, including the 'X-ray' style, which displays the internal organs and bone structure of animals, also appeared around this time.

By about 1000 years ago many of the salt marshes had turned into freshwater swamps and billabongs. The birds and plants that provided new food sources in this landscape appeared in the art of this time.

From around 400 years ago, Indigenous artists also depicted the human newcomers to the region – Macassan traders and, more recently, Europeans and other non-Indigenous people – and the things they brought, or their modes of transport such as ships and horses, and species such as cattle and buffalo, which severely impacted upon the environment.

There are a number of cultural tours owned and managed by local traditional custodians, such as Kakadu Cultural Tours in Kakadu National Park. Key visual arts communities across Arnhem Land include Gunbalanya/Oenpelli in western Arnhem Land, Maningrida, Milingimbi and Ramingining in central Arnhem Land, and Yirrkala in northeast Arnhem Land. The Tiwi Islands of Bathurst and Melville Islands are also home to a number of art centres.

Dot Painting

Western Desert painting, also known as 'dot' painting, evolved from 'ground' or 'sand' paintings, which formed the foundation of ceremonial practices. These were made from diverse media including pulped plant material, natural pigments and feathers, with the designs created on the ground and/or body using particles (dots) of this material. Dots, or stippling effects, were also used in other ways: to outline objects in rock paintings and to highlight geographical features or vegetation.

While these paintings may look abstract, they depict Ancestral Tjukurrpa/Jukurrpa (Dreaming) stories, and can be read in many ways, including as aerial, topographical and underground geographical maps, though not always literally. Many paintings feature the tracks of birds, animals and humans, often identifying key ancestral beings. Subjects may be depicted by the imprint they leave in the sand: a simple arc depicts a sitting person, a *coolamon* (wooden carrying dish) is shown by an oval shape, a digging stick by a single line, a campfire by a circle. Men or women are identified by the objects associated with them: gathering tools and objects for women, hunting tools and objects for men. Concentric circles generally depict ancestral sites, or places where ancestors paused in their journeys.

Although these symbols are widely used, only the artist and the people closely associated with his or her story – either by clan or by the Tjukurrpa/Jukurrpa – know their meaning in each individual painting since different clans apply different interpretations to each painting's subject matter. In this way sacred stories can be publicly portrayed, as the deeper meaning is not revealed to uninitiated viewers, but coded by layers of stippled acrylic paint, literally and metaphorically concealing sacred information from uninitiated people. Many recent works are far more coded in their imagery with few or no figurative symbols, using colour and application to achieve optical effects denoting the power inherent in the stories portrayed.

Bark Painting

It is difficult to establish when bark was first used, partly because it is perishable, so the oldest pieces in existence date from the late 19th century and none of the early works were created in the format that we know today. The paintings were never intended to be permanent records but were painted on the bark shelters in much the same way as the art on rock galleries. Non-Indigenous explorers travelling through the region in the early 19th century observed the practice of painting the inside walls of bark shelters, and later in the 19th century and early in the 20th century the trade in examples of bark paintings brought them to the notice of natural history/ethnographic museums around the world.

One of the main features of Arnhem Land bark paintings is the use of *rarrk* designs. These designs identify particular clans, and are based on body paintings handed down through generations. More recently, senior artists are recognised by their specific stylistic signature, while retaining communal clan designs. The paintings can also be broadly categorised by their regional styles. In the region's west the tendency was towards naturalistic and figurative images and plain backgrounds, although many renowned artists from western and central Arnhem Land cover the entire surface of the bark or carving in intricate line work to create a sense of power emanating from the imagery depicted. To the east, the use of geometric, abstract designs is more common, with the artists of northeast Arnhem Land renowned for their use of *kaolin* (white) in their ever-innovative paintings and sculpture.

The art reflects themes from ancestral times that vary by region. In eastern and central Arnhem Land the most prominent ancestral beings are the Djan'kawu Sisters, who travelled the land with their elaborate dillybags (string carry bags) and digging sticks (for making waterholes), and the Wagilag/Wawilak Sisters, who are associated with snakes and waterholes and creation of the clans of the regions. In western Arnhem Land, the significant being (according to some clans) is Yingarna, the Rainbow Serpent, as is one of her offspring, Ngalyod. Other groups paint Nawura as the principal ancestral being – he travelled through the rocky landscape creating sacred sites and giving people the attributes of culture. Another powerful ancestral being is Namarrkon, the Lightning Man, associated with the monsoon season.

The mimi spirits are another feature of western Arnhem Land art, on both bark and rock. These mischievous spirits are attributed with having taught the Indigenous people of the region many things, including hunting, food-gathering and painting skills. More recently, many of the most senior artists have become renowned for their highly innovative depictions of ancestral stories, with works of art held in major national and international public and private collections. The Museum & Art Gallery of the Northern Territory (p147), on the gorgeous location of Bullocky Point, Darwin, presents changing displays from its extensive collection of work from communities across the NT.

Contemporary Art

Since the early 1970s there have been burgeoning centres of creativity throughout remote regions, often where clan connections cross government borders, particularly throughout the Anangu/Pitjantjatjara/Yankunytjatjara (APY) Lands, which include parts of South Australia, the Northern Territory and Western Australia. In the late 1980s to mid-1990s, critical and popular focus centred on artists and work from the communities of Utopia, Haasts Bluff, Papunya and Yuendumu in central Australia, and Ngukurr in southeast Arnhem Land. In the 1990s, work being created in communities across Arnhem Land gained national and international acclaim.

The most significant developments over the past three decades have come from urban and rural-based artists, living in the regions that have experienced the longest impact of colonisation. Their individual and collective contributions challenged the status quo of the time, being that 'authentic' Aboriginal art could only be created by artists from remote communities – those regions that supposedly were more 'traditional'. This misconception overlooked the strong cultural connections held by Aboriginal people whose families and communities had been moved off their customary homelands, had children forcibly removed and placed in government- and church-operated institutions, lost access to language and customs, yet who intrinsically retained a sense of Indigenous identity, which was represented – overtly or subtly – in the work they created.

Much of this work was created by artists/activists living, studying and working in major metropolitan centres across Australia such as Sydney, Brisbane, Melbourne, Adelaide and Perth. Artist-run initiatives such as Boomalli Aboriginal Artists Co-operative in Sydney in 1987, Dumbartung in Perth in 1989, Tandanya National Aboriginal Cultural Centre in Adelaide in 1989, and Campfire Group (later Fireworks Gallery) in Brisbane in 1990, were established as a political response to the exclusive nature of the contemporary mainstream art scene; the impact of these venues and the artists involved on the uninformed art world continues to resonate nearly three decades later.

Subject matter ranged from identity politics, land and cultural rights, Stolen Generations and cultural revival, while media included paintings, sculpture, textiles, photo-media and film, new media and installation and conceptual work. Works on paper have long been created by

The *art+soul* DVD series (2011, Sydney: ABC Sales & Hibiscus Films) is produced by one of Australia's most respected Indigenous curators and educators, Hetti Perkins. The series covers a diversity of artists who have had a significant impact on the development of the contemporary Indigenous art scene over the past two decades.

artists from all regions across the country – urban, rural and remote, with many art centres producing their own works on paper or working with specialist organisations. Fine-art prints are now produced by many artists and communities, assisted by master printmakers and organisations such as Northern Editions at Charles Darwin University. These works of art are sought after due to their affordability.

Discussion has long surrounded the 'contemporary' vs 'traditional' debate, but perhaps the biggest change has been the involvement of Indigenous curators of Aboriginal and Torres Strait Islander art working in artist-run spaces, state and federal public art galleries and museums, which ensures that visual art and culture is presented from an Indigenous perspective.

Artefacts & Contemporary Objects

Objects traditionally made for utilitarian or ceremonial practices, such as weapons, hunting and gathering tools and musical instruments, often feature intricate and symbolic decoration. In recent years many communities have also developed nontraditional forms of weavings and objects that have generated cultural revival and pride, employment and income. In central Australia, artists have created idiosyncratic works such as *mukata* (beanies or hats), *tjanpi* (woven natural grasses, brightly coloured wool, seeds and beads) objects ranging from birds, animals and humans to the more quirky – the near-life-size *Tjanpi Toyota* by Tjanpi Desert Weavers (p206), which won the overall Telstra National Aboriginal and Torres Strait Islander Art Award (NATSIAA) in 2005 and is on permanent display at the Museum & Art Gallery of the Northern Territory (p147) in Darwin.

Buying Indigenous Art Ethically

The rising interest in Aboriginal art in Australia and overseas has been accompanied by an increase in unethical actions by individuals who have not always had the rights of the artists and their communities as a priority.

Very few galleries in SA or the NT are owned and directed by Indigenous people, but there are many Aboriginal art centres that are governed by Aboriginal people. The best place to buy art is either directly from the communities that have art collectives, or from galleries and outlets that are operated or supported by Indigenous arts and advocacy groups – the general standard in such places is the artists receive around half of the proceeds from any sale of their work. In most major cities and towns there are also commercial galleries that have established long-term relationships with artists and communities. These usually display a notice stating they are a member of the Australian Commercial Galleries Association (ACGA) and/or the Indigenous Art Code.

Spirit Country: Contemporary Australian Aboriginal Art (2004), by Jennifer Isaacs, is a stunning treatment of modern Indigenous art, with sections on The Desert, the Kimberley, Arnhem Land, Tiwi Islands and the Gulf Country.

DIDGERIDOO

The most widespread craft objects seen for sale these days are didgeridoos. There has been a phenomenal boom in their popularity and they can be found in outlets around the country, although not always made by an Indigenous artisan. A hollow drone instrument, the didgeridoo is played by a musician who has mastered the art of circular (non-stop) breathing and is now used by Indigenous and non-Indigenous musicians due to its unique and amazingly diverse sound. It has been used in traditional, crossover, country, rock and classical music.

Although it is often considered a universal Aboriginal musical instrument, the didgeridoo originates from Yolngu culture in northeast Arnhem Land, where it remains a revered cultural object and is known as the *yidaki*.

There is a plethora of publications on the market but a key resource is *One sun, one moon: Aboriginal art in Australia* (2007, Sydney: Art Gallery of New South Wales).

Art Centres

The NT has dozens of excellent, community-run art centres. The following are some of our favourites:

Injalak Arts & Crafts Centre (p176) Fabulous collection and many artists in residence at Gunbalanya (Oenpilli), close to Kakadu.

Ghunmarn Culture Centre (p191) Outstanding west Arnhem Land collection in Beswick (Wugularr).

Warlukurlangu Art Centre (p198) One of the longest-established art centres in the NT, out in the Tanami Desert at Yuendemu.

Buku Larrnggay Mulka Art Centre & Museum (p178) Treasure trove of artistic creations from east Arnhem Land.

Ngukurr Arts Centre (p192) A west Arnhem Land special along the Roper River.

Merrepen Arts (p164) Quiet outpost of Indigenous artworks in Daly River.

Waralungku Arts Centre (p193) Fascinating collection of figurative paintings and other art in remote Borroloola.

Art Galleries

There are a number of privately owned art galleries that have an excellent record in their dealings with the Indigenous artists whose work they display. Usually based in cities and larger towns, they can be good alternatives to the more remote art centres. Some community art centres also have city shopfronts that are well worth exploring.

Darwin

Mason Gallery (p143) Dot paintings from the Western and Central Desert regions and works from Arnhem Land and Utopia.

Outstation Gallery (p155) The works of nine different Aboriginal art centres from Arnhem Land to the Western Desert.

Mbantua Fine Art Gallery (p155) Paintings from Utopia.

Nomad Art Gallery (p155) Contemporary Indigenous art in a range of forms.

Katherine

Djilpin Arts (p181) Aboriginal owned, with art from the Ghunmarn Culture Centre in west Arnhem Land.

Mimi Aboriginal Art & Craft (p184) Aboriginal-owned and not-for-profit, Mimi has works from the Katherine and Tanami Desert regions.

Top Didj Cultural Experience & Art Gallery (p181) A good place to see Aboriginal artists at work.

Alice Springs

Papunya Tula Artists (p206) Alice Springs shopfront for paintings from the Western Desert.

Jila Arts (p207) Contemporary paintings from the Western Desert.

Mbantua Gallery (p206) Extensive exhibits of works from the renowned Utopia region, and watercolour landscapes from the Namatjira school; a fine collectors' gallery out the back.

Ngurratjuta Iltja Ntjarra (p207) Watercolour and dot paintings from all over central Australia.

Talapi (p206) Central Desert Indigenous art.

Tjanpi Desert Weavers (p206) Central Desert weaving from 18 remote communities.

The Outback Environment

Australia's outback is home to some of the country's most extreme environments, but the deserts are also extremely varied in their shape, from vast salt pans and scrubby plains to rugged red-rock desert massifs and seas of sand dunes. Up north, the Top End, with its abundant seasonal rainfall, is another world altogether.

The Land

Deserts

Deserts cover an estimated 18% of the Australian mainland, and up to one-third of the country's mainland could technically qualify as desert based on rainfall levels alone. The Great Victoria Desert, in Western Australia and South Australia, is Australia's largest at around 350,000 sq km, or nearly 5% of mainland Australia.

Parts of the Australian outback are among the world's oldest land surfaces. Australia's last great mountain-building events took place more than 300 million years ago, and it's hard to believe that Uluru was once part of a mountain range that would have rivalled the Andes in height. Erosion and the relentless cycle of drought and flood have leached the nutrients away from Australia's ancient soils and prevented the creation of new soils, resulting in the vast sandy plains of the Australian outback.

The Stuart Hwy passes through some of the lowest, flattest and driest parts of Australia, but there are numerous ranges and individual mountains scattered through the outback. At 1531m, Mt Zeil is not remarkable by world standards, but it is the highest mountain west of the Great Dividing Range. The rocky ranges of the outback provide important refuges for a diverse collection of plants and animals, and are significant in the ancient song lines and stories (accounts of the Dreaming which link into the law) of the traditional Aboriginal custodians of these areas.

In the outback you will also drive past huge salt pans or claypans that rarely fill with water. These may be dry for years, but when there is an abundance of rain they become important arid wetland systems: they hold water long after the surrounding landscape has dried out and are crucial to the survival of many plants and animals, especially those that require inundation during their life cycles. Lake Eyre, Australia's largest lake, is the most obvious example.

Sand dunes are less visible than you might think out here – grasslands, desert scrub (including the ubiquitous spinifex grass) and salt pans are far more common. There are seas of sand dunes, but most tend to occur in the deserts' more accessible reaches – the Simpson Desert, which extends across the NT, SA and Queensland, is estimated to be the world's largest sand-dune desert and is home to what could the world's longest parallel sand dunes.

SA's low and unreliable rainfall has resulted in water from the Murray River being piped over long distances to ensure the survival of many communities, including Adelaide. More than 50% of South Australians depend entirely on the Murray for their water supply, and this figure can rise to 90% in drought years.

The Top End

While spectacular geological formations are characteristics of the outback's arid interior, it is the extensive river systems and wetlands that herald your arrival in the Top End. The sandstone escarpment and plateau of western Arnhem Land is a magnificent sight, but the life-sustaining floodplains at its base are just as impressive.

Kakadu and Arnhem Land are thought to be home to some of the oldest rocks on earth. Geologists estimate that the Arnhem Land plateau was formed a mind-boggling 1650 million years ago. For much of the period from 500 million to 140 million years ago, the region lay beneath the surface of a shallow sea, and it was the Arnhem Land Escarpment – visible across the region, but most easily at Nourlangie and Jim Jim Falls – that provided the cliff-bound shore.

For millions of years, the escarpment was a continuous body of rock, but the erosion by the sea's waters gradually created the sandstone outliers that still ripple down into the interior today. The most obvious examples are Nourlangie and, further afield, Nitmiluk (Katherine) Gorge.

The Land & Indigenous Peoples

Professor Irene Watson

Bruce Pascoe's *Dark Emu – Black Seeds: Agriculture or Accident* (2014) makes a convincing argument that Indigenous Australians lived far more than nomadic lifestyles prior to the arrival of white settlers and actually planted crops and lived in otherwise-sophisticated societies.

The earth is our sacred relative; it is a relationship that is based on nurturing, caring and sharing. From birth we learn of the sacredness of all living things. Every aspect of the natural world is honoured and respected, and we learn to tread lightly on the earth.

The spirit of creation is in all things, for all life forms are related. The philosophy of respect for all living things is an idea central to Aboriginal spirituality and is an idea that nurtured and kept the land in a pristine state prior to colonisation.

Managers & Bosses

There are both managers and bosses for country, and each party has a different responsibility or right. The manager is the custodian and the boss is the owner. Naming the parties a manager or a boss is simply a way of discerning between custodian and owner, although in reality these two roles are not always strictly separate and are often merged to become one.

Some of these responsibilities are made known to the members of an Aboriginal community through songs and ceremonies. For example, there may be a particular obligation not to kill the females of a certain animal, in order to preserve the species.

When traditional custodians and/or owners approach their country they will talk to the spirit ancestor of the place. They will tell them who they are and also who they may have brought with them to the place. When food is taken from the land, thanks are given to the ancestors. Nothing is assumed or taken for granted, not even the next meal. We are always seeking permission from the spirit world for our actions.

The boundaries between different Aboriginal clans or nations are sometimes marked. These boundaries are not straight lines but may be determined by the footsteps and tracks of the ancestors, by bends in the creek or the river, the rain shadow, trees or rocks. Some regions were shared between different Aboriginal peoples and some were restricted, with strict rules for obtaining permission to travel across the country.

The Relationship to the Land

The idea of the land being 'terra nullius', or a vast empty space across which we range sporadically, is a myth. We know the land intimately:

every rock and every river has a name and is remembered in the Dreaming, as it is still remembered today.

To own the land as a piece of real estate, as a 'property', is an idea remote to Aboriginal people. Our relationship to the land is considerably more complex. The land cannot be treated as a consumable, which can be traded or sold. We believe the land cannot be sold.

We have always lived as a part of the natural world, and we take from the environment only what is needed to sustain life; we nurture the land as we do ourselves, for we are one.

The land is both nurturer and teacher from which all life forms grow; all life is inseparably linked. The Aboriginal relationship to the land carries with it both obligations and rights. The relationship to land is at once one of traditional owner and of custodian. It is a relationship that is difficult to explain in a foreign language, because the term 'owner' has different meanings across cultures. Ownership is not viewed in relation to ownership of material goods, but is more accurately viewed as in possession of other values: knowledge, culture and law business, a relationship, a problem, a dispute, a ceremony.

The idea of Aboriginal ownership is not exclusive, and it does not define the owned object as a commodity. Instead, that which is owned is defined as the concern of a limited group of people who stand in a particular relationship to the owner, and whose various responsibilities depend on that relationship.

The Spirit in the Land

The land is sacred because the essence of our spirituality lies in the earth; our spirit guides are resting in the mountains, in the rocks and in the rivers, and they are everywhere in the land. The land is sacred because it carries the footsteps of our spirit ancestors as they walked every part of it, laying tracks and spiritual songs across the country. The ancestors lie sleeping deep in the earth and we are responsible for the care of their places of rest, for their creative powers are alive and influence all things still in the natural world.

If these spirits are disturbed, so too are the natural order and cycles of life. Where sacred sites are destroyed we believe the ancestors are disturbed and will no longer protect or provide for the people. As a result of damaged or destroyed sacred sites, natural disasters and sickness may occur and afflict communities who have not fulfilled their cultural obligations as custodians. By neglecting our spiritual and cultural obligations we bring disharmony to the country and the community.

Wildlife

The timing of your visit to outback Australia will determine the variety and types of wildlife you are likely to see. In January a flooded wetland in the north will be teeming with wildlife, whereas a searing hot January day in the desert may leave you wondering if anything lives there at all apart from flies and ants.

Lake Eyre has filled only a handful of times in the last century. When filled, it takes up an area of about 9500 sq km and attracts countless waterbirds. In recent years, much of the lake has been close to full of water, including in 2009 and the years immediately following. Lake Eyre is also Australia's lowest point, at 15m below sea level.

THE OUTBACK ENVIRONMENT WILDLIFE

Wildlife Parks

To catch a glimpse of the astonishing richness of the outback's wildlife, take the time to explore the Alice Springs Desert Park, one of the best of its kind in Australia. Also excellent is the Territory Wildlife Park near Darwin.

VOLUNTEERING FOR THE ENVIRONMENT

Want to get you hands dirty? Conservation Volunteers Australia (www. conservationvolunteers.com.au) is a not-for-profit organisation focusing on practical conservation projects such as tree planting, walking-track construction, and flora and fauna surveys. You'll meet like-minded people and get to visit interesting areas of the country. Most projects are either for a weekend or a week and all food, transport and accommodation is supplied in return for a small contribution to help cover costs.

Animals

Birds

The rivers and wetlands of both SA and the NT are home to an incredible variety of birds, as well as hosting great flocks of migratory birds from other parts of Australia and the world. In Kakadu look out for regal pairs of Jabiru storks and brolgas among the massive flocks of magpie geese.

Away from the wetlands, birdwatchers will need to put in more time and effort, as the birds of the dry desert regions are generally more mobile, only visiting waterholes for a quick drink before disappearing into the void. The waterholes of the MacDonnell Range can teem with

ABORIGINAL LAND MANAGEMENT

For more than 50,000 years Aboriginal and Torres Strait Islander peoples have occupied the full range of environments within Australia. Indigenous peoples have successfully utilised and renewed the country, using an accumulated intimate knowledge of the land, and have implemented innovative management regimes with traditional customs to keep the country healthy and productive.

Through this long-term use and occupation, Indigenous peoples developed an intimate understanding of the environment, including the flora and fauna, and the environmental conditions. This knowledge was crucial for long-term survival in a land that can be harsh and uninviting at the best of times. The land has always nurtured and provided for Indigenous peoples, through meats like kangaroo and emu or vegetables like yams and sweet potatoes. However, the land means a great deal more than that – it also provides spiritual strength. Through story places (where special Dreaming events occurred) and Dreaming tracks throughout the landscape, our attachment to land provides us with our identity – where we come from as Aboriginal people, who we are, where our land is, our languages and our social structure.

The land is all important. However, with invasion many Aboriginal people were denied access to their land – they were killed, dispersed or taken away to Aboriginal missions. This has had a variety of effects on Aboriginal people, including separation from family, loss of identity and the myriad social problems that accompany these things, such as alcohol abuse and unemployment.

Nevertheless, Aboriginal occupation and day-to-day use have been, and in many places continue to be, significant factors in maintaining the landscape. Fire-stick farming (burning off) is a well-documented technique Aboriginal people used to renew and manage the land. In most areas burning off the country with fire was, and in some areas continues to be, an annual occurrence. In the north of Australia it is carried out at the beginning of the cool dry season. Fire-stick farming serves two main purposes. One is to decrease the chance of a bushfire by reducing the vegetation build-up after a wet season. This vegetation could be fuel for a major fire. Secondly, fire is used to clear the country and encourage new growth. This new growth attracts wildlife such as kangaroos and other species, which are drawn to nibble on the soft, new shoots sprouting after the fire.

Although much of the special knowledge of the environment has been lost due to the various impacts upon traditional culture, a great deal still exists. Aboriginal people's special attachment to land is tied to their social, cultural and economic wellbeing. Understanding this attachment can provide a good insight into the way Aboriginal people used and continue to use the land, and their aspirations for looking after their 'country'. Many Aboriginal and Torres Strait Islander people want to play a role in managing their country. Since invasion, Australia has lost a large percentage of its native vegetation and many native species are in danger of extinction. For Australia to maintain its unique environmental credentials, it needs Aboriginal people and their knowledge to play a role in environmental management.

colourful and noisy zebra finches and budgerigars only to be abandoned a few minutes later. Keep an eye out for emus near the road
around Coober Pedy – even at the hottest time of the day!

Early morning and late afternoon are the best times for birdwatching. Some species are rarely seen, while others hang around in flocks so
large that you can't possibly miss them. Australia is in fact the perfect
place for lazy birdwatchers because many of our birds are noisy and
easily identifiable, such as pink cockatoos, red-tailed black cockatoos,
sulphur-crested cockatoos, galahs, kookaburras, parrots and corellas.
Australia's majestic wedge-tailed eagles are a common sight along the
Stuart Hwy and you will often hear a whistling kite before you see it.

Mammals

Of the larger marsupials, you are most likely to see mobs of Australia's
unique marsupial macropods, either bounding away from you, grazing
quietly with ears twitching or resting in the shade of a tree. Look for
a joey poking out from the female's pouch. In southern and central
Australia, the most common macropod species is the red kangaroo, the
world's largest marsupial. Males are a reddish brown colour and can
grow to 2m, while females are smaller with blue-grey colouring. Robust
euros (wallaroos) can be seen around Alice Springs and yellow-footed
rock wallabies are making a comeback in the Flinders Ranges, thanks
in part to a feral-animal eradication program. In the north, the most
common macropod species is the agile wallaby, which grows to about
1m and has a distinct white line from the tip of its nose to its eye.

Not all Australian mammals have pouches. You may see the occasional solitary dingo; usually slinking away annoyed at being discovered. But many of Australia's mammals are small, secretive and
nocturnal, so you're unlikely to see them in the wild unless you go
spotlighting with a knowledgable guide or visit one of the excellent
wildlife parks in Alice Springs and Darwin.

Reptiles

Despite their abundance in Australia, most reptiles are difficult to
observe because many of them are inactive during hot summer days
and hibernate during winter. Snakes tend to move around more
between October and April, when you may also spot a large, active
daytime predator such as a perentie or a sand goanna. In southern and
central Australia, following an ant trail in the red desert sand may lead
you to a small thorny devil taking lunch.

In the tropical woodlands of the north, the larger frill-necked lizards spend most of their days in trees eating insects and termites.
When a 'frilly' is frightened or defending its territory, its defensive
strategy is to open its mouth, widen its impressive frill and hiss. This
menacing show is all bluff and a frilly will generally run very fast on its
two hind legs in the opposite direction when the show is over. In June
and July, when many other reptile species are hibernating, Australia's
best-known reptiles – the freshwater and estuarine crocodiles – can be
seen warming themselves on the banks of Top End rivers.

Feral Animals

The introduction of animals from other countries in the last 200 years
has contributed significantly to the fragmentation of ecosystems
and the extinction of native animals in Australia. Introduced species
include foxes, rabbits, cats, pigs, goats, donkeys, horses, camels, star-
lings, sparrows, cane toads, mosquitofish and carp. They each bring
a unique suite of problems as they carve out a niche for themselves in

THE OUTBACK ENVIRONMENT WILDLIFE

If you stay overnight in Alice Springs, a visit to Simpsons Gap early morning or just before dark is your best bet for seeing black-footed rock wallabies in their natural environment.

Join a community 'toad muster' to help keep the cane-toad count down. To learn more about how cane toads affect biodiversity, and how you can help, go to www.frogwatch.org.au.

their new environment – some as predators of native animals, others as competitors for the limited resources of food, water and shelter.

By one estimate, there are 15 million feral cats in Australia, and the Australian Wildlife Conservancy (AWC; www.australianwildlife. org) warns that each cat could be eating five native animals every night – that's 75 million across the continent *every* night! While other scientists warn that these figures are too high – one recent study put the number of feral cats in Australia at closer to 2.3 million – no one disagrees that feral animals are an existential threat to Australia's native wildlife.

The AWC currently runs at least eight wildlife sanctuaries in NT and SA. Some of these sanctuaries are vast and some are fenced to keep out feral animals once they have been eradicated within the fenced areas. By then being able to restore ecosystems and, in some cases, reintroduce native mammal species, AWC hopes to repopulate parts of the outback with species that haven't been seen in decades. One such sanctuary, which you can visit, is Pungalina – Seven Emu Wildlife Sanctuary (p197) up on the Gulf of Carpentaria east of Borroloola.

Plants

There is a great diversity of vegetation between Adelaide and Darwin, reflecting the sweeping range in climate and rainfall. Much of the Top End receives an annual rainfall of around 1600mm, while the desert regions of SA receive less than 150mm (median) of annual rainfall.

Known as wattles in Australia, acacia species dominate the woodlands occupying large areas of the arid zone, with mulga varieties having by far the largest representation. Mulga has varying forms, from a multibranched shrub of 1m to an erect tree of 7m. Once used by Aboriginal people to make spear throwers and long, narrow shields, the wood is extremely hard and today it is used for turning, craftwork and fence posts. Gidgee is another acacia that covers large areas of central Australia.

Some of the deserts of southern and central Australia are surprisingly well vegetated, usually with tough, dry chenopod shrublands (such as saltbush) and spinifex-dominated hummock grasslands. After heavy rains, seeds that have been lying dormant are triggered into life and the desert is then blanketed in wildflowers. The brightly coloured poached-egg daisy is one of the most abundant and conspicuous wildflowers.

You'll see a wide variety of eucalypt species, from multistemmed mallee to giant, shade-giving river red gums, such as those majestic specimens lining the Todd River in Alice Springs and the creeks of the Flinders Ranges. These massive, spreading trees offer refuge to a variety of wildlife, such as bats, birds, small mammals, lizards and insects. The glossy green leaves and stark white bark of the ghost gum are another common sight in central Australia, and it's around Alice that they've achieved most of their fame, largely through the work of artists such as Albert Namatjira.

One of the dominant Top End eucalypts is the Darwin woollybutt, a tall tree that produces large clusters of bright orange flowers (usually from May to August). Whether flowering or not, it is easily recognisable by the 'stocking' of rough, dark-coloured bark on its lower trunk, which is in stark contrast to the smooth, white upper trunk and branches. This is the tree's inbuilt protection from grass fires. Many a termite-eaten woolybutt ends up as a didgeridoo.

There are numerous guides to Aussie mammals on the market but some are more suited to your reference library than your suitcase. One exception is the excellent *A Field Guide to the Mammals of Australia* (3rd edition, 2011) by Peter Menkhorst & Frank Knight, with just enough detail, maps and fine illustrations. A terrific companion is *The Complete Guide to Finding the Mammals of Australia* (2015) by David Andrew.

A visit to the 200-hectare Australian Arid Lands Botanic Garden (p124), on the Stuart Hwy in Port Augusta, is a great way to see a range of different arid-zone plants in one place.

Survival Guide

Deadly & Dangerous

ENVIRONMENTAL HAZARDS

Bites & Stings

Calamine lotion or Stingose spray will give some relief to many insect bites and stings and ice packs will reduce the pain and swelling. Wash well and treat any cut with an antiseptic. Where possible avoid bandages and Band-Aids, which can keep wounds moist.

Crocodiles

The risk of crocodile attack in tropical northern Australia is real but predictable and largely preventable. Discuss the local risk with police or tourist agencies in the area before swimming in rivers, waterholes (even far inland) and in the sea, and always heed warning signs.

Marine Animals

Stings Stings from jellyfish (box jellyfish, irukandji) occur in Australia's tropics, particularly during the Wet (November to April). Warning signs and stinger nets exist at popular affected beaches. Never dive into water unless you've checked that it's safe. First aid consists of washing the skin with vinegar followed by transfer to a hospital; antivenin is available.

Spikes & spines Marine spikes found on sea urchins, stonefish, scorpion fish and stingrays can cause severe local pain. If this occurs, immerse the affected area in hot water (as high a temperature as possible). Keep topping up with hot water until the pain subsides and medical care can be reached. Stonefish antivenin is available.

Sharks

Despite extensive media coverage, the risk of shark attack in Australian waters is no greater than in other countries with expansive coastlines. That said, check with local surf life-saving groups and surfers about risks.

Snakes

Risks Australian snakes have a fearful reputation, but the actual risk to travellers and locals is low. Snakes are usually quite timid and, in most instances, will move away if disturbed. Prevent bites by wearing protective clothing (such as gaiters) around the lower legs when bushwalking.

Treatment If bitten, prevent the spread of venom by applying pressure to the wound and immobilising the area with a splint or sling before seeking medical attention. Firmly wrap an elastic bandage (or a T-shirt) around the entire limb, but not so tight as to cut off the circulation.

Spiders

Australia has several poisonous spiders. In central Australia, redback spider bites cause increasing pain at the site, profuse sweating, muscular weakness and nausea. If bitten, apply ice or cold packs to the bite then transfer to hospital.

Heat Exhaustion, Heatstroke & Dehydration

Heat Exhaustion Heat exhaustion occurs when fluid intake does not keep up with fluid loss. Symptoms include dizziness, fainting, fatigue, nausea or vomiting, and pale, cool and clammy skin. Treatment consists of rest in a cool, shady place and fluid replacement with water or diluted sports drinks.

Heatstroke Heatstroke is a severe form of heat illness that occurs after fluid depletion or extreme heat challenge from heavy exercise. Extreme heatstroke is a true medical emergency, with heating of the brain leading to disorientation, hallucinations and seizures.

Dehydration A number of unprepared travellers die from dehydration each year in outback Australia – preventable by following these simple rules:

➡ Carry sufficient water for any trip, including extra in case of vehicle breakdown.

➡ Always let someone, such as the local police, know where you are going and when you expect to arrive.

➡ Carry communications equipment.

➡ Stay with the vehicle rather than walking for help.

Hypothermia

Hypothermia is a risk during winter. Early signs include the inability to perform fine movements, shivering and the 'umbles' (fumbles, mumbles, grumbles and stumbles). Treatment includes minimising heat loss, removing wet clothing and adding dry, wind- and waterproof layers. In severe cases, shivering actually stops – a medical emergency requiring rapid evacuation.

Insect-Borne Illnesses

Various insects can be a source of irritation and, in central Australia, may be the source of specific diseases (eg Ross River fever). Protection from mosquitoes, sandflies, ticks and leeches can be achieved by a combination of the following strategies:

➡ Wear light, loose-fitting, long-sleeved clothing.

➡ Apply 30% DEET to all exposed skin and repeat every three to four hours.

➡ Impregnate clothing with permethrin (an insecticide that kills insects but is believed to be safe for humans).

Sunburn

Ultraviolet (UV) exposure is greatest between 10am and 4pm, so avoid skin exposure during these times. Always use SPF 60+ sunscreen, apply it 30 minutes before going into the sun and repeat application regularly.

Surf Beaches & Drowning

The surf can be unpredictable in SA. Check with local surf life-saving organisations before entering the water, and always be aware of your own limitations.

Traveller's Diarrhoea

If you develop diarrhoea, drink plenty of fluids – preferably an oral rehydration solution containing lots of salt and sugar. You should also begin taking an antibiotic (usually a quinolone drug) and an antidiarrhoeal agent (such as loperamide). If diarrhoea is bloody, persists for more than 72 hours or is accompanied by fever, shaking chills or severe abdominal pain, seek medical attention.

INFECTIOUS DISEASES

Giardiasis

Giardia is widespread in waterways around Australia. Drinking untreated water from streams and lakes is not recommended. Use water filters and boil or treat water with iodine to help prevent the disease. Symptoms consist of intermittent bad-smelling diarrhoea, abdominal bloating and wind. Effective treatment is available (tinidazole or metronidazole).

Meningococcal Disease

This occurs worldwide and may be a risk if you have prolonged stays in dormitory-style accommodation. A vaccine exists for some types of this disease, namely meningococcal A, C, Y and W. No vaccine is presently available for the viral type of meningitis.

Ross River Fever

This is caused by a virus that's widespread throughout Australia, and is spread by mosquitoes living in marshy areas. In addition to fever, it causes headache, joint and muscular pains and a rash that resolves after five to seven days.

Sexually Transmitted Diseases (STDs)

Rates of infection are similar to most other Western countries. The most common symptoms are pain while passing urine, and a discharge. Infection can be present without symptoms, so seek medical screening after any unprotected sex with someone new – though you should always use a condom with a new sexual partner. Throughout the country you'll find sexual-health clinics in all of the major hospitals. Condoms are readily available at chemists and through vending machines in many public places, including toilets.

Viral Encephalitis

Also known as Murray Valley encephalitis virus, this is spread by mosquitoes and is most common in northern Australia, especially during the Wet (November to April). This potentially serious disease is normally accompanied by headache, muscle pains and sensitivity to light. Residual neurological damage can occur and no specific treatment is available. However, the risk to most travellers is low.

TAP WATER

Tap water is usually safe in central Australia. All other water should be boiled, filtered or chemically disinfected (with iodine tablets) to prevent traveller's diarrhoea and giardiasis (giardia).

Directory A–Z

Accommodation

South Australia & the Northern Territory have excellent accommodation possibilities, but choice is limited outside major towns and tourist sites.

➡ **Hotels, motels and pubs** Hotels are often restricted to major cities. Pub accommodation is usually very basic and motels are typically clean, convenient, conventional and everywhere.

➡ **Roadhouses** One-stop shops along the highways; from camp sites to basic dongas (small, transportable buildings) with shared facilities to modern motel rooms.

➡ **Caravan parks** Most caravan parks have cabins as well as caravan and camping sites. Many have swimming pools and restaurants.

➡ **Hostels** Found in the more major towns, hostels tend to be highly social affairs ideal for young travellers.

B&Bs

The atmosphere and privacy of B&Bs can be hard to top.

Most B&Bs are 'self-catering', meaning breakfast provisions are provided for you to cook. Rates are typically $100 to $200, though they can climb higher. B&Bs are largely restricted to SA and, to a lesser extent, Darwin – it's an idea that has yet to catch on elsewhere in the NT.

The South Australian Tourist Commission (SATC) publishes a B&B booklet. Online resources include:

➡ www.babs.com.au

➡ www.australianbed andbreakfast.com.au

➡ www.ozbedandbreakfast. com

➡ www.bandbfsa.com.au

Camping

Bush camping at remote sites or in national parks is a highlight of any trip in outback Australia. In the desert, where rain and mosquitoes are often not an issue, you don't even need a tent – just slip into a swag.

Payment is often made into honesty boxes (around $3.50 to $15 per person per night).There are plenty of free camping places out here, including roadside rest areas. In national parks camping is usually only permitted in designated areas, where facilities can range from a fireplace and simple pit toilet to hot showers and free gas barbecues.

Caravan Parks

Caravan parks are excellent value, charging from $22 to $34 for two people camping, slightly more for a powered site. Most have basic cabins with shared facilities (from around $60) and ensuite cabins with cooking facilities ($80 to $160). Book ahead for powered sites and cabins in peak season.

Most parks have a camp kitchen, laundry, BBQs and a shop or kiosk, and all offer toilets and hot showers. If the gods are smiling there might even be a swimming pool and perhaps a restaurant.

Farm & Station Stays

For a true country experience, stay on a farm or working cattle station. Some let you kick back and watch workers raise a sweat; others rope you in to helping with day-to-day chores. Most accommodation is very comfortable – B&B-style in the main homestead (dinner on request), or in self-contained cottages. Some farms also provide budget outbuildings or shearers' quarters.

One shining example of the genre is **Mt Bundy Station** (☑08 8976 7009;

SLEEPING PRICE RANGES

The following price ranges refer to a double room with bathroom in high season.

➡ **$** less than $130

➡ **$$** $130 to $250

➡ **$$$** more than $250

www.mtbundy.com.au; Haynes Rd; unpowered/powered sites $22/30, s/d $70/100, cottage d from $140; ☒), close to Adelaide River.

Online, see:

➡ www.farmstay campingaustralia.com.au

➡ www.stayz.com.au/ farm-accommodation

➡ www.bandbfsa.com.au

➡ www.frabs.com.au

Hostels

Hostels are a highly social and low-cost fixture of the outback Australian accommodation scene, although they're usually only found in larger towns.

A dormitory bed costs around $22 to $35, and most also have comfortable private rooms from around $60 ($70 to $100 with ensuite).

Most hostels have kitchens with fridges, stoves, microwaves and cooking utensils; communal areas with TV; a laundry; internet access (including wi-fi); travellers' noticeboards and tour-booking services.

Hotels & Lodges

Fancy hotels and resorts are all around SA but are limited to Darwin, Alice Springs, Yulara, Kings Canyon and Kakadu in the NT. Most have fabulous facilities and locations, but a few five-star places are clinical and corporate in atmosphere. Although rack rates are high, discounts and deals mean you'll rarely pay full price (except in peak season).

Out in the wilds of Kakadu National Park, Mary River National Park and Arnhem Land up in the NT, safari-style lodges are all the rage. With fabulously remote locations they offer a mix of semi-luxurious four-walled cabins and elevated canvas tents with ensuite bathrooms.

Motels

For comfortable, midrange accommodation, motels are

BOOK YOUR STAY ONLINE

For more accommodation reviews by Lonely Planet authors, check out lonelyplanet.com/hotels. You'll find independent reviews, as well as recommendations on the best places to stay. Best of all, you can book online.

the way to go. Even in smaller towns, there always seems to be one around. They proliferate in cities and larger towns, and many outback roadhouses also have motel rooms out the back.

Expect to pay at least $90 for a double and up to $160 for more upmarket (or remote) places.

The average motel is a modern (but anonymous), low-rise affair with parking and tidy rooms with bathroom, tea/coffee facilities, TV, telephone, air-con, a fridge humming in the corner and – if you're lucky – a swimming pool.

Pubs

For the budget traveller, pubs ('hotels' that serve beer) are cheap, central options. Many pubs were built during boom times, so they're often the largest, most extravagant buildings in town.

Pub singles/doubles with shared facilities start at around $50/70, more if you want a private bathroom. Few have a separate reception area – just ask at the bar.

Some pubs have been restored as heritage buildings, but generally rooms remain small and old-fashioned, with an amble down the hall to the bathroom. If you're a light sleeper, avoid booking a room above the bar, and be aware that pub rooms don't always have air-con.

Roadhouses

Outback roadhouses are an Australian institution, the sort of place where you can fill your car, get a filling meal or takeaway food, and find a motel or camp site for the night. They're usually

no-frills, but sometimes come brimful of personality and even they can seem like an oases after long desert kilometres.

Customs Regulations

When entering Australia you can bring most articles in free of duty, provided customs is satisfied they're for personal use or that you'll be taking them with you when you leave. Duty-free per-adult quotas:

➡ **Alcohol** 2.25L

➡ **Cigarettes** 50

➡ **Dutiable goods** Up to the value of A$900

Narcotics, of course, are illegal, and customs inspectors and their highly trained hounds are diligent in sniffing them out. Quarantine regulations are strict, so you must declare all goods of animal or vegetable origin – wooden spoons, straw hats, the lot. Fresh produce – particularly meat, cheese, fruit, vegetables and flowers – is also prohibited. There are disposal bins located in the airport where you can dump any questionable items if you don't want to bother with an inspection.

For more information, consult the Department of Immigration and Border Protection (www.border.gov.au)

Discount Cards

Senior Cards

The Seniors Card (www.seniorscard.com.au) is available to permanent residents over the age of 60, giving discounts on everything from accommodation and tours to car hire and meals (with participating businesses, of course). The card is free; apply online. Even without a card, seniors with proof of age receive a discount on admission to many attractions in central Australia.

Student Cards

A student card entitles you to a wide range of discounts, from transport and tour charges to admission fees. The most common is the International Student Identity Card (www.isic.org). To get one you need proof of full-time student status.

The same organisation also produces the International Youth Travel Card (IYTC) with benefits equivalent to the ISIC, issued to people between 12 and 26 years of age and not full-time students. Another similar card is the International Teacher Identity Card (ITIC), available to teaching professionals.

All three cards are issued by student unions, hostelling organisations and student-travel companies.

Electricity

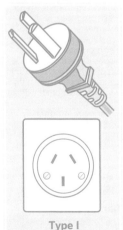

Type I
230V/50Hz

EATING PRICE RANGES

The following price ranges refer to a standard main course:

⇒ **$** less than $15

⇒ **$$** $15 to $30

⇒ **$$$** more than $30

Food

Eating in outback Australia can be as pricey or prudent as you like: a roadhouse hamburger can taste just as good as a fine-dining morsel in a haughty winery bistro.

Health

Dr David Millar

Healthwise, Australia is a remarkably safe country in which to travel, considering that such a large portion of it lies in the tropics. Few travellers to SA and the NT will experience anything worse than sunburn or a bad hangover and, if you do fall ill, the standard of hospitals and health care is high.

Availability & Cost of Health Care

Facilities Australia has an excellent health-care system. It's a mixture of privately run medical clinics and hospitals alongside a system of public hospitals funded by the Australian government. There are also excellent specialised public-health facilities for women and children in major centres.

Medicare The Medicare system covers Australian residents for some health-care costs. Visitors from countries with which Australia has a reciprocal health-care agreement are eligible for benefits specified under the Medicare program. Agreements are currently in place with Finland, Italy, Malta, the Netherlands, Norway, Sweden and the UK – check the details before departing these countries. For further details, visit www.medicareaustralia.gov.au/public/migrants/visitors.

Over-the-counter medications Widely available at chemists throughout Australia. These include painkillers, antihistamines for allergies, and skincare products.

Prescriptions You may find that medications readily available over the counter in some countries are only available in Australia by prescription. These include the oral contraceptive pill, some medications for asthma and all antibiotics.

Recommended Vaccinations

⇒ The World Health Organization (www.who.int/wer) recommends that all travellers be covered for diphtheria, tetanus, measles, mumps, rubella, chickenpox and polio, as well as hepatitis B, regardless of their destination. The consequences of these diseases can be severe and, while Australia has high levels of childhood vaccination coverage, outbreaks of these diseases do occur.

⇒ Since most vaccines don't produce immunity until at least two weeks after they're given, visit a physician four to eight weeks before departure. Ask your doctor for an International Certificate of Vaccination (otherwise known as 'the yellow booklet'), which will list all the vaccinations you've received.

⇒ If you're entering Australia within six days of having stayed overnight or longer in a yellow fever–infected country, you'll need proof of yellow fever vaccination. For a full list of these countries, visit Centers for Disease Control & Prevention (wwwnc.cdc.gov/travel).

Insurance

Level of cover A good travel insurance policy covering theft, loss and medical problems is essential. Some policies specifically exclude designated 'dangerous activities' such as scuba diving, motorcycling and even bushwalking. Make sure the policy you choose fully covers you for your activity of choice.

Health You may prefer a policy that pays doctors or hospitals directly rather than requiring you to pay on the spot and claim later. If you have to claim later make sure you keep all documentation. Check that the policy covers ambulances and emergency medical evacuations by air.

Worldwide travel insurance is available at www.lonelyplanet.com/bookings. You can buy, extend and claim online anytime – even if you're already on the road.

Internet Access

Wi-fi is increasingly the norm but connections are less common in remote areas.

Libraries Most public libraries have internet access, but generally they're provided for research needs, not for travellers to check their emails – so book ahead.

Internet cafes With the expansion of wi-fi (usually free), many internet cafes have fallen by the wayside. Most youth hostels can hook you up, as can many hotels and caravan parks.

Legal Matters

Most travellers will have no contact with Australia's police or legal system; if you do, it's most likely to be while driving.

Driving There's a significant police presence on Australian roads; police have the power to stop your car, see your licence (you're required to carry it), check your vehicle for roadworthiness, and insist that you take a breath test for alcohol (and sometimes illicit drugs).

Drugs First-time offenders caught with small amounts of illegal drugs are likely to receive a fine rather than go to jail, but the recording of a conviction against you may affect your visa status.

Visas If you remain in Australia beyond the life of your visa, you'll officially be an 'overstayer' and could face detention and expulsion, then be prevented from returning to Australia for up to three years.

Arrested? It's your right to telephone a friend, lawyer or relative before questioning begins. Legal aid is available only in serious cases; for Legal Aid office info see www.nla.aust.net.au. However, many solicitors do not charge for an initial consultation.

LGBTI Travellers

Northern Territory In the NT you'll find active gay and lesbian communities in Alice Springs, though homophobic attitudes do exist beyond the main towns.

South Australia Attitudes towards homosexuality in SA are fairly relaxed, but as you'd expect, homophobia does rear its ugly head the further you travel into the outback. Adelaide has plenty of gay-friendly venues, and a dedicated annual gay and lesbian cultural festival, **Feast** (www.feast.org.au; ☉Oct/Nov), held over two weeks in November. For info on the LGBTI scene, pick up a copy of Blaze (www.gaynewsnetwork.com.au) magazine, available around Adelaide.

Resources For general information, check out the Gay & Lesbian Tourism Australia website (www.galta.com.au), which has information on gay-friendly businesses, places to stay and nightlife. See also www.gaystayaustralia.com.

Maps

Hema Maps (www.hemamaps.com) publishes some of the best maps for desert tracks and regions, from the *Great Desert Tracks* road atlas (which has high-level overview text for the major tracks) to the three-sheet HEMA Great Desert Tracks fold-out map series – *Western Sheet, Central Sheet* and *Eastern Sheet* (all 1:250,000). Hema also publishes useful maps that include:

➜ *Central Australia* (1:2,000,000)

➜ *Flinders Ranges* (1:400,000)

➜ *Northern Territory* (1:1,750,000)

➜ *Red Centre: Alice Springs to Uluru* (1:750,000)

➜ *Savannah Way – Cairns to Broome* (1:750,000)

➜ *South Australia* (1:1,700,000)

➜ *Top End and Gulf* (1:650,000)

➜ *Top End National Parks: Litchfield, Katherine, Kakadu* (1:160,000 to 1:850,000)

Hema maps are available online and from some bookshops in the region.

Touring and 4WD maps are also available from the **Automobile Association of the Northern Territory** (AANT; ☑08 8925 5901; www.aant.com.au; 2/14 Knuckey St; ☉9am-5pm Mon-Fri, to 12.30pm Sat) or the **Royal Automobile Association of South Australia** (RAA; ☑08 8202 4589, Roadside Assistance 13 11 11; www.raa.com.au; 55 Hindmarsh Sq, Adelaide, SA; ☉8.30am-5pm Mon-Fri, 9am-4pm Sat).

Geoscience Australia (☑1800 800 173; www.ga.gov.au) publishes large-scale topographic sheet maps for bushwalking and 4WD explorations.

You can hire a GPS from the major car-hire companies (subject to availability).

Money

ATMs & Eftpos

ATMs There are 24-hour ATMs in most substantial towns in SA and the NT (including Yulara at Uluru and Jabiru and Cooinda

PRACTICALITIES

DVDs Australian DVDs are encoded for Region 4, which includes Mexico, South America, Central America, New Zealand, the Pacific and the Caribbean.

Newspapers The main newspapers are the *Advertiser* (Adelaide & SA), the *NT News* (Darwin), and the *Central-ian Advocate* (Alice Springs). The *Age*, *Sydney Morning Herald* and *Australian* newspapers are readily available.

Radio Tune in to Triple J (ABC youth radio station) and the multicultural SBS National Radio.

TV On TV you'll find the government-sponsored ABC, the multicultural SBS, Imparja (an Aboriginal-owned station), the three major commercial stations: Seven, Nine and Ten; plus additional digital channels. Not all stations will be available in remote areas, although satellite dishes often solve that 'problem'.

Smoking Banned on public transport and in pubs, bars and eateries.

Weights & Measures Australia uses the metric system.

in Kakadu National Park). All accept cards from other Australian banks, and most are linked to international networks. Stuart Hwy roadhouses also have ATMs.

Eftpos Most service stations and supermarkets have Electronic Funds Transfer at Point of Sale (Eftpos) facilities allowing you to make purchases and even draw out cash with your credit or debit card.

Credit Cards

Credit cards (especially Visa and MasterCard) are widely accepted throughout central Australia. A credit card is essential if you want to hire a car, and can also be used for cash advances at banks and from ATMs (depending on the card). Diners and AmEx cards are not widely accepted.

Lost credit card contact numbers:

American Express (☑1300 132 639; www.americanexpress.com.au)

Diners Club (☑1300 360 060; www.dinersclub.com.au)

MasterCard (☑1800 120 113; www.mastercard.com.au)

Visa (☑1800 450 346; www.visa.com.au)

Currency

Australia's currency is the Australian dollar, comprising 100 cents. There are 5c, 10c, 20c, 50c, $1 and $2 coins, and $5, $10, $20, $50 and $100 notes. Prices in shops are often marked in single cents then rounded to the nearest 5c when you come to pay.

Debit Cards

A debit card allows you to draw money directly from your home bank account using ATMs, banks or Eftpos machines. Any card connected to the international banking network – Cirrus, Maestro, Plus and Euro-card – should work with your personal identification number (PIN). Expect fees.

Companies such as Travelex offer debit cards (Travelex calls them 'Cash Passport' cards) with set withdrawal fees and a balance you can top up from your personal bank account while on the road.

Taxes & Refunds

The Goods & Services Tax (GST) is a flat 10% tax on all Australian goods and services, with some exceptions such as basic food items (milk, bread, fruit and vegetables etc). By law, the tax is included in the quoted or shelf prices. All prices we provide are GST inclusive.

Opening Hours

Banks 9.30am to 4pm Monday to Thursday; until 5pm on Friday

Cafes 7am to 5pm, or late into the night

Petrol stations and road-houses 8am to 10pm; some open 24 hours

Post offices 9am to 5pm Monday to Friday; some from 9am to noon on Saturdays

Pubs Open for drinking from lunchtime until late; food from noon to 2pm and 6pm to 8pm

Restaurants Noon to 2pm and 6pm to 8pm, often later

Shops and businesses 9am to 5pm Monday to Friday; until noon or 5pm on Saturday

Supermarkets 7am until at least 8pm

Post

Australia's postal services are reasonably cheap and efficient. Post offices are open from 9am to 5pm Monday to Friday, and you can also buy stamps at some newsagencies. Check out Australia Post (www.auspost.com.au) for postal rates and post office locations.

Public Holidays

National and statewide public holidays observed in SA and the NT:

New Year's Day 1 January

Australia Day 26 January

Easter Good Friday to Easter Monday inclusive; March/April

Anzac Day 25 April

May Day 1st Monday in May (NT only)

Adelaide Cup Day 3rd Monday in May (SA only)

Queen's Birthday 2nd Monday in June

Picnic Day 1st Monday in August (NT only)

Labour Day 1st Monday in October (SA only)

Christmas Day 25 December

Boxing Day 26 December (NT only)

Proclamation Day 28 December (SA only)

Local Holidays

Alice Springs Show Day 1st Friday in July (local only)

Tennant Creek Show Day 2nd Friday in July

Katherine Show Day 3rd Friday in July

Darwin Show Day 4th Friday in July

School Holidays

➡ The Christmas-holiday period is part of the long summer school vacation. This is low season in the NT, so you're unlikely to find crowds (except around Uluru) or accommodation booked out (but you will in SA).

➡ There are three other school-holiday periods during the year: from early to mid-April (including Easter), late June to mid-July, and late September to early October.

Safe Travel

Bushfires

Bushfires are an annual event. In hot, dry and windy weather, be extremely careful with any naked flame – cigarette butts thrown out of car windows have started many a fire – and make sure your fire's out before you decamp. On total-fire-ban days it's forbidden even to use a camping stove in the open – penalties are harsh. Campfires are banned in conservation areas during the Fire Danger Period (FDP), which varies from region to region but is usually from 1 November to 31 March (30 April in some places).

Bushwalkers should seek local advice before setting out. When a total fire ban is in place, delay your trip until the weather improves. If you're out in the bush and you see smoke, even a long distance away, take it seriously – bushfires move quickly and change direction with the wind. Go to the nearest open space, down-hill if possible. A forested ridge, on the other hand, is the most dangerous place to be.

Crime

SA and the NT are relatively safe places to visit but you should still take reasonable precautions. Lock hotel rooms and cars, and don't leave your valuables unattended or visible through car windows. In Darwin, Alice Springs and Katherine, petty crime can be a problem, particularly late at night. Avoid walking alone in unlit areas.

In response to several reports of drugged drinks in pubs and clubs, Darwin authorities are advising women to refuse drinks offered by strangers in bars and to drink bottled alcohol rather than from a glass.

On the Road

As a rule, Australian drivers are a courteous bunch, but risks can be posed by rural rev heads, inner-city speedsters and fatigue- or alcohol-affected drivers. Road distances are HUGE so take regular breaks to avoid fatigue and be aware of animals, which can be a real hazard on country roads, particularly at dusk.

If you're keen to explore the outback, do some careful planning and preparation. Driving on dirt roads can be tricky if you're not used to them, and travellers regularly encounter difficulties in the harsh outback conditions. The golden rules are to always carry plenty of water and tell someone where you're going.

At the Beach

Popular beaches are patrolled by surf lifesavers. Safe areas are marked by red-and-yellow flags. Even so, surf beaches can still be dangerous if you aren't used to the local conditions. Undertows (or 'rips') are the main problem. If you find yourself being carried out by a rip, don't panic or try to swim against the rip, which will exhaust you. In most cases the current stops within a couple of hundred metres of shore – you can then swim parallel to the shore for a short way to escape the rip and make your way back to land. If you swim between the flags, help should arrive quickly; raise your arm (and yell!) if you need help.

A number of people are paralysed every year by diving into waterholes or waves in shallow water and hitting the bottom – look before you leap.

Always assume that there are crocodiles in waterholes and rivers in the Top End – seek local advice before jumping in.

Telephone

Australia's main telecommunications companies:

Telstra (www.telstra.com.au) The main player – landline and mobile phone services.

Optus (www.optus.com.au) Telstra's main rival – landline and mobile phone services.

Vodafone (www.vodafone.com. au) Mobile phone services.

Virgin (www.virginmobile.com. au) Mobile phone services.

GOVERNMENT TRAVEL ADVICE

The following government websites offer travel advisories and information for travellers.

Australian Department of Foreign Affairs & Trade (www.smartraveller.gov.au)

Canadian Department of Foreign Affairs & International Trade (www.voyage.gc.ca)

French Ministère des Affaires Étrangères et Européennes (www.diplomatie.gouv.fr/fr/conseils-aux-voyageurs)

Italian Ministero degli Affari Esteri (www.viaggia resicuri.mae.aci.it)

New Zealand Ministry of Foreign Affairs & Trade (www.safetravel.govt.nz)

UK Foreign & Commonwealth Office (www.gov.uk/foreign-travel-advice)

US Department of State (www.travel.state.gov)

Information & Toll-Free Calls

➡ Numbers starting with 190 are usually recorded information services, costing anything from 35c to $5 or more per minute (more from mobiles and payphones).

➡ Many businesses have either a toll-free 1800 number, dialled from anywhere within Australia for free, or a 13 or 1300 number, charged at a local call rate. None of these numbers can be dialled from outside Australia.

➡ To make a reverse-charge (collect) call from a public or private phone, dial 1800 738 3773 or 12 550.

International Calls

➡ You can make international subscriber dialling (ISD) calls from most phones, but the cheapest deals come through phonecards, with calls to the UK and USA that can be as low as 1.5c per minute.

➡ To call overseas from Australia, dial the international access code from Australia (0011 or 0018), the country code, the area code (minus the initial '0'), then the local phone number.

➡ Dialling Australia from overseas, use the 61 country code, then the state/territory STD area code (minus the initial '0'), then the local phone number.

Local Calls

Local calls cost 50c from public phones; 25c from private phones – there are no time limits. Calls to/from mobile phones cost more and are timed.

Long-Distance Calls

Australia uses subscriber trunk dialling (STD) area codes for long-distance calls. The area code for SA and the NT is 08. Long-distance calls are timed; rates vary depending on distance, service provider and time of day – they're cheaper off-peak (usually between 7pm and 7am).

Mobile Phones

European phones will work on Australia's network, but most American or Japanese phones won't. Use global roaming or a local SIM card and prepaid account.

NUMBERS, NETWORKS & PROVIDERS

Numbers Australian mobile-phone numbers have the prefix 04 and contain 10 digits (04xx xxx xxx).

Reception Australia's mobile networks service more than 90% of the population but leave vast tracts of the country uncovered. Adelaide, Darwin and most of central Australia's settled areas get good reception, but as the towns thin out, so does the service. Don't rely on coverage in outback areas, except in Yulara.

Networks Australia's digital network is compatible with GSM 900 and 1800 (used in Europe), but isn't compatible with the systems used in the USA or Japan.

Providers It's easy and cheap to get connected short term – the main service providers all have prepaid mobile systems.

Phonecards

A range of phonecards ($10, $20, $30 etc) is available from newsagencies and post offices, and can be used with any public or private phone by dialling a toll-free access number and then the PIN on the card. Rates vary from company to company – shop around.

Time

➡ SA and the NT are on Central Standard Time, half an hour behind the eastern states (Queensland, New South Wales, Victoria and Tasmania), and 1½ hours ahead of Western Australia.

➡ Central Standard Time is 9½ hours ahead of GMT/UTC (London), 13½ ahead of New York, 15½ ahead of LA, 2½ ahead of Jakarta and 2½ hours behind Wellington (New Zealand).

➡ 'Daylight savings' does not apply in the NT, WA or Qld during summer, so from October to March (approximately), most eastern states are 1½ hours ahead of NT time, and SA is one hour ahead of NT time.

Toilets

➡ Toilets in SA and the NT are sit-down style (though you mightn't find this prospect too appealing in some remote outback pit stops).

➡ See www.toiletmap.gov.au for public toilet locations.

Tourist Information

Almost every decent-sized town and the larger national parks have a visitor information centre of some description, with a proliferation of brochures and maps and professional staff. In smaller towns or tourist centres, they're usually staffed by volunteers (some with sketchy knowledge of tourism).

The best online resources include:

South Australian Tourism Commission (www.tourism. sa.gov.au)

Tourism Australia (www. australia.com) The main government tourism site with visitor info.

Tourism NT (www. northernterritory.com) Bountiful info on the NT outback. Also produces *The Essential NT Drive Guide*, a great booklet with driving distances, national parks, and outback info and advice for 2WD and 4WD travellers.

Tourism Top End (www. tourismtopend.com.au) Helpful office with hundreds of brochures; books tours and accommodation.

Travellers with Disabilities

Disability awareness in Australia is pretty high and getting higher. New accommodation must meet accessibility standards, and discrimination by tourism operators is illegal. Many key attractions provide access for those with limited mobility, and sometimes for those with visual or aural impairments; contact attractions in advance.

Long-distance bus travel isn't viable for wheelchair users, but the *Ghan* train has disabled facilities (book ahead). Some car-rental companies (Avis, Hertz) offer rental cars with hand controls at no extra charge for pick-up at the major airports (advance notice required).

Download Lonely Planet's free *Accessible Travel* guide from lptravel.to/AccessibleTravel.

Australian Resources

Deaf CanDo (Royal South Australian Deaf Society; 08 8100 8200; www.deafcando.com.au)

Deafness Association of the Northern Territory (08 8945 2016; www.deafnt.org.au)

Guide Dogs SA/NT (08 8203 8333, 1800 484 333; www.guidedogs.org.au)

National Information Communication & Awareness Network (Nican; 1300 655 535, 02 6241 1220; www.nican.com.au) Australia-wide directory providing information on access, accommodation, sports and recreational activities, transport and specialist tour operators.

South Australian Royal Society for the Blind (08 8417 5599; www.rsb.org.au)

Vision Australia (1300 847 466; www.visionaustralia.org.au)

International Resources

Access-Able Travel Source (www.access-able.com) A US-based site providing information on disabled-friendly tours and hotels.

Mobility International USA (www.miusa.org) In the US, it advises disabled travellers on mobility issues; it primarily runs educational exchange programs.

Society for Accessible Travel & Hospitality (www.sath.org) In the US; offers assistance and advice.

Visas

Obtaining a Visa

➡ All visitors to Australia need a visa – only New Zealand nationals are exempt, and even they sheepishly receive a 'special category' visa on arrival.

➡ There are several different visas available, depending on your nationality and what kind of visit you're contemplating.

➡ See the website of the Department of Immigration & Border protection (www.border.gov.au) for info and application forms (also available from Australian diplomatic missions overseas and travel agents), plus details on visa extensions, Working Holiday Visas (417) and Work & Holiday Visas (462).

eVisitor

Many European passport holders are eligible for a free eVisitor visa, allowing stays in Australia for up to three months within a 12-month period. eVisitor visas must be applied for online (www.border.gov.au). They are electronically stored and linked to individual passport numbers, so no stamp in your passport is required. It's advisable to apply at least 14 days prior to the proposed date of travel to Australia.

Electronic Travel Authority (ETA)

Passport holders from eight countries which aren't part of the eVisitor scheme – Brunei, Canada, Hong Kong, Japan, Malaysia, Singapore, South Korea and the USA – can apply for either a visitor or business ETA. ETAs are valid for 12 months, with stays of up to three months on each visit. You can apply for the ETA online (www.eta.immi.gov.au), which attracts a nonrefundable service charge of $20.

Tourist Visa (676)

If you're from a country not covered by the eVisitor and ETA, or you want to stay longer than three months, you'll need to apply for a Tourist Visa. Standard Tourist Visas (from AUD$135) allow one (in some cases multiple) entry, for a stay of up to 12 months, and are valid for use within 12 months of issue.

Working Holiday Visa

On a normal visa you're not allowed to work in Australia, but you may be eligible for a 12-month working-holiday visa, which lets you supplement your travels with casual employment. People from 19 countries (including the UK, Canada, Korea, the Netherlands, Malta, Ireland, Japan, Germany, France, Italy, Belgium, Finland, Sweden, Norway and Denmark) are eligible, but you must be between 18 and 30 years old at the time of lodging your application; the government was considering raising the eligible age to 35 years at the time of writing, although nothing was confirmed. A visa subclass is available to residents of Chile, Thailand, Turkey and the USA.

The emphasis on casual rather than full-time work means that you can only work for six months at a time with any one employer – but you are free to work for more than one employer within the 12 months. There's a limit on the number of visas issued each year, so apply as early as possible to the Australian embassy in your home country before you leave.

Volunteering

Lonely Planet's *Volunteer: A Traveller's Guide to Making a Difference Around the World* (2013) provides useful information about volunteering.

Australian Volunteers International (www.australianvolunteers.com) Places skilled volunteers into Indigenous communities in northern and central Australia (mostly long-term placements). Occasional short-term unskilled opportunities too, helping out at community-run roadhouses.

Conservation Council of SA (☑08 8223 5155; www.conservationsa.org.au; 111 Franklin St Adelaide; ◷9am-5pm Mon-Fri) South Australian volunteer opportunities including restoration of swamps, grasslands and other natural habitats, and recovery programs for threatened bird species.

Conservation Volunteers Australia (www.conservationvolunteers.com.au) Nonprofit organisation involved in tree planting, walking-track construction, and flora and fauna surveys.

Earthwatch (www.earthwatch.org) Respected worldwide NGO with a wildlife and environmental focus that sometimes has Australian expeditions for volunteers.

Nature Conservation Society of South Australia (☑08 7127 4630; www.ncssa.asn.au) Survey fieldwork volunteer opportunities in SA.

Women Travellers

Travelling in SA and the NT is generally safe for women, but everyone should exercise common sense.

➡ Avoid walking alone at night and be wary of stopping for anyone on the highway.

➡ Sexual harassment is rare though some macho (and less enlightened) Aussie males still slip – particularly when they've been drinking.

➡ Hitching is not recommended for anyone. Even when travelling in pairs, exercise caution at all times.

➡ Lone women should also be wary of staying in basic pub accommodation unless it looks safe and well-managed.

➡ The Adelaide-based Women's Information Service (www.wis.sa.gov.au) provides information, advice and referrals.

Work

Work visas If you come to Australia on a tourist visa then you're not allowed to work for pay: you'll need a Working Holiday Visa (417) or Work & Holiday Visa (462) – visit www.border.gov.au for details.

Finding work Backpacker magazines, newspapers and hostel noticeboards are good places to source local work opportunities. In SA, seasonal fruit picking and vineyard work abounds.

Resources

➡ **Career One** (www.careerone.com.au) General employment site; good for metropolitan areas.

➡ **Gumtree** (www.gumtree.com.au) Classified site with jobs, accommodation and items for sale.

➡ **Job Active – Harvest** (www.jobsearch.gov.au/harvest) Harvest job specialists.

➡ **National Harvest Labour Information Service** (☑1800 062 332) Info on when and where you're likely to pick up harvest work.

➡ **Seek** (www.seek.com.au) General employment site; good for metropolitan areas.

➡ **Travellers at Work** (www.taw.com.au) Excellent site for working travellers in Australia.

➡ **Workabout Australia** (www.workaboutaustralia.com.au) Gives a state-by-state breakdown of seasonal work opportunities.

Transport

GETTING THERE & AWAY

Australia is a long way from just about everywhere – getting there usually means a long-haul flight. If you're short on time on the ground, consider internal flights – they're affordable (compared with petrol and car-hire costs), can usually be carbon offset, and will save you some *looong* days in the saddle. Flights, tours and rail tickets can be booked online at lonely-planet.com/bookings.

Entering the Country

There are no restrictions regarding citizens of foreign countries entering Australia. If you have a current passport and visa, you should be fine.

Air

Flying around Australia is the fastest, safest and often cheapest way to get from state to state or city to city.

Airports & Airlines

The main airports in South Australia and the Northern Territory are at Adelaide, Darwin, Alice Springs and Yulara (for Uluru).

Some airlines fly directly into **Adelaide Airport** (ADL; ☑08 8308 9211; www. adelaideairport.com.au; 1 James Schofield Dr) and **Darwin International Airport** (☑08 8920 1811; www. darwinairport.com.au; Henry Wrigley Dr, Marrara), but most utilise east-coast hubs (Sydney, Melbourne, Brisbane) from where you can book domestic flights to Adelaide, Darwin and regional centres.

The major Australian domestic carriers – **Qantas** (☑13 13 13; www.qantas.com),

Virgin Australia (www. virginaustralia.com) and **Jetstar** (www.jetstar.com. au) – fly all over Australia, operating flights between Adelaide and Darwin and other centres. Both Qantas and Virgin also fly to Alice Springs and Uluru, while Jetstar flies to Uluru.

Airnorth (☑1800 627 474; www.airnorth.com.au) is a small airline with flights from Darwin to Broome and Kununurra in Western Australia, and Mt Isa and Townsville in Queensland. They also fly to/ from East Timor.

Tickets

High season for flights to/ from Australia is between December and February, except in the tropical north where it's around June to September.

Round-the-world tickets can be a good option for getting to Australia: Adelaide is an easy inclusion, but Darwin is a little trickier.

CLIMATE CHANGE & TRAVEL

Every form of transport that relies on carbon-based fuel generates CO_2, the main cause of human-induced climate change. Modern travel is dependent on aeroplanes, which might use less fuel per kilometre per person than most cars but travel much greater distances. The altitude at which aircraft emit gases (including CO_2) and particles also contributes to their climate change impact. Many websites offer 'carbon calculators' that allow people to estimate the carbon emissions generated by their journey and, for those who wish to do so, to offset the impact of the greenhouse gases emitted with contributions to portfolios of climate-friendly initiatives throughout the world. Lonely Planet offsets the carbon footprint of all staff and author travel.

DEPARTURE TAX

The Australian international departure tax ($55) should be included in your airline ticket – check when you book.

Qantas (☑13 13 13; www.qantas.com.au) offers a discount-fare Walkabout Air Pass (www.qantas.com/travel/airlines/walkabout/us/en) for passengers flying into Australia from overseas with Qantas or American Airlines. The pass allows you to link up around 80 domestic Australian destinations (including Adelaide, Uluru, Alice Springs and Darwin) for less than you'd pay booking flights individually.

Land

If you're a keen driver, central Australia was made for you! There's not much traffic here, roads are in good condition, and there are there are plenty of opportunities for off-road exploration.

South Australia Bitumen highways link the huge distances between Adelaide in SA and other Australian cities, including Melbourne to the east and Perth to the west. The Stuart Hwy runs across north–south across the entire country to Darwin.

Northern Territory Getting to the NT overland means a lot of travel through empty country, but there's no better way to appreciate Australia's vastness. The nearest state capital to Darwin is Adelaide (a tick over 3000km), while Perth and Sydney are both around 4000km away – about the same distance as New York to Los Angeles and more than 2½ times the drive from London to Rome! More manageable paved road links are to the provincial towns of Mt Isa (Qld) and Kununurra (WA), while numerous unsealed roads cross state borders somewhere out in the outback – two of the best-known are the Tanami Road (p198) and the Savannah Way (p186) (www.savannahway.com.au).

State Border Crossings

There are no international land border crossings here, but a few state or provincial ones.

➡ The main routes into SA include Hwy 1 from WA (across the Nullarbor Plain), and the Stuart Hwy from the NT (via Alice Springs).

➡ From Victoria, there are two main crossings: the Princes Hwy (via Mt Gambier and/or Great Ocean Rd), and the more direct (but more dull) Dukes Hwy (via Bordertown and Vic's Western Hwy).

➡ Outback 4WD tracks aside, there are three main (sealed) roads into the NT: the Victoria Hwy from WA (via Kununurra), the Barkly Hwy from Qld (via Mt Isa), and the Stuart Hwy from SA (via Coober Pedy).

Bus

Many travellers prefer to access outback Australia by bus because it's one of the best ways to come to grips with the area's size – also the bus companies have far more comprehensive route networks than the railway system (and they have good air-con!). Discounts are available for members of backpacker associations/international student ID card holders.

Major long-haul operators include:

Firefly Express (☑1300 730 740; www.fireflyexpress.com.au) Runs between Sydney, Canberra, Melbourne and Adelaide.

Greyhound Australia (www.greyhound.com.au) Australia-wide bus network including the Top End.

V/Line (☑1800 800 007; www.vline.com.au) Bus and bus/train services between Adelaide and Melbourne.

BUS PASSES

If you're planning on doing a lot of bus travel in central Australia, a **Greyhound Australia** (☑1300 473 946; www.greyhound.com.au) bus pass will save you money. For a full list of passes and routes, check out www.greyhound.com.au/passes.

Km Pass These are the most flexible passes, giving you specified amounts of travel starting at 1000km ($189), going up in increments to 25,000km ($2675). Passes are valid for 12 months, and you can travel where and in what direction you please, stopping as many times as you like. Use the online kilometre chart to figure out which pass suits you. Make sure you reserve your seat in advance.

Short Hop Pass You have 30 days to travel and you can get on and off as many times as you like between two preselected major cities – Adelaide and Alice Springs ($229) or Alice Springs and Darwin ($225).

Hop-On, Hop-Off Pass Passes of longer durations for longer journeys along prescribed routes. You have 90 days to make the journey. The only route relevant to outback Australia is Alice Spings to/from Cairns in Qld ($385).

Train

The famous *Ghan* train connects Adelaide with Darwin via Alice Springs. From Adelaide there are rail connections with Sydney and Perth on the *Indian Pacific* and Melbourne on the *Overland*. You can also join the *Ghan* at Port Augusta, the connection point on the Sydney–Perth *Indian Pacific* route.

➡ From Adelaide, the *Ghan* departs Adelaide for Alice Springs on Sunday and Wednesday (18 hours), continuing on to Darwin arriving on Tuesday and Friday (another 24 hours).

It returns from Darwin to Alice Springs on Wednesday and Saturday, continuing to Adelaide and arriving on Friday and Monday.

➡ From Melbourne, the *Overland* has day trains to Adelaide (10 hours) on Tuesday, Thursday and Saturday, returning on Monday, Wednesday and Friday.

➡ From Sydney, the *Indian Pacific* departs on Wednesday (plus Saturday in September and October) for Adelaide (25 hours, arriving Thursday), continuing to Perth (another 40 hours, arriving Saturday). The return leg chugs out of Perth on Sunday (plus Wednesday in September and October),

COSTS & CLASSES

Classes The *Ghan* and *Indian Pacific* no longer offer economy or seat class, and instead there are Platinum and Gold sleeper classes that involve cabins with different kinds of foldaway seats and beds. Pricier sleepers have ensuites and private restaurant-car dining.

Discounts Booking at least six months ahead will secure a discount (up to 20% off) on Gold Service cabins.

Motorail The Motorail service allows you to put your vehicle on the train.

RESERVATIONS

Book tickets through **Great Southern Rail** (☑1800 703 357, 08 8213 4401; www. greatsouthernrail.com.au). Advance bookings are recommended, especially for Motorail spaces.

Sea

There are no scheduled international passenger-ferry services to/from SA or the NT, but it's possible – with a bit of graft and good fortune – to sail to northern Australia from Asia by hitching rides or crewing on yachts. Ask around at harbours, marinas or yacht clubs. Darwin is a good place to try to hitch a ride to Indonesia, Malaysia or Singapore. Try contacting the **Darwin Sailing Club** (☑08 8981 1700; www.dwnsail.com. au) at Fannie Bay, or the Darwin Port Corporation (www.darwinport.com.au).

GETTING AROUND

Outback Australia is vast: buses and trains can shuttle you between the major centres, but you'll be getting behind the wheel for most other destinations.

Car & 4WD To explore SA and the NT properly you'll need your own wheels (4WDs for outback tracks). There are car-hire outlets in cities and most large towns. Drive on the left.

Bus Useful, affordable, regular connections between major centres: good for covering long distances on a budget.

Train Expensive, infrequent long-distance routes: more for romance and scenery than expedience.

HISTORY OF THE GHAN

The legendary *Ghan* was named after the Afghan cameleers who helped forge tracks through central Australia. It is now considered one of the best railway journeys in the world, but it wasn't always that way.

The *Ghan* saga began in 1877, but the line took more than 50 years to reach Alice Springs after construction began in the wrong place. The creek beds north of Marree were bone dry and nobody had ever seen rain out there, so the initial stretch of line was laid right across a floodplain. When the rain came, the line simply washed away.

This wasn't the end of the *Ghan*'s early problems. At first the line was built as a wide-gauge track to Marree, then extended in 1884 as narrow gauge to Oodnadatta. But the foundations were flimsy, the sleepers too light and the grading too steep, and the whole thing meandered hopelessly. The top speed of the old *Ghan* was a flat-out 30km/h! Early rail travellers went from Adelaide to Marree on the broad-gauge line, changed there for Oodnadatta, then made the final journey to Alice Springs by Afghani-led camel train.

In 1929 the line was extended from Oodnadatta to Alice Springs. Though the *Ghan* was a great adventure, it was slow and uncomfortable as it bounced and bucked its way down the badly-laid line. Worst of all, a heavy rainfall could strand it at either end, or even somewhere in the middle. Parachute drops of supplies to stranded train travellers became part of outback lore, and on one occasion the *Ghan* rolled into Alice 10 days late!

In the early 1970s the South Australian state railway system was taken over by the Federal government and a new, standard-gauge, $145-million line to Alice Springs was planned. In 1980 the line was completed ahead of time and on budget. In 2004 the Alice Springs to Darwin section was finally opened, completing the trans-Australia crossing from Adelaide to Darwin – 2979km and 42 hours of track.

Air

It is possible to fly between Adelaide, Alice Springs and Darwin with **Qantas** (☑13 13 13; www.qantas.com.au), **Virgin Australia** (www.virginaustralia.com) or **Jetstar** (www.jetstar.com.au), depending on the route.

Within SA, the main regional airlines are:

Altitude Aviation (☑1800 747 300; www.altitudeaviation.com.au) Charter flights (including helicopters) to/from pretty much anywhere in central Australia.

Regional Express (Rex; ☑13 17 13; www.regionalexpress.com.au) Flies between Adelaide and Kingscote on Kangaroo Island, Coober Pedy, Ceduna, Mt Gambier, Port Lincoln and Whyalla, plus Mildura and Broken Hill interstate.

Rossair Charter (☑08 8234 4219; www.rossaircharter.com.au) Adelaide-based charter flights around SA.

In the NT, the main regional operator is **Airnorth** (☑1800 627 474; www.airnorth.com.au), with flights from Darwin to Broome, Kununurra and East Timor, as well as small airports across Arnhem Land.

Bicycle

South Australia SA is a great place for cycling. There are some excellent bike tracks in Adelaide, thousands of kilometres of quiet, flat country roads, converted railway tracks in wine regions and the **Mawson Trail**, an 800km mountain-bike track from Adelaide to Parachilna Gorge in the Flinders Ranges.

Northern Territory Darwin also has a network of bike tracks, and Katherine and Alice Springs have plenty of pancake-flat riding opportunities. However, actually using a bicycle as your mode of transport in the NT is another matter. Dehydration and the availability of drinking water are the main concerns. It can be a long way between towns and roadhouses, and those isolated bores, creeks and tanks shown on your map may be dry or undrinkable.

Practicalities

Make sure you've got the necessary spare parts and bike-repair knowledge. Carry a good map and let someone know where you're headed before setting off. Check road conditions and weather forecasts, and make conservative estimates of how long your journey will take. Beware of road trains: if you hear one coming, get right off the road. No matter how fit you are, take things slowly until you're used to the heat, wear a hat and plenty of sunscreen, and drink lots of water.

Bicycle Hire

➡ In SA you can hire bikes in Adelaide, McLaren Vale, Victor Harbor, the Barossa and Clare Valleys and the Flinders Ranges.

➡ In the NT you can hire bikes in Darwin, Alice Springs, Yulara and Wauchope.

➡ Costs start at around $25 per day, usually including helmet, lights and lock.

Buying a Bike

➡ If you want to buy a reliable new road or mountain bike, your absolute bottom-level starting point is $500 to $650. Throw in all the requisite on-the-road equipment (panniers, helmet etc), and your starting point becomes $1500 to $2000.

➡ Second hand bikes are worth checking out in the cities, as are the post-Christmas sales and midyear stock takes, when newish cycles can be heavily discounted.

➡ To sell your bike, try hostel noticeboards or online at www.tradingpost.com.au.

Transporting Your Bike

➡ If you're coming to SA and the NT specifically to cycle, it makes sense to bring your own bike – check with your airline for costs and the degree of dismantling/packing required.

➡ While you can load your bike onto a bus to skip the boring/difficult bits, bus companies require you to dismantle your bike, and some don't guarantee that it will travel on the same bus as you.

Boat

South Australia The only passenger ferries in SA are between Cape Jervis and Kangaroo Island, run by **SeaLink** (☑13 13 01; www.sealink.com.au), and across Spencer Gulf between Wallaroo on the Yorke Peninsula and Lucky Bay on the Eyre Peninsula, run by **SeaSA** (☑08 8823 0777; www.seasa.com.au). Both are smooth, efficient operations (if a little pricey).

Northern Territory In the NT **SeaLink** (www.sealinknt.com.au; adult/child one-way $52.50/27.50, return $105/55) has passenger ferries that operate between Darwin and Mandorah and the Tiwi Islands.

Bus

Bus transport in central Australia is regular, safe, efficient and (usually) cost-effective – distances can be *very* long.

LEGALITIES

Bike helmets are compulsory in all states and territories, as are white front lights and red rear lights for riding at night.

Northern Territory

In Darwin, interstate and intra-NT buses use the **Transit Centre** (www.enjoy-darwin.com/transit-bus.html; 69 Mitchell St).

Greyhound Australia (www.greyhound.com.au) runs the major long-distance regional routes in the NT, including Alice Springs to Uluru and Kings Canyon; Alice to Darwin via Katherine and Tennant Creek; and Darwin to Kakadu.

The **Bodhi Bus** (☑08 8971 0774; www.thebodhibus. com.au; 6/27 Katherine Tce) has a Katherine–Tennant Creek service but is better known for its much-needed services along remote, less frequented routes that include Katherine to Timber Creek, Borroloola and either Numbulwar (in the Dry) or Ngukurr (in the Wet).

South Australia

In SA, Adelaide's **Central Bus Station** (☑08 8221 5080; www.adelaidemetro. com.au/bussa; 85 Franklin St; ⊙6am-9.30pm) has ticket offices and terminals for all major statewide and interstate services, including long-distance operators **Greyhound Australia** (☑1300 473 946; www. greyhound.com.au), **Firefly Express** (☑1300 730 740; www.fireflyexpress.com.au) and **V/Line** (☑1800 800 007; www.vline.com.au).

Premier Stateliner (☑1300 851 345; www. premierstateliner.com.au) is the main service provider within SA. It runs to destinations including McLaren Vale, Victor Harbor, Mt Gambier, Port Augusta, Port Pirie, Naracoorte and Penola, among many others.

Other regional SA bus companies include:

➥ **LinkSA** (☑08 8532 2633; www.linksa.com.au) Covers the lower Murray River region, Barossa Valley and parts of the Adelaide Hills.

INTERSTATE QUARANTINE

Within Australia, there are restrictions on carrying fruit, plants and vegetables across state and territory borders. This is in order to control the movement of disease or pests – such as fruit fly, cucurbit thrips, grape phylloxera and potato cyst nematodes – from one area to another.

Most quarantine control relies on honesty and quarantine posts at the state/territory borders are not always staffed. However, the Western Australia border is permanently manned and sometimes uses dogs to sniff out offending matter. This may seem excessive, but it's taken very seriously. It's prohibited to carry fresh fruit and vegetables, plants, flowers, and even nuts and honey across the Northern Territory–Western Australia border in either direction. The controls with South Australia, Victoria, New South Wales and Queensland are less strict – there's usually an unmanned honesty bin for disposal. Check at the borders.

➥ **Southlink** (☑08 8186 2888; www.southlink.com. au) Fleurieu Peninsula and Adelaide's far northern suburbs.

➥ **Yorke Peninsula Coaches** (☑08 8821 2755; www.yp coaches.com.au) Clare Valley, Yorke Peninsula and southern Flinders Ranges.

Car & Motorcycle

The ultimate freedom within SA and the NT is to have your own wheels. Driving distances are long, but you can take it at your own pace and branch off the main roads to places public transport doesn't go. Shared between three or four people the cost of hiring a car or even a 4WD or campervan can be reasonable but, before you drive off into the sunset, you need to know a few things about outback travel.

2WD or 4WD? To truly explore outback areas you'll need a well-prepared 4WD vehicle, but there are plenty of routes open to a conventional (2WD) vehicle. Even the legendary Oodnadatta Track can, in theory, be tackled in a 2WD, but we wouldn't recommend it.

Motorcycle Born to be wild? The central Australian climate is good for bikes for much of the year, particularly in SA, and the many small tracks from the road into the bush lead to perfect spots to spend the night.

➥ A fuel range of 350km will cover fuel stops along the Stuart Hwy.

➥ The long, open roads are really made for large-capacity machines above 750cc.

➥ Contact the **Motorcycle Riders Association of SA** (☑0408 607 788; www.mrasa. asn.au) for info.

Automobile Associations

Official automobile associations offer emergency breakdown services and useful advice on motoring, including road safety, local regulations and buying/selling a car. The following organisations have reciprocal arrangements with similar organisations overseas and interstate.

➥ **Automobile Association of the Northern Territory** (AANT; ☑08 8925 5901; www. aant.com.au; 2/14 Knuckey St; ⊙9am-5pm Mon-Fri, to 12.30pm Sat)

ABORIGINAL LAND PERMITS

If you wish to travel through the outback independently, particularly in the Northern Territory, you may need special permits if you're passing through Aboriginal land or visiting a community. Generally, such land has government-administered reserve status or it may be held under freehold title vested in an Aboriginal land trust and managed by a council or corporation.

Exclusions In some cases permits won't be necessary if you stick to recognised public roads that cross Aboriginal territory, but as soon as you leave the main road by more than 50m you may need a permit. If you're on an organised tour the operator should take care of permits – check before you book.

In the NT a transit permit is required for most of Arnhem Land, the Mereenie Loop (from the West MacDonnell Ranges to Kings Canyon) and the Yulara–Kaltukatjara (Docker River) Rd, but not for either the Tanami Rd or the Sandover Hwy where these cross Aboriginal land. Travellers may camp overnight without a permit within 50m of the latter two routes.

Applications The easiest way to apply for a permit is to download a form from the relevant land council and send it by email. Alternatively you can send it by post or fax. Allow plenty of time: transit permits can be approved within 24 hours, but others can (and very often do) take 10 working days. Keep in mind that your application may be knocked back for a number of reasons, including the risk of interference with sacred sites or disruption of ceremonial business. Also, some communities simply may not want to be bothered by visitors without good reason.

The following places issue permits:

➡ **Northern Land Council** (www.nlc.org.au) For western Arnhem Land and much of the Top End.

➡ **Central Land Council** (www.clc.org.au) For areas around Alice Springs and Uluru.

➡ **Dhimurru Aboriginal Corporation** (☑08 8939 2700; www.dhimurru.com.au; Arnhem Rd, Nhulunbuy) Eastern Arnhem Land.

➡ **Tiwi Land Council** (☑08 8981 4898; www.tiwilandcouncil.com; 162/2 Armidale St, Stuart Park) For the Tiwi Islands.

➡ **Royal Automobile Association of South Australia** (RAA; ☑08 8202 4589, Roadside Assistance 13 11 11; www.raa.com.au; 55 Hindmarsh Sq, Adelaide, SA; ⏱8.30am-5pm Mon-Fri, 9am-4pm Sat)

Driving Licences

Foreign driving licences are valid in Australia as long as they are in English or are accompanied by a translation. You can also get an International Driving Permit from automobile associations in your own country.

Fuel

➡ Unleaded, diesel and LPG fuel are available from urban service stations and highway roadhouses.

➡ Distances between fill-ups can be long in the outback, so check locations and opening times of service stations and carry spare fuel.

➡ Prices vary from place to place depending on how remote they are, but fuel in outback central Australia is some of the most expensive in the country: at the time of writing unleaded petrol prices were hovering around $1.15 in Adelaide, $1.30 in Darwin, and climbing as high as $1.85 in remote areas. Regardless, expect to pay 20% more in Darwin than in the east coast capitals, and up to 50% more in small outback towns.

Hire

There are plenty of car-rental companies ready and willing to put you behind the wheel. Competition is fierce so rates vary and special deals pop up and disappear again. The main thing to remember when assessing your options is distance – if you want to travel far, you need *unlimited kilometres*. The major companies offer this, or 100km a day free plus however many cents per kilometre beyond 100km (make sure you do your sums!). Darwin offices in particular seem reluctant to offer unlimited kilometres, but miraculously seem happy to do so if you book through a travel agency or local tourist information office.

Age You must be at least 21 years old to hire from most firms – if you're under 25 you may only be able to hire a small car or have to pay a surcharge.

One-way Hire One-way hire into or out of the NT and SA may be subject to a hefty repositioning fee; however, some big rental hfirms offer good deals from Alice Springs to Adelaide or Adelaide to Melbourne. Ask about this before deciding on one company over another.

Relocations For budget car-hire experience, relocations can often work well: when a rental company requires a certain vehicle to be moved to a certain location, they'll sometimes offer a cheap rate for someone to drive it there. Lucky you!

Insurance & Excess Most car-rental companies include insurance in the price, but in the event of an accident the hirer is still liable for a some-times-hefty excess. Most offer an excess-reduction daily rate on top of the base rental rate. Most firms won't let you drive after dark in the outback due to the risk of hitting kangaroos – read the fine print.

Costs Daily rates, including insurance and taxes, are typically about $40 to $80 a day for a small car (Toyota Yaris, Hyundai i20), $70 to $100 a day for a medium car (Holden Cruze, Toyota Corolla) or $90 up to $120 a day for a big car (Holden Commodore, Hyundai i45). Local firms are almost always cheaper than the big boys – sometimes half-price – but cheaper hire often comes with crippling restrictions. It's cheaper if you rent for a week or more and there are often low-season and weekend discounts.

The main players:

➡ **Avis** (☑13 63 33; www.avis.com.au)

➡ **Budget** (☑13 27 27; www.budget.com.au)

➡ **Europcar** (☑1300 131 390; www.europcar.com.au)

➡ **Hertz** (☑13 30 39; www.hertz.com.au)

➡ **Thrifty** (☑1300 367 227; www.thrifty.com.au)

CAMPERVAN

Many people find a campervan is the best way to explore the outback, and it's hard to disagree. From a two-berth to a full-blown family camper, they offer a home on wheels, allowing you to pull up anywhere, save on accommodation costs and crank up the ACDC as loud as hell! Most have some sort of cooking facilities and there are a few 4WD models. They typically cost from $100 to $150 a day.

4WD

Having a 4WD vehicle is essential for off-the-beaten-track driving into the outback. And there might even be room to sleep in the back! The major car- and campervan-hire companies also do 4WDs.

Costs Renting a 4WD vehicle is affordable if a few people get together: something like a Nissan X-Trail (which can get you through most, but not all, tracks) costs around $100 to $150 per day; for a Toyota LandCruiser you're looking at around $150 up to $200, which should include unlimited kilometres.

Exclusions Always read the fine print of your rental and insurance agreements. The excess (the amount you pay in the event of accident) and policies might not cover damage caused when travelling off-road (which they don't always tell you when you pick up your vehicle). Some also name specific tracks as off limits and you may not be covered by the insurance if you ignore this. At the time of writing, these include the Ernest Giles Rd (south of Alice Springs) and the Jim Jim Falls Rd (Kakadu).

Insurance

Excess Rather than risking paying out thousands of dollars if you do have a crash, you can take out comprehensive insurance on the car or pay an additional daily amount to the rental company for an 'insurance excess reduction' policy. This reduces the excess (the amount of money for which you're liable before the insurance kicks in) from between $2000 and $5000 to a few hundred dollars, though it pushes the rental cost up.

Exclusions Be aware that if you're travelling on dirt roads in a 2WD you often won't be covered by insurance unless you have a 4WD – in other words, if you have an accident you'll be liable for all costs involved. Also, most companies' insurance won't cover the cost of damage to glass (including the windscreen) or tyres. Similarly, because of the risk of hitting an animal, most companies void your insurance if you travel outside city limits between dusk and dawn. Always read the small print.

Purchase

Buying your own vehicle to travel around in gives you the freedom to go where and when the mood takes you, and may work out cheaper than renting in the long run. Some dealers will sell you a car with an undertaking to buy it back at an agreed price, but don't accept verbal guarantees – get it in writing. It's your responsibility to ensure the car isn't stolen and that there's no money owing on it: check the car's details with the Personal Property Securities Register (www.ppsr.gov.au).

PAPERWORK & REGISTRATION

When you buy a vehicle in Australia, you need to transfer the vehicle registration into your own name within 14 days. Each state has slightly different

ROAD DISTANCES (KM)

	Adelaide	Adelaide River	Alice Springs	Barrow Creek	Coober Pedy	Darwin	Elliot	Erldunda	Glendambo	Katherine	Kulgera	Larrimah	Marla	Pimba/Woomera	Port Augusta	Port Pirie
Adelaide River	2903															
Alice Springs	1524	1379														
Barrow Creek	1808	1095	284													
Coober Pedy	835	2068	689	973												
Darwin	3020	117	1496	1212	2185											
Elliot	2284	619	760	476	1449	736										
Erldunda	1324	1579	200	484	489	1696	960									
Glendambo	590	2313	934	1218	245	2430	1694	734								
Katherine	2702	201	1178	894	1867	318	418	1378	2112							
Kulgera	1250	1653	274	558	415	1770	1034	74	660	1452						
Larrimah	2522	381	998	714	1687	498	238	1198	1932	180	1272					
Marla	1068	1835	456	740	233	1952	1216	256	478	1634	182	1454				
Pimba/Woomera	485	2418	1039	1323	350	2535	1799	839	105	2217	765	2037	583			
Port Augusta	300	2603	1224	1508	535	2720	1984	1024	290	2402	950	2222	768	185		
Port Pirie	225	2678	1299	1583	610	2795	2059	1099	365	2477	1025	2297	843	260	75	
Tennant Creek	2032	871	508	224	1197	988	252	708	1442	670	782	490	964	1547	1732	1807

requirements and different organisations to do this. Similarly, when selling a vehicle you need to advise the state or territory road transport authority (p272).

Some considerations:

Transfer of registration form In the NT, you and the seller need to complete and sign this form. In SA there is no form, but you and the seller need to complete and sign the reverse of the registration certificate.

Roadworthy certificate In the NT and SA you don't need to provide a roadworthy certificate when selling a vehicle.

Changing state of registration Note that registering a vehicle in a different state to the one it was previously registered in can be difficult, time consuming and expensive.

'Rego' is usually renewed annually Australia-wide. This generally requires no more than payment of the registration fee, but SA and the NT have some extra considerations:

➡ **South Australia** You can pay for three, six, nine or 12 months registration.

➡ **Northern Territory** Vehicle roadworthy inspections are required once the vehicle is three years old. Vehicles older than three years, but less than 10 years old, require a roadworthy inspection every two years until they reach their 10th year. Vehicles over 10 years old require an annual roadworthy inspection.

ROAD TRANSPORT AUTHORITIES

South Australia (www.sa.gov.au/topics/driving-and-transport)

Northern Territory (www.transport.nt.gov.au)

WHAT TO LOOK FOR

It's prudent to have a car checked by an independent expert – automobile associations offer vehicle checks, and road transport authorities have lists of licensed garages – but if you're flying solo, things to check include:

➡ tyre tread

➡ number of kilometres

➡ rust damage

➡ accident damage

➡ oil should be translucent and honey-coloured

➡ coolant should be clean and not rusty in colour

➡ engine condition; check for fumes from engine, smoke from exhaust while engine is running and engines that rattle or cough

➡ exhaust system should not be excessively noisy or rattle when engine is running

➡ windscreen should be clear with no cracks or chip marks. When test-driving the car, also check the following:

➡ listen for body and suspension noise and changes in engine noise

⇒ check for oil and petrol smells, leaks and overheating

⇒ check instruments, lights and controls all work: heating, air-con, brake lights, headlights, indicators, seatbelts and windscreen wipers

⇒ brakes should pull the car up straight, without pulling, vibrating or making noise

⇒ gears and steering should be smooth and quiet.

WHERE & WHEN TO BUY

If you're buying a second-hand vehicle, keep in mind the hidden costs: stamp duty, registration, transfer fee, insurance and maintenance.

BACKPACKERS

Hostel noticeboards and online noticeboards such those on www.taw.com.au and the Thorn Tree travel forum at www.lonelyplanet. com are good places to find vehicles for sale.

DEALERS

Buying from a licensed dealer gives you some protection. They are obliged to guarantee that no money is owing on the car and you're usually allowed a cooling-off period (usually one day). Depending on the age of the car and the kilometres travelled, you may also receive a statutory warranty. You will need to sign an agreement for sale; make sure you understand what it says before you sign.

ONLINE

Private and dealer car sales are listed online on websites such as Car Sales (www. carsales.com.au) and Trading Post (www.tradingpost. com.au).

PRIVATE ADS

Buying privately can be time consuming, and you'll have to travel around to assess your options. But you should expect a lower price than that charged by a licensed dealer. The seller should provide you with a roadworthy certificate (if required in the state you're in), but you won't get a cooling-off period or a statutory warranty.

Road Conditions & Hazards

Sealed roads In SA, all major highways into Adelaide are bitumen and in good condition. Further north in the outback, the Stuart Hwy and the main roads into Lyndhurst, Roxby Downs and Wilpena Pound are the only bitumen roads – the rest are unsealed. In the NT, the Stuart Hwy into Darwin is sealed, as is the loop road through Kakadu and the main highways into WA and Qld.

Unsealed roads Driving on unsealed roads requires special care, as cars perform differently when braking and turning on dirt. Conditions vary from well-maintained gravel to rough corrugations, deep sand and dust. Heavy rain will quickly turn some roads into muddy skating rinks, many impassable when wet. If a road is officially closed because of heavy rain, you can be fined up to $1000 per wheel for travelling on it. Under no circumstances exceed 80km/h on dirt roads; if you go faster you won't have time to respond to a sharp turn, stock on the road or an unmarked gate or cattle grid. Take your time and don't try to break the land-speed record.

Road condition reports For up-to-date South Australian road conditions, call 1300 361 033 or check www.dpti.sa.gov.au/ OutbackRoads; in the NT call 1800 246 199 or check www. roadreport.nt.gov.au.

Animal hazards Collisions with kangaroos, cattle, camels, brumbies and emus can be a real hazard. The result of a collision with an animal at high speed in a car can be disastrous. Kangaroos are most active around dawn and dusk, and often travel in groups. If you see one hopping across the road in front of you, slow right down – its friends are probably just behind it. If one hops out right in front of you, hit the brakes and only swerve to avoid the animal if it is safe to do so. If possible, avoid travelling at night on the highway.

Road trains Road trains are a prime-mover truck with two or three trailers stretching for as long as 50m. On dual-lane highways they pose few problems, although you need some distance and plenty of speed to overtake. On single-lane bitumen roads you should get right off the road if one approaches. On dirt roads you also need to pull over, and often stop altogether while you wait for the dust cloud to clear.

Fatigue Driving long distances (particularly in hot weather) can send you to sleep at the wheel. On a long haul, stop and rest every two hours or so – stretch, do some exercise, change drivers or have a coffee.

Hitchers A couple of incidents in recent years have led to warnings against stopping for people, or vehicles, on isolated stretches of road – even if they wave you down.

OUTBACK DRIVING

Resources The **RAA** (RAA; ☑08 8202 4589, Roadside Assistance 13 11 11; www.raa. com.au; 55 Hindmarsh Sq, Adelaide, SA; ⊙8.30am-5pm Mon-Fri, 9am-4pm Sat) and **AANT** (AANT; ☑08 8925 5901; www.aant.com.au; 2/14 Knuckey St; ⊙9am-5pm Mon-Fri, to 12.30pm Sat) can advise on preparation, and supply maps and track notes.

Preparations Apart from being well prepared with spare parts and tyres, plenty of water (5L per person per day and extra for the radiator) and a basic knowledge of outback driving (things such as deflating tyres to get through deep sand), an extra safety net is to carry a high-frequency (HF) radio transceiver or satellite phone to contact Royal Flying Doctor Service bases, a Global Positioning System (GPS) unit and/

or an emergency position-indicating radio beacon (EPIRB). The big car-hire companies also hire out GPS units from around $60 a week.

Seasons It's wise not to attempt tough tracks during the heat of summer (November to March) when the dust can be severe and water scarce, making a breakdown more dangerous. Travel during the Wet (November to April) in the north may be hindered by flooding and impassable mud.

Tell someone There are still many unsealed roads in central Australia where the official recommendation is that you report to the police before you leave, and again when you arrive at your destination. If not the police, tell friends, family and/or your car-hire company what you're up to.

In trouble? If you do run into trouble in the back of beyond, always stay with your car. It's easier to spot a car than a human being from the air, and you wouldn't be able to carry a heavy load of water very far anyway. Police suggest that you carry two spare tyres (for added safety) and, if stranded, set fire to one of them (let the air out first) – the pall of smoke will be seen for kilometres.

Road Rules

Australians drive on the left-hand side of the road.

Give way When driving, 'give way to the right', meaning that if an intersection is unmarked (common in the outback, but not in cities), you *must* give way to vehicles entering the intersection from your right.

Speed limits The general speed limit in built-up areas is 50km/h (25km/h or 40km/h near schools at certain times – look for the signs), and 110km/h on highways in SA. In the NT, the speed limit on the open highway is either 110km/h or 130km/h.

Seatbelts Seatbelts must be worn by law.

Drink-driving You must not drive with a blood-alcohol content 0.05% or more.

Mobile phones Talking on a mobile phone while driving is illegal in Australia (excluding hands-free technology).

Hitching & Ride-Sharing

Hitching (or picking up hitchers) is never entirely safe – we do not recommend it. Hitching to or from SA across the Nullarbor is definitely not advisable as waits of two or three days are common. People looking for travelling companions for the long car journeys interstate often leave notices on boards in hostels and backpacker accommodation: ask around.

Ride-Sharing

Ride-sharing is a good way to split costs and environmental impact with other travellers. Hostel noticeboards are good places to find ads, as well as online classified sites like www. catchalift.com and www. needaride.com.au.

Local Transport

In SA, Adelaide has an extensive public bus network, a not-so-extensive public train system and one tram line (which is surprisingly useful). All are run by **Adelaide Metro** (☑1300 311 108; www.adelaidemetro.com. au; cnr King William & Currie Sts; ◷8am-6pm Mon-Fri, 9am-5pm Sat, 11am-4pm Sun).

In the NT, Darwin and Alice Springs have handy public bus networks run by the **Department of Transport** (☑08 8924 7666; nt.gov. au/driving/public-transport-cycling/public-bus-timetables-maps-darwin).

Train

The historic *Ghan* train runs between Adelaide and Darwin and is one of the world's great train journeys.

Classes

The *Ghan* isn't cheap or fast – it's more expedient to fly – and the easing out of economy-class sleeper seats has pushed the cheapest tickets up considerably – the choice is now only between gold or platinum sleeper cabins. That said, the experience of rolling through the vast, flat expanse of the 'dead heart' is magical, and it's great to wander around the train, enjoy a beer and a meal, and share desert tales with other travellers.

Train Fares

Fares drop if you make your reservation more than six months in advance, or if you travel in the low season (changes depending on journey and direction of travel). Price for children aged between four and 15 is 80% of the accompanying adult fare. Standard adult high-season fares:

JOURNEY	GOLD SERVICE ($)	PLATINUM SERVICE ($)
Adelaide–Darwin	2599	3989
Adelaide–Alice Springs	1419	2749
Alice Springs–Darwin	1419	2749
Adelaide–Perth	2049	3299
Sydney–Adelaide	999	1619

Both levels of service include sleeper cabins and all-inclusive dining and beverages. Platinum cabins are more spacious and include an en suite, plus access to a separate dining car, the Platinum Club.

Behind the Scenes

SEND US YOUR FEEDBACK

We love to hear from travellers – your comments keep us on our toes and help make our books better. Our well-travelled team reads every word on what you loved or loathed about this book. Although we cannot reply individually to your submissions, we always guarantee that your feedback goes straight to the appropriate writers, in time for the next edition. Each person who sends us information is thanked in the next edition – the most useful submissions are rewarded with a selection of digital PDF chapters.

Visit **lonelyplanet.com/contact** to submit your updates and suggestions or to ask for help. Our award-winning website also features inspirational travel stories, news and discussions.

Note: We may edit, reproduce and incorporate your comments in Lonely Planet products such as guidebooks, websites and digital products, so let us know if you don't want your comments reproduced or your name acknowledged. For a copy of our privacy policy visit lonelyplanet.com/privacy.

WRITER THANKS

Anthony Ham

A very big thank you to Tasmin Waby for sending me out into some of Australia's most beautiful corners and for her commitment to good writing. Thanks also to Liam, Sticks, Mandy Dwyer and so many others who made my stay in the Northern Territory so memorable. And to my family who always keep the home fires burning – *os quiero* and I can't wait to take you there next time.

Charles Rawlings-Way

Huge thanks to Tasmin for the gig, and to all the helpful souls I met on the road in South Australia who flew through my questions with the greatest of ease. Biggest thanks of all to Meg, who held the increasingly chaotic fort while I was busy scooting around in the sunshine ('Where's daddy?') – and made sure that Ione, Remy, Liv and Reuben were fed, watered, schooled, tucked-in and read-to.

ACKNOWLEDGEMENTS

Climate map data adapted from Peel MC, Finlayson BL & McMahon TA (2007) 'Updated World Map of the Köppen-Geiger Climate Classification', *Hydrology and Earth System Sciences*, 11, 163344.

Cover photograph: Vineyard, Barossa Valley, Stefano Scata/4Corners ©

BEHIND THE SCENES

THIS BOOK

This 7th edition of Lonely Planet's *South Australia & Northern Territory* guidebook was researched and written by Anthony Ham and Charles Rawlings-Way. The 6th edition, *Central Australia: Adelaide to Darwin*, was researched and written by Charles, Meg Worby and Lindsay Brown. Lindsay also updated the Outback Environment chapter originally written by Dave Fuller, Kylie Strelan and Dr Irene Watson. The 5th edition was written by the same team, with the added assistance of Paul Harding. This guidebook was produced by the following:

Destination Editor
Tasmin Waby

Product Editors
Hannah Cartmel, Shona Gray

Senior Cartographer
Julie Sheridan

Book Designer
Virginia Moreno

Assisting Editors
Michelle Bennett, Melanie Dankel, Sandie Kestell, Rosie Nicholson, Lauren O'Connell, Charlotte Orr

Assisting Cartographer
Hunor Csutoros

Cover Researcher
Naomi Parker

Thanks to Carolyn Boicos, Jennifer Carey, Daniel Corbett, Liz Heynes, Claire Naylor, Gabrielle Stefanos, Jeroen Wesselink, Janet Whiteway, Tracy Whitmey, Alison Young.

Index

EMMA NEUVONEN

LONELY PLANET IN THE WILD

Send your 'Lonely Planet in the Wild' photos to social@lonelyplanet.com
We share the best on our Facebook page every week!

Map Legend

Sights
- Beach
- Bird Sanctuary
- Buddhist
- Castle/Palace
- Christian
- Confucian
- Hindu
- Islamic
- Jain
- Jewish
- Monument
- Museum/Gallery/Historic Building
- Ruin
- Sento Hot Baths
- Shinto
- Sikh
- Taoist
- Winery/Vineyard
- Zoo/Wildlife Sanctuary
- Other Sight

Activities, Courses & Tours
- Bodysurfing
- Diving/Snorkelling
- Canoeing/Kayaking
- Course/Tour
- Skiing
- Snorkelling
- Surfing
- Swimming/Pool
- Walking
- Windsurfing
- Other Activity

Sleeping
- Sleeping
- Camping

Eating
- Eating

Drinking & Nightlife
- Drinking & Nightlife
- Cafe

Entertainment
- Entertainment

Shopping
- Shopping

Information
- Bank
- Embassy/Consulate
- Hospital/Medical
- Internet
- Police
- Post Office
- Telephone
- Toilet
- Tourist Information
- Other Information

Geographic
- Beach
- Hut/Shelter
- Lighthouse
- Lookout
- Mountain/Volcano
- Oasis
- Park
- Pass
- Picnic Area
- Waterfall

Population
- Capital (National)
- Capital (State/Province)
- City/Large Town
- Town/Village

Transport
- Airport
- Border crossing
- Bus
- Cable car/Funicular
- Cycling
- Ferry
- Metro station
- Monorail
- Parking
- Petrol station
- Subway station
- Taxi
- Train station/Railway
- Tram
- Underground station
- Other Transport

Note: Not all symbols displayed above appear on the maps in this book

Routes
- Tollway
- Freeway
- Primary
- Secondary
- Tertiary
- Lane
- Unsealed road
- Road under construction
- Plaza/Mall
- Steps
- Tunnel
- Pedestrian overpass
- Walking Tour
- Walking Tour detour
- Path/Walking Trail

Boundaries
- International
- State/Province
- Disputed
- Regional/Suburb
- Marine Park
- Cliff
- Wall

Hydrography
- River, Creek
- Intermittent River
- Canal
- Water
- Dry/Salt/Intermittent Lake
- Reef

Areas
- Airport/Runway
- Beach/Desert
- Cemetery (Christian)
- Cemetery (Other)
- Glacier
- Mudflat
- Park/Forest
- Sight (Building)
- Sportsground
- Swamp/Mangrove

CONTRIBUTING WRITERS

Cathy Craigie is a Gamilaori and Anaiwon woman from northern New South Wales. She is a freelance writer and cultural consultant and has extensive experience in Aboriginal Affairs. Cathy contributed to the Aboriginal Australia chapter.

Brenda L Croft was born in Perth and now lives on the south coast of New South Wales. She is a Senior Research Fellow at the University of NSW. Brenda is from the Gurindji, Malngin and Mudpurra peoples in the NT on her paternal side, and has Anglo-Australian, German and Irish heritage on her maternal side. She has been involved in the arts and cultural sectors for three decades as an artist, arts administrator, curator, writer, academic and consultant. Brenda contributed to the Indigenous Visual Arts chapter.

David Fuller & Kylie Strelan wrote the Outback Environment chapter. David has worked for more than 20 years as a parks and wildlife ranger, and Kylie is an editor with an environmental consultancy. They lived for more than 10 years in national parks throughout the Northern Territory, including Garig Gunak Barlu, the West MacDonnells and Nitmiluk. With a passion for road trips (and family to visit in Adelaide), David and Kylie have driven the length of the Stuart Hwy more times than they care to recall.

Professor Irene Watson wrote the section headed The Land & Indigenous Peoples in the Outback Environment chapter, first published in Lonely Planet's *Aboriginal Australia & the Torres Strait Islands: Guide to Indigenous Australia*. Professor Watson is now working with the University of South Australia. Professor Watson writes: 'I am a Tanganekald and Meintangk woman; my ancestors are the sovereign peoples of the Coorong and the southeast region of South Australia.'

OUR STORY

A beat-up old car, a few dollars in the pocket and a sense of adventure. In 1972 that's all Tony and Maureen Wheeler needed for the trip of a lifetime – across Europe and Asia overland to Australia. It took several months, and at the end – broke but inspired – they sat at their kitchen table writing and stapling together their first travel guide, *Across Asia on the Cheap.* Within a week they'd sold 1500 copies. Lonely Planet was born.

Today, Lonely Planet has offices in Franklin, London, Melbourne, Oakland, Dublin, Beijing and Delhi, with more than 600 staff and writers. We share Tony's belief that 'a great guidebook should do three things: inform, educate and amuse'.

OUR WRITERS

Anthony Ham
Northern Territory Anthony is a freelance writer and photographer who specialises in Spain, East and Southern Africa, the Arctic, the Middle East and Australia. When he's not writing for Lonely Planet, Anthony writes about and photographs Spain, Africa and the Middle East for newspapers and magazines in Australia, the UK and US. Anthony also contributed to the Indigenous Art & Culture and Ultimate Outback themed spreads.

Charles Rawlings-Way
South Australia Charles is a veteran travel writer who has penned 30-something titles for Lonely Planet – including guides to Singapore, Toronto, Sydney, Tasmania, New Zealand, the South Pacific and Australia – and numerous articles. After dabbling in the dark arts of architecture, cartography, project management and busking for some years, Charles hit the road for Lonely Planet in 2005 and hasn't stopped travelling since. Charles also contributed to the Plan, Understand and Survival sections.

 RS

onely Planet Global Limited

2017

Photographs © as indicated 2017

Although the authors and Lonely Planet have taken all reasonable care in preparing this book, we make no warranty about the accuracy or completeness of its content and, to the maximum extent permitted, disclaim all liability arising from its use.

t of this publication may be copied, stored in a retrieval system, or transmitted in any form by any means, electronic, herwise, except brief extracts for the purpose of review, and no part of this publication may be sold or hired, without the blisher. Lonely Planet and the Lonely Planet logo are trademarks of Lonely Planet and are registered in the US Patent and r countries. Lonely Planet does not allow its name or logo to be appropriated by commercial establishments, such as ls. Please let us know of any misuses: lonelyplanet.com/ip.